The End is just The Beginning

Preface to Second Printing of
U.A. Whitaker book "The End is Just the Beginning"

The first printing of 10,000 copies of this book was in 1980. Although the book centers on the life of U.A. Whitaker, it has also been used extensively to gain a better understanding of AMP Incorporated. Mr. Whitaker founded AMP in 1941 after a very successful career as an engineering executive. He served as its Chairman and Chief Executive Officer until 1972, and as Chairman until his death on September 16, 1975.

Events since his death have dramatically confirmed that the foundations he laid in goals, policies and people, for both AMP and various philanthropic projects, were very sound. AMP's sales have increased through the years at approximately a 15% compound annual growth rate. Since 1975, the Company has grown from sales of just over $400 million and 13,000 employees to a current annual sales rate approaching $2 billion and 22,000 employees in the U.S. and 26 other countries. Similarly, the various charitable, scientific, and medical activities which he conceived and funded have also made excellent progress.

Thus the impact of Mr. Whitaker's life continues to grow. On this 11th anniversary of his death, we wish to again acknowledge the invaluable "legacy" he has left to AMP and society as a whole from his energy, imagination, wisdom, and generosity. His life will continue to inspire people for many years to come. We are therefore pleased to now make this second printing available.

Walter F. Raab
Chairman and Chief Executive Officer

The End is just The Beginning

U.A.Whitaker

Biography of an
Engineer

by W.H.Cohn

Published by Carnegie-Mellon University, Pittsburgh, Pa. 15213
Manufactured in the United States of America

80-66231
ISBN 0-915604-92-2

First Printing 1980 - 10,000 Copies
Second Printing 1986 - 15,000 Copies

Acknowledgments

This biography was undertaken at the suggestion of Carnegie-Mellon University President Richard M. Cyert, who correctly believed there was an interesting story in the life and career of U.A. Whitaker. L.F. Schaefer, chairman of the Carnegie-Mellon University History Department offered me the opportunity to recreate that story. Jack Johnson, then vice-president for Development, followed the project through to its end and spent many valuable hours arranging interviews and discussing with me the progress of the biography.

Of the many people who helped, Mrs. Helen F. Whitaker, wife of the founder of AMP Incorporated, deserves a special note of thanks for her time-consuming and painstaking work in reading the manuscript at various stages. Mr. C.J. Fredricksen, chairman of the board of AMP Incorporated, offered continuous encouragement and a storehouse of accurate information about U.A. Whitaker and the development and growth of the corporation. Others at AMP Incorporated were equally forthcoming —President and Chief Executive Officer, J.D. Brenner; Vice-President and Chief Financial Officer, Walter F. Raab; Vice-President, Research, S.W. Pollock. Others associated with AMP Incorporated for many years, Kenneth L. Neijstrom, Albert F. Curtis, Morton Brown, G. Earle Walker, Marshall Holcombe and Truman S. Safford, also contributed valuable information and insights. Another special note of thanks goes to Mrs. Margaret Rahm, U.A. Whitaker's personal secretary, for her kindness and generosity. Miss Mary Fran Walsh and Miss Naomi Early also deserve mention for their help and cooperation.

U.A. Whitaker's personal friends and associates outside of AMP Incorporated aided my work immensely. Longtime friends Samuel L. Williams, George Misner and George Hastings, who knew U.A. Whitaker for most of his adult life, added a good deal of color to the story. I also had the full cooporation of A.H. Gordon of Kidder, Peabody & Company, James C. Olson of Booz, Allen and Hamilton, Dr. Irwin W. Sizer of the Massachusetts Institute of Technology and Marcia Magill, a close friend of both U.A. and Helen Whitaker.

To librarians, any author must confess his dependence — the entire reference staff at Carnegie-Mellon's Hunt Library and especially Dorothea Whitehead; Karen M. Duree of the State Historical Society of Missouri, Columbia, Missouri; and Warren Seamans, Director of the Massachusetts Institute of Technology Historical Collection.

Among others who contributed immeasurably were various members of the Whitaker family —Mrs. Ruth Holmes, U.A. and Helen Whitaker's daughter, and Glaucus Burnell, one of U.A. Whitaker's nephews, as well as those family members and family friends residing in the vicinity of Weaubleau, Missouri who helped reconstruct life in that rural setting in the early years of the century.

Finally and inevitably my gratitude to my wife Jan Cohn, who too often neglected her own professional responsibilities to lend an editorial hand.

William H. Cohn
Reston, Virginia

Table of Contents

INTRODUCTION

The Origins and Development of
an Entreprenurial Career

A good deal of nonsense — both condemning and praising entrepreneurial types as they have emerged in the past 200 years — has been written about the role of business and businessmen in American history. Attempts to understand the history of business in American life have too often led to cycles of historical revisionism in which the image of the entrepreneur, usually of the tycoon variety, has shifted alternately from hero to villain as the vicissitudes of contemporary life demanded. It is certainly time to reject the "praise or blame" approach and to work toward an understanding of the story of business and businessmen as an integral part of American culture.

The origins and development of U. A. Whitaker's career is the story of an American "nontycoon" who quietly and successfully built AMP Incorporated, founded in 1941, into one of the world's leading electrical engineering firms. A producer of electrical terminations and connectors, the company is now among the nation's 500 largest. The Whitaker-AMP story is an instructive example of a business venture in post-World War II America, beginning with a simple idea — the solderless electrical termination — and developing into a multinational and multimillion dollar business in fewer than thirty-five years. In one sense, Whitaker's career is unique — very few businessmen succeed on the scale he did. In another sense, the story is a typical, mainstream American story — "Uncas Whitaker's Better Mousetrap," — as *Forbes* termed it in a 1969 article.

The origins of U. A. Whitaker's career can be traced from his family associations, through his professional training, and in his early work experiences. Although Whitaker once claimed that he had no roots, his rural origins provided a significant number of entrepreneurial models that influenced his thinking. For all their lives, his father and most of his other male relatives were associated with small town Missouri banking and land transactions, as well as farming. Relatives, both male and female, were charged with running schools or school districts at one time or another. Whitaker's professional education exposed him to the intricacies of business enterprise as well as the technical aspects of mechanical and electrical engineering. His early work experience at Westinghouse Air Brake (1923-29), at the Hoover Company (1929-38), and at American Machine & Foundry (1939-41) involved business management in addition to engineering invention, innovation, and technology.

A man of considerable energy and intellectual curiosity, Whitaker earned a pilot's license while working at the Hoover Company, and he bought the controlling interest in a bootstrap operation called McKinley Air Transport. A good number of his early entrepreneurial ideas were tested on that small organization during the late 1930s. In addition to his full-time employment at Hoover and his part-time concerns with the air transport company, Whitaker found time to earn a law degree at night school.

Whitaker's early work experiences served him well when he undertook the organization of the company that became AMP Incorporated, but the decision making necessary to form and sustain the company in its first years taxed even Whitaker's engineering and management expertise. The company struggled to stay afloat during the Second World War, caught in the complex relationship between business and government during that time of national crisis. The experience of doing business during World War II profoundly affected Whitaker's thinking in the postwar years. The young company's total dependence on government war contracts and the associated problems of dealing with the government as prime contractor convinced Whitaker to try to make AMP Incorporated as independent of government-related defense business as possible in the future.

It is generally known and acknowledged that public policy had a considerable impact on private enterprise during the years 1941-45. What is less well known is how private decision making during this period contributed to the shaping of public policy. Despite a wartime environment and the predominance of war-oriented markets, competition between companies in the same industry was not suspended for the duration. As a result of this continuing competition, certain private business decisions proved to have important public policy implications for the general war effort.

It is against the background of defense and war needs, as well as the imperatives of the competitive market place, that the development of the internal organization of AMP Incorporated can be documented. Business functions, such as general management, marketing, financing, public relations, employee relations, and research and development, reflected these pressures. At the same time, the company made its plans for the postwar business world. After the war, the needs of the consumer market, tempered by the onset of recession, further shaped various business functions and key entrepreneurial decisions. The continued effects of competition within the industry are visible in all major areas relating to the growth and development of AMP Incorporated. The complex relationship between profit, research and development, and the market on the one hand, and public policy on the other, can be analyzed during several postwar phases of AMP Incorporated's expansion program, which eventually directed the company to overseas markets and to a position of multinational leadership.

A great deal of emphasis is placed in this study on U. A. Whitaker's world view — on the ideas, manners, and morals which most affected the professional, business, and personal choices he made throughout his life and career. Much attention, therefore, is given to Whitaker's relationship to his rural western origins, to his ties both to the land and to his family. Whitaker's father, Oliver Barr (O.B.) Whitaker, a longtime Missouri legislator, educator, and minister with some substantial claim to local fame, was immensely influential in his son's life, and the devotion and loyalty of the two men to one another form a crucial part of the overall story of U. A. Whitaker's life. The conservative values of rural, small-town American life before World War II are evident in numerous facets of Whitaker's own professional and business life.

The narrative addresses a broad spectrum of questions interesting both to the business historian and the entrepreneurial biographer. Part One, The Apprentice Engineer, focuses on those formative influences — family background, educational training, and early work experiences — which seem to have a direct bearing on Whitaker's later activities as the leader of his own business organization. Part Two, The Journeyman Manager, and Part Three, The Master Entrepreneur, are, on one level, a further elaboration of U. A. Whitaker's personality and world view as they affected managerial decision making. But, they are also a description of a specific set of stages through which the business organization progressed from its inception in 1941 to its entry into the select circle of America's top 500 firms.

Behind the relatively anonymous and certainly private character of

U. A. Whitaker existed another kind of personality, one who, like his father O. B., lived a part of his life in the world of his own imagination. Although, unlike his father, he was an immensely practical man, he drew heavily on the resources of nature. He loved the outdoors and the camaraderie of men together around the campfire. In such an environment — while hunting or fishing — he enjoyed those recreational activities that are part of the "man's world" of American culture. And in relation to that world he could find and express a wit and imagination that echo his father's and that help us to see, beyond the engineer-entrepreneur, the whole man. U. A. Whitaker, who brought AMP Incorporated into the circle of *Fortune's* 500, was also the "Whit" his friends knew, a man who claimed expert knowledge of the fur-bearing trout and of the difference between the right-handed and the left-handed flounder:

> In reference to George's letter of October 21st in which he sends a picture of the "Hicken's Fur Bearing Trout," I am sorry to advise you that George is wrong *just this one time.* George is an absolute authority on almost everything, such as shooting grouses, finding difficult places to haul wood out of ravines, making flapjacks, etc., etc. He is particularly an expert on rattlesnake stories. The fish that he shows is actually Salvelinus fontanalis. These fish naturally grow fur as the water grows colder, and I am surprised that George didn't know this. If he will wade out into one of the streams next time he goes to his camp, excuse me, "lodge," he will find that the fish in the stream running past his hunting and fishing lodge are by this time growing a coat of fur and, come February, they will look like the picture he encloses and, if he wades in the water, he will probably grow fur. It amazes me how some people who are authorities on fish do miss on certain items. I had a friend that did a lot of fishing and caught a lot of Flounder and didn't know that the winter Flounder are right-handed and the summer Flounder are left-handed. Can you imagine that???

1. Origins

*Where are the blossoms of those summers! — fallen one by one: so all
of my family departed, each in his turn, to the land of spirits. I am on
the hilltop, and must go down into the valley; and when Uncas follows in
my footsteps, there will no longer be any of the blood of the sagamores,
for my boy is the last of the Mohicans.*

— *James Fenimore Cooper, The Last of the Mohicans*

Uncas Aeneas Whitaker, born March 22, 1900, was a Missouri farm
boy who went to work in Pittsburgh, Pennsylvania in 1923 at an
hourly wage of sixty cents. In 1941 he founded a business that in 1965
entered the select circle of the top 500 companies in the United
States. At the time of his death, in 1975, AMP Incorporated of
Harrisburg, Pennsylvania stood 343 on the list of America's largest
corporations and was still growing. A Horatio Alger success story?
The saga of a poor farm boy who came to the city to seek fame and
fortune and by a combination of pluck and luck traveled the path
from rags to riches? Well, not quite. The Whitaker family was neither
poor nor rich; rather, it was respectable and comfortable. The success
part of the story is that very few Americans, either from the farm or
the city, grow up to head a multimillion dollar, multinational
corporation.

Contrary to Horace Greeley's advice, Uncas Whitaker went East to
earn his fortune. Earlier generations of the Whitaker clan had gone in
the other direction. Great grandfather Joshua Whitaker, whose
English antecedents are unknown, was born in Virginia in 1811. In his
early twenties, Joshua married Nancy NesSmith. The first two of
their eight children, Joseph and Thomas, were born in Virginia in
1834 and 1838, and a third son, John, Uncas' grandfather, was born
in Ohio in 1842. The Joshua Whitaker family began its trek westward
about 1840, living for a number of years in Ohio, then for about a
decade in Iowa; finally, in 1859 the Whitakers settled in southwestern
Missouri in the vicinity of the little village of Weaubleau (pronounced
Wah-blow), in Hickory County.

During the Civil War both John Whitaker and his older brother
Joseph served in the Missouri militia; in that badly divided border
state, they fought against fellow Missourians who had opted for the
Southern cause. John Whitaker, who enlisted as an orderly sergeant,

was ordained a Christian minister in 1863. As the story is told, John's ordination occurred following a skirmish that left scores of dead and wounded on the field of battle. Because there were so few chaplains available to minister to the dying, John, who had joined the Christian Church at the age of eleven, took it upon himself to provide religious reassurance as the final moment approached.

After the war, the Whitaker brothers returned to Weaubleau. In 1867 Joseph was elected to the 23rd General Assembly of the Missouri Legislature as a Republican (ten years later he would be elected to the 30th General Assembly as a Greenbacker) while brother John, who had married Emeline Earnest in 1866, organized the Weaubleau Christian Church. At first John Whitaker and a few faithful followers held services and meetings in his mother's home on the outskirts of the little town, but John looked forward to a more permanent center, specifically planning a two-story brick building to be used both for religious and educational purposes. Land for the building was donated, appropriately by John's brother Joseph and his wife Sarah, and the building begun in 1867, and, after some delay, was finished in 1871. That year only six students enrolled in the newly founded Weaubleau Christian Institute, and in 1877 the first class was graduated.[1]

In 1869 Oliver Barr Whitaker, first son of John and Emeline Earnest Whitaker (and Uncas Whitaker's father), was born. With his wife and young child, John now moved to Merom, Indiana. Apparently he felt the need for some formal education, for he attended Union Christian College, graduating in 1873. Union Christian College, like the Weaubleau Christian Institute, trained students primarily to be teachers and school administrators. With his new degree John Whitaker soon became a school superintendent, although just where he held his first position is not clear. In the late 1870s the family was homesteading in Ford County, Kansas, where John Whitaker held the post of superintendent of Ford County schools.[2] His son Oliver's recollections of these years bring back a vanished America.

> The first distinct Xmas I remember was our first Xmas in Kansas. That was in 1878 I think. I was 8, Minnie 10, Syd 4 and Joe a baby not quite a year old. Our homestead was on the western bleak plains. Indians, prairie fires and horse thieves were our greatest dread, unless it was hunger. . . . Father and Ma rarely left the homestead. . . . How that . . . picture comes back to me . . . the level far-stretching prairie of buffalo grass, flocks of antelope sometimes within less than a quarter mile of our home, wild geese

and cranes that often blackened whole acres of land, the dreaded prairie fires, and Indian scares.[3]

"That was in the Wild West days of Dodge City," his brother Syd Whitaker recalled many years later. In a letter to his nephew Uncas, he spoke "of Bat Masterson and the other noted characters of that day. We grew up for a few years within the influence of all that lore, and all that kept you from being the son of a cowboy, was a later change of ideals of your father."[4] Images of the West dominated Oliver Whitaker's imagination for the rest of his life and in a very real sense shaped his career as well as his consciousness. Son Uncas, who grew up in the atmosphere a generation or so later, would inherit this western legacy from his father and it would have an important effect on the shaping of his own personality, too.

In the early 1880s, John Whitaker returned to Weaubleau to carry on his duties as church minister and head of the school he had founded. The state of Missouri now had a population of about two million. Approximately ten thousand lived in Hickory County, located between Springfield on the south and Kansas City on the north; they were scattered in numerous villages, none of which numbered over 400. A weekly newspaper, *The Index*, described the village of Weaubleau in 1885.

> Weaubleau . . . situated in the western part of the county . . . has three dry goods stores, two hotels, one drug store, one grocery store, two shops, a fine brick school house, The Weaubleau Christian Institute, and a fine grade school; also a good two-story frame public school building, and fine flourishing mill.[5]

The first hotel was erected in 1882, and two more followed before the turn of the century. The hotel boom is explained today by old-timers in the mood for a tall tale. If a traveler, they say, came to Weaubleau, he was forced to stay overnight, so tired was he from battling the Main Street mud, "knee deep to horse."[6]

In its 1886 description of Hickory County, however, *The Index* downplayed the frontier aspect, stressing the peace and civility of the local citizenry.

> The people socially and morally, of the county will compare favorably with those of any state in the Union. Our criminal docket is generally small and most of the cases are misdemeanors. No man was ever convicted of murder in the county and hanged, and but one has been sent to the penitentiary for murder during the last 20 years. Hickory County has quiet, peaceable, orderly citizens, and as many of them to her population as any county in America.[7]

The placid self-assurance of this article brings to mind the classic western movie and the words of a typical frontier mayor just before the outlaws ride into town, and, in fact, it was little more than two months later that an outlaw gang hit nearby Wheatland. *The Index*, in mid-June 1886, published a supplement describing the "Terrible Shooting Affray!" One of the infamous Clayton boys rode into town looking for trouble:

> For some days there had been bad blood between the three Clayton boys and Thos. G. Allen, the town marshall. It was expected by a good many citizens of the place that bloodshed would result from their feud, and today their fears were realized.

Charley Clayton picked a fight with the marshall, a shooting match followed, the marshall killed Clayton, Clayton's brothers learned of the killing and rode into town to take their revenge on the marshall. The Clayton boys succeeded in wounding a bystander and "perhaps fatally wounding" the marshall, who, according to *The Index*, lingered precariously between life and death.[8]

Oliver Barr Whitaker grew up in a world that shifted between the drama and violence of the Wild West and the diligence and piety of small-town America. Because Oliver Barr, affectionately known as O. B., was to have a particularly profound influence on his son Uncas, and because his remarkable letters continued to bring to Uncas the idea and spirit of the American West, it is necessary that considerable attention be given to this man.

Oliver Barr Whitaker (1869-1942) was born in Weaubleau and educated wherever his father John happened to be teaching. He graduated from Weaubleau Christian Institute and College in the class of 1888. Discouraged by his father from going on to a career in law, O. B. went on to complete his training for a career in education. Along the way, he gathered a total of five degrees — B. S., M. S., A. M., Ph. D., and D. D. In 1887, O. B. took his first teaching job in St. Clair County, and 1891 found him attending normal school in nearby Bolivar, Missouri to earn further teaching credentials. In 1892, at age twenty-three, he was superintendent of schools in Stockton, Missouri. In the spring of 1893, O. B. returned to Weaubleau to take charge of the calisthenic and elocution classes at his father's institute and to prepare for his wedding to Annetta Ruth Boyles, a fellow student at Weaubleau Christian Institute. There was, as well, a leap upward on the vocational ladder.[9]

The wedding announcement in the weekly *Index*, published on July 27, 1893, described O. B. Whitaker as "the son of Prof. John

Whitaker. . . a bright light in the educational world, having recently accepted the position of President of Lincoln College Kansas." On the forty-eighth anniversary of his wedding day O. B. reminisced about his marriage ceremony and his new position.

> I recall dimly that I was a very important personage that day — son of the President of Weaubleau Christian Institute, which distinction fades largely in face of the fact that *I* was PRESIDENT-elect of Kansas Christian College, a paralyzing fact that I feared might not constantly be dominating the minds of those present. All I knew of the college I was soon to take active charge of was what my rather obscure father had told me about it. I had never met a member of the trustees or any other soul connected therewith. I had been employed solely on the fact of the relation to my father (solely because the trustees did not know that the contrasts between father and son were far more striking, even glaring, than similarities). I doubted also that the bride was duly appreciative of her great fortune — soon to be the wife of a COLLEGE PRESIDENT!!! And such a college!!![10]

O. B.'s lament, "and such a college!!!" was justified. At the time of his arrival in little Lincoln, Kansas in 1893, the college consisted of one finished room, an "endowment" represented by a $3,000 mortgage on the property and a student body of seven. O. B. recognized a challenge when he saw one. He put about $600 of his own money into the unpromising venture, borrowed another $200 from his father so that he and his new bride could make it through the year, and then proceeded, over the next twelve years, to increase the enrollment to more than 200 students. Since Kansas Christian College, like Weaubleau Christian Institute, prepared young people for teaching careers, O. B. decided that the success of the institution would be judged on the basis of the success of his graduates in achieving the highest scores on the county teachers' examination. The Kansas Christian graduates did just that and as a result received the majority of available teaching certifications. With such success, the school grew and at the end of O. B.'s presidential term was out of debt.[11]

O. B. Whitaker loved a challenge. In this sense he provided a model for his son Uncas, a model reinforced by recollections and anecdotes. For example, he talked of the time when, at the age of seventeen, he ran a footrace against the fastest boy on an opposing baseball team. Despite his father's prohibition against gambling, O. B. challenged the fellow and bet him a silver dollar that he could beat him. He won the silver dollar. More pious ends were met in

Lincoln, Kansas, where O. B., in addition to his struggle at the college, took on the "wets" in the town and succeeded in closing all the saloons. Gambling aside, O. B. followed his own father's model in most ways and like him was a lifelong opponent of drinking and a proponent of temperance efforts of all kinds.[12]

The Whitakers took their principles seriously. The search for, and the achievement of, a moral life were viewed as a man's highest accomplishment. The purpose of education, according to John Whitaker, was to provide for "the enlargement or expansion of the mind," which in turn would allow the individual to increase his "ability and disposition to lead a healthy, happy, and a morally worthy life." The stated aim of Weaubleau Christian College is instructive in this respect: "What we grow to be is of more importance than what we come to know." That liberal, progressive educational philosophy informed the college catalogue:

> The school has ever been under the liberal control of the Christian Church (designated in the late U.S. Census as *Christian Connexion* to distinguish it from another organization called Christians, Disciples, etc.). The plan of the school is such that it is patronized by persons of all religious beliefs, and all are made to feel at home, without any attempt to proselytize. The school is designed to be *Christian and not sectarian.*[13]

Christian colleges, such as the one founded at Weaubleau in 1871, were in actuality four- or five-year secondary schools at which university preparatory courses could be taken. Most students, however, completed their education at these institutions and went on from them to the world of work. Although the normal course, the program for the training of teachers, was the standard program, some schools, like Weaubleau Christian College, added commercial programs in the 1890s. The emphasis on character was maintained as the college attempted to meet the needs of a changing society:

> The management of this school from its incipiency have aimed to keep abreast of the times with respect to curriculum studies, methods of instruction and management, and in whatever pertained to the future success of its students. The school is intended to meet the present and future demands. Old obsolete ways are readily abandoned for new practical ones.

The addition of courses in accounting, shorthand, business law, penmanship, and other "practical Business [were] carefully arranged with a view to a successful business life."[14]

Whatever curricular changes might occur, a rigorous and moral life remained at the center of the school experience. In addition to teaching a nondogmatic but principled approach to Christianity, John and Oliver Whitaker insisted on "teaching subordination to properly constituted authority" and "cheerful compliance with all the rules of the school." Those rules reflected in their restrictiveness a sense of a world made up of moral snares:

- All students are required to be in their rooms after the ringing of the bell at 7 o'clock or 7:30 in the evening.

- The use of tobacco in the building is prohibited.

- Sedentary games of chance or skill are not allowed.

- Party going is not allowed.

- Students are prohibited from riding or walking with the opposite sex after sundown.

- Intoxicating drinks must not be used by anyone connected with the college.

- Students are not allowed to ride or walk beyond certain specified limits without special permission from the president.

- Before boarding or rooms are secured, students must consult the president.[15]

It is said that John Whitaker made nightly rounds to ensure that students were in their rooms at the proper time. And about O. B. Whitaker it was noted by one of his former students that "if you didn't learn from him you didn't stay." Later in his own life Uncas Whitaker commented on the atmosphere in this way: "It was Hell fire and Damnation to take a drink in my day."

If there was any one obsession for O. B. Whitaker, it was the matter of drink. O. B.'s saloon-closing campaign in Lincoln, Kansas provided the background material for his first published novel, *Herbert Brown* (1906). Autobiographical in much of its material, imitative of Horatio Alger in character, plot, and moral message, *Herbert Brown* went through multiple printings, achieving a mildly successful sale of around twenty thousand copies. The melodramatic novel consists mainly of heroics of Herbert Brown (a thinly disguised O. B. Whitaker) in his efforts to help overcome the insidious effects of the local saloons on the well-meaning, but often misguided, people of the town. The book presents a set of characters seen almost wholly in relation to drink: the loving mother whose son is seduced by the saloon keeper into a drinking life; the saloon keeper himself, a bully against whom Herbert Brown is drawn into physical battle; several powerful business and professional types who control the town's government and allow the saloons to exist contrary to state law. Pathos comes in the inevitable death of the mother, whose poverty compounds her illness and her grief and the consequent demise of her wayward son, whose death from drink brings home the obvious moral lesson.

A second novel, *Dick Haley* (1910), had its source in a popular lecture O. B. developed as early as 1893. Originally entitled "Poor Dick and Winning Willie," the lecture focused on the problem of the poor boy and the lack of attention he received in public school.[16] To criticize public schools, especially their callous teachers, O. B. invented the story of a poor child on whom the impact of his teachers' shabby treatment is so strong as to lead him into evil paths, straight to drink, and finally to death and oblivion. Meanwhile, the favored child, Winning Willie, from a family of affluence and power, gets the advantages and succeeds in school and life over the prostrate bodies of the Poor Dicks of the world. In the novel, O. B. Whitaker fully expressed his contempt for the rich and mighty and for the narrow-mindedly religious, while stressing the importance of loving mothers, a proper home atmosphere, and a high moral code to live by.

In his years in Lincoln, Kansas, O. B. Whitaker also found expression for his entrepreneurial talents. A biographical sketch of his life published in the Kansas City *Star* in 1935 called him "one of the busiest men in Kansas." He acquired farm property, raised Hereford cattle, horses, and grains, and participated in the organization of two banks, one of which he headed as president and the other as vice-president. The atmosphere in which young Uncas Whitaker grew up was filled with talk of business and finance and discussions about land values and cattle prices.

By the time O. B. Whitaker returned to Weaubleau in 1913, his family of four children had all been born — two daughters, Portia in 1893 and Minnie in 1898 — and two sons, Uncas in 1900 and Sidney in 1903. With the exception of the school year 1906-07, when O. B. served as head of Weaubleau Christian College following his father's retirement, he had been away from the small southwestern Missouri town for nearly twenty years. He had gone from Kansas Christian College to Meron, Indiana, to act as President of Union

Christian College, where his father John had received his education years earlier. The family lived on the college campus, and the older children, Portia, Minnie, and Uncas, apparently attended elementary school in the town.

In Weaubleau, O. B.'s career took a different turn. The growth of the public school system and new state standards for teaching certification took their toll on the small independent nonsecular church schools. Weaubleau Christian Institute and College survived only until 1914. John Whitaker, its longtime driving force, had died in 1910 after a distinguished career as educator, clergyman, banker, state representative (1904-08), and a supervisor of the Census, during the Taft administration. O. B., persuaded by his father's friends to take up a political career, entered the race for representative to the Missouri Legislature in 1913, winning in his first attempt for the office. In addition to politics, O. B. now needed to spend a considerable amount of his time looking after his various farming interests in and around Weaubleau. In addition to the farm property he had inherited from his father, O. B. increased the family holdings by trading property he held in Lincoln County, Kansas for comparable land in southwest Missouri. His 1,320-acre Shady Bend Ranch near Lincoln brought him about $19,000 in cash when he exchanged it for a smaller tract of land a short distance outside Hickory County, Missouri.[17]

While O. B. Whitaker had been absent from Weaubleau, the town and the surrounding county had grown more prosperous. John Whitaker and other influential citizens of Weaubleau had succeeded in obtaining an extension of a nearby railroad for the town in 1898, and like so many western towns favored with railroad facilities, Weaubleau, and its townspeople, anticipated unlimited growth. The weekly newspaper reflected this optimism:

> The town is taking on new life in consequence of the near completion of the great 'Blair' line of railroad. Three large business houses are now under process of erection and several houses are in prospective construction. Hammering, howling, and painting seem to be the order of the day.

The "Frisco Line," as it came to be called, now connected Weaubleau with the cattle and grain markets in Kansas City, and the population of the town, according to some estimates, swelled to about one thousand by the turn of the century. Other members of the Whitaker family had also been active in the growth that accompanied the coming of the railroad. John Whitaker's brother

Joseph and his children — Laura, Thomas, Ida, and George — organized the Bank of Weaubleau in July 1899 with a paid up capital stock of $5,000. Along with young Tom, designated cashier of the Bank of Weaubleau, John built a spacious two-story brick building on Main Street, which housed the druggist and the general merchandise store on its bottom floor.[18]

Turn of the century Weaubleau was an unexceptional place, much like many other small western towns. The news largely revolved around births and deaths, parties and minor accidents, and an occasional cultural event like theatre performances by a traveling group. For example, *The Index* in the winter of 1900, the year of Uncas Whitaker's birth, reported that "the Wheatland Opera Troupe presented their latest drama, *Because I Love You,* at Weaubleau Saturday night," and that "the play was well received here."[19]

At the turn of the century, however, Weaubleau had reached its peak of development. Today it is a quiet town, somewhat depressed since the railroad ended its operations a quarter century ago. Old-timers there remember the Whitakers very well. O. B. remains a kind of culture hero to many, for a good number of the older citizens were taught by O. B. , either at the old institute or in the public high school after the institute closed its doors. About young Uncas Whitaker, though, little is remembered, save that he liked to hunt and fish and to run around town in an old Model T Ford, which, according to one account, "he glued together to keep it running."

Uncas, in fact, spent little time in Weaubleau because O. B. elected to send him to school outside the town. He attended high school at Drury Academy in Springfield, Missouri, some fifty miles south of Weaubleau. While at the academy, probably for the four or five years from 1913 to 1918, young Whitaker took a normal college preparatory course consisting of four units of English, three of algebra and geometry, four and one-half of history, one of Biology, one-half of physics, one of Latin, as well as bookkeeping, political economy, physical geography, and physiology.[20]

In the fall of 1918, better than a year and one-half after America's entry into World War I, eighteen-year-old Uncas began his college career at Drury College, also in Springfield. With the broadening of the draft eligibility to the ages of eighteen to forty-five, Uncas Whitaker, along with thousands of other college-bound youths, faced the prospect of becoming a soldier in the United States Army. But at Drury College, as on campuses across the nation, a plan was devised to allow those going to college and those already in college to continue their education. Uncas became part of the Student Army Training Corps (SATC), and, like his fellow draftees, spent half of each long, twelve-hour work day in academic classrooms and the other half in classes of military instruction and close-order drill on whatever served as the parade ground. That arrangement ended with the war, and Uncas received his honorable discharge from the United States Army, having served all of two months under its jurisdiction. His academic record in the one year at Drury College was largely undistinguished although he did manage As in surveying and sophomore level physics. In English and mathematics he did satisfactory work, while chemistry apparently presented a somewhat greater challenge.[21]

The following school year found Uncas enrolled in the mechanical engineering program at the Missouri School of Mines and Metallurgy in Rolla, a little less than one hundred miles east of Weaubleau. He took a series of basic engineering and mathematics courses appropriate to the engineering schools of that day, doing his best work in the electrical engineering lab, where he ranked number one of twelve, in mechanics, where he stood seventh in a class of fifty-one, and in machine shop where he finished second among seventeen students. In most other courses, Uncas could be found in either the top twenty-five or fifty of the class. Spanish, however, and something called shop and forge were evidently less to his liking, and in both instances he ended embarrassingly close to the bottom. Nevertheless, in his year in Rolla, Uncas achieved a respectable enough average (a strong B plus) to allow him to gain entry to the Massachusetts Institute of Technology the following year.[22]

Many years later, U. A. Whitaker wrote a letter to a young nephew with advice about future schooling and he revealed his own educational strategy in the years following World War I. "As to the school," Whitaker wrote,

> I have never considered that too important. Purdue does have a pretty good reputation, Michigan a better reputation, Carnegie and Case even better, but any of them would be very good and the education depends more on the student than on the school anyway.
>
> Another plan that would work out very well would be to go to your local college . . . for say two years, specializing in mathematics, physics, science, etc., and then transfer to an engineering school. Many educators consider that this is the best plan, as you then get some experience in two different types of schools. (It happens to be the plan I followed.)[23]

Whether U. A.'s father O. B. was one of those educators who considered this plan the best is not known. Neither is it clear why Uncas Whitaker chose to complete his engineering education at MIT, other than that it had an outstanding reputation. That reputation, however, had to compete against O. B.'s hostility towards eastern schools and eastern institutions in general, a hostility that would be transferred to his son. In another letter expressing educational advice, Whitaker told an old friend whose son was trying to choose between the University of Michigan Engineering School and MIT, that "Michigan, I think, develops a better rounded person and being a midwestern school I believe their boys tend to fit in better no matter where they go."[24]

With whatever uncertainties and prejudices, Whitaker left Weaubleau Missouri for Boston and MIT in the fall of 1920 equipped with two years of college education, a lifetime of western rural experience, and the name Uncas Aeneas, a liability or an asset depending on how greatly his new friends and acquaintances were admirers of James Fenimore Cooper. Among Cooper's most fervid fans, of course, was O. B. Whitaker. "I have just reread *Deer Slayer*," he wrote in one of his frequent family letters. "I think the hero in his various characters in the *Leather-Stocking Tales* is the finest character in American fiction, and those are my favorite novels. His standard of Christianity is to my mind admirable and infinitely superior to the 'Orthodox' creedal standards."[25] In Cooper's romances, O. B. found the fullest expression of all he admired: the world of the frontier, that curious blend of Christian and individual moral strength, and the American hero of American romance. The friendly, public, disputatious, and even garrulous father passed those enthusiasms on to his son. Uncas adopted the attitudes, but not the personal model his father provided; he would grow into a quiet, private man, a man to keep his own counsel. His later deeds, however, would prove to be talk enough.

2. The MIT Years

In the midst of the 1920's presidential campaign, advertised by at least one of the political parties as an opportunity to return the nation to the path of "normalcy," Uncas Aeneas Whitaker arrived in Cambridge to complete his undergraduate engineering education. Some of young Whitaker's relatives back home wondered out loud whether the expense of sending the boy to MIT would be worth it. Uncle Syd Whitaker was probably not one of the doubters, for he admired his bright young nephew. As he told O. B. a year or so after nephew Uncas had graduated from MIT: "Have always enjoyed Uncas' company and he and I have had a common ground of mechanics besides his naturally mature mind and fine manly outlook on the world."[1] In Uncle Syd's opinion, the money was well spent, although the cost was not modest. College officials estimated that a full year at MIT would run an individual student about $900 — tuition, $300; student tax, $9; board, $238; room, $109; clothes, $91; books, $62; other items, not including carfare, $68. Scholarships were awarded only for need. Who paid? O. B., periodically short of cash, borrowed some of the money from his brother Syd through his bank in Brownington, Missouri. Moreover, Syd probably provided some financial help outright.[2]

Carfare, at least, was no problem. Although young Whitaker lived off campus, his residences on Beacon Street were within reasonable walking distance of the university. No doubt, on that first day Uncas came a few blocks down Beacon, turned on Massachusetts Avenue, then across the Charles River and into Cambridge. Like Eric Hodgins, a fellow student (MIT, 1922), later famous as the author of *Mr. Blandings Builds His Dream House*, Uncas' first reaction to MIT may have been both exciting and sobering. Hodgins wrote of his experience as follows:

> I took leave of my parents as soon as I could and trudged across Longfellow Bridge to Cambridge. . . . I finally arrived opposite the Dome and Colonnade that stood between the two out-flung arms and pylons that enclosed the massive Great Court. I must have stood in awe for ten minutes, seeing with my own eyes the words incised in foot after foot of Indiana limestone: MASSACHVSETTS INSTITVTE OF TECHNOLOGY, and thinking to myself, "I am here. I am here."

Hodgins, like Uncas Whitaker, was a transfer student and had come to Cambridge during the summer to determine the possibilities of entering what he described as "the most difficult seat of learning to get into and to get out of in the United States." What Hodgins discovered was that come fall term he had to "go the rounds of professors" to see if, as a transfer student, he might be accepted with advanced standing. No doubt Whitaker had to do the same.[3]

U. A. Whitaker's MIT transcript indicates that he did receive credit for much of the work he had taken at Drury College and at the School of Mines at Rolla. He enrolled in the Mechanical Engineering Course II, described by the catalogue as a course that "prepares students to enter into any one of a number of branches of that profession."

> Beside machine design, with its specialties, engine design, power plant design, locomotive construction, steam turbine engineering, and mill engineering, courses are offered in the upper years preparing for heat and ventilating engineering, refrigeration and hydraulic engineering, factory construction, and industrial management There is also some work in Electrical Engineering, sufficient for the handling of ordinary problems.[4]

Eric Hodgins (a major in chemical engineering) later analyzed his education in terms that might reasonably be applied to Whitaker's experience: "Indeed, it comes over me, as I think of it now that in the 1920s we were taught seventeenth century mathematics, eighteenth century mechanics, and that most of the *ideas* of the nineteenth century were presented by — of all things — the English Department." Steam power and the magnificent Corliss Engine represented the focus of the mechanical engineering program in Uncas Whitaker's time.[5]

Uncas Whitaker did not have a distinguished academic career at MIT. At the close of the school year in June, 1922, a notation on the transcript indicates that student Whitaker was "referred to Professor Johnson in view of unsatisfactory record." In that academic term Whitaker had failed Applied Mechanics 223, Heat Engineering 224, and Materials of Engineering 230. Fortunately, MIT had a system that entitled those receiving a grade of F the opportunity to be reexamined. (There was a grade lower than F — FF — which apparently did not allow for this privilege.)[6]

Despite the rigorous grading at MIT and whatever deficiencies and educational disadvantages Whitaker might have brought with him from Drury and the School of Mines, it is possible that highly skilled and patient teaching might have helped his academic work. Apparently such teachers were rare at the time; at least Eric Hodgins' descriptions of his teachers give that impression. Hodgins describes the professor of applied mechanics as "Slave-Driver Smith," and adds that "even the best students conceded that Slave-Driver Smith deserved his title. He was a dry, bald Yankee, a martinet who piled on the workload and was a ruthless marker-down of even the most strenuous student efforts." As Whitaker's transcript indicates, applied mechanics was perhaps his worst experience at MIT.[7]

By the fall term of his final year at MIT, Uncas was managing to do better work. He successfully took the three previously failed examinations and passed all of them. In the remainder of this senior year, he passed all his courses except for elements of electrical engineering, which he failed in the middle term but passed upon reexamination. Having successfully passed all his courses by June, 1923, student Whitaker was — as his transcript records — recommended for the degree of Bachelor of Science in Mechanical Engineering.

As a student at MIT, Uncas Whitaker had received not only an engineering education but had also taken rigorous courses in English (learning, no doubt, the "ideas of the nineteenth century") and in political economy. The studies in political economy at MIT must surely have helped MIT earn its reputation for providing first-rate training not only for engineers, but for future business administrators as well. Political Economy 31 and 32 dealt generally with "the analysis and description of the existing economic structure of society, a brief study of economic theory and the application of that theory to some of the more important economic questions." Political Economy 33 gave particular attention to business administration, emphasizing such processes as "principles of accounting, corporate organization and finance, credit, banking, labor problems, and business management."[8]

University records provide a sketch of Whitaker's academic life at MIT, but no such records survive to tell us much about his personal life. He did apparently have close friends with whom he roomed on Beacon Street, just a few blocks from Massachusetts Avenue on the Boston side of the Charles River. Two roommates from 811 Beacon Street remained in correspondence with Whitaker over the years. Myron E. Doucette (MIT, 1925) and S. D. (Sargent) Heath (MIT, 1924) recalled the good old days in brief letters written in the 1960s. "Remember the old house at 811," S. D. Heath reminisced in a note to Whitaker in 1961. "The place where Doc Turnbull and the Mrs. used to hold forth [is] gone now. . . a new building there." In his reply, school friend Whitaker referred to their old buddies — Myron Doucette and Joshua Kingham (MIT, 1924) — and suggested to Heath "that maybe at an MIT homecoming a special effort could be made to get as many [of the old group] together as possible."[9]

Perhaps Uncas Whitaker's closest friend, and certainly the man with whom his longest lasting friendship was made at MIT, was Samuel Longfellow Williams, a New Hampshire native who, like Whitaker, earned a degree in mechanical engineering in 1923. Williams and Whitaker would both begin their professional careers soon after graduation with Westinghouse Air Brake Company in Pittsburgh and remain closely in touch in the years ahead.

The two men met during their junior year, Whitaker's first term at MIT, and because both were enrolled in the university's mechanical engineering course, they frequently attended the same classes. Williams recalls that Whitaker occasionally reminisced about life in Missouri — with Whitaker flourishes of humor and the tall tale.

> Whit talked about experiences at the school of mines, about experiences as a page in the Missouri legislature and about fishing in Missouri, mostly about catfish, which sounded like they were improved in the telling.

Williams has little recollection of Whitaker's activities outside of his academic life at MIT, partly because they lived on opposite sides of the Charles River. Moreover, academic life came first. "While at our school work," recalls Williams, "I guess it could be said we paid attention to the frequent admonishment by one of the Profs. that 'Tech is a place for men to work not for boys to play.'" As Williams emphasizes, both he and Whit took that admonishment seriously.[10]

Uncas Whitaker's education at MIT culminated in the senior year thesis project required of all graduating students. Like most senior theses, Whitaker's project, unglamorously entitled, "The Design of a Rubber Heel Testing Machine," demanded a great deal of work. Whitaker had to choose a subject-project, locate an appropriate adviser, find a local company with which to cooperate in developing the project, do the research, define the problem, and then solve it to the satisfaction both of the company and the professor. The project is interesting for two reasons. First, the thesis manifests an important aspect of Uncas Whitaker's character: the practical, down-to-earth mind at work. In his introduction to the project, Whitaker states the problem simply, at the same time posing it as something that everyone who wears shoes with rubber heels has had cause to think about: "Tests are usually made to determine resistance to abrasion, percent of elongation, strength in tension, hardness and the relation of strain to stress. There is, however, no test that will in itself determine whether a heel will give good service or poor." The purpose of the research was "to design a machine that will so test a heel that the results obtained will give an accurate index to the ability of the heel to resist wear in actual service. The criterion of the machine will therefore be its capability in differentiating between heels of any serviceableness."[11]

The other interest in the project lies in the approach Whitaker took, one that would remain his professional modus operandi. According to a recent history of MIT, the mechanical engineering program was not particularly oriented to application at this time.[12] Although the program was in Whitaker's time strong in the field of materials testing, Whitaker found in his project the opportunity to develop the practical approach to problem raising and problem solving in the field of engineering that would become the trademark of his professional career. In this specific instance — and the point of view would remain paramount for Whitaker — he did not try to figure out how to convince a customer to buy and use a machine for a need either unrecognized or, more to the point, nonexistent. For Whitaker, the problem was how best to design a machine to serve the requirements of a customer. A related point of view, probably part of Whitaker's thinking as early as 1922, was that the customer for an engineering project had the responsibility to collaborate creatively with the engineer. The engineer's corollary responsibility to understand completely the need of his customer would become a major tenet of Whitaker's later engineering and business philosophy.

Whether Uncas Whitaker conceived of his thesis subject independently is problematic. It is possible that the query about the feasibility of constructing a rubber heel testing machine came from the Plymouth Rubber Company, which may very well have asked the Institute for advice and information on the problem. Such a relationship between MIT and outside companies was not new, but before 1919 the university had no systematic method for handling requests of this kind. In 1919, however, MIT was in the midst of an endowment campaign, raising funds for more teachers and new facilities to cope with the increasing enrollment in technical and engineering education encouraged by the needs of World War I. In the course of that campaign, the Technology Plan was devised to offer the research capabilities and technical facilities of MIT to industry and business, for the purpose of bringing in outside income to meet the Institute's growing educational needs.[13]

The scope of the Technology Plan provided for contractual arrangements with various corporations, companies, and private individuals, "to undertake research work in their behalf." Even before Uncas Whitaker arrived on campus, the plan had, after its first full year of operation, worked out contracts with over two hundred clients amounting to $1.2 million, and a new division had been created — the Division of Industrial Cooperation and Research (later shortened to the Division of Industrial Cooperation) — to administer the contracts.[14] In the years ahead, U. A. Whitaker would become an active participant in the program, not only as a contractor, but also as an important alumni advisor and friend. It would be the first important link between Uncas Whitaker and the MIT educational community and it would be a significant one.

Professor William H. Walker, who first headed the Division of Industrial Cooperation and Research, believed firmly in the principles of the plan. In his report, submitted after the division's first year of operation, he explained the advantages to MIT. "The principles of the Technology Plan are sound," and provide MIT needed financial aid, but in addition to the financial benefits:

> Intimate contact with progressive manufacturing concerns has proved a great stimulus to the educational and research activities of the different departments. The fact that work of moment is being carried on in its laboratories and that great industries are looking to the Institute for the solution of many of their basic problems becomes known throughout the instructional force and student body, permeating even to the members of the Freshman class. A keener interest is thus taken in acquiring that knowledge and experience which is being daily shown to be of value and importance alike in the enrichment of the individual, and in the progress of the community.[15]

C. L. Norton, Walker's successor as director, reported the following year that, despite the recession (1920-21), "the most striking development of the year is the extent to which the Division of Industrial Cooperation and Research has become the real point of contact betwen technology and industry on matters relating to science and engineering."[16]

By the beginning of Uncas Whitaker's final year at MIT, the Division of Industrial Cooperation and Research was in its fourth year of existence and there can be little doubt that he knew of the operation. In addition to Walker's belief that the consciousness of every undergraduate on campus was permeated with the idea, Whitaker's advisor on his senior thesis, Professor Harrison W. Hayward (MIT, 1896), had begun already his own tenure as a directing member of the division. Therefore, Hayward, who was an expert in the area of materials testing, may well have made the contact with the Plymouth Rubber Company that led to young Whitaker's project involving the rubber heel testing machine.[17] In any event, Uncas grew well acquainted with the kinds of services institutions like MIT could provide industry, and later, as the head of his own company, he took full advantage of them. By the same token, understanding the value of these arrangements to the university, he remained a strong supporter of their continuance despite the powerful opposition that emerged in the 1960s. Ironically, even in those early days before talk of the military-industrial complex, there was opposition to the plan from faculty members who wanted to keep education separate from business. From the perspective of the present it would be easy to misinterpret this opposition as essentially political in nature; in fact, the response was more along the lines of "ivory tower" thinking, thinking that the university countered with the argument that the plan could serve them well as one way to keep industry from stealing their best people.[18]

The MIT Endowment Campaign, begun in 1919, had already received pledges amounting to about $4 million when an anonymous matching donation was announced. Guessing about the identity of "Mr. Smith" went on for months until on January 20, 1920, about nine months before Uncas Whitaker made his first appearance on campus, an alumni dinner was held for the purpose of revealing the actual identity of the donor. "Mr. Smith" turned out to be George Eastman of Eastman Kodak. This dramatic example of university philanthropy could not have escaped Whitaker's attention, but it would never have occurred to him during his years as a student that some day he too would be in a position to make the kind of contribution George Eastman had made to MIT.[19]

* * * * * * *

Commencement exercises for the Class of 1923 — the second largest in MIT's history to that date — were held Tuesday, June 12, beginning at 10:30 A. M. The exercises were to be held outdoors, in the Great Court (later renamed for George Eastman), before the Dome and Colonnade. The day before, Samuel Wesley Stratton had been inaugurated as MIT's eighth president, and he presided over a ceremony awarding 545 undergraduate degrees to a class that included a son of Thomas Alva Edison and a future president of MIT, Julius Adams Stratton (no relation to Samuel). The 1923 graduation ceremony was unique: for the first time in MIT's history, all members of the class wore caps and gowns. That new decorum was intensified as diplomas were, again for the first time, handed out individually to graduates rather than being presented to the class en masse, avoiding the usual mad scene at the end of commencement when grads participated in a "wild scramble for degrees."

Perhaps because of Edison's presence at the graduation (it is reported that Edison, who disapproved of formal engineering education, snoozed through the ceremonies), someone decided to take motion pictures of the inauguration, the commencement ceremonies, the processions, and a variety of informal scenes of commencement day activities. The film does, with the expected home-movie elements of self-consciousness, show a clean, magnificently landscaped, and uncluttered campus — a view of a more leisured and orderly past.[20]

The major concern of the commencement organizers, not surprisingly, was the weather. Would it rain and force the exercises and the 3,000 spectators into the stuffy Cambridge Armory? The memory of the preceding year's graduation did not alleviate their worry, for in 1922 a high wind had blown over the huge tent set up to accommodate the graduation crowd. Eric Hodgins, a survivor of the '22 commencement, also attended the ceremonies in 1923, now as a member of the staff of MIT's alumni publication, *The Technology Review*.

> The Weather Bureau had been useless. It would neither deny nor confirm, comfort nor warn. There might be rain; there was a good chance of it. But there might not be; there was also a good chance of that. The official verdict was Unsettled, meaning that the Bureau would remain officially unastonished at showers, thunderstorms, floods, seismism, or a volcanic eruption from a hitherto undiscovered crater on Beacon Hill.

These grave possibilities notwithstanding, the graduation went off without a hitch. The main invited speaker that year was Elisha Lee (MIT, 1892), vice-president of the then flourishing Pennsylvania Railroad who told the graduates, among other things, that "you are starting your active careers in the most interesting and stirring period of the world's history." Within the context of the development of science and industry of which he was speaking, Lee's prediction was not the overstatement it might appear. Between Lindbergh's Atlantic flight, four years in the future, and manned flights to the moon, late in Whitaker's life, lay astonishing scientific and technological breakthroughs in which Uncas Whitaker and a good number of his classmates would be involved.   There was more prediction than cliche, after all, in Lee's statement that he could "scarcely avoid a feeling of envy for the limitless opportunities which lie before the generation to which you belong."[21]

Thus, Uncas Aeneas Whitaker, along with 544 fellow undergraduates received his degree under what the *Technology Review* described editorially as "the happiest and most impressive conditions any class has known."[22] As Eric Hodgins reported the degree granting:

> Each man of the . . . carefully alphabetized class marched to the platform, ascended a runway in which the Schuberts could have taken pride, approached the Presidential position, and received from the Presidential hand, that for which he had spent four years of more effort or less. Then he marched down another runway, quit of Technology forever, if he wished it so. When the last man of the last course had marched down again . . . the 56th Commencement was over. The Class of 1923 broke ranks and spread like mist that is scattered by a wind.[23]

Uncas Whitaker, "quit of Technology," made his way immediately to his new job; it was time to apply what he had learned to the real world as it was represented at the Westinghouse Air Brake Company in Pittsburgh. Some years later, though, Whitaker would return to MIT as a valued alumnus, and he would remain a significant member of the MIT community until his death.

3. The Engineer on the Job: Westinghouse Air Brake

In January 1923, when Uncas Whitaker was completing his next to last academic term at MIT, his father O. B. Whitaker was in Jefferson City, Missouri, beginning his fourth term as representative from Hickory County in the 52nd session of the Missouri Legislature. According to the Kansas City *Times*, the elder Whitaker, now Republican floor leader, "coming from the smallest county in the state, showed himself to be the most dominant force in a Democratic legislature." But O. B., voraciously reading biographies of heroes and heroines — Gladstone, Cromwell, Teddy Roosevelt, Abraham Lincoln, Paul Kruger, Helen Keller — was not a happy man. When he was not busy on the house floor, O. B. suffered loneliness and frustration that he did not hesitate to share. In the extraordinarily long and personal letters he sent in multiple copies from the capitol to family members back home, he expressed discouragement in many areas, even about his political future. "I can't see any issues now that would justify my candidacy again," he reported. And although he was at the height of his political power in the state, O. B. told the St. Louis *Star* in March about his feeling also. The *Star* disclosed on March 18, 1923, that "Whitaker who has come nearer controlling the Democratic House than any other legislator, said today that he has served his last term in the legislature unless some unusual issue arises."[1]

These and similar accolades did not mitigate O. B.'s melancholy. Lonely for his family, he wrote: "I always remember you in my prayers every night. After all, the only perfect ideal is the Christian life, and that standard is the only correct measure of the value of our lives." And directly to his son, who had served as a page in the Missouri House during some of his father's earlier terms, he wrote, "Uncas, I sometimes think of you when a big debate is on, for I remember how you seemed to enjoy that, and I am also proud of your ability to logically analyse and understand propositions." But now, separated by distance from his loved ones, alone in a housekeeping room in Jefferson City with his typewriter as his only companion, he wrote page after page reporting events and examining his thoughts and emotions.[2]

I shall be glad to get home, and I wish I could have something that kept me busy all the time, something that I could feel was worthwhile. When I am not fully occupied, I sometimes am very lonely. I often think I am surely the saddest member of the legislature — but I guess I should not write that.[3]

O. B. Whitaker, having developed the habit of communicating to his family whatever was on his mind, produced, no doubt, a mixture of guilt and sympathy in those who chose to take him too seriously. For nearly thirty years, from 1912 until his death in 1942, the elder Whitaker pounded out letter after letter chronicling his life, his feelings, and his attitudes and judgments. Their effect on son Uncas would not be minimal.

The year 1923 found both father and son wrestling with personal and professional decisions. For Uncas Whitaker it was a question of where to begin his engineering career — he chose the Westinghouse Air Brake Company in Pittsburgh. For O. B. Whitaker, it was a question of where to continue his political career — he chose to run for the United States Congress in 1924. While Uncas had few worldly possessions to carry with him from Boston to Pittsburgh, his father had the responsibility of maintaining a half dozen pieces of farming property totaling over 1,500 acres. Wearying of that responsibility he decided to spread it among his children, a significant decision in its effect on Uncas Whitaker, for it would involve him continuously in Missouri farm affairs for twenty-five years at the same time that he was engaged in furthering his own engineering and business career.

While O. B. was electing to divide his land among his children, the voters in his congressional district were electing his opponent to Congress. O. B., disheartened over the loss, began to dwell more intently on his personal affairs and proposed the following to his children:

What to do with my property and indebtedness has been a question with me lately. It is next to impossible to sell land now, and if sold it would have to be a very low price. I am thinking of offering to divide my land and indebtedness among you. I do not know whether you would want to accept this or not, but I believe you could each take your part and keep it for say ten years and each have a good property. Anyway I will suggest my plan and you can consider it, and maybe we all will be together Xmas and can talk it over.[4]

Uncle Syd Whitaker, who became the family banker for this arrangement, complimented O. B. on his generosity, telling him he had "done handsomely by your children." Uncas, however, found himself at age twenty-four saddled with mortgage notes totaling $8,000.[5] By the time the arrangements were approved in December, 1924, Uncas had been with WAB for about a year and a half and was earning approximately $130 a month.[6] That the farmland in Missouri would appreciate in value over the coming years was a belief that O. B., Syd, and Uncas Whitaker clung to for many years. All three predicted that land ownership was the only possible hedge against the inflation they constantly predicted, even during the depths of the depression. Consequently, land deals of all kinds became a major obsession with the family all through the 1920s and 1930s. Unfortunately, although the family optimism remained, land values in southwest Missouri never appreciated.[7]

Uncle Syd, through the State Bank of Brownington, offered Uncas very favorable terms as he always did when dealing with family matters. The day after the new year, 1925, began he wrote his brother O. B.:

> As for payment, tell Uncas to just suit his own convenience about that. I am in a position to carry it the year for him, to take any payment he may want to make at any time he likes, stopping interest, of course on the payment amount at the time of payment, or to take full payment any day that he may make arrangements that suit him better. There is no occasion for him to borrow anything from his bank or anyone else unless he can get cheaper money.[8]

It was nearly four years before Uncas Whitaker had the resources to begin repaying the principal on the $8,000 note.[9]

* * * * * * *

In 1890, a little over twenty years after George Westinghouse had formed the Westinghouse Air Brake Company, then located near downtown Pittsburgh, a new plant was erected in the newly incorporated borough of Wilmerding in East Pittsburgh. Two years before, in 1888, the Pennsylvania Railroad had established a flag stop station there, and George Westinghouse soon after purchased the farmlands in the area for his expanding air brake business. In 1889 ground was broken for the new plant construction and a town was built to provide housing and other facilities for the plant employees. In 1901, the company acquired the old Glen Hotel on Marguerite Avenue in Wilmerding "for the purpose of providing for unmarried male employees of the engineering department and general office." Renamed the Tonnaleuka Club, after a famous Indian chief, it became, some twenty-two years later, the residence of Uncas A. Whitaker, an unmarried male employee of the Westinghouse Air Brake engineering department.[10] It was his home for the six years he remained with the company. That son Uncas was quartered in a home named after an heroic Indian chief must have amused, even pleased his father.

Air brake technology essentially began with George Westinghouse in 1869. Although Westinghouse is not necessarily credited with the invention of the air brake himself, he has been assigned the more important credit of creating a new art. Others, that is to say, may have had the original idea, but Westinghouse was the first to apply the invention in practical ways. In brief, Westinghouse solved the problem of stopping trains safely. Between 1869 and 1907, Westinghouse filed 103 air brake patents beginning with a simple mechanical straight-air system and finally introducing a fluid-pressure automatic brake mechanism in which the air valves were controlled electrically.[11]

After 1907, Westinghouse left the further development of the air brake to others, as his interests and area of responsibilities shifted. Engineers from the ranks at Westinghouse Air Brake carried on his work, expanding and extending the basic existing principles of the prior art. As one of Westinghouse's important inventive successors put it, "it is truly remarkable that through all subsequent improvements not one of the original functions of the triple valve has been discarded, but that they have been extended and expanded, and many new functions added."[12] Uncas Whitaker and engineers like him would be engaged in this process, working to further air brake technology. By the 1920s, if not before, the atmosphere in those areas responsible for developing new patents was extremely conducive to that kind of creativity. At Westinghouse Air Brake, patent producing engineers were allowed the broadest latitude in the area of engineering problem solving. To let the talented engineer make his own successes and suffer his own failures was a philosophy Whitaker would apply to his own engineering department some years later.

****

On June 14, 1923, just two days after graduation ceremonies at
MIT, Whitaker left Boston for his new job with Westinghouse Air
Brake Company in Pittsburgh. Whitaker's old friend, Sam Williams,
recalls the trip west and reveals something of Whitaker's playful side:

> In our senior year, we attended together many of the meetings with
> representatives of companies seeking graduates [writes Williams].
> We both applied to WAB , received job offers and accepted them.
> Whit proposed that we 'bum our way' to Pittsburgh cropping rides
> on freight trains. He may have been testing me and having fun. He
> was quite persistent and since he was adventuresome and got
> pleasure from testing himself, I thought he was serious. If I had
> agreed I think he would have done it.

Feeling less adventuresome than "Whit" and wanting some
vacation between school and job, Williams left Whitaker to go off
alone to Pittsburgh to find a place for the two of them to live.
Whitaker traveled to Pittsburgh, not by riding the rails as he
proposed, but as a regular passenger on a regularly scheduled
railroad. Nevertheless, there is some evidence to suggest that young
Whitaker had jumped a freight train or two in his Missouri school
days.

Whitaker arrived in Wilmerding only to discover that WAB's
Tonnaleuka Club had no vacancies. He was fortunate in finding a
room in a private house just down the street from the Club and
located immediately behind the company's headquarters building.
Two weeks later, Williams arrived and moved into the private
residence with his school chum. Their tenure in the house proved to
be brief; Whitaker's playfulness and innovative urges apparently
hastened their departure. Sam Williams recalls the episode:

> We managed to get rooms in the Tonnaleuka Club after a few
> weeks as a result of one of Whit's inventions. To help cool our
> room an electric fan was purchased. It was small, high speed and
> very noisy especially located on the wall between the two windows
> where it was found to be most effective. Whit decided to make a
> control that would automatically shut the fan off after a period to
> allow time for us to go to sleep. A shoe tied to the fan switch would
> operate it when dropped. A string passed around a candle held the
> shoe up until the candle burned down to the string when it
> permitted the shoe to drop. This worked so it was set up and we
> went to bed with the fan noisily at work. When we awoke the next
> morning, the fan was still noisily at work. The candle had gone out.
> When the landlady saw us she suggested we find another room as

she had decided she didn't wish to rent the room any longer.

Whitaker's inventive talents, usually more successful, could be employed towards more interesting and constructive ends. He and Sam Williams decided to use some of their spare time to assemble a large radio receiver complete with a loudspeaker. Radio at that time was still largely a "do-it-yourself" affair and a few stores, one in East Pittsburgh, had begun to stock the parts necessary for radio assembly. As Sam Williams remembered the project, Whitaker's major motivation was to construct a set that could pull in stations from as far away as possible. "KDKA was close by and dominated the local air. We wanted to be able to reach outside and get other stations. The further, the better. Whit was the instigator, the director and the chief workman."

The project itself came to affect the living arrangements of the two newly hired WAB engineers. Whitaker and Williams decided to reallocate the space in the two rooms assigned them, making one a bedroom and the other a combination living room and workshop. Given the size of the equipment for the radio project, the workshop part of the living room came to dominate the available space. Tubes, dials, batteries, and tools could be found everywhere as Whitaker and Williams labored through the construction process. According to Williams, Whitaker did most of the work, including the soldering of what seemed to be an infinite number of electrical connections. Perhaps, Williams later hypothesized, "all that work helped him to see the potential for AMP's solderless connectors when he ran across the opportunity there."[13]

Now comfortably installed in their rooms at the Tonnaleuka club, Whitaker and Williams settled down to work at WAB. At first, both young men entered WAB's special apprenticeship program for newly graduated engineers. It had been inaugurated some years earlier when WAB selected its engineering apprentices from the railroad yards themselves. More recently, "shop" engineers were being replaced with university-trained engineers, but the apprenticeship training program was retained and largely conducted in the same manner as before.[14] The prospect of yet more schooling after four years of formal education may not have been an attraction, but Whitaker, Williams, and about ten other recent college graduates entered WAB's apprenticeship class in 1923, a six-month program paying each man an hourly wage of sixty cents. "For six months," as Sam Williams described the program, "we studied air brake devices and braking equipment as directed by the supervisor of special training. Whit was continually after me to study the pamphlets so those from the other colleges wouldn't 'show us up.' We were rather impatient with the additional schooling and Whit was a leader in persuading WAB to assign us activities . . . at current jobs in the engineering department."[15]

After the six-month apprenticeship ended, the class was "graduated" and assigned to a variety of jobs at WAB. Although the records at WAB for that period are not complete, they do show that U. A. Whitaker moved into the engineering division as an assistant foreman in the testing department, a reasonable assignment considering his testing experience at MIT. At this point Whitaker was earning $130 a month, a considerable increase over his beginning apprenticeship wage.[16] Next, he appears to have been shifted into the very recently created rubber parts department of the engineering division, where he assisted in development work using parts made of rubber.[17]

Whitaker's ambitious nature and persuasive personality impressed his superiors, and he was given additional duties of importance both to WAB and to his own career development. "Whit was the first in our class to get an assignment where he repesented WAB to the customers," Williams remembers. "Some extra large freight cars were being built for the Virginia Railroad. . . in McKees Rocks. Whit was responsible that the brake equipment was correctly applied and functioned as intended. For . . . several weeks he commuted between Wilmerding and McKees Rocks. The rest of us envied him."[18]

Such opportunities made WAB an attractive firm to young Whitaker. Moreover, there was the possibility of experiencing a variety of jobs, not the least interesting of which was in the area of original development work. After the initial shifting around, as noted above, men of Whitaker's inventive talent were provided the opportunity to contribute innovations in a variety of areas. Whitaker, in a resume of his work experience written some years later, underscored this point in the description of his accomplishments at WAB:

> Upon finishing school, a connection was made with Westinghouse Air Brake Company. The last two years with this Company were concentrated on original development work and as a result of these two years of development, the Westinghouse Company has taken out over 20 U. S. patents and over 30 foreign patents in my name.

In fact, several of Whitaker's patents on air brake equipment were important improvements on an original invention made by George Westinghouse himself in the latter part of the nineteenth century. There is no doubt that WAB was pleased with Whitaker's work during the six years he was with the company. As Whitaker succinctly put it in his resume, "the opinion of the Westinghouse Air Brake Company of the work done while there is perhaps best indicated by the fact that when advised of my intention of leaving, they offered a salary increase exceeding 50 per cent and a choice of several positions of definite advancement."[19]

In this open-ended environment, Uncas Whitaker was encouraged to produce and he flourished. In those final two years at WAB, Whitaker filed some twenty-seven of his patentable ideas, an amazing record for one person in so short a period. George Westinghouse's truly phenomenal inventive record aside (no mere mortal could match it), only a few other engineers in the history of WAB compiled a list as long as Whitaker's. Probably no one (again, George Westinghouse aside) was able to do it in so short a time. It is not suprising that WAB officials tried to keep Whitaker with the firm by offering him such a substantial salary increase and various possibilities for rapid advancement.[20]

In addition to the lessons he learned from his development experience in the WAB engineering patent-producing departments, Whitaker, in his years in Wilmerding, Pennsylvania, was exposed to certain other Westinghouse Company policies and attitudes that also affected his later thinking and business decision making. George Westinghouse, like most late nineteenth century American entrepreneurs of his type, believed in paternalism. Open shop principles prevailed; the Saturday half-holiday was instituted in 1881; safety and sanitation features were built into his early factory buildings; emergency medical treatment was available in case of accident; a pension system at company expense went into effect in 1906; and a plan for the sale of stock to employees was also available fairly early on. Whitaker's later concerns for his own employees incorporated a number of these ideas, updated to serve new conditions. Whitaker also had the opportunity to become acquainted with WAB's long-established international operation, which, at the very least, suggested to him the unlimited possibilities of trading and manufacturing overseas, another crucial aspect in the development of AMP Incorporated.[21]

But in the mid-1920s, Uncas Whitaker had more pressing short-term goals in mind. To better prepare himself for his assignment in original development work at WAB, Whitaker decided to attend night school at Carnegie Institute of Technology (now Carnegie-Mellon University), situated in the Oakland section of Pittsburgh. Large companies, then as now, encouraged employees like Whitaker to upgrade and improve themselves through further education. It is even possible that Whitaker's superiors suggested that some additional course work in electrical engineering would enhance his chances of advancement within the company. More to the point was the growing need to know more as engineering science and technology expanded, for Uncas Whitaker's formal engineering education to this point was somewhat inadequate for the responsibilities a company like WAB was ready to offer him.

Whether Whitaker knew it consciously or not, he was in the right place at the right time to gain some further engineering education. It had always been Andrew Carnegie's notion that night school would be valuable for uplifting the individual worker to a higher and better job opportunity. Of course, when he conceived the idea at the turn of the century, he had in mind the shop mechanic and not the professionally trained engineer. The original night school clientele of 607 in 1905-06, therefore, differed considerably from the 4,829 in attendance (both in day school and night school) during the 1929-30 academic year. By the late 1920s at least one-quarter of those attending had college degrees or had taken some college courses. The administration and faculty of the Carnegie Institute of Technology wisely recognized these changing needs and revamped its program accordingly. As one historian of Carnegie Tech, writing in 1937, put it:

> A double decade ago it was a commonly held view that a college graduate was a more or less finished product. Today, with the rapid expansion of man's knowledge, particularly in science and technology, even the college graduate finds his training inadequate unless he continues his studies. So, at Carnegie, it became necessary in 1926 to offer a series of post-graduate courses at night.

Such a new series of courses might well have convinced Uncas Whitaker to attend Carnegie Tech in the spring term beginning January, 1927.

Thomas Baker, then president of Carnegie Tech, soon recognized the need to work more closely with industry to establish firmer contacts with companies interested in hiring the school's graduates. Through face-to-face discussions with the management of various industries, officials at Carnegie Tech learned "what types of training would be most advantageous to both employer and employed." That this kind of industrial cooperation could be successful was evidenced by the presence on the campus of employees from eleven hundred separate companies by the latter part of the 1920s. The very large firms in the area, like WAB, were represented in significant numbers.[22]

The enrollment in Whitaker's night school program in electrical engineering numbered well over 200 when he began in 1927. The standard night school program leading to a bachelor's degree in engineering took so many years (up to six and sometimes more) that not a very large number of students worked toward a degree.[23] Whitaker, however, having completed one undergraduate program at MIT, was able to earn a B. S. in electrical engineering in five semesters. Having successfully completed the requisite core courses before entering Carnegie Tech, he had only to take a half-dozen additional courses and write a senior thesis, all of which he accomplished successfully by June, 1929.[24]

During his first semester at Carnegie Tech, he made the trip from Wilmerding on Thursdays to attend lectures and recitations in the basic electrical engineering course and on Tuesdays to work in the concurrent lab course, which dealt with electrical measurements. The second semester, fall 1927, Uncas Whitaker, anticipating the new research responsibilities that were soon to come at WAB, decided to increase his course load. As he explained to his father, "I just got back from registering at Carnegie. Will go to school two nights a week and will write my thesis this year if I can for I will have a good deal more work next year."[25] As it turned out, he did not write his thesis that year, instead choosing to put off that exercise till the following year.

In his final two semesters, taken during the academic year 1928-29, Whitaker enrolled for an even heavier course load. In addition to the work on his senior thesis and a course and lab in alternating current machinery, he took a full year in the design of electrical machinery. On June 11, 1929, a little over four months before the stock market crash, Uncas Aeneas Whitaker received a degree in electrical engineering along with only eighteen others at Carnegie Institute of Technology's twenty-second commencement.[26] Although his record at Carnegie Tech was not brilliant, it was respectable, and apparently what he learned there was substantial enough for him to be able to make numerous outstanding contributions to contemporary air brake technology.

Meanwhile, along with his studies at Carnegie and his development work at WAB, Uncas Whitaker had often to turn his attention to things back on the farm. He remained alert for that hoped-for rise in land prices about which he received conflicting messages from his Missouri informants. In late September, 1927, he received a note from his father, suggesting prices to ask for the 560 acres of farmland O. B. had given him. Always irrepressibly optimistic when it came to land prices, O. B. suggested that collectively the land at sale should bring about $14,000. Uncle Syd, however, perhaps closer to the financial reality of the situation on account of his banking activities, put the problem in its proper perspective when he wrote his nephew shortly after Christmas, 1927, that "the trouble with land value is the placing on the market of so much land that loan companies have taken over. Until this land is sold, the values are bound to be kept down and land sales more difficult at reasonable value." This situation grew continually more serious and farmers had ever greater difficulty realizing enough on their crops and livestock to meet mortgage payments.[27]

Nevertheless, Uncle Syd, despite his measured judgment about land values in 1927, remained essentially optimistic. One year afterwards he advised his nephew to hold on, things could only go up now:

> I think farming will be better in the next few years and that farm land will regain its standing as an investment. Good farmers who are in condition to take advantage of present prices are making money. And I believe better rather than poorer conditions are directly ahead of us in farming communities. You are apt to have more demand for your farm and a better income. . . . The general conditions are better and are getting better.[28]

Nephew Uncas took his Uncle's advice and held on — for the next twenty years. New pieces of land were added and old ones sold, but Uncas Whitaker's relationship with Missouri farming and farm land produced only aggravation and tax write-offs (and minimal ones at that). More significantly for our story, those losing investments did succeed in keeping Whitaker directly tied to his Missouri origins.

If landed investments were not enough to keep engineer Whitaker's mind on events back home, his father's ever-fluctuating career decisions and state of mind were. Late in 1926, Uncas learned from his father that he was contemplating a return to Lincoln, Kansas and the possibility of securing a church there. Interest on mortgage payments, taxes, and outstanding bank loans, coupled with the fact that he had as yet no regular income, left O. B. in a precarious financial position. Somehow or other son Uncas, who by spring 1928 could not have been earning much more than $200 per month at WAB, got his hands on $1,000, which he promptly sent to help his father out. O. B. needed the money desperately. Although he had, by 1928, succeeded in finding a church in Truro, Iowa, the condition of his voice was such that he could not preach on Sundays, and O. B. was, as a result, not yet being paid his monthly salary. A long history of throat trouble, which often left O. B. so hoarse he could not speak above a whisper, led the family to fear its cause might be cancer.[29]

Although O. B. needed money, he was not entirely happy about taking a gift of $1,000 from his considerate son. He wrote to Uncas, worrying about how the money had been raised: "I am suspecting that you have borrowed the money you sent me or have disposed of your securities to raise it. I do not want you to do that." On the other hand, O. B. was in financial need, and he suggested that Uncas lend him any monies he could spare. "If you have a part of it not in use I will be glad to borrow it."[30]

O. B. managed somehow to struggle through both financially and psychologically. When his voice gave out and he could not preach, he kept himself occupied at his typewriter, turning out stories. Apparently, he had sustained his ambition to become a writer and in 1929 he gave serious consideration to undertaking writing as a profession. While still in Truro, he wrote yet another version of the story of a young man who succeeded in closing the saloons in town. This time the story was altogether autobiographical, exploiting details from O. B.'s experience as head of Kansas Christian College back in 1893. Uncas received thirty-two pages of O. B. 's manuscript and the opportunity to read about and, surely, comment on his father's early years in what was an increasingly legendary American West.[31]

In the fall of 1928, O. B. returned to Weaubleau to run once more for the state legislature. Reelected, O. B. Whitaker and his wife Nettie traveled to Jefferson City for the opening of the 55th General Assembly of the Missouri Legislature. Uncas, beginning his final term at Carnegie Tech and busy with his development work at WAB, had been out of touch with his parents for some days, long enough to prompt a threat from his father that he would send him a collect telegram if he did not write soon. O. B. was joking, as he often did when Uncas failed to write home, but now he had a reason. O. B.'s throat problem had become so severe that he had scheduled a

February visit to the Mayo Clinic in Rochester, Minnesota. He warned Uncas that his mother would be alone in Jefferson City for a time and ordered him to write a letter every other day for the period he was at Mayo.[32]

O. B. felt considerable anxiety, and the possibility of throat cancer must have been on everyone's mind. Certainly it was on O. B.'s mind as his letters made plain. As an outpatient, he stayed at a YMCA near the clinic, and in his small room at night, with his typewriter as companion and with cancer on his mind, he wrote of death and dying. The letters received by the members of the family, Uncas included, must have been difficult to deal with:

> I have no fear of death, but I do not want to linger useless and suffering with a loathesome disease, a burden to my loved ones. Speaking of death — not that I think I am going to die, but the fear of cancer of the throat had led me to consider much the relative preference of death to cancer of that kind. (For I am of the opinion that cancer of the throat would be one of its most dread forms.)

O. B., understandably, was feeling sorry for himself; moreover, he was rethinking his views on death and found that his attitude had changed markedly:

> I used to think, with almost unbearable agony, of dying and leaving Mamma and the children, a feeling that it would be a loss to them, that they needed me. Recently that feeling is quite gone, and I feel that they will be just as well off without me as with me. The children are all independent, and should I go first I know Mamma will be cared for — Uncas will see to that, and no boy has ever had a more loving worshipful mother to care for.

O. B. went on to describe the suffering resulting from the operation he had just undergone. "I am not writing this in tears. I am perfectly calm and enjoying saying these things. . . . Nor is it the effect of morphine, for at my request the doctor did not give me any — I would rather suffer a little more under the operation than experience the terrible effect that morphine always has on me." Then the tone of the letter changes:

> I think we all often attach too much significance and importance to the significance of our lives in relation to our loved ones — thinking ourselves indispensable, when in truth it may matter little to them whether we live or die.

O. B., who often mixed the historical with the personal, went on to explain:

> I am thinking of so many of our greatest and best men who were deprived of their mothers or fathers when they were babes or children — Lincoln, Garfield, Hoover. I am thinking of dear sister Minnie. When the telegram reached me at Lincoln, Kansas [1893], of her death I thought of her three little girls, almost babies; and it seemed to me cruelly unjust to them to take their mother from them — and such a mother! — unselfish, loving, devoted, intelligent, wise; but would her three chilren have accomplished more than they have or been better women had she lived — and that was the only reason she wanted to live.

There was more, much more, in this vein before O. B. decided he had exhausted the subject. Things must have looked grim to the family the day this letter was received, but the emotions called forth by this maudlin account were of short duration. O. B. found out he would live![33]

The day following his thoughts-on-death letter, O. B. wrote another, equally long, reflecting on the possibility of having cancer, how he had come to believe it, what might happen next, etc. After completing several single-spaced typed pages on this topic, O. B. was interrupted by a visit from his doctor. When the customary doctor-patient amenities were concluded, O. B. decided to confront the issue directly: "Doctor," he asked, "do I or do I not have throat cancer?" According to O. B.'s account, a look of amazement passed over the doctor's face, and he asked O. B. where he had gotten that idea. O. B. explained that a few moments after his operation, when he was still in the operating chair, he had heard the doctor talking on the telephone about a patient whom he was scheduling for cancer treatment, and O. B. assumed the doctor was referring to him. In fact, the doctor was talking to a colleague about another patient. The crisis had passed, but O. B., undoubtedly embarrassed, decided to turn humorous. He expressed his disappointment on hearing the good news: "Well you just can't sympathize with me now, I almost wish it was cancer; for wouldn't cancer with honor be better than no cancer and no fame at all? Anyway I can't help feeling glad and grateful." Gratitude notwithstanding, O. B. regretted the hours wasted on his long letters and for a while considered sending the cancer story out to his friends and fellow legislators despite the fact that it was not true. The widespread sympathy he would gain thereby seemed too valuable to overlook, but in the end, his legislative friends, if not his family, were spared.[34]

O. B. Whitaker, in any of his moods of expression, was a strong personality. Like his own father, he made the rules, set the moral tone, and insisted that father knew best. Uncas, like the rest of the family, respected and acknowledged his father's authority and even after reaching adulthood he remained dutiful and generous in his treatment of O. B. But as a mature young man, Uncas had already begun to show signs of his own ability to influence and lead people, and within his family he began to establish himself as someone whose advice and counsel should be heeded. O. B., too, recognized his son's influence with the family, no doubt with some pride intermingled with reservations stemming from his own frustrations and disappointments, among them a recent loss in a tough legislative fight. A portion of his "sermonizing" letter written from the Mayo Clinic, apparently in response to some advice from Uncas, reflects these ambivalent feelings.

> Uncas I got your fine letter today. Somehow, consciously or unconsciously, you have assumed the same role in our family that Brother Syd has in my father's family (Uncle Joe calls it "self-constituted authority" when referring to Uncle Syd). You speak with authority in our family. It is not just your mother that recognizes you as such, but your sisters do the same, and I have discovered that I do also — tho I am more ashamed to confess it.

But writing about Uncas' advice to his immediate family, O. B. expressed no chagrin at all, only a fatherly pride. He was sufficiently impressed with what Uncas had to say to quote it in its entirety to other family members:

> As for feeling bad about losing, you ought to have a lesson from my boss [wrote Uncas]. On any argument as to how a device or equipment is to be built he is always glad to see the other side win, even if he is sure he's right. He says that if you are right, and it is decided to make the device the way you want it, the fact that you are right and the others wrong will soon be forgotten; but if you are right, and it is decided to make the device the other way it is sure impressed on everyone that you were right in the first place.[35]

Uncas, who would continue in his role as family counselor for the rest of his life, handled awkward situations with tact and a gentle manner. O. B. found his son's arguments logical and, no doubt, admired the man-to-man tone.

By early spring, 1929, O. B. Whitaker was back in the legislature making battle, showing off his parliamentary prowess, and still looking for other things to do. Purina Feeds of St. Louis wanted O. B. to sell their products in Weaubleau, and a representative from a nearby county wanted him to consider editing a Republican newspaper there. But O. B. decided to take up a writing career seriously. He chose to take a correspondence course called "Post-Graduate Short Story Writing," and enter his own efforts in writing contests.[36]

Son Uncas, perhaps more constructively, was also doing some thinking about his next move. Although WAB wanted Whitaker to stay on, and was prepared to pay him a substantial salary increase, the attraction of a better paying and more challenging job was what the young engineer had in mind. After six productive years at WAB, he wanted a job that combined engineering development work with a large measure of management responsibility. The Hoover Company in North Canton, Ohio, had just such a job available. On August 3, 1929, Uncas Whitaker worked his last day at WAB. He moved immediately to North Canton to begin, that first week in August, what would be nearly ten years of employment at Hoover.[37]

4. At the Hoover Company

Uncas Whitaker survived the Roaring Twenties. For him, as to millions of Americans, the "return to normalcy" meant merely business as usual. In Whitaker's case, life in the twenties revolved around education, first at MIT and later at Carnegie Tech, and around career building. Whitaker was not unaware of prohibition, bathtub gin, the Charleston, Babe Ruth, wild youth, and loose morals — the media of the day being filled with *ad nauseum* accounts of the banal and the sensational. But what attracted his attention and informed his consciousness of those years were the great technological advances being made day by day in a variety of areas. From Whitaker's base in Pittsburgh, many of these changes were already visible.

In 1920, for example, the first commercial radio broadcast originated in Pittsburgh over station KDKA. Engineers and inventors were making great strides in the electrification of locomotives, and Whitaker made his own contributions to the modernization of all types of equipment necessary for rail transportation. In May, 1925, Westinghouse Electric tested the world's largest electric locomotive in its East Pittsburgh yards. Evidence that the automobile was here to stay was impressed upon the minds of Pittsburghers with Henry Ford's announcement in early 1923 of plans for the first Ford plant in the area. The continuing and growing importance of the steel industry was underlined by Jones & Laughlin's announcement that it was going public and for the first time placing its stock on the open market. If one missed that November 1923 announcement, graphic evidence of the use of steel could be seen in the construction of skyscrapers in Pittsburgh.

But perhaps the advances in technology that most captured Whitaker's imagination were those associated with the development of the airplane and the future possibility of commercial air travel. Whitaker, who would later have his own personal love affair with planes and flying, might very well have attended the large air show mounted in 1926 for the purpose of formally dedicating Pittsburgh's first commercial airfield. During the next two years a series of firsts occurred — the first airmail service was inaugurated, the first express parcel service was begun, and passenger service was instituted from Pittsburgh. Lindbergh's trans-Atlantic flight in May, 1927, was the

decade's greatest story, and his subsequent visits to cities like
Pittsburgh that summer kept his accomplishment in the headlines for
months. The growth of interest in flying in the several years ahead
took impetus from the Lindbergh accomplishment and Uncas
Whitaker would be one of many to try his hand at flying. A final
reminder that the air age had arrived could not have escaped future
flyer Whitaker's attention. In the late winter of 1929, the tallest
building in Pittsburgh, the thirty-seven-story Grant Building, was
completed and opened for occupancy. At the very top was an airplane
beacon that spelled out "Pittsburgh" in Morse code to inform flyers,
who for some time would be flying "by the seat of their pants," of
where they were.[1]

Close to the end of the decade, in early August, 1929, Uncas
Whitaker quit the technology of air brake development and
manufacturing to take on the technology of vacuum cleaner
production. Almost eighty-seven years to the day after grandfather
John Whitaker was born in Ohio, grandson Uncas arrived in the state
to settle in North Canton (called New Berlin before World War I),
where the Hoover family had settled at about the same time Joshua
Whitaker brought his family to Ohio. Nearby was Canton, a town of
about 100,000, where President William McKinley had practiced law
before the turn of the century.

The Hoovers, who had started out clearing land for farming in
typical frontier fashion, found themselves in the leather business by
the latter part of the nineteenth century. But with the development of
the automobile they quickly realized that harnesses and other tackle
would be in decreasing demand. The opportunity arose, in 1908, of
moving into the sweeper field, when the Electric Suction Sweeper
Company of New Berlin, Ohio went into bankruptcy. The Hoovers
took the company over in August, 1908, and demonstrating credible
acumen, saw at once the advantages in advertising. In December of
that year their first ad appeared in the mass circulation weekly, *The
Saturday Evening Post.* Two sacks of mail arrived the following week,
and the Hoovers were on their way. By the time Uncas Whitaker
arrived in later summer 1929, mass production had turned Hoover
into a large American company just on the verge of going overseas to
expand its operation and its market.[2]

Hoover established an engineering department on January 1, 1919,
and it had from the very beginning a division called Development
and Design, which Whitaker was hired to head early in 1930 after
several months of orientation. Whatever engineering problems

Hoover had hired Whitaker to solve, the depression created a new one. Whitaker later described his job at Hoover in terms of the new economic situation:

> Having been made Director of Development and Design of the company in 1930, the development and placing in production of an electric cleaner to sell at a price to meet depression incomes was one of the first major problems undertaken. This problem of designing a cleaner for sale in the low priced field had been previously undertaken several times without success.[3]

In fact, Hoover had already entered the low-priced field. In 1908 the original electric suction sweeper was offered for the relatively high price of $125; succeeding models had been developed in mass production procedures, which resulted in dramatically lower prices as the years went by. However, no radically new model had been developed since 1926. It was that projected new model Whitaker was engaged with, and it emerged on the market in 1936, after about five years of development work.[4]

The production of a new, low-priced vacuum cleaner called for a radically new approach to design and manufacturing problems. As Whitaker explained:

> To reach a successful solution, it was necessary to completely reorganize the method of designing and to change to a large extent, the procedure then in use in regard to cost estimating, coordination between Engineering, Production and Purchasing and relations with suppliers. The result was a product well within the allowable manufacturing cost, affording the Company an adequate profit, and a product meeting the quality standards of the company. This new model and the related line that followed was one of the major contributions in making it possible for the Hoover Company to maintain its cash position throughout the depression.[5]

No doubt Whitaker was correct about Hoover's ability to maintain its cash position throughout the depression as a result of this kind of product improvement. But it is also fair to say that the Hoover Company was never in real trouble during the depression years, and this was true even before the production of the model Whitaker helped develop. In 1932, one of the most desperate years of the decade, the Hoover Company actually increased its share of the market by seven percent. It is one of those historic ironies that vacuum cleaner companies benefited by the depression as they seem to do in all periods of recession. As one of the Hoovers explained:

One of the apparent reasons for this was that when depression struck many women could suddenly no longer afford maids. Such households would typically be large, containing great areas of carpeting. Faced suddenly with the unfamiliar task of cleaning a huge house, these women wanted all the labor-saving appliances their husbands could afford. A further factor may well be that during depression men are home from work. The house gets dirtier quicker. It needs more frequent cleaning — more Hoovers.[6]

The major market for Hoover vacuums was the newly poor middle class and that was apparently not an unsubstantial market. One might not think that clean carpets would be a matter of great concern compared with the more desperate issues of longtime unemployment, but as we have learned, keeping up the trappings of respectability during the 1930s was an important psychological need for a good portion of America.

None of this, it should be noted, takes anything away from Uncas Whitaker's contribution to the company's profitability. Since the problem of the depression was never solved until the onset of World War II, what he accomplished in engineering products for a changed economy was a significant factor in keeping the Hoover Company "depression proof" over that long decade. But more important for our story is what Whitaker actually experienced in his years with Hoover and how those experiences would prepare him for his own entrepreneurial venture later.

To begin with, the Hoover Company, long before Whitaker's arrival, understood the importance of engineering to sales profitability It was at Hoover that Whitaker learned the lesson that would come to form the basic philosophy of his own business career. In an article he wrote for the April, 1936, issue of *Product Engineering* he spoke directly to this subject:

It may be difficult to understand how 130 men can be profitably employed in the engineering department of the Hoover Company, which makes only one product and that of such apparent simplicity as an electric vacuum cleaner. The explanation lies in the unusual set up of the concern.

The management, directors, and stockholders have almost exclusively only the one business interest, this being the manufacture of electric vacuum cleaners. In view of the nondiversity of its product the company has considered as wise insurance the maintenance of a large enough engineering department to place it in a predominant position in relation to the rest of the industry as to technical knowledge, patents and other phases. This insurance offsets, to a large degree, the otherwise hazardous condition of depending entirely on one product for the success of the company.

Succinctly put, this means — take one product and engineer the hell out of it. This is how Whitaker would later explain his own venture into solderless electrical terminations. The 1936 article gives us his first public statement of this idea and tells us where he learned it.

The article, entitled "Development and Engineering Procedure," also provides material on Whitaker's approach to problem solving, then in electric cleaners and later in the field of electrical terminations. Crucial is the importance of design as the first step in the long and involved process of product development. The key role of the Development and Design division of the engineering department, according to Whitaker, is to initiate the preliminary plan for a new model — in this case, the vacuum cleaner. He points out the long period of research necessary before development begins — about five years in advance — and that the engineering department as a whole is usually working on four or more different ideas at one time. After the first plan for a new model is originated in Development and Design, specifications are drawn up and the new model plan submitted to management for approval. If approved, preliminary development gets underway with staff engineering coordinating the new plan with sales, purchasing, production, advertising, and patent departments. In the preliminary stage, design weaknesses, patent problems, and costs are checked and double checked so that modifications can be made early, at less expense than later. Then comes the working-model stage, and the same process is repeated with all departments in the company so that further modifications will suit the needs of cost, production, suppliers, sales, and, of course, the ultimate consumer. Finally, if all goes well, the testing of the final models begins before mass production gets underway.[7]

Obviously, the design, development, and engineering procedures outlined superficially here are much more complicated and time-consuming (and filled with battles of all kinds, it might be noted) than might appear from this brief description. Practically speaking, Whitaker's charge to produce a vacuum cleaner at low price for a depression market involved other matters than just a low-cost product. In the case of the vacuum cleaner, as with many consumer products, lightness was a desirable factor. But with lightness in such equipment comes the problem of maintaining quality. Weight reduction, at least as it affected the vacuum cleaner, necessitated much more rigorous quality control than was previously required. As Whitaker explained shortly after he became director of Development and Design at Hoover:

> In recent years the pressure on the designer to reduce weight has made the use of careful tests necessary if the quality of the product is to be improved or even maintained. Insistence of present day managements that improvements in design be taken advantage of as quickly as possible makes it desirable that test results be obtained in a shorter time than they could be secured by field or service tests. As a result it is necessary to depend largely on the data obtained from accelerated tests for preliminary design work.[8]

The testing of the vacuum cleaner was not dissimilar to the rubber heel testing machine problem that occupied student Whitaker at MIT, and his explanation of the problem recalls the language of his senior thesis. "The designer of an ordinary bridge or building framework might make a satisfactory and dependable design without tests to check his calculations, but no amount of calculation would enable a designer to determine accurately how long the wheels of an electric cleaner or a switch of a washing machine would last in actual service."[9] Will the product — heel, wheel, switch, electrical termination, etc. — give good service or poor? Good service or poor — the question had arisen with the rubber heel testing machine and at Westinghouse Air Brake; now it surfaced again at Hoover. It would continue to be *the* question, *the* problem, that Whitaker's career was ultimately dedicated to answering.

More practically, Whitaker made his contribution toward solving the specific problem of reduced weight. In an article describing the new Model 150 Hoover cleaner, which went on the market in 1936, Whitaker explained the problem and outlined the solution. "There has always been some complaint that the electric vacuum cleaner is too heavy, and it was therefore specified that this new machine be much lighter than the machine it was to replace. To accomplish this and at the same time include the new features it was necessary that something different in materials be used."[10] He goes on to explain how magnesium die castings came to replace aluminum and how phenolic plastics were used in various structural parts of the new machine. Whitaker, in a career resume prepared in 1940, suggests that he was largely responsible for the decision to employ these lighter weight materials:

> The manufacture in the Hoover plant of magnesium die castings and the installation of a department to manufacture plastics were the result of my recommendation and supervision. The technique of moulding plastics was developed in the Engineering Department and the installation of the Bakelite Plant was under the supervision of and in accordance with the recommendations of the Engineering Department. This was also the case with the introduction of magnesium die castings. No one in the company, either in production or engineering, had previous experience with either of these materials, yet the results obtained in both departments have been quite outstanding.[11]

Presumably Whitaker, like the others in engineering and production, was without experience in the use of these materials. In that case, his recommendations are even more impressive.

As indicated, the new Model 150 cleaner was a radical improvement over the model produced ten years earlier. The Hoover Company's advertising strategy, at least as it appeared in *The Saturday Evening Post*, emphasized its use of new materials as well as the cleaner's new streamlined design. All through the 1930s, the Hoover Company took one yearly ad in the *Post*, appearing always early in December. Attractive gift packages helped promote the Hoover as a Christmas present, and typically each advertisement pictured Father, with Son or Daughter, standing before a Hoover display contemplating which model to buy for Mother. The 1936 advertisement is typical except that more than usual emphasis is given the new features of the redesigned Model 150. The double page spread read like this:

> First basically new cleaner in ten years. Most efficient ever built . . . *made with new metal* — Magnesium — one third lighter than aluminum . . . New streamlined beauty designed by Henry Dreyfus. Non-marring ripple finish in Stratosphere gray (easy to keep clean) . . . *a complete cleaning ensemble* . . . attached in one second without turning the cleaner over or even stopping the motor . . . *new efficiency* — stronger suction with even quieter operation. . . *Automatic Rug Adjuster* . . . rugs of any thickness . . . *Time to Empty Signal* . . . *Dirt Finder* . . . broad beam of light . . . plus exclusive Hoover principle of *Positive Agitation.*

The new Hoover 150 sold for $79.50, plus $16.50 for the cleaning tools. Terms were offered — $1.50 weekly, payable monthly. Readers of *The Saturday Evening Post* surely took notice of the Hoover advertisement, sandwiched between the pages of the sixth installment of Agatha Christie's serialized mystery, *Poirot Loses a Client.* Unlike

Hercule Poirot, the Hoover Company gained clients, for the Hoover 150 cleaner was a success.[12]

That Uncas Whitaker the inventor made some significant contributions to the Model 150 and other Hoover cleaners that followed is attested to by the several patent applications that were filed in his name. One in August, 1933, concerned an improvement in agitator constuction; another in April, 1934, dealt with eliminating the interference to radios caused by the electric motor of the sweeper. An August, 1935, patent had to do with a motor bearing unit that included an oil circulating system. In November, 1935, with two other engineering associates, Whitaker filed a patent for an improved suction and blowing system for both on-the-floor and off-the-floor cleaning. A final Hoover vacuum patent, again in collaboration with two associates, was filed in 1940 after Whitaker had left the firm; it involved adjusting mechanisms for raising or lowering the wheels to accommodate the suction nozzle to different carpet thicknesses.[13]

Whitaker's work at the Hoover Company earned him a great deal of admiration from the Hoover family, who at that time tightly controlled the corporation. Like Whitaker's own family, the Hoover descendants had come from tough frontier stock, and they held values very similar to those of Whitaker's own people. That the Hoovers appreciated Whitaker's work is apparent from the salary increases he received over the years. Beginning in August, 1929, at somewhere in the range of $3,000 to $3,200, Uncas Whitaker had doubled his salary by the end of the 1930s. His income from the Hoover Company in his last full year in its employ was $6,441, a not insignificant sum for the depression period.[14]

* * * * * * *

If the sensational aspects of the 1920s had little affected Whitaker, caught up in his own career and more attracted to technology than to the technicolor exploits of flaming youth, he could not so easily remain impervious to the 1930s. The traumatic conditions of the depression made their impact on him although he did not personally suffer any deprivation. For a brief time in 1932-33, he had to accept, along with many others, a salary cut, which was soon restored when increased sales encouraged the Hoover Company to increase production.[15] Therefore, despite the fact he was seriously worried at times about economic trends, Whitaker did not carry with him into the postdepression period the kind of depression mentality that afflicted so many others of his generation.   As we shall see, Whitaker's personal financial stability in the 1930s had a significant and a positive effect on his decision making in his own organization.

The depression occurred for Uncas Whitaker on two fronts. At Hoover he worked to help a major business weather the economic storm. At the same time, he was constantly made aware of the effects of the depression on the farm economy. But in late July, 1930, when he went back to Weaubleau for his vacation, little had as yet changed. The previous summer, engaged in changing jobs, son Uncas had forgone his yearly visit home. Now, settled and more relaxed in his new position at the Hoover Company, he returned home and took part in the family routine. As O. B. reported after the visit had ended, "Uncas spent about all his time while here helping me with my farm work. We cut timothy and shocked it and baled some hay and set up a baler I got from Uncle Syd and a lot of other things."[16]

Uncas' visits were important to the whole Whitaker family, and when he left, father, mother and sister Minnie felt his absence profoundly.   After this particular visit, sister Minnie and her father amused themselves and kept Uncas' visit alive in their minds by adopting one of his "swear words" for their own use, which, according to O. B., was to "break their loneliness:"

> Minnie went with me over to the North and we dug our dawlgarned potatoes, I dug the dawlgarned things and she picked the dawlgarned things up, and and then I hitched up the dawlgarned old mare and put the dawlgarned potatoes in the house over there. I may put the dawlgarned things in the cellar later as we have a dawlgarned good cellar there. Minnie thinks [dawlgarned] is characteric of Uncas — just suits him, and Mamma thinks it far better than my assortment.[17]

Another of O. B.'s reports to the family told them about how Uncas shot a rabbit while back home. The little story enforces one's sense of how deep were O. B.'s attachments to basic American idioms and how intensely he tried to impress these on his son. In this case, the story of Uncas and the rabbit takes on many characteristics of James Fenimore Cooper's tales. In *The Last of the Mohicans,* where young Whitaker's namesake, the Indian hero Uncas, appeared, there is a scene in which Uncas comes upon his father Chingachgook and Hawkeye in the forest. The two are discussing the coming fight with the evil Maguas, but after a bit the conversation turns to food.

> Chingachgook: "Hawkeye, let us eat to-night, and show the Maguas that we are men tomorrow."

> Hawkeye: "I am as ready to do the one as the other; but to fight the
> Iroquois 'tis necessary to find the skulkers; and to eat to-night
> 'tis necessary to get the game — talk of the devil and he will
> come; there is the biggest pair of antlers I have seen this
> season, moving the bushes behind the hill!"

Hawkeye then bets Uncas that he can bring down the moose with
one shot:

> Hawkeye: "I will bet my charger three times full of powder, against
> a foot of wampum, that I take him atwixt the eyes, and nearer
> to the right than to the left."

> Uncas: "It cannot be!" . . . All but the tips of his horns are hid."

> Hawkeye: "He's a boy! Does he think when a hunter sees a part of
> the cretur', he can't tell where the rest of him should be!"

Hawkeye raises his rifle to shoot, only to be warned by
Chingachgook that the noise of the rifle report will bring the Indian
enemies running to the camp. Acknowledging his near-disastrous
mistake, Hawkeye replies: "I must leave the buck to your arrow,
Uncas, or we may kill a deer for them thieves, the Iroquois, to eat."
Cooper's narration continues:

> The instant the father seconded this intimation by an expressive
> gesture of the hand, Uncas threw himself on the ground, and
> approached the animal with wary movements. When within a few
> yards of the cover, he fitted an arrow to his bow with the utmost
> care, while the antlers moved, as if their owner snuffed an enemy in
> the tainted air. In another moment the twang of the cord was heard,
> a white streak was seen glancing into the bushes, and the wounded
> buck plunged from his cover, to the very feet of his hidden enemy.

In O. B. Whitaker's letter, the story of Uncas and the rabbit looked
like this:

> O yes. I must tell you about Uncas' shooting with his new pistol (for
> which I deserve most of the credit). One evening I called him and
> said, "if you will bring your pistol I believe we can find you a
> rabbit." He came and I said, "Now, if I show you a rabbit, and you
> don't shoot it you will give me a nickel, and if I show you one and
> you do shoot it, we will count it even, and if I don't show you one I
> will give you a nickel." He agreed. I saw one 35 steps away and
> pointed it out to him as it hopped into a patch of grass. He thought
> he saw its ears and asked me if it was. I was not sure but said I
> thought so. He took deliberate aim (thinking all the time, no doubt,
> about the nickel) and fired. The rabbit leaped into the air, and
> thinking it wounded I ran to it. The bullet went through the head an
> inch below the ear.[18]

Even in more serious contexts, particularly in relation to ethical questions, O. B. mixed moral reflection with Western American humor and the suggestion of the tall tale. Uncas was the recipient of this curious blend of piety and folk comedy in his father's letters. In one instance, O. B. wrote of his heartfelt relief at a young niece's recovery from a long illness. He turned next to moral philosophy.

> When I received the good news of Lulu's recovery I wrote [brother] Joe that after all, our financial troubles dwindle into insignificance in the presence of the really important things in life. In truth, I entertain serious doubts as to whether I was ever really entitled to the property I once owned or to anything more than a comfortable living — or even that. For is not the accumulation of wealth, in its last analysis, the result of the application of superior ability; and is it unquestionably right to take from others what their inferior ability cannot keep? Is it quite Christian? I am bitterly condemning the powerfully organized moneyed interests of the nation for robbing the poor, yet am I not guilty of the same thing in my heart, and lack only the opportunity?

But the philosophy was incomplete without fanciful exemplification

> For instance suppose Jack should become universally known as I know him — the greatest mule in the world, and suppose that a millionaire should miraculously develop a more sensible taste for distinction, and want to own the greatest mule in the world, and I should learn that I could get a million dollars for Jack. Wouldn't I demand it, notwithstanding the fact that he cost me less than $25 to raise, and his society [companionship] has been worth a hundred?

If one "for instance" was good, two were better.

> Or suppose the great showman of the world should learn about Watch what Mamma and Minnie and I know about him — that he is the most intelligent pup that ever beheld the dawning of a glorious day, or killed a chicken, or ate one that had been dead two months in hot weather — and should bid him up to five hundred thousand dollars, would we say, "For every penny that pup has cost us he has brought us a dollar's worth of joy. He has therefore cost us nothing. Take him at actual cost."

O. B. concludes his parable with the observation that neither Mamma, Minnie, nor he would be that self-sacrificing. Rather, as O. B. put it in droll self-deprecation, "I would assume a pained look as I accepted the last dollar I thought I could get for him." In characteristic fashion, he added, "There! I set up a beautiful argument in the first part of the letter, and now I have shot it all to pieces — have a notion to cut the letter in two in the middle, and send you only the first half."[19]

Of course, he did not cut the letter in two. Hard moral choices were everybody's business, not just O. B.'s, and certainly the serious business of those who sought success. Son Uncas would face his own choices later in his career as he fulfilled his Uncle Joe's judgment about all the Whitakers — that they were "by nature and instinct and training. . . ambitious."[20]

In addition to moral choices, there were political choices to be made. Party choices, certainly, presented no problems for the Whitaker family. Hickory County, Missouri was a Republican county, and the Whitakers were and always had been Republicans. All, that is, with the exception of John Whitaker's brother, Joseph. Joseph, who had been born in Frederick County, Virginia in 1834 and had come to Hickory County in 1859, was first elected to the 23rd Missouri General Assembly in 1867 as a Republican. He continued to carry that party's label until the election of 1878, when he entered the 30th General Assembly as a Greenbacker. That particular election had been close — Joseph Whitaker won by only seven votes over the runner-up and by fourteen over the third place finisher. The *Index*, Hickory County's most vocal Republican weekly, made great fun of the Greenbackers who were proponents of "soft" money as opposed to the more limited gold specie available. Although it never attacked Joseph Whitaker personally (the country had too much respect for the Whitaker family), it violently opposed the Greenback philosophy and the Union Labor Party (ULP) eventually created to serve the needs of many discontented farmers and workers. In 1888 the ULP selected Joseph Whitaker as its candidate for Congress and made him chairman of the state ULP. But the congressional district did not know and appreciate the Whitaker name as did Hickory County, and Joseph Whitaker was not sent to Congress. He ran a bad third in a field of three, gaining only 167 of about 1,800 votes. Later, Joseph Whitaker apparently decided to return to the Republican fold.[21]

Placed in historical perspective, Joseph Whitaker's political choices are not as unusual as they appear. Like many small farmers and businessmen living in rural areas like southwestern Missouri, Joseph Whitaker developed a profound contempt for Eastern "money-lenders." Later, Republicans like O. B. Whitaker (Greenbacker Joe's nephew) came to cherish similar antipathies and in essence, at least in the context of southwestern Missouri, the philosophies of the two parties were not that far apart. Republi-

canism in O. B. Whitaker's time and in the part of the country from
which he came, carried specific meaning and values. It is important to
understand these, for Uncas Whitaker's mature political views grew
very largely out of those espoused by his relatives back home.

Not surprisingly, as late as O. B. Whitaker's adult days, the Civil
War was still being fought in Missouri. Democrats were associated
with Civil War "Rebels" and Republicans with the Union cause.
Joseph and John Whitaker had fought on the Union side, and John
had married a woman whose father was seen as a Civil War hero.
The shotgun that Grandfather Earnest had used during the war was a
prize that O. B. obtained in 1932, trading twenty-five pounds of seed
for it with a man who did not understand its importance. The
complicated negotiations completed, O. B. announced his triumph to
the family: "I have grandfather Earnest's old famous and feared
shotgun. . . . He chased a whole company (about 12) of rebels once
with that gun on the open prairies, and he had it in his hands when
he was treacherously shot and killed."[22] Stories like this one lingered
on for many years, and their legacy carried over into the political
arena with practical effects, as O. B. clearly indicated on the occasion
of the opening of the 1931 legislative session:

> This morning's paper says that the Democrats in caucus yesterday
> decided to allow the Republicans no clerks. I can hardly believe
> that. But I said to Mamma, "O, there are lots of fine Democrats,
> but politically they are descendants of the old Civil War Rebels, and
> it is harder for the party that's whipped to forget and forgive than it
> is for the victorious party. You may say and think what you please
> to the contrary, but the old rebel spirit still lingers to a degree in
> the hearts of the majority of Democrats. The first session I was here
> (1913) the Republicans had to try three times before we could get a
> U. S. flag put in the House; and before that, when my father was a
> member, it was impossible to do so. Many of them (tho they all lie
> about it) still hate that old flag."[23]

O. B., as we have seen, had strong principles. To comprehend his
brand of Republicanism, it is necessary to understand that party
loyalty was secondary to political principles. He saw himself primarily
as a Jeffersonian type, which meant for him the responsibility of
upholding the life-style, and the property rights, of the small
independent farmer and businessman. Like William Jennings Bryan,
whom he greatly admired, O. B. Whitaker hated monopolists, the
gold standard, "wets," and big bankers; and, also like Bryan, he
fought a lifelong battle to preserve the rural world of southwestern
Missouri, which he understood and loved. For O. B., big cities like

Kansas City and St. Louis represented evil and immoral ways —
especially those propagated by the liquor interests. But more than
that, the growing urban centers represented a real threat to the
maintenance of a viable rural existence. When, for example, a vital
state highway bill came before the legislature in the 1929-31 period,
he battled against those urban interests that were concerned only
with connecting the large cities, being content to leave the less
populous areas to fend for themselves. O. B. and his associates won
the day, however, and the Centennial Highway Bill, passed in 1931,
connected the whole state, not just the major cities.   At that time,
Missouri's was called the best highway system in the United States.[24]

O. B. Whitaker was a proponent of free enterprise, but not of the
mindless variety that allowed the big man to run over the little
fellow. He believed that government was instituted to protect people
and their interests but not to support bigness on the one hand and
furnish welfare to its victims on the other. For instance, he struggled
long and hard against those elements in the state who wanted tax
monies from a proposed sales tax (which he violently opposed as
regressive) to be used largely for state-funded educational institutions like the rapidly developing university system. As an educational
entrepreneur in his own right, O. B. believed strongly in private
education and standards of intellectual excellence rather than those
standards of education imposed by the state legislature. The
institution of state standards effectively eliminated those small
Christian schools which trained so many of the state's teachers in
O. B.'s day. What a prospective teacher really knew came to be less
important than his or her ability to pass state-determined required
courses. As far as public education was concerned, O. B. was a strong
supporter of local control of school systems. O. B. opposed, and beat,
bills in the legislature that proposed state tax monies to support local
districts and threatened as a result the existence of rural schools. In
poorer districts, school consolidation into larger and larger areas
would, he feared, replace smaller local efforts to educate children. As
a result of Whitaker's opposition, state taxes were allocated to local
districts and local control. The larger, more prosperous areas were
forced to share the wealth.[25]

O. B. Whitaker fought the wealthy vested interests all his life. He
always found himself beleaguered and outnumbered, but his
parliamentary skills frequently won the day and prevented unjust and
inequitable legislation from passing, at least for a time. The "Lone
Ranger" position he often found himself in may account in large part

for his continual feeling of loneliness. As a lover of Western lore and Western literature, he adopted the metaphor of the peaceman-law-enforcer to describe his position. He wrote of his own legislative role in terms heavy with frontier mythology.

> In a miniature way I am like Bat Masterson. When he was asked by the President to accept the position of United States Marshall for Arizona (Teddy Roosevelt appointed him) he declined saying: "If I took it inside of a year I'd have to kill some fool boy who wanted to get a reputation by killing me." That's exactly my position in the House, except that I have neither the power or desire to kill anybody. It has become sort of conspiracy among a few to "roll" on me on parliamentary issues. They watch for their chance to do so.[26]

O. B. had plenty of opportunity himself to draw a bead on those in the opposition party (as well as a few of his own party), but during the 1930s, especially after 1933, O. B. reserved his political six-shooters for F. D. R., the New Deal, and the Roosevelt family. As O. B. saw it, the greatest threat to American Democracy had begun its destructive tyranny over the nation.

* * * * * * *

In 1931, however, self-improvement rather than politics was on Uncas Whitaker's mind. Indirectly, the family back home received news that he had once again added night school to his full-time work schedule. Now he undertook the study of law. Sister Portia in Alliance wrote the news to sister Minnie, who in turn sent Portia's letter along to O. B. and Nettie. The family rallied in concern; now their worry was Uncas' eyesight. Both Minnie and O. B. wrote with fears and warnings.[27] Uncas' decision to study law may have been a result of his involvement in patent work and his developing recognition of the usefulness of understanding law as it applied to business. After he was made director of Development and Design at Hoover, he became a member of the company's Operating Committee, and he became involved in all aspects of the business of the concern, which included, according to his own accounting, "manufacturing, sales, service, patents, cost accounting, personnel relations, legal, and foreign operations."[28]

Whether Uncas had discussed the possiblity of going to law school with his father is not clear. It is an interesting coincidence, however, that O. B., like Uncas, was also "reading law," as the family put it. It is clear that O. B. began first. In September, 1931, he wrote Uncas after hearing the news from Portia:

Just received your letter from Minnie enclosing one from Portia, in
which she says you are studying law. Mamma and I are very fearful
of your overworking your eyes from too much reading. Do not do
that. I mean do not endanger your eyes. Otherwise I am very much
taken with the thought of your studying law, not with a view to a
profession (which I assume you do not consider), but as a matter of
equipment for your present business and life in general.[29]

O. B. was proud of his son, but he was not one to ignore
competition when he saw it. Writing from his own experience,
essentially guided reading in the nineteenth century tradition, O. B.
asked: "What work are you reading? Are you under a tutor? How
extensively are you going into it?" In the next statement O. B. lays
down the not-too-veiled challenge: "The work I am reading is
American Law and Procedure, 14 volumes, about 400 pages to the
volume. I am now reading Volume 13."[30] O. B., unlike his son
Uncas, would never pass the law exams, although he tried more than
once. That series of failures only added to his personal frustration.[31]

By the middle of 1931, the effects of the depression began to hit
home in Missouri. O. B. lost about $60 in a local bank that closed in
June but later recovered the small sum when the bank reopened. A
month later Uncle Syd was involved in a bank robbery. Once again,
events in the Whitaker family had the flavor of myth. In an episode
reminiscent of Bonnie and Clyde or John Dillinger, several masked
bandits invaded the Brownington Bank and held up a teller at
gunpoint. Small rural banks were often the target of gangs of robbers,
and the Missouri area had already had enough such incidents so that
bankers like Syd Whitaker carried guns. On this occasion, a bank
employee managed to sound an alarm. Uncle Syd drew his weapon
and began firing as he, wisely, fell to the floor. One of the bandits
returned the fire, narrowly missing the falling Uncle Syd. Syd was
sanguine about the whole affair, as he would be about his bank's
survival chances during the depression. Some months later he wrote
his brother O. B. a letter expressing his toughness and character.
O. B. passed along the salient parts of the letter to his family, quoting
Syd directly:

I, myself, have a pretty high opinion of the State Bank of
Brownington. They did not have much success in burglarizing us,
the attempted holdup would not be called the most successful, they
can't break us, and I am very strongly convinced that this bank will
never close its doors as long as it is under its present management,
whatever may happen at Clinton and elsewhere.

The Whitakers were made of strong stuff. It was, after all, a family tradition to be tough and uncompromising in the face of such perils. The old homesteading, frontier legacy worked well even in the twentieth century.[32]

The effects of the depression were also being felt in North Canton, Ohio, by Uncas Whitaker. By the end of 1931, the Hoover Company was beginning to cut back a bit on the salaries of its employees, and Uncas was one who took a small cut. In addition, his own bank failed, and like many Americans he lost some of his money. Uncle Syd, informed of these setbacks in his nephew's annual interest-paying letter, told Uncas that good banking procedures these days were hard to find. "Too many banks," he added "have been run in the interest, private interest, of the officers of the bank, and when closing comes it is found that the active officers and their families and business associates have been using the funds extensively — generally quite legally."[33] Uncas would learn that this technique could be applied outside of banking, in businesses of all kinds. He would, therefore, be wary in his later career of the kind of management that ran an ongoing business into the ground by taking undue advantage of its position — nice legal considerations notwithstanding.

By March 1932, Whitaker's salary had been cut by about thirty percent, the largest reduction he would have to accept. It was necessary, as a result of this cutback, to request some relief from the New Smyrna Investment and Loan Company in New Smyrna, Florida. He was making payments on property his father had purchased in Florida, which had become Uncas' responsibility some years earlier. The investment and loan company was understanding and provided an acceptable payment figure with which Uncas could live.[34]

Through the remainder of the year Uncas carried on his work at Hoover and his law studies at the Cleveland Law School. Evidently pleased that he and his father were both studying law, he wrote home occasionally with news of his progress.[35] O. B. replied with news from Weaubleau, an example of which was the report that the old college building had burned down in February, 1932. Fortunately, O. B., who among other pursuits sold insurance, had seen to it a bit earlier that a lapsed $5,000 fire insurance policy had been renewed. It was O. B.'s opinion that the proceeds from that policy should be used to refurbish the Christian Church and provide for the future upkeep of both the church and the adjoining cemetery, where members of the family were buried. As O. B. put it to son Uncas, "I think that would

come as near father's [John Whitaker] wish as I can imagine it."
Years later, Uncas Whitaker would want the same for the church and
the cemetery as his father and his father's father. The tradition of
family responsibility towards its past would remain strong down
through the years.[36]

Uncas made his annual summer visit in 1932, and, when he left
for the East again, the family was lonely and despondent as usual. In
the fall of 1932, O. B. reported that Uncle Joe was in financial trouble
but indicated that the family was prepared to help him over that
particularly rough time. Meanwhile, O. B. was reading the life of
Ghandi and reluctantly running for yet another term in the
legislature. Demonstrating his reluctance for office by refusing to
answer the charges of his opponents, O. B. fully expected to lose. He
sincerely believed that Herbert Hoover bore responsibility for this
outcome. O. B., who had been one of the Republican platform
committee members in the state of Missouri, had voted with the
minority that recommended that Hoover and the party remain firm
on the prohibition plank. Because Hoover and the party had
crumbled under the pressure from the liquor interests supporting the
wet plank in the national platform, O. B. believed that the national
election, along with his own, was lost.[37]

He hated fellow Republican Hoover for reasons other than
Hoover's compromise on the drinking issue. According to O. B.,
Hoover hurt his chances when he decided to support the union labor
wage scale; when he appointed the president of International
Harvester ("the great monopolistic robber of the farmers in the
world") chairman of the Farm Marketing Board; when he appointed
an incompetent Missouri automobile dealer who knew nothing about
farming as secretary of agriculture; and finally when he announced
that had the great Dawes Bank failed the whole banking system
would have followed, implying that the big eastern banking house
controlled the nation's economic system and needed more support
than the little banker. It was O. B.'s considered judgment that Hoover
was not a Republican at all. He told his family that the Republican
Party was responsible for the mistake "when four years ago it
nominated and elected a Democratic President." As it turned out, of
course, Hoover was not elected. But O. B. was, one of only nine
Republicans sent to Jefferson City. Those results prompted O. B. to
comment, "Well Hoover and I will have to part company. He just
simply can't keep up with me — and he tries and I don't. There's the
great difference between us." Despite all his criticism of Hoover,

O. B. preferred him to Roosevelt. As early as November 9, 1932, he knew that the victorious F. D. R. would put an end to prohibition. Later he would have considerably more reason to "roll" on F. D. R.[38]

In the months between the election of 1932 and Roosevelt's inauguration in March, 1933, banks were closing all over America. Southwestern Missouri was no exception. Uncle Syd reported to his nephew that a number of banks all around him were going under.[39] O. B., upset by the general state of things as well as by a repeated failure in his bar examination, unleashed a series of polemics on a series of topics; farmers, the feeders of the world, who could not pay on their mortgages or their debts; Wall Street Bankers; the rich getting richer; farm products as legal tender; and so on. He informed Uncas that he had sold the bank building (at a considerable loss) and paid off the mortgage on the Weaubleau home with the proceeds. "I would like to live to see you get out from under the big debt I put you," he wrote. "I think I wrote you that I paid the mortgage off on the old home at Weaubleau, and as that is in your name maybe that will help you out a little." O. B. was concerned that Uncas was suffering from further salary cuts, the falling stock market and other financial reverses. Not having heard from his son for over a month, he was also lonely for his company: "I do not think I ever felt such a longing to take an outing — just get away from work and cares, out fishing, and having you for a companion for a week or two."[40]

From Uncas Whitaker's situation things looked more optimistic than from his father's. No doubt he buoyed his father's spirits during the spring of 1933 by proposing that they buy more cattle for investment purposes, which they did. In May, Uncas reported on conditions in his area; "Things are looking very much better in this section, but will have to improve a great deal more before conditions will be good. . . . Big men in business seem to be more optimisitic than they have been for two years and most of them have switched over to Roosevelt."[41]

Uncas did not say whether he had switched over; certainly his father was of no such mind. He began his attacks on all things Roosseveltian during the summer of 1933. O. B.'s letters gave son Uncas the opportunity to consider his father's plan for restoring currency stability, a twentieth century version of an eighteenth century Physiocrat point of view, in which O. B. suggested that the nation adopt his "legal-tender wheat theory," pegging currency to wheat and other farm products.[42] But for O. B. the problems of the nation went well beyond solving the currency situation. The issue was at base a moral one, and the cause of a deteriorating moral fabric was the Roosevelt family itself. Commenting sarcastically on a Roosevelt son who was seeking a divorce after a week of marriage, O. B. generalized:

> Teach our young people — especially our "cultured young people" — to marry today and get divorced tomorrow and marry again in the afternoon of the same day, teach girls to drink intoxicants while they are young so that they will know how to drink properly when they are older — repeal the 18th amendment and the prohibition laws and the laws relating to marriage and adultery, and then watch the progress of the next generation.[43]

Clearly, the world was moving too fast for O. B. Whitaker; too many changes, and none of them good ones. For Uncas Whitaker, the message was a familiar one. He had heard variations of it all of his life.

Uncas Whitaker's year-end message to the family back home was optimistic despite hard times. Although he was able to pay only the interest on his $8,000 indebtedness to Uncle Syd's bank, conditions were looking hopeful from North Canton:

> Since the first of July . . . things have improved very steadily and at a fair rate in this section. The company is running well out of the red at the present time and will probably do a little better than break even for the total year's business, which is certainly very much better than anybody expected at the end of the first half. During the first half men were laid off continuously and salary cuts were the order. Now more people are being employed and some wage increases are being put through. . . .. Things at the present time, I believe, look about the brightest that they have been since the depression started.

Uncle Syd, speaking for the farmers, was not at all sure that New Deal policies were working as farm prices fell lower and lower. Borrowing one of F. D. R.'s memorable phrases, he told Uncas that "possibly we are just the *forgotten man* under the present dispensation."[44]

Early 1934 found O. B. again wrestling with the decision to run for the state legislature. Such New Deal action as calling in all gold certificates outraged O. B., who remarked to fellow legislators that if any individual had done what the government was doing he would be sent to jail. Now his perennial (one should say biennial) disenchantment with politics had had added to it the special irritant of F. D. R. and the New Deal, providing O. B. new reasons not to run for office. Moreover, his fears of growing older surfaced again. "What is it all worth in the end," he asked his family. "The reason life becomes sadder as we grow older is that so many things that seemed worthwhile in youth or prime resolve themselves into rainbows or jack-o'lanterns as we come to know better." He concluded with a typical, sympathy-seeking sentence: "Wish I had something to do the remainder of my days that I could feel was worthwhile."[45]

Not surprisingly, O. B. ran again. Rightly fearful of the opposition within his own party for his seat, he won the nomination by only four votes, not helping himself by his own indifferent campaigning.[46] In the general election, he ran against the New Deal, haranguing at length against the appropriation of the citizens' gold by the federal government, an issue which very likely affected few of his constituents. More to the point were his comments on general government encroachment on the lives of all Americans. As those familiar alphabetic agencies spewed out of congressional hoppers, along with piles of legislative acts affecting all manner of societal problems, the ones directed toward business and business recovery were particularly irritating to the Whitakers. Uncas noted that in his part of the country "the main thing that is retarding a real business improvement . . . is the fear of inflation [and] restrictive legislation." His view was seconded by his father and Uncle Syd, the latter telling Uncas: "I feel as you express yourself that the uncertainty as to governmental movements is retarding recovery. Also I cannot help but feel that most of the recovery measures have been a great retarding influence, but as your own father can express my opinion of the New Deal much more fluently than I can, I am sure you know how he feels and thinks." Uncas knew, and he had no ground for disagreement regarding government in business. Nor would he years later.[47]

By the end of 1934 things had settled down into a routine for the Whitaker family. O. B. was again preparing to go to Jefferson City; Uncle Syd at the Brownington Bank was closing his books on another successful year (the bank had managed to stay in business — and that was success in 1934); and Uncas in North Canton was in the final stages of development work on Hoover Cleaner Model 150. The first half of the depression decade was over, although none of them knew it at the time. The first year of its second half, 1935, would bring exciting new prospects and adventures for both father and son.

5. Investments

Uncas Whitaker was a man who kept his own counsel. Typically he told his family very little about his personal or professional life. His privacy both amused and irritated his father and mother. Their emotional investment in all of their children was great, and, like most parents, they enjoyed those occasions when letters brought news of their children's activities. Uncas' letters brought precious little personal information to his parents, and they learned to be grateful for what news arrived secondhand. Sometimes, however, they had to settle for thirdhand news. "Received a letter from Portia saying among other things . . . that Coyla [Portia's daughter] has learned that Uncas 'has a steady girl,' but they can't get any further information from Uncas," O. B. pointedly informed the family. "What's it all about Uncas," O. B. asked, "When and how is the 'steady girl' business to end? Mamma wants to know if she is a good cook and whether she reads *Good Housekeeping* or novels." There was no reply to these questions from Uncas.[1]

Although Uncas had completed law school and taken the Ohio bar examination in June, 1935, his parents did not learn of his accomplishment until they arrived in North Canton for a visit early in July. From North Canton, O. B. announced this latest news to the family back home:

> Uncas has just finished his bar examination. He graduated the month before from the McKinley School of Law, and got his L. L. B. degree (tho he had not even told us that). He lacked but one-tenth of one percent of making the highest grades of any graduate from that school in its history.

O. B. was proud of his son's accomplishments ("your life is a constant joy and pleasure and satisfaction to us," he had written him on his thirty-fifth birthday in March, 1935), and he wanted his family to share those successes:

> I think Uncas has made a remarkable record as a student since he graduated from MIT and began work in his profession. In addition to his exacting professional work he has now completed courses in two important lines — graduating from Carnegie Institute in Electrical Engineering and from McKinley School of Law. He now holds three degrees, two of them, I believe, from the greatest institutions of the world in their line.[2]

Perhaps O. B. lectured his son on keeping the family better informed about his life, because as soon as Uncas received the results of the bar examination, he wrote his father that he "got a good grade, 84.5%, the high grade of the state being 89.5%." And he added, "Now that I have finished it, will probably not do anything with it for the time being at least."[3]

There was certainly one piece of information Uncas Whitaker did not pass along to his parents when they visited him in North Canton in July, 1935. He was going to begin taking flying lessons early in the following month, and he must have reasoned that this was news his parents could do without. Private flying was not exactly a widely accepted sport in the mid-thirties, especially to people like the Missouri Whitakers, who for some years to come would consider the overflight of the mail plane a marvelous event.[4]

If Uncas Whitaker was by nature taciturn and even secretive, it may well have been because his father did enough talking for everybody. Uncas may have taken after his grandfather John, who dealt with his own exploits as modestly as Uncas. It was not until 1934, for example, that O. B. Whitaker learned that his father John, who had preceded him in the legislature, had earned a reputation as an outstanding parliamentarian. Surprised at such reticence, he wrote the family, "why didn't he tell the world — especially all his kin folks. I'm not going to make the mistake father did. — The first time I get a chance I am going to tell you all what a great parliamentarian I am."[5] O. B. had been making that point to his family for nearly twenty years, but he never tired of repeating it. It is amusing to speculate that perhaps every other generation of male Whitakers produced a modest one.

If Uncas Whitaker did not talk about his life during the summer 1935 visit of his parents, O. B. certainly took the occasion to talk about his. Earlier in the year he informed his son that some associates were urging him to run for governor of Missouri. Feature stories about O. B. began to appear in several Missouri papers that spring, as word of his possible candidacy began to circulate. Encouraged by this interest in his running for higher office, O. B. considered the alternative possibility of running for Congress again (he had made the race unsuccessfully in 1924). Uncas was aware of both possibilities when O. B. and Nettie arrived for their visit in July, and the two no doubt exchanged views about which might be the wiser choice. After all, O. B.'s reputation for tough-mindedness and principled action was known far beyond the borders of tiny Hickory County. Neither alternative was that farfetched.[6]

Another matter for discussion during the July visit was the New Deal, which by that time O. B. described as "saturating and contaminating the whole nation with its insincerity, disregard for all established standards and its dishonesty." (Soon thereafter he simply labeled the administration a "gang of lunatics.") Specifically, the rising national debt appalled the Whitaker men, and the fear of drastic future inflation was on their minds as they discussed ways to hedge against its arrival. Uncas and O. B. had no trouble agreeing with Uncle Syd's more measured criticism of what he called "this corps of experimenters," when he said, "The general course of the administration is exactly contrary to all my training and all my judgment of finances." Spending money you did not have or could not secure with proper collateral was not the Whitakers' idea of sound fiscal practice. Simply stated, it was not good business. As the elder Whitakers left for home ("probably our last long trip," said O. B.), the question of what to do about the expected inflationary spiral was left unresolved.[7]

The problem continued to bother Uncas, however. Early in August, 1935, he wrote his father about it. "Have been thinking about some way to get into position so as to capitalize on any inflation that we get over the next few years should such occur. What would you think of borrowing from the Government on the cattle at the Mansfield Place and buying as many more head as could be purchased with the money? Would imagine there would be plenty of grass for twenty or thirty more. Let me know what you think about this." O. B. liked the idea, for he too wanted to capitalize on any future inflation. He suggested that, in addition to enlarging the stock, they also consider the acquisition of more land. Uncas gave O. B. the go-ahead: "I believe, like you, that there is going to be some inflation and I think equities in farms are about as good a guess as any." For Uncas Whitaker, intuition was often a safe guide to investment decisions, and all of his life he believed that he could guess at least as well as the experts.[8]

The fall and early winter of that year produced a flurry of correspondence between father and son over properties available, deals that might be made, deals that could not be made, deals that were consummated, property that was bought, and property that was sold. In the midst of his involved work at the Hoover Company and the considerable amount of time devoted to learning how to fly, Uncas still found the time and energy to debate at length with his father about the latest land possibility. So enthusiastic was he, that he even interested a friend in North Canton in investing a small amount in Missouri real estate. He told his father about it early in October: "I have a friend here who would like to invest a very small amount of money in an equity in a farm out in that section. We agreed that he would put up the money and loan me enough for my half of the deal, and we would buy the place in partnership." For once Whitaker was in a talkative mood about his personal affairs. "Was over at Portia's last night and told her about our latest investments. She was quite excited about the proposition but wondered how we were going to pay all the mortgages. I explained that we were broke already and that there were no degrees of brokeness, and that if the thing went the way we expected, we might get unbroke." Despite evidence of further slumping cattle markets and depressed land values, both men remained optimistic.[9]

Uncas Whitaker, far away from the Missouri scene, would sometimes base his investment judgments on conditions in North Canton. For example, rents were rising all over town (his own was increased $6.00 a month); he interpreted this as one good illustration that "there are rather certain signs of price inflation or a going up in this section of the country." Additionally, he was encouraged by the general business improvement in the area, noting particularly that the Hoover Company was running about fifty percent ahead of the previous year in sales. If none of this seems to resemble a scientific approach to investing one's money, Whitaker would have been the first to agree. For Whitaker at this time, expertise in investment was a lot like expertise in duck shooting. As he told his Uncle Syd after explaining in meticulous scientific detail his theory on wing shooting, "This is all very fine theory but I have found that someone that doesn't know the slightest thing about the science can nevertheless kill birds right and left."[10] Asked directly, he would have said the same thing about investment — as he did on numerous occasions in the future.

In the midst of Hoover engineering and his own land deals, Whitaker was spending a lot of time at the local airfield. He began his flight training shortly after his parents returned to Missouri, probably about the first of August, 1935. By August 19 he had logged some four hours of flying time and after that date flew almost every day for about thirty minutes or an hour at a time. By Labor Day he had soloed, and for the remaining months of 1935 and through the first half of 1936 he practiced his flying on a regular basis. By July, 1936, he had become an experienced flyer, for during that month and the next he took three business trips for the Hoover Company, flying his rented plane to Reading, Pennsylvania, New Haven, Connecticut, and Toledo, Ohio. Flying quickly became a passion with him.[11]

Uncas Whitaker's love affair with flying soon extended into a major business involvement. Just when he decided to buy a half-interest in McKinley Air Transport (MAT), located at the local airport, is not clear. What is clear, is that by the time O. B. Whitaker decided to make a run for Congress, in mid-January, 1936, his son Uncas had already committed himself to running an airport.[12] Although he would always claim he was in the commercial aircraft business for fun rather than for profit, this never seemed to prevent Whitaker from trying to make a return on his investment in the decade or so he remained in that business. Whitaker's commercial flying operation proved a valuable training ground for his later business ventures.

Through December, 1935, and early January, 1936, Uncas Whitaker worked to consummate the airport deal with his future partner, Earl Kail, who had been Whitaker's flying instructor. During the same period, O. B. Whitaker was working to make up his mind about which political path to take. The elder Whitaker assessed his congressional chances day by day — or rather week by week, as his decision to run or not to run depended heavily on the *Literary Digest* weekly political poll. The *Literary Digest* had been his own father's favorite magazine, and O. B. recalled later that he could always remember it around when he was a boy. His dependence on the information in the *Literary Digest* was to prove politically fatal because during this crucial period the journal insisted weekly that anti-New Deal sentiment was growing, not only in the state of Missouri but across the country. Coupled with O. B.'s perception of increasing prosperity, which he believed was changing people's minds about the New Deal, the magazine's message seemed plausible, no doubt because the anti-New Deal trend it reported was exactly what O. B. Whitaker wanted to believe. On that score, the magazine never disappointed him, right up to the time it predicted a landslide victory for Kansas' Alf Landon.[13]

His hopes were encouraged by his son Uncas, who did not read the *Literary Digest.* Two days before Christmas, 1935, O. B. received a letter from his son with a check for $650 in payment for a seventy-acre tract of land the two of them were buying and an endorsement of O. B.'s congressional candidacy. O. B. had estimated that such a campaign would cost about $1,000, roughly the same amount he had spent in 1924, and Uncas had some advice about that as well.

> I am 100% in favor of your making the race for Congress this year as I feel, with you, that this will probably be a turning point in sentiment back towards a logical and proven government and business problems. Along this line if this . . . farm deal is going to place us in a position too short of finances, I would recommend that we do not go through with it because I feel it would be a mistake to try to conduct a campaign on too limited a fund. To succeed in anything like that undertaking requires a little good luck but it also requires some money along with the qualifications and background which there is no doubt about your having.[14]

If the tone and substance of this message suggest that Uncas Whitaker intended to get involved financially in his father's campaign, he meant it that way.

O. B. took his son's advice and held up on another farm deal they were considering, but despite Uncas' encouragement he did not make up his mind right away. He continued to weigh his options. Shortly after the first of the year he wrote: "'To be (a candidate for Congress), or not to be: that is the question.' I am not sure whether that was Shakespeare or Eleanor Roosevelt, but it is the question now with me. Four propositions are before me: Governor, Congress, Missouri House or retire from public life. All have their enticements — all have their objections." A week later, he was still undecided. "I'm doubtful as to the race for Congress. If I knew the answers to all questions I think I would know what to do." But the favorable anti-New Deal projections made by the *Literary Digest* and his own conscience eventually determined O. B. to throw his hat into the congressional ring. The decision was applauded by his son: "Was most pleased to hear you had announced for Congress. I think you are doing the absolutely right thing. It looks more and more like the New Deal can be defeated next fall." Then, in what would become Whitaker's rhetorical trademark, just a note of caution followed by a disclaimer of that caution; "Of course something might happen to change the trend but this seems unlikely."[15]

Of more immediate importance was Uncas' willingness to help finance the campaign despite his own tight money situation. He outlined his plan in a January letter:

> The financial side of the race I think important and I think you should not try to be too economical. After the investments I made there in the farms and with an investment that took over $900 that I made here last month I have used about all my cash and credit. I

had an investment in a savings club at Westinghouse that was to pay out this spring that would have given me about $2,000 cash but just got notice that they had decided to postpone paying out for another six months so that makes that source too late.

The $900 invested in Canton, of course, had gone into the McKinley Air Transport deal Whitaker had made with Earl Kail. With the substantial amount tied up in the savings club in Wilmerding, Uncas had another suggestion: "In thinking it over I think the best place to raise money is to sell the cattle on the Mansfield place. You put most of the money in them to start with and I would be more than happy to use the small amount I put in to defray the campaign expenses." Uncas also promised additional cash later. He took pains to emphasize again the dangers of skimping on campaign spending, for he did not believe such a race could be made for under $1,000.[16]

As O. B.'s self-appointed campaign-manager, Uncas advised him first to get a new car so that he could safely and effectively travel to all parts of the congressonal district to meet the voters. O. B. replied promptly. He declined the idea of a new car for the present (and the money his son offered to send for it), but he indicated that later he might reconsider. Somewhat embarrassed at taking advantage of his son's largesse, O. B. tried to make a joke of it: "Hope your new investments will prove profitable. Most any sound investment now, except in campaigns, ought to prove profitable, it seems to me — except (possibly) in Government bonds."[17]

In early February the *Literary Digest* poll must have raised O. B.'s spirits to an extremely high level. In no uncertain terms he blurted out an election prediction:

Franklin Delano Roosevelt will never again be elected President of this nation. He won't come near it. He won't carry 20 states — more accurately, he won't carry 17 states (and only one of them with a large electoral vote) — and that will be 25 more than he ought to carry. THE NEXT PRESIDENT WILL BE A REPUBLICAN no matter who is nominated, and if it's Landon it will be a landslide almost equal to 4 years ago.

So confident was candidate Whitaker that he began thinking about buying more farmland, despite Uncas' warnings against it. "Pete Hardy just stopped me and asked if you would buy his 80 acres adjoining the 70 we bought from the county on the south," O. B. wrote in February. Uncas, who had been out of town for a few days, replied politely that he wanted to think it over but made it clear that he did not have the cash to spare and would have to raise the necessary money should he decide to take up Pete Hardy's offer.[18]

Towards the middle of March, 1936, the campaign was under way. O. B. wrote to Uncas that he had accepted two invitations to speak and that requests were coming in every day. Uncas' sister Minnie, now married to John Frost, was in Weaubleau with her daughters — Uncas' nieces, Ruth and Portia — and O. B. sent along their greetings to him, "on your 35th birthday," his father wrote. Actually, Uncas Whitaker was thirty-six, but neither his father nor mother could remember exactly in which year he was born. Son Uncas replied to the yearly oversight with Whitaker humor:

> Mamma, you are just one year off on my age. I am now 36 having been born in the year 1900 according to the 'hearsay' evidence I have at hand. Also Minnie is off on her age I think but I won't tell her if she wants to appear young. [Sister] Portia still seems to be truthful about her age but I suppose she will begin to forget a year or so too pretty soon.

In addition to their uncertainty about Uncas' birthday, O. B. and Nettie were also unclear as to his birthplace — whether it was the farm just outside of Lincoln, Kansas or the college campus.[19]

Campaign advice continued to travel from Uncas to O. B. He counseled his father to take it easy and rest up for the arduous months ahead, and reassured him that the money would be there when he needed it. Now Uncas spoke of being able to get his hands on $3,000 by September. "I think we are all almost as interested in your succeeding as you are and I would be more than glad to put any or all of the $3,000 in the fund." For the moment he offered to raise $500, which he believed he could get out of the Westinghouse Air Brake Company fund if he gave them proper notice. Although he was short of cash at the moment, he assured his father he was in good financial shape.

> Now if there is any need at all for this money you be sure to say so. The only reason I don't just send it to you is that I don't have it at hand. . . . Even if I should let you have $2,000 for the campaign I still would be to the good as far as our financial dealings are concerned [meaning cattle, crops and farms]. I am somewhat short of ready cash but my income is good and is fast getting better. Had a $55 per month increase the other day which makes my salary $400 and I get a bonus that runs from $25 to $50 per month. With this income I have no difficulty handling my obligations.[20]

If Uncas Whitaker was private about most of his activities, he was quite open when it came to discussing his earnings. His total Hoover earnings in 1936 were $5,350, up $850 from his 1935 salary of $4,500.

Evidently he was able to save an impressive part of his income because the obligations he referred to were certainly growing. In addition to his initial $900 investment in McKinley Air Transport, he began, early in 1936, making frequent cash advances to MAT for supplies and for operating money. MAT was and would remain a shoestring operation, and over the coming years Whitaker's frequent cash advances grew into a tidy sum. Fortunately for Whitaker, $5,350 was a good deal of money to live on in 1936. His rent, for example, averaged less than $30 per month, and he was not a lavish spender in any case.[21]

O. B. thanked his son for offering to invest money in his campaign and indicated that he would take advantage of his generosity but, as O. B. put it, "not to the extent you have offered." As things turned out, O. B. would take full advantage of that generosity. He was already considering Uncas' suggestion about buying a new car for the campaign. At the same time, despite hopeful signs from the *Literary Digest*, a note of caution was beginning to creep into O. B.'s assessment of his political situation, for, emotional enthusiasm aside, he remained capable of shrewd analysis. The New Deal policy of what he called "mixing politics with relief" was becoming clear to him, and he did not like what he saw. As he told Uncas, "I don't know whether the influence of the millions on federal payrolls was fairly reflected in the Digest or not. If not that too must be reckoned with." The ability of the Roosevelt administration to "buy" the election was beginning to dawn on O. B. Whitaker.[22]

Interestingly, O. B. unwittingly proved just how pervasively inclusive the New Deal could be, even among such articulate dissenters as himself. Early in April he informed Uncas that he was "making a study of the present complicated fool federal farm program to see whether we can get anything worth bothering about under it." He added, "if so will apply. Since we have to pay for it I think we should get what we can out of it."[23] For the present, Uncas did not disagree with his father's approach, and they did in fact come to accept some minimal money from the federal farm support program. Later, however, Uncas grew unalterably opposed to federal research and development money, a position he maintained for both ethical and business reasons.

Just after the first of April, the mail brought a copy of Uncas Whitaker's "Development and Engineering Procedure" article, published in *Product Engineering*. "Just received your letter enclosing clipping containing a scientific article by you," O. B. replied. "Seems to me quite a distinction, tho I would have a better ground for conclusion if you had told us more." Judging by Uncas' past performances in keeping his parents informed, O. B. should have been grateful to receive a copy of the article. Apparently he was not, as his reports to the family indicate.

> About all we know is that he is doing a little work for the [Hoover] Company for a salary and that he got an Electrical Engineering degree from night school from Carnegie Institute at Pittsburgh and an L. L. B. from McKinley Law School in Ohio, and we have been wondering what he was doing with his time. We were pretty sure he was into something. Find out about it Portia.[24]

The summer of 1936 brought the nomination of Landon and Knox ("they are good Christian men — Landon a Methodist and Knox a Congregationalist," O. B. commented) and of O. B. Whitaker, as well as perhaps the worst drought of the decade. Uncas continued to supply campaign money, and early in August sent checks for $250 and $300. By the first of October, O. B. had been on the campaign trail for over a month, traveling in his new Ford Coupe purchased with a trade-in and $300 of Uncas' money. But more money was needed. O. B. sold some cattle at a disastrous loss and asked Uncas for an additional $200 to finish the campaign. That check arrived on October 11 following by several days the arrival of twelve inches of much needed rain. Another $350 check came ten days later.[25]

Money and moral support were not enough in Uncas' mind, and he decided to campaign actively for his father. He thought up a particularly dramatic technique, deciding to spend the final week of the campaign carrying his father from town to town by airplane! Despite Uncas' experience (he had logged some 220 hours of flying time), the piloting he had in mind was not easy. With few airfields in Missouri, landings would typically be made in farmers' fields. The heavy rains, which O. B. normally would have welcomed, now worried him. "Everything is wet and soggy," he warned Uncas; "I expect the best landing place would be in the Neil Morton pasture."[26]

On October 16, 1936, O. B. wired his son: "Expect you last week October. Will print circulars. Letter follows." O. B.'s campaign plans for that last effort, explained in the letter that followed, were rigorous, presenting a challenge even to an accomplished pilot. "I think we can cover the district in two days. I will prepare manuscript and order 50,000 little 6-page folders printed, which will cost $80 to $100 I think. I will probably speak each night and possibly in the afternoon part of the time." A little nervous about the prospect of flying for the first time, O. B. typically tried to cover his anxiety with humor. "I don't know much about this airplane business, as I was never in one of those contraptions — but guess might as well take a 'nose-dive' (whatever that is) just before as just after election."[27]

For the moment, things looked bright. Uncas was coming, and he was to bring sister Portia along as well. On October 24, 1936, Whitaker and his sister took off from McKinley Airport for the seven-and-one-half hour flight to Jefferson City, Missouri, where Uncas would pick up O. B. and start out on the final speech-making and distribution of handbills. After resting a day in Jefferson City, the men took off in the single-engine Rearwin on the first leg of the trip. In an hour and one-quarter they arrived in Marshall, Missouri, where O. B. spoke and distributed circulars. In small boldface type above O. B.'s picture, the printed bill carried a modest statement of O. B.'s immodest pleasure. "Many of these leaflets are distributed from airplane piloted by Mr. Whitaker's son. Kindly read and carefully consider."[28]

The campaign handbill, entitled "Why You Should Vote for O. B. Whitaker for Congress," demonstrates O. B.'s belief in principles. An accomplished parliamentarian and constitutional expert, O. B. believed that what was written down and accepted in a party platform was the gospel regardless of the personal predilections of the individual candidate. He believed this deeply; it was not merely campaign rhetoric. For O. B. Whitaker, the Democrats under F. D. R. had violated most, if not all, of their pledges, as they were documented in the 1932 party platform. Pledges to reduce spending and balance the budget had been ignored, making the platform in question "a scrap of paper." In brief, F. D. R. and all his congressional "lackeys" had lied to the people, broken their covenant, and gotten themselves elected dishonestly. Appealing to history, O. B. went on to offer a definition of a Democrat: "A Democrat is one who believes in the basic principles laid down by Thomas Jefferson, the founder of the Democratic Party, and who faithfully keeps the pledges of his party platform when entrusted with office."[29]

From his point of view, his incumbent opponent and all those who had voted with F. D. R. in Congress had violated that trust. Therefore, none could really be considered Democrats. A real Democrat, according to O. B.'s printed statement, would have voted to reduce expenditures, abolish governmental waste and useless offices, and create a fair system of taxation based on ability to pay. A real Democrat would have voted against boondoggling and against government entry into private enterprise except in those areas (public works, natural resources) affecting the common good. Finally, had O. B. been an elected Democrat in Congress in 1932, he "would have voted against any act that I believed to be in violation of the Constitution I was sworn to support."[30] O. B. Whitaker would have done just that, regardless of party or issue.

Friends and acquaintances who knew Uncas Whitaker later in his career described him as a man who cared a great deal about his country, "a quiet devout patriot."[31] Much of what he cared about he learned from his father, who was unquestionably devoutly patriotic, although not necessarily quiet about it. For O. B. Whitaker, Americanism was not flag-waving of the kind demonstrated by the "sunshine patriots" who appeared only once a year on the Fourth of July. Rather, Americanism for O. B. Whitaker, and for his son, was individual and personal liberty as it was outlined and described in the American Constitution. Agreeing with Gladstone's statement that "the Constitution of the United States is the greatest work ever struck off at any one time by the mind and purpose of man," O. B. often explained to his constituents that the Founding Fathers had written the Constitution "to preserve Americanism." And he would add, "if you do not know that you do not know your country's Constitution."[32] The legal, constituted way was the Whitakers' way.

The day following the Marshall, Missouri stop, Uncas Whitaker flew more than four hours around the vicinity distributing handbills. In the course of the next seven days he logged over thirty air hours traveling around the district. He landed in more farmers' fields than he could later remember. He flew even on election day, taking off from Neil Morton's pasture in Weaubleau for Jefferson City in a final effort to help swing the election to his father. Election Day, Tuesday, November 3, was a bad day for O. B. Whitaker: the Democrats outpolled the Republicans by 2 to 1, and O. B. lost.[33]

Wednesday, November 4th, was an even worse day for the losing candidate — his son and daughter took off for home. Pathetically, on the reverse side of an extra "O. B. Whitaker for Congress" flyer, he wrote the family both pieces of sad news. O. B. was indeed morose, but he could still count his blessings:

> What blessings have been ours in the last few days — infinitely better than an old seat in Congress. Portia, Minnie and Uncas and Minnie's two little angels . . . were all here, and one evening Syd and Homer [another brother] drove up. We all took a ride in Uncas'

airplane — Mamma enjoyed it most. When Uncas and Portia sailed away in the airplane, we watched with a mingled feeling of mystery, joy and sadness. Mamma's eyes filled with tears. Minnie and the little angels had gone before. Gee it was lonesome here for a while. I finally said to Mamma, "let's go and sit on the sofa and put our arms around each other and take a big cry." She said, "I sure feel like it."[34]

A month later the loneliness persisted, and O. B. felt compelled to tell his son the same thing. In the telling the story had grown more elaborate, but it remained equally pathetic.

Uncas . . . we are on the airplane mail line, and a number of planes pass over every day and night, and I guess Mamma and I never see or hear one but that we think of you. I cannot describe our feeling when you and Portia left us at Weaubleau for your Ohio homes. There was something unspeakably sublime and beautiful yet sad as your plane rose so majestically and sailed to the westward, rising in the face of the wind and then circled and came back high above us speeding eastward. We were waving at you but could not tell whether you saw us or not, and we watched you sail out of sight. When I turned and looked at Mamma, her eyes were filled with tears.[35]

With that letter in the mail, O. B. and Nettie Whitaker left for their modest place in Forida. O. B. would as usual feel sorry for himself, contemplate all the things he might do — preach, teach, write — reject them all as unfeasible and then ruminate over the fact that he was getting too old to do anything. And as usual, he generously shared these thoughts with all of his family. He had made sure to bring his carbon paper and second sheets to Florida. The usual seven copies went out.[36]

* * * * * * *

In the midst of the depression thirties, America experienced a recession in 1937. Uncle Syd Whitaker summed up the family's attitude about America at that point, when he wrote his nephew Uncas that "The New Deal and crop failure are too much for us." In Brownington, Missouri, half of the town's businesses had gone under during the past half dozen years. The buildings they had formerly occupied were falling apart. The town looked and was depressed. So was Syd Whitaker. His description of the disrepair of his own residence might very well have been applied to the whole town and other towns like it. "Everything we have," he wrote, "is worn out and breaking down."[37]

O. B.'s despair was global compared to Uncle Syd's. "To me the most loathed name in American history is Franklin Roosevelt," he informed his family, "and I make no exception, not even Benedict Arnold, Aaron Burr or Al Capone." If the nation had set off for hell in a handcart during the 1920s, from O. B.'s perspective it had arrived fully at that destination by 1937. "What's the Use?" he exclaimed.

What can we do when those in official control bribe millions of voters with public funds, refuse to count votes cast against them or change them into votes for themselves, sneer at the Constitution and laws, while masses of their voting supporters organize themselves into gangs of outlaws, seizing millions of dollars worth of private property, driving out their rightful owners, and clubbing, wounding or killing officers that attempt to enforce the laws and orders of the courts — while the President, the real cause of it all, admittedly the biggest liar and the greatest perjurer of the nation, whose paralyzed legs are less afflicted than his conscience, with his booming laugh and idiotic smile, approves, condones and encourages it all.[38]

By "the gangs of outlaws," O. B. meant the auto workers in Detroit who had invented the sit-down strike and the concept of factory occupation. The labor turmoil that occurred in 1937 obviously appalled O. B. Whitaker. Uncas, in North Canton, was less hysterical, but worried nonetheless. "There has been considerable nervousness here," he informed his father early in July, "but nothing serious has happened in Canton, and it looks as if it is going to pass without any very bad trouble."[39] But Uncas Whitaker would not soon forget the labor problems of the 1930s.

O. B. Whitaker went on a land-buying spree in 1937 despite his lack of confidence that the nation would survive the New Deal. He and Uncas purchased two additional farms that year, the latter borrowing heavily on his government life insurance policy to cover part of the purchase costs. In the process, Uncas Whitaker accumulated more mortgage notes to add to the ones on which he was already paying.[40] Before O. B. mailed the letter outlining one of the farm deals he was considering, he read it to Nettie and asked her to OK it and sign it. She replied, "I won't do it." O. B. commented on her refusal by saying, "Mamma acts on the principle that any business I favor is bad — a logical conclusion from over forty years actual observation and experience," but in the end Nettie signed.[41]

Nettie Whitaker wrote her son Uncas very infrequently. Once in a while she would tack on to one of O. B.'s letters a handwritten postscript. On this particular letter she did just that; she had a "business" proposal of her own for Uncas' consideration.

P. S. In reference to the above I would suggest you give up your job there and move your aeroplane business here and buy the Crosse property here and settle down in dear old Weaubleau. It can be had for $1,300. There is 200 acres of land, three large barns, 7 room house and other buildings. We could trade this on it for $200 and move in with you until you took the girl to wife I have picked out for you. She is small and has dark hair, sharp as a tack book keeper for King Bros. Hardware. . . 25 years old. So just come home soon and look over everything.

A week passed with no reply from son Uncas. His father wrote, "Uncas why didn't you answer your mamma's letter the other day in which she advised you to give up your job there and bring your airplane business back here and marry the girl she has picked out for you?" There is no evidence that Uncas Whitaker answered his father about this matter.[42]

Not surprisingly, O. B. was in the red most of the year. Uncas helped all he could, sending expense money every so often to pay for needed farm repairs and for buying seed and other supplies.[43] At the same time he was pouring money into his airplane operaton. During 1937 he advanced MAT nearly $3,000; by the summer of 1938 MAT's balance sheet listed an entry which read: Mortgage held by U. A. Whitaker — $4,150.52. The company's assets, which included two single-engine airplanes, totaled approximately $6,500 at that time, matched of course by liabilities of the same amount.[44]

By the end of 1937, O. B. Whitaker's predictions of rising farm prices, large crops, and higher land values clearly did not materialize. Reacting to his nephew's judgment that business conditions in North Canton were "rather gloomy," Syd Whitaker dismissed newspaper statements to the contrary as merely New Deal propaganda. Uncas, who subscribed to several business forecasting services, was a bit dubious about their predictions for an improved second half in 1938, commenting to Syd that "these big advisers are wrong almost as often as the average fellow." Although he granted that "they were worth paying some attention to," Whitaker always read these forecasts with a healthy scepticism. As one of the "average fellows," he could often do just as well. He was, however, in agreement with those forecasts that called for a very slow, if not outright bad, first half in 1938. Consequently, he suggested to his father that they sell most of their cattle on the assumption that prices would fall lower in the spring. Good common sense told him that poor live stock prices would accompany a bad general business situation, and he was correct.[45]

By the autumn of 1938, U. A. Whitaker, the Hoover Company's director of Development and Design, had been with the firm nine years. An organization chart dated September 7, 1938, indicates that some forty-three people, in three separate sections — staff engineering, design, drafting — comprised his division.[46] Although Whitaker did not know it then, several of the engineers on that list — F. L. Pierce, V. E. Carlson, Q. Berg, and S. W. Pollock — would later join him in his own engineering business venture a few years in the future. As we shall see, the network among engineers was a tight one, and in recruiting many of the key personnel for the new firm Whitaker turned largely to former associates at the Hoover Company and, in at least one instance, at Westinghouse Air Brake Company. Whitaker's relationship with the Hoover Company would always remain a close one, and in the early years of his own business he frequently called upon Hoover's engineering department for help.

For the present, U. A. Whitaker's position at Hoover was secure. His contributions to Hoover's profitability were, by 1938, earning him a salary of nearly $6,500 a year. But the currency of Hoover's 1938 organization chart would be brief. Perhaps even at the moment of its first appearance in September, its director of Development and Design was already entertaining the idea of changing jobs. It is not unlikely that because of his outstanding record at Hoover, Whitaker might have had several possible positions to choose from. Although he was not actively seeking a new position, he was open to offers. One of Whitaker's business trademarks was to investigate opportunities whether or not he was serious about taking advantage of them.

American Machine & Foundry Company was looking for an engineering business type to reorganize its entire engineering function, and U. A. Whitaker looked exactly like the kind of man they needed to accomplish this goal. American Machine & Foundry Company must have wanted him badly. When negotiations were completed by the end of the year, U. A. Whitaker had accepted the job at a starting salary of $13,500, better than double what he was making at Hoover. A salary of this magnitude in 1939 placed Whitaker in an income bracket enjoyed by very few of the American population. It would turn out to be a very good investment for American Machine & Foundry Company, but an even better one for U. A. Whitaker.[47]

6. The Move to American Machine & Foundry Company

In the late summer of 1938, while U. A. Whitaker was thinking about his future, his father, O. B. , was obsessively dwelling on the past. It had been two years since he had lost his second congressional race but the experience still burned in his memory. He recalled election night, 1936, for his family: "Uncas had already abandoned hope, but I hadn't — I clung to that ill-fated *Literary Digest* poll. By nine o'clock all hope was gone, and we retired soon after. I wish I could hand Uncas back the money he spent in his unstinting effort to help me win an impossible victory." Admitting with hindsight that the *Literary Digest* had done him in and that his chances had always been impossible, O. B. still allowed himself the luxury of considering what might have been, "Suppose Roosevelt had never been elected."[1]

A month later, shortly after Neville Chamberlain returned from Munich with the scrap of paper that guaranteed "peace in our time," O. B. was feeling his old self again. Always a vocal isolationist, O. B. understood fully the implications of England and France's "act of betrayal," as he made plain in a letter to Uncas: "If they think that this is the way to prevent a world war, they are in the same class of lunatics with a man who throws a lamb to a pack of wolves when they bark for them in order to teach wolves not to kill sheep. The only way to stop Hitler and Mussolini is war or disgraceful surrender to all they demand." And by November, when Uncas was deeply involved in his American Machine & Foundry Company negotiations, O. B. was already correctly predicting that the United States would become involved in that war. He hated even the idea of war and was especially dismayed by the probability of American participation in it.[2]

News from North Canton was sparse. Son Uncas took too long to answer O. B.'s questions on farm matters and the latter was irritated. So was Uncas' mother. O. B., underscoring his own feelings, wrote: "And Mamma wants to know WHY YOU CAN'T WRITE SOMETHING ABOUT YOURSELF AND YOUR WORK SO WE CAN KNOW HOW YOU ARE AND WHAT YOU ARE DOING."[3] Not until after Whitaker had accepted the job with American Machine & Foundry Company did O. B. and Nettie hear anything about it, and then the news came not from Uncas but from sister

Portia. O. B. pressed Uncas for details, got them in due course, and reported at length to the rest of the family shortly before Christmas, 1938:

> Last week we had a letter from Portia saying that she supposed we knew that Uncas was going to locate in New York, that she could not keep back the tears as she thought of his moving so far away from them, but that she was glad of his promotion, etc. Well, that was the first inkling we had of the matter. We were of course interested and so I wrote him some pointed questions, accompanied with demand for immediate answer. The answer came in characteristic Uncas style — nothing exciting or remarkable or worth mentioning, but admitting that he had taken a new position with a new company — the American Machine & Foundry Company, "about the size of Hoover Co., and like the Hoover Co., has always made money, even during the depression." In answer to another point-blank question he said his salary would be $13,500.[4]

That apparently was all Whitaker wrote to his father about his situation, but that was not all there was to be said about it. Again it was from Portia that O. B. got the rest of the account, and he, as was his habit, quoted those portions of his daughter's letter that explained the details of this latest development in Uncas' career:

> I certainly was surprised when Uncas told us he was leaving the Hoover Co. I told him I didn't know he was looking for work somewhere else, and he said he wasn't. It seems that the American Machine & Foundry Company was looking for a man who was capable of reorganizing their plants and putting them on a more satisfactory working basis, and after looking up several men and studying their ability, accomplishments and education decided Uncas was the man they wanted, and, if I understand it right, the President of the Company sent a man to Canton instructed not to come back without getting him. He didn't succeed in getting him, but he did get a promise that he would go to New York and have a talk with the President. While there the President was able to get Uncas favorably interested in the work he wants him to undertake, and he signed up for a salary of $13,500 the first year, and I think it is to increase after the first year.[5]

It was on November 22, 1938, that U. A. Whitaker checked into New York's Statler Hotel and hurried over to the executive offices of American Machine & Foundry Company, at 511 Fifth Avenue for a discussion of the position they wanted him to fill. That evening Whitaker returned to North Canton, promising Morehead Patterson, the ranking American Machine & Foundry Company vice-president, that he would think the offer over and reply in a few days.

Whitaker's reply was affirmative and Patterson acknowledged it on the first of December: "Thank you for your letter of November 27th, which confirms all the matters of which we have talked. I look forward with the greatest pleasure to the initiation of the arrangements contained therein and have the greatest confidence that the results will be everything that could be wished."[6]

In mid-December Whitaker received a batch of documents relating to the current organization of the company in order that he might begin to familiarize himself with the internal workings of the firm. Whitaker discovered that things at American Machine & Foundry Company were in a state of flux. The latest approved engineering organization chart dated from 1934; the one that the company was currently developing had already been revised several times without any consensus being reached. That, of course, would be a main part of Whitaker's job. In the meantime, Patterson told Whitaker to take it easy and get rested up for his anticipated start at American Machine & Foundry Company, on January 1, 1939.

By that time Whitaker had nearly ended a month's vacation generously given him by the Hoover Company and in fact was already at work studying the American Machine & Foundry Company situation, preparing to make some initial recommendations. Sister Portia saw her brother at that time and reported to her father that Uncas looked well and rested.

He says it does feel good just to rest his mind, and not to have to feel any responsibility for awhile. Says he is just taking it easy and resting up before starting in on his new work. He says he thinks there will be a lot of fine experience and enjoyment in his new job, but it will also carry with it a lot of worry and responsibility.[7]

The Hoover Company, appreciative of the work Whitaker had done for them for nearly ten years, presented him with a wrist watch (which Portia described as being just like the one worn by Earl Hoover, vice-president of the Company, for which he had paid $500). Engraved on the back were the words, "To U. A. Whitaker by The Hoover Company as an expression of gratitude for the valuable services he has rendered our company."[8]

On December 21, Whitaker received a note from Morehead Patterson asking him to choose one of four titles for the name of the new engineering department Whitaker was to head. None of the four sugggestions — Division of Standards and Methods, Engineering Methods, Methods and Processes, Research and Methods — pleased Whitaker because to pick a title before defining clearly the division's

functions was to place the cart before the horse. So important was
this distinction to Whitaker that he felt compelled to make his point
before arriving in New York to start work. Vacation or not, Whitaker
was doing his homework, as he always would. The day after
Christmas, 1938, he sat down to write Patterson a letter containing
his views. He began diplomatically, never actually stating that
Patterson had things backwards: "In reply to your letter of
December 21, I have some suggestions for a name for the new
division of the American Machine & Foundry Company, but should
like to discuss first the probable activities of this new division."

He then proceeded to list ten assignments he might undertake,
indicating his own preferences by noting that "items 1, 5, and 8 have
been given some thought." The ten activities listed by Whitaker
exemplify the blend of engineering and business talents he had been
developing over the years.

> 1. Study the technical departments of other companies who have
> been successful along engineering lines, and especially those having
> engineering problems similar to those of our Company. From the
> background gained, decide upon the general type and size of
> organization best suited to the present needs and future
> developments of the Company.

Whitaker's Hoover experience had qualified him well to identify successful engineering divisions for study.

> 2. Work out a long term plan for gradually bringing the present
> organization into line with the proposed organization.

When Whitaker joined American Machine & Foundry Company, the
company manufactured various kinds of equipment through a
number of separate divisions. At least six of the more important —
International Cigar Machinery, General Tobacco Machinery, Sewing
Machine, General Bakery Machinery, Glen Mixer, Contract — had
fairly independent engineering divisions. Whitaker's major task was to
centralize engineering functions to serve the various divisions, and in
a little over a year he accomplished this fully for four of the divisions
and partially for the others.

> 3. Decide upon a policy for developing present personnel and
> bringing in new personnel, as required, for the new organization.

During his business life, Whitaker was always concerned with the
continuing improvement of his engineering personnel and the
recruiting of topflight new technical people to assure the flow of new
ideas and approaches to the solving of engineering problems.

4. Review the present engineering activities, and set up a general work program covering immediate engineering items considered most important by the management.

Whitaker had done just this at the Hoover Company and not long after this time instituted the concept of the work program for the McKinley Air Transport operation in much the same manner as suggested here for American Machine & Foundry Company

5. Analyze the cost of producing merchandise now being manufactured, and determine which items offer the best possibilities in making cost reductions, either by improved manufacturing methods or changes in design.

This was among Whitaker's high priorities. As at the Hoover Company, Whitaker would press for cost estimating BEFORE a design was brought forward, rather than after completion of the design. This approach became a major part of his later total engineering concept as it was applied to electrical termination devices.

6. Determine whether worthwhile savings in manufacturing cost could be effected by better standardization or reduction in the number of models, or by further standardizing of sub-assemblies or individual parts.

At both Westinghouse Air Brake and Hoover standardization was the order of the day. Whitaker's experience along this line was extensive. Beginning as early as his MIT project on the rubber heel testing machine, Whitaker had learned to think in terms of more and more standardization wherever applicable.

7. Review the cost-estimating system to determine whether it is adequate for engineering needs.

This activity is a corollary to number 5. Again, Whitaker would begin with the needs of engineering, the problems to be solved, and then analyze the cost-estimating procedures to see that needs were balanced with realistic cost budgets.

8. Review the present activities in establishing new merchandising lines, and set up a regularly organized program for uncovering desirable new lines.

This was another of Whitaker's priority items, perhaps the most important of the three he enumerated. His emphasis on research in his own engineering business would prove to be a major building block. New products, Whitaker believed, were the lifeblood of manufacturing concerns like American Machine & Foundry Com-

pany and, later, AMP Incorporated. Funds for that purpose, he
reasoned, should always be available in generous amounts.

> 9. Provide a definite system by which intimate contact is maintained
> between Engineering and Sales, Service, Consumer, Production and
> Patent Departments.

This is the way it had been at the Hoover Company, step-by-step
communciation all along the path of product development. Constant
consultations and revisions when necessary BEFORE the final
product went on the market.

> 10. Undertake such special assignments of a more or less
> management nature, but on subjects for which a technical group
> should be fitted to make recommendations. The problem of
> determining possible advantages in moving the plant from Brooklyn
> to some other locality would be a good illustration of a problem of
> this type.

Beyond the obvious good sense of involving technical types in
major management decision making, the example Whitaker chose to
illustrate his tenth suggested activity is significant as foreshadowing
later decisions Whitaker would make with his own company.[9]

Whitaker's rural backround never left him without some
uneasiness over big city locations for manufacturing companies. His
experience in George Westinghouse's company town of Wilmerding
and in the small suburban community of North Canton, where the
Hoovers set up shop, reinforced his inbred preference for nonurban
environments. Beyond western prejudice, Whitaker believed, like
many other entrepreneurs of his generation, that the rural worker
was more dependable than his urban counterpart. It was not
altogether the question of organized versus unorganized labor,
although that played a part, but rather the idea that people in the
nation's more rural areas adhered to values much closer to his own
than those in major American cities.

Only after U. A. Whitaker had made all of these points in his reply
to Morehead Patterson, did he return to the question of a title for
the new engineering division. In place of Patterson's four options,
Whitaker had some ideas of his own. "As to a name for this
division, I feel it should indicate a broader field than indicated by the
four names suggested. Something like (1) Staff Engineering
Division, (2) Technical Staff Division, (3) Technical Advisory
Division, and (4) Technical Control Division would seem to be more
descriptive. I shall be interested in discussing this further when I see
you."[10]

Whitaker's discussion with Patterson and others about the name for the division did not go his way. He lost on that issue, but he won where it counted — his list of activity priorities was largely adopted, as can been seen in a letter Whitaker wrote in February, 1939. L. E. Jermy, editor of *Machine Design*, had written requesting information about Whitaker's new position at American Machine & Foundry Company.

> At the American Machine and Foundry Company I have the title of Director of Research and Standards — which title might be a little misleading. I report to the Operating Committee of the Company and will undertake assignments of a rather broad nature. At the present time my efforts are directed toward three major problems. One is to reorganize the design and cost-estimating and coordinate the design, manufacturing and cost estimating activities so that cost of any particular machine can be established before the design is started rather than after the design is completed. The reduction of manufacturing costs will be included in this assignment. The second problem is a study of the entire technical activities of the company, with a view to working out a long-term plan for the future development of the engineering and other technical divisions. The third problem I have at present is a similar study in cooperation with the Patent Department of the patent activities of the Company.

Whitaker told editor Jermy that he was satisfied with the way things were working out at American Machine & Foundry Company, and optimistic about the future, concluding that "there are plenty of opportunities to show some real accomplishment."[11]

Technically, Whitaker reported to the Operating Committee at American Machine & Foundry Company, but he was also generally involved in major management problems. He participated in Executive Committee meetings with the four vice-presidents and the firm's comptroller. Thus, he gained valuable experience about and insights into decision making at the highest corporate level, and he later adopted some similar management committee models for his own firm. Moreover, some key personnel from American Machine & Foundry Company later became associated with Whitaker's new business venture. George Ingalls, later the president of AMP Incorporated, was then head of general accounting at American Machine & Foundry Company; for a number of years, before joining AMP Incorporated in 1957, he was an important financial advisor to Whitaker. Frank Wells, whom Whitaker had first known at Westinghouse Air Brake, followed Whitaker to American Machine & Foundry Company, and then later joined AMP Incorporated as its chief research engineer. George Hastings, American Machine & Foundry Company's patent counsel, became a lifelong friend of Whitaker's and in the early months of AMP Incorporated's formation rendered valuable patent advice to Whitaker about the state of electrical termination art.[12]

But early in January, 1939, all of this lay in the future for Whitaker. For the moment he was staying at the Hotel St. George in Brooklyn to be near the American Machine & Foundry Company plant, but he soon determined that he was not going to be happy living there. By the first of February, he moved to New York City and into the McAlpin Hotel at Broadway and 34th Street, where, as he told his father, he was more comfortable. There was, however, one clear disadvantage to living in New York State, as he pointed out to O. B. early in February: "Looks as if my income taxes are going to run over $1,000 this year since the State of New York has an income tax almost as great as the Federal Tax." He was not exaggerating; in those days the New York State tax tables were only slightly less than those governing federal taxes. Under the circumstances, Whitaker asked his father to send along any farm expense records that would legitimately allow him his fullest deductions. As has been indicated, farm losses were not hard to come by in the 1930s.[13]

* * * * * * *

Although Whitaker had left North Canton, he was still intimately involved in the operation of his commercial flying venture, McKinley Air Transport. Major and minor business matters called forth considerable correspondence. Furthermore, Whitaker often flew into Canton on weekends to attend to things personally. MAT was still a two-person operation — Earl Kail was in effect the general manager, and Miss Lou Ritzman handled the office, battling to balance the books and keeping the checks from bouncing. At this time, she was also learning to fly, and letters kept Whitaker up-to-date on her progress in the air as well as the progress of the operation. Whitaker's removal to New York made a rather tenuous business situation yet more tenuous, and a good deal of foot-dragging was going on in the administrative center of MAT. Ritzman's report of January 8, 1939, lists the work program, as instituted by Whitaker, but notes rather casually that nothing specific was being done about it, and somewhat less casually comments that they both felt the absence of their friend: "I wish you were still here. It seems funny not to see you popping in at the door and putting on your flying suit."[14]

Perhaps the lack of progress irritated Whitaker, but if so, he did not show it. The next report, dated January 12, looked better and Whitaker, who gave credit where credit was due, sent back a note of encouragement:

Dear Miss Ritzman:

Your January 12th report looks very good, and, certainly wish to compliment you and Earl on the action in connection with the work program. I believe you will show results — if you keep up that activity.

"Miss Ritzman," apparently struck by a new note of formality, advised "Whit" that she preferred to remain "Lou" in correspondence A late January note carried the "Dear Lou" salutation and referred to one of Whitaker's weekend visits. The business might be floundering in his absence, but there was only so much he could accomplish long distance.

Dear Lou:

Would certainly have liked to spend more time at the Airport when I was there, but unfortunately, I have another business, possibly not as interesting but for the time being more profitable.[15]

Profit at the McKinley Air Transport operation would prove to be a sometime thing. Problems, however, were commonplace, and adjustment after Whitaker left took several months. During this period, Ritzman and Kail had words — Kail evidently pointing out some of her shortcomings — and Whitaker had to fly in to smooth things over the last weekend in February. After that particular visit, Ritzman wrote Whitaker:

I'm so glad I talked with you Sunday — had a talk with Earl as you suggested and it has helped very much already. He said he had been meaning to talk to me for some time. I'll certainly endeavor to make some progress along the lines that you and he have suggested. Thank you from the bottom of my heart for giving me the "Dutch Uncle" talk.[16]

Whitaker was in an expansive mood by early spring. Things were going well at American Machine & Foundry Company, and his flying operation seemed at last to show some progress. He was pleased enough with one report from MAT to add a small Easter bonus to Lou Ritzman's weekly salary of $2.50.[17] On the same day, still expansive, he wrote Kail of a plan he had to add income to their operation.

At Floyd Bennett [Field] they will let me operate off the line and
they suggested that we put the Stimson on the line hopping
passengers there. . . . With a 5 place airplane . . . I believe a good
profit could be made. . . . According to my calculations, the best
proposition would be for me to keep the Cessna [here] at Floyd
Bennett and hop passengers myself on Saturdays and Sundays. I
figure 15 hours a month would net about $180 profit that way and I
would only have to spend a few hours at the airport.

Such a proposal from a man fully employed as a major executive
and engineer was at least unrealistic. Earl Kail's reply revealed his
own incredulity, but he did not attempt to quash the project. "I can't
imagine YOU YOURSELF hopping passengers on Saturdays and
Sundays, athough it may be a good idea."[18]

When Whitaker used the phrase, "according to my calculations,"
he meant that he had studied the problem thoroughly before making
a judgment, and this case was no exception. Although he did not yet
own the Cessna airplane he had referred to, Whitaker had worked
out a complicated scheme of trade-ins designed to bring them the
Cessna, which Whitaker believed would produce a "margin of profit
. . . greater than . . . the Stinson." Facts and figures accompanied the
plans; little was left to guesswork. As Kail put it: "You certainly
must have gone into the matter thoroughly at Floyd Bennett to get
all those statistics." And indeed Whitaker had — he had even
calculated to the penny the amount of gas each five- to seven-minute
hop would take![19]

Despite Whitaker's energy and Kail's continued optimism that
business would improve if only the weather would, MAT's prospects
were not bright in the spring of 1939. A controversy over the use of
McKinley Airport threatened MAT's location, and both Whitaker and
Kail began talking about moving the business elsewhere. Kail even
hinted that he might have to start looking for other employment. The
possiblility of "going under" was a reality that had to be faced. Fully
aware of this possibility, Whitaker tried to make sure that, if it
happened, MAT's creditors would be adequately protected, along
with his own reputation as a man who promptly paid his bills.[20]

With the coming of summer and better weather, business at MAT
should have improved, but it did not, and Kail and Whitaker began
talking about selling the operation. Whitaker flew to Canton the first
weekend in September to talk with Kail about prospective buyers,
and Kail was left with the unpleasant task of explaining their plan to
Lou Ritzman. "Oh, Whit," she wrote, on September 7, 1939,

Earl just told me about selling the company, and I do feel so bad about it, though I knew it was merely a matter of time till it happened. You know the way you kid yourself into not believing something you don't want to believe. It has been such a pleasure to work with people like you and Earl, and — oh, I don't know the way to say it. I want to stay in the flying field — don't think I'd be happy without the hum of Cubs. . . . Have been happier the past year and a half than at any other time in my life.[21]

Whitaker surely felt just as bad as Ritzman; he, too, loved the "hum of Cubs."

Kail dragged his feet on the sale of the company, probably hoping for some miracle although no sign of one was apparent. Less than a week after Kail and Whitaker had discussed MAT's sale, Whitaker had to send a check of $350 just to cover shortages in the MAT account. Things grew worse, and Kail soon began negotiations for the sale and thought about becoming a copilot for United or American Airlines, provided he could pass the test for an instrument rating.[22]

As shaky as the airplane business looked in the summer and early fall of 1939, Whitaker's investments in Missouri agriculture looked worse. His father's assessment was not encouraging in late June: "The agricultural situation has just about gone smash all over the country. . . . I do not know what your ideas may be touching the matter, as to whether land will 'come back' and if so when. . . . Mine are not worth telling." Uncas admitted his own perplexity over the apparent hopelessness of conditions, but added that whatever the chances of land values coming back, "there seems to be nothing else that one can invest in with much of a chance to get a good return on the investment, so I suppose land is about as good as anything. If we should have real inflation it would seem that land would be about the best possible investment." While son Uncas continued to talk about hedging against inflation, O. B. suddenly began to predict another "crash." Still, he agreed that land and cattle investments were the best alternatives in either case. O. B. 's judgment that "this is the most discouraging agricultural outlook I ever faced," prompted Uncas to send $1,000 to his Uncle Syd's bank for the purchase of additional cattle, no doubt hoping to improve his father's outlook.[23]

In Canton, MAT's business picked up a little by October, but the temporary improvement only convinced Kail that it was imperative to sell the operation immediately. Through October and November the sale of the company dominated the thinking of Whitaker, Kail, and Lou Ritzman. Every other weekend, Whitaker prepared to fly into

Canton, "to help complete the deal," but nothing concrete emerged as those weekends came and passed.[24]

Then the miracle occurred. With feigned casualness, Earl Kail announced it at the end of a letter dated December 1, 1939. Kail had been notified by the Civil Aeronautics Agency (CAA) that MAT had been "selected for the noncollege student training program [flight instruction] . . . which certainly makes MAT look up in a big way." Then he added, "that is the real news I wanted to give you." And real news it was! Kail predicted that between thirty and fifty students would be participating in the program and that as far as he could see it would be a continuing contract provided MAT could do the job. How this all came about is not entirely clear. Kail evidently had learned of such programs through a certain Major Barnhill in Cleveland. Barnhill had asked Kail a couple of months earlier if he would be interested in training student flyers enrolled in nearby Baldwin Wallace College, which had received a CAA contract for that purpose. It is entirely possible that Kail made his own inquiries and subsequently convinced CAA officials that MAT was qualified to undertake a similar arrangement for the noncollege flying aspirants. In any event, MAT got the contract.[25]

Despite this potential windfall, the cash flow situation at MAT was terrible. At the end of January, 1940, Whitaker found MAT's bank balance overdrawn and wrote Kail asking for an explanation. In answer, he received a tale of woe; Kail had borrowed money on his personal possessions to keep the operation going. Lou Ritzman supplied the appalling details:

> The bank balance is $13.78 — we owe two months field rent ($50) — Earl is behind in his room rent $8 and a car payment $44 an airplane ticket for around $40 — 2 months phone bill for $40 — a $20 check on Earl's personal account (that will bounce) to reimburse a company loan borrowed from his brother, back wages for me $8 — Kenny $5.

With undiminished optimism, Ritzman concluded her account: "but this *is* a low spot, and things have righted themselves before."[26]

To make matters at MAT even worse (if that were possible), Earl Kail was responsible for a couple of costly mistakes. He worked out a deal to buy a six-seat Ryan airplane to fly people to the World's Fair in New York, but the company had come out on the short end, paying more for the plane than it was worth. Whitaker had warned Kail originally that the idea did not look promising — the plane was old, and he was afraid it would cost more in trouble than it would bring in profit. Additionally, Kail trapped himself in a bad settlement of a case contesting MAT's exclusive right to the McKinley Airport. The price for settlement escalated as Kail failed to reach an agreement. Whitaker eventually paid for both errors. On February 2, 1940, he bailed Kail out of the Ryan deal with a check for $600. Ten days later, Kail finally came to a legal settlement at great expense to the management: ("Sorry, had to accept a figure of $819," he reported to Whitaker.) Whitaker was understandably irritated: "Was not particularly pleased with that deal you finally made . . . as I think we got pretty badly taken." Whitaker, however, seldom wasted energy over things that could not be undone. "Since it's settled, it is off our minds," he told Kail, adding, "let's hope for the best as far as the Ryan is concerned."[27]

Under the circumstances, Whitaker's patience was a necessary virtue, for he next received a note from his father. "Believe it or not," O. B. informed him, "I have spent nearly all the thousand dollars you deposited in the bank at Brownington and also my own." In reply, Whitaker offered to help out by buying O. B. 's interest in two farms. Shortly after that came another bad monthly statement from Lou Ritzman in Canton, and Whitaker sent along another check to keep the MAT bank account alive.[28]

It is not surprising that Whitaker was increasingly eager to sell MAT. A new prospect appeared in May, 1940, and the proposition looked good, as Whitaker explained to Kail:

> [The prospective buyer agreed] to pay me $4,300 for the loan I have made the Company . . . $500 for my stock, and pay you whatever you ask for your stock. . . . He would then take all assets listed on our statement of April 24, and assume all liabilities.

The prospective buyer, whom Whitaker expected at the airport in the near future, did not make an appearance. A month passed. By then, Kail was maintaining his optimism with the hope of finding another buyer should this deal fall through: "We should have no trouble in finding another buyer," he insisted, "I really believe that with a huge government-subsidized training program MAT should get a sizeable amount of business. I have never seen the interest [in flying] being shown as it is now."[29]

Nearly another month passed with no potential buyers on the scene. Business was looking up, at least on paper, for people continued to sign up for the government-subsidized flying course, but money difficulties remained severe. The government was very slow at paying; moreover, the paperwork was considerable. Under the circumstances, Whitaker encouraged Kail to seek further CAA contracts, and he outlined a program for improving the overall profit picture at MAT in the event of a prospective purchaser.[30]

In late June Kail stepped up his efforts to get new CAA contracts by flying to Washington for interviews with CAA officials. Confidence restored, Kail suggested that the long-dormant offer to buy MAT was now laughable, for they had $15,000 worth of government contracts in the offing. Finally, in July, that reluctant buyer showed up at the MAT offices, having gotten wind of those "contracts in the offing." He regretted, according to Lou Ritzman, that he had not bought the company out and tried to pry more details about the contracts from her. These efforts were met with "no comment" from Ritzman as she sent the man on his way.[31]

After a weekend visit to Canton in early August, Whitaker sent Kail and Ritzman a work plan that included a newly established weekly goal: "make a drive to build student business up to $500 next week." Over the next couple of weeks, the goal had been translated into a "quota": "Hope you will go over the top next week," he wrote on August 17, and on the twenty-second, "Last week's statement looks pretty good, but it seems that you can't quite get the volume up to quota. Hope you are doing better this week." When they failed to make the quota that week, Ritzman commented, "that *business* figure has come to be more and more of a Pike's Peak or bust, and it *won't* be bust."[32]

Kail and Ritzman soon learned that government contracts brought their own special difficulties. "There certainly is a lot of red tape connected with this program," Kail informed Whitaker in October; "There are myriad reports and forms to be filled out." Ritzman, of course, had the job of filling them out and fairly soon began to feel overworked and underpaid. She complained to Whitaker that the Civilian Patrol Training Program "stuff takes a lot of time . . . came in at 2:45 AM to get the regular report out." Anticipating future profits, she asked Whitaker about the chance for some kind of bonus when MAT completed the first round of training — perhaps $100. "I'm sure it's worth it from the amount of work there is," she explained. Whitaker's response was cautious: "If the company actually does as well as indicated, I will be favorable toward some sort of bonus and I will talk this over with Earl."[33]

Whitaker let the issue drop for the time being; those anticipated profits were not yet in hand. By the first part of December, however, they appeared within reach. On the third, Whitaker received a wire from Kail that a new contract was nearly certain. On the fifth he was notified by Ritzman that the government had finally come through with $810 of the money it owed MAT. Finally the bank balance had a balance! Ritzman was exuberant at MAT's progress and, anticipating her bonus, she discussed the matter with Earl Kail. To her dismay, she learned that her request for a bonus had seriously annoyed her two bosses. Angry over the way the matter had been handled, or rather, not handled, Ritzman wrote to Whitaker expressing her disappointment:

> Was very much disturbed Tuesday night when Earl told me both you and he resented my asking for a bonus. Heavens, Whit, I wish you had come right out and said so at the time. I am always frank with you and Earl and thought you were with me too. Earl said the fact that I mentioned a definite figure was the most annoying part of it.

A bonus, she explained, had seemed more appropriate than a raise. Raises had gone to other people on the payroll (people who were not, in her judgment, working harder than she). Furthermore, those employees, unlike herself, were not company people; that is, they did not know about nor care particularly that MAT had a cash shortage. Because she was aware of the cash problem, Ritzman had not asked for a raise, and that was why she had suggested the bonus plan. She felt, she said, badly about being misinterpreted. She felt badly about the way Whitaker and Kail reacted. But more than that, Ritzman was distressed to learn that the two men had talked together about their annoyance and had not spoken with her. "Whit, if in the future there is any cause for criticism of me — I shall welcome it directly. I think the part I hate most is that you didn't *tell* me how you felt." Turning the tables on her boss, she announced that this was a "Dutch Uncle Letter." Whitaker got the point. "The next time I get down," he wrote, "we can have a general discussion of any question that may be on your mind."[34]

Whitaker's experiences with MAT in these years taught him a good deal about the minor irritations inherent in running a business, about the need to pay attention to small details. Better management procedures had to be instituted in order to control the flow of cash, and also the flow of events. Loyal employees were essential; on the other hand, so were competent employees. Early in 1941, Whitaker removed the MAT bookkeeping operation from Canton to New York; the financial aspect of the company, at least, would become more orderly.

Probably the most important lesson taught Whitaker by his commercial flying venture was that dealing with the United States government as customer had its costs as well as its benefits. In his yearly letter to Uncle Syd, Uncas mentioned the benefits — and the dangers:

> My little company out at Canton is showing signs of making a profit but this depends entirely upon continuation of Government contracts for training pilots. We are just completing one contract and have been assured that we will get another. The dangerous thing, however, is that we are having to buy additional equipment and there is a serious question as to how much value this equipment will have should the contracts be terminated.[35]

Whitaker might have been worried, but his father could find the comic side and pass that, too, on to Uncle Syd.

> I read Uncas' letter to Nettie in which he said his airplane company was getting some good government air contracts and expected more, and I added, "Uncas will just about turn New Dealer." Nettie said, "Pooh!" I said, "What would you do if Uncas should come out for the New Deal and Roosevelt?" She hesitated a moment, and then said, "I wouldn't vote."[36]

Nettie's son Uncas had no intention of turning New Dealer. But whatever his distrust of government contracts, it seems clear enough that without the coming threat of United States involvement in the war, MAT would not have remained in business. Whitaker's flying firm capitalized on this reality as would the electrical termination enterprise he founded in 1941. Whatever the costs and difficulties, the government as buyer directly and indirectly provided Whitaker the impetus for his new undertaking. As one of his longtime associates would put it years later, Whitaker was in the right place at the right time.[37]

His position at American Machine & Foundry Company, and the perilous financial situation at MAT plunged Whitaker ever deeper into business problems and decisions; nevertheless, his engineer's mind was far from inactive. He still spent a considerable amount of time flying — logging some 150 air hours in 1940 — and as one result grew increasingly knowledgeable about the construction of airplanes.[38] In the summer of 1939, he had ordered his first brand-new airplane, a Rearwin three-seater Cloudster, with delivery scheduled for April, 1940. For over a year, Whitaker tinkered, ordered modifications, altered specifications, until he was satisfied with its performance.

Letters to the Rearwin factory indicate how much practical and theoretical knowledge Whitaker had gained about airplane construction. Normally a patient man, Whitaker finally grew angry over design defects in the airplane, particularly those associated with the landing gear. Long after he had received the plane, the problems remained unsolved. Examining a newer Cloudster, housed in his airplane hanger, Whitaker discovered the answer to his own landing gear problem and wrote the chief engineer at Rearwin a detailed analysis of what he believed was wrong. His frustration was evident in the final paragraph of the letter:

> This will make the fourth time we have taken this landing gear apart and this has been quite an expense to me as well as being extremely annoying, especially since no improvement has been accomplished. I imagine you are getting equally tired of hearing about it. Therefore, in order to clear things up promptly, please give this your immediate attention and write me return airmail when these parts can be shipped. Please get them to me as soon as you can but be sure they are right before shipping.[39]

Annoyance aside, Whitaker loved working out mechanical problems in his own way. As he wrote to a fellow flying enthusiast, "I suppose that before you and I die of old age, airplanes will be made so that you can buy them already assembled and with all the necessary parts attached, instead of having to not only build them, but design them after they are bought. That may take a little fun out of it though."[40]

Time spent flying and tinkering made it seem reasonable for Whitaker to move from the McAlpin in New York to Long Island for the summer of 1939. There he could be closer to Roosevelt Field and his airplane.[41] After the summer, he moved into the Shelton Hotel at Lexington and 48th in New York City, where he lived until the beginning of June, 1940. Then, consolidating home, office, and airfield, Whitaker moved to the residential Hotel Granada in Brooklyn, only fifteen minutes from his American Machine & Foundry Company office, and he moved his plane from Roosevelt Field to nearby Floyd Bennett Field.

* * * * * * *

By 1940, engineers were increasingly in demand, and talented engineers like U. A. Whitaker were hard to come by. Whitaker's reputation in his field had grown to such an extent that he received frequent inquiries asking for information about top-notch engineers to fill a variety of responsible positions across the country. The restlessness of the engineering troops at the Hoover Company kept him busy on this front for a good portion of the year. Several of the men involved — V. E. Carlson, F. L. Pierce, S. W. Pollock, — later joined Whitaker as key men in the business venture. While Whitaker did not believe in "raiding" a company for its employees, he did feel strongly that when a man wanted to better himself (even one of his own employees) he would do all he could to help.[42]

Whitaker, however, did set ethical limits on job hopping. For example, one engineer at Hoover was considering taking a job with a well-established Hoover competitor, and he wrote Whitaker for some advice and guidance. Whitaker had a talent for giving his opinion, yet somehow forcing the other fellow to assume the responsibility for his own decisions. He wrote to the Hoover engineer:

> As to the ethics of the proposition, you would be somewhat on the ragged edge, I guess, since you do have a lot of intimate information of the future plans of the Hoover Company. . . . This matter of ethics, however, I think everyone has to decide for themselves, and I would say that it wouldn't necessarily be unethical to take a job with a competitor, though you should certainly consider this part of the proposition. . . . I believe that both in choosing a wife and a job, the person involved is about the only one who can make the decision.

The engineer declined the job and remained at Hoover.[43]

Whitaker was not looking for a new job in 1940; nevertheless, he was approached about taking a top executive position at a small vacuum cleaner manufacturer. In this case, it was not ethics that determined Whitaker's decision but shrewd business sense. He was sought out by the important business management firm of Booz, Fry, Allen and Hamilton who had learned that Whitaker would be an outstanding candidate for the job, for his successes at Hoover were well known in the industry. Since Whitaker was the type who neither rejected nor accepted anything without investigating its possibilities, he agreed to look the company over. Subsequently, he met with Booz, to tell him he was not interested in the job. Booz, suspecting that perhaps the salary being offered was not high enough for a man of Whitaker's talents, volunteered to intervene with the company to get the offer raised. To his astonishment, Whitaker replied that the trouble with the job was not that the salary was too low but rather that it was too high.

Booz, who had felt himself in command of the interview, now sat down and asked for an explanation. How could Whitaker make this judgment after such a brief visit? According to one of Whitaker's later close associates, his answer went something like this:

> Whit said that the trouble with the job he was offered was that it was a "bail out" proposition. It had been mismanaged to a point where they had to have a drastic change of management, but they could not afford to pay more than had been offered to him. He could see that to contract to pay a higher salary might be good from the point of view of improving their management, but that it would give them a new problem, which would make it necessary to economize drastically. Whit did not want to be in a position of having his job dry up under him so he said the company should not pay more than it had originally offered him.

Booz found it hard to believe what he was hearing. He prodded Whitaker for more information about the company's management, and Whitaker told him what he had learned by "asking a few questions here and there." Booz, who had considered Whitaker merely a successful engineer, now saw him as a potentially brilliant businessman, and he promised the American Machine & Foundry Company engineering executive that he would be on the constant lookout for something in which he might be interested. Whitaker told Booz that he would be interested only in "a long term connection which he could build into something big." The interview with Booz would prove to be a major turning point in Whitaker's professional life.[44]

Whitaker made another very significant connection in 1940, in this instance, a renewal of an old connection — with MIT. Among the requests for recommendations he was receiving were a number from MIT's Division of Industrial Cooperation's Placement Officer, Nat Sage. Besides its important industrial research contracts, the division had also taken on some responsibility for placing MIT's engineering graduates. Now, in a seller's market, Sage frequently called upon Whitaker for men already in the field who wanted to relocate. Then, in the spring of 1940, Whitaker was invited to serve as an alumni representative on the Departmental Visiting Committee for the Division of Industrial Cooperation, an honor and a responsibility Whitaker readily accepted. Whitaker's formal liaison with MIT was thus begun, and in the future the reciprocal relationship benefited both the man and the institution.[45]

At the same time, the spring and summer of 1940, news centered around the war in Europe and the coming presidential election. In Missouri, O. B. was running once again for the legislature under the

Republican banner held now by Wendell L. Willkie, in his attempt to
wrest the White House away from Franklin D. Roosevelt. O. B. was
fast becoming a firm supporter of Willkie, and Uncas had been
impressed with the man even before he was nominated that
summer.[46] News from Missouri was not all politics. O. B. wanted to
buy more land, cattle, and sheep, but Uncas was not enthusiastic.
The problem was money. O. B. requested that Uncas take over his
livestock, and Whitaker replied that, while he liked the idea, "there is
some question whether I will have enough money to do it. I am
trying to get some money out of my airport interest in Canton, but
so far I have had to keep putting more in as business there has
expanded rapidly." Whitaker's multiple responsibilities were making it
hard for him to answer his father's frequent requests for information
about farm affairs. Occasionally, Uncas would put one of his father's
letters in his coat pocket and ignore its existence for some days.
Once, when O. B. remonstrated, Uncas replied, "The trouble is that I
have found you go ahead and do what you think best, anyway, and I
suspect that the reason you write for my advice is simply to do a little
visiting, which is all right too." With that off his chest, Uncas
followed with detailed advice on rams, cattle, hogs, repairs, farmland
and the like.[47]

In the fall, O. B. Whitaker stepped up his campaigning. His
admiration for Willkie increased, although he was not sanguine about
his defeating Roosevelt. "Willkie is a marvelous and remarkable
man," he wrote to his son, "and making a remarkable campaign; and
if only those who (on the basis of intelligence, honesty and
patriotism) ought to vote were allowed to vote he would sweep the
U. S. by 4 or 5 to 1." On November 1, O. B. reported to Syd that
Uncas was predicting a Willkie victory, but Uncas' letter on the
subject did not really represent an unqualified victory prediction.

> It looks now as if Willkie might make it. There has been a strong
> swing toward him here in the last two weeks. Unless Roosevelt can
> pull some slick trick in the last few days to scare some voters back
> believe he may lose. Believe if I were betting today I would put my
> money on Willkie — tho I wouldn't be very sure.[48]

O. B. Whitaker, who had chosen to run for the Missouri House
once more at the age of 70 ("I here and now bury my ambition for
anything higher than Representative in the Missouri House"), won
his seat for what would turn out to be the last time.   Wendell
L. Willkie, of course, lost in his bid to prevent an American president
from being elected for the third time. O. B. fought for Willkie's

election right down to the wire. On the last night of the campaign, he made a spontaneous eleventh hour appeal for Willkie, speaking to a handful of people on a street corner in Weaubleau. That speech exhausted O. B. , leaving him hardly able to walk home, as he told his family in a postelection letter. When he finally arrived home, he fainted. Nettie, at first frantic and then furious, criticized him for making the speech at all, but O. B. only grew more grandiose: "If my speech would make Willkie the vote that would elect him I would gladly give my life for the vote." On consideration, he added: "When my time comes I think that's the way I would like to go."[49] As it turned out, O. B. Whitaker would not live to see another presidential election, but he would live long enough to have the satisfaction of seeing his son Uncas embark on the next, and most exciting, chapter of his professional career.

7. Industrial Manufacturers Inc.

On the evening of December 29, 1940, President Franklin D. Roosevelt delivered his fifteenth fireside chat to the American nation. The Oval Office was jammed with statesmen, politicians, newsmen, and a sprinkling of show business people, notably actor Clark Gable and his actress wife Carole Lombard. Millions of Americans tuned in their radios at 9:30 P.M. anticipating, as *Time* put it a few days later, that "his words might mark a turning point in history." Roosevelt did not disappoint his audience: "If Great Britain goes down, all of us in the Americas would be living at the point of a gun." "We must be," the President concluded, "the arsenal of democracy.[1]

O. B. Whitaker, listened to the fireside chat in his housekeeping room in Jefferson City, Missouri, waiting for the 57th General Session of the Missouri Legislature to convene; he was depressed but not surprised. Like many Americans, O. B. was unreconciled to the prospect of United States entry into a foreign war. He continued to fight that prospect in the months to come, writing to his son Uncas that F. D. R. was deliberately intending "to lead the U. S. into war."[2]

O. B. was not well — his heart was giving him trouble, and he was lonely, once again. On one day he would write of his loneliness; on another he would recount his present and past triumphs; on still another he would muse about life and approaching death. In between, he took the floor of the Missouri House and attacked F. D. R. and the New Deal. In May, 1941, for example, O. B. Whitaker introduced a resolution in support of Charles A. Lindbergh, whom F. D. R. had refused to call back to active duty because of Lindbergh's vocal opposition to American intervention. The America First Committee, which sponsored Lindbergh's cross-country speaking tour in support of continued American isolation policies, was so impressed with O. B.'s actions that it invited him to St. Louis to sit on the platform with Lindbergh at a scheduled rally that same week. O. B. profoundly admired Lindbergh; yet, he decided not to accept the invitation. Perhaps he was too tired and too ill to attend; more likely he was resigned to the inevitable. Towards the end of the legislative session he wrote Uncas: "In this mad whirl of New Deal lunacy, I have about quit trying to think or reason. I'm like a cowboy that has lost his balance on a bucking bronco — I'm just waiting for the fall, and wondering where and how I'll light."[3]

Uncas Whitaker, back in New York City, was also waiting, in this case, for a "rise" rather than a "fall." Late in March, 1941, Carl L. Hamilton, of Booz, Fry, Allen and Hamilton, placed a long distance call from his Chicago office to Henry Dreyfus in New York. Dreyfus was the famous industrial designer who had worked with Whitaker on the 1936 Hoover Cleaner Model 150. Dreyfus reported the call to Whitaker, saying that he had given his "usual good report" about Whitaker. Whitaker thanked his friend for his help and added, "the information . . . that Mr. Hamilton has called you was of interest to me as this matter is only in the preliminary stages as far as I am concerned." Just exactly what matter Whitaker was referring to is not clear. Following Edwin Booz's first unsuccessful attempt to place Whitaker, he and his associates brought him a number of promising opportunities for consideration. What Whitaker wanted, he had told Booz, was something well financed and a product requiring, and responsive to, good engineering. In the meantime, he was occupied at American Machine & Foundry Company.[4]

At American Machine & Foundry Company, Whitaker had the opportunity to enlarge the scope of his experience considerably, most importantly in regard to understanding the value of competition and its relationship to engineering, engineering research, and company profits. At the Hoover Company Whitaker had been forced to work with a very small budget to produce a vacuum cleaner (about 1 percent of gross sales), but the situation in several of the divisions of American Machine & Foundry Company was quite different — little or no attention was paid to costs. Because competition among vacuum cleaner manufacturers was fierce, Hoover engineers had to design low-cost products. Nevertheless, despite Whitaker's complaints about limited funds for Hoover engineering research, he recognized his experience with stringency as valuable. Still, the changed situation he encountered at American Machine & Foundry Company provided Whitaker rich new opportunities.

At American Machine & Foundry Company, Whitaker not only managed engineers, he also worked as one. An early chance came in relation to the Glen Mixer Division, which, unlike the cigarette and cigar machine divisions of the company, operated in a very competitive market. When Whitaker came on the scene, American Machine & Foundry Company had not yet been able to develop a vertical mixer for commercial bakeries to sell at a profit. Whitaker's investigations revealed that the Glen Mixer Division was trying to produce an intermediate size mixer in competition with firms that could do it better and cheaper. A much more promising alternative was to find an area in which Glen Mixer could compete successfully. He found it; on a large mixer — of a 340-quart variety — American Machine & Foundry Company could be competitive. Whitaker and his associates applied their engineering talents to developing a 340-quart mixer, and it proved to be American Machine & Foundry Company's one profitable vertical mixer over the years. Competition he always maintained, was good for a company and even better for engineering creativity, which in the first and final analysis was the lifeblood of any industrial manufacturing concern. Creativity and profits were inextricably interwoven in Whitaker's mind. Without competition there would be neither significant creativity nor significant profits.[5]

For Uncas Whitaker the roles of engineer and businessman were not distinct. According to long time friend and American Machine & Foundry Company associate, George Hastings, Whitaker was always profit-minded. He "did not just want to design things; he wanted to design things for a price." The people who came to work under him at American Machine & Foundry Company, Hastings added, "paid a lot of attention to what things cost. . . . Whitaker was always able to arouse a good deal of loyalty in his engineers (the ones who came to American Machine & Foundry Company). . . . When he had his own company a lot of them were determined to go with him." As American Machine & Foundry Company's patent counsel, Hastings had frequent contact with Whitaker and taught him a good deal about patenting products. Hastings in turn became acquainted with Whitaker's business and engineering theories. As Hastings described it, "Whitaker's theory was that the way you built a business was to out-engineer all the others" — his philosophy was "to engineer the hell out of his products." "Engineering the hell out of products" would become the semiofficial slogan of the new company Whitaker founded in 1941.[6]

Whitaker's ideas about engineering, engineering research and engineering management did not come entirely or exclusively from his work experience. He read a great deal and associated himself with national societies that met to discuss problems common to engineering business firms. He was American Machine & Foundry Company's representative to the Division of Engineering and Industrial Research of the National Research Council, which, as a result of World War I, had become committed to the promotion and dissemination of scientific research and knowledge. The engineering and industrial research division, one of eleven in the council, kept its member organizations up to date on matters relating to engineering research.[7]

A good example of the kind of reading material Whitaker typically received and carefully examined was a reprint of an article, "Industrial Research in Your Own Business," originally published by Dun and Bradstreet and reissued by Arthur D. Little, Inc. The article came to Whitaker in the latter part of 1940, at the time when he was beginning seriously to investigate possibilities of acquiring his own engineering business. Although the article was general enough to have been useful in his work at American Machine & Foundry Company, at least half a dozen of the author's sixteen suggestions resemble very clearly some of the basic tenets that would underpin research and development at AMP Incorporated.

> Approach the establishment of your research activities with a determination so to set up your research department and to man it that it will command your management's respect and confidence.

> Although you establish the department separately, see to it that your entire organization becomes "research conscious."

> Inventory your problems. Clarify in your own mind what you need to do or what you hope to do, study previous attempts to do it, find out why they failed — and then turn your research department loose.

> Remember that research is a service department, charged with its own entirely respectable responsibilities and with its own share of your practical operations. Never let it be thought that research is a critic, a faultfinder, or spy.

> Scan all findings in the light of the facets of your business; but bear in mind that successful research results can come only when research work is accepted as receptively as is the work of any other independent department.

> Whatever the size of your company, equip your research department with facilities adequate to the tasks you assign it.

As Whitaker's own company developed, he had to reaffirm these and other corollary points on many occasions to keep his whole organization on an even keel. The author's conclusion about industrial research coincided with Whitaker's own philosophy:

Research is nothing more mysterious than an organized hunt for facts. It is an orderly investigation, a system of planned experiments designed to yield useful facts before those facts are revealed by chance. It is the hunt for facts — and here it touches the concern of the most "practical" among us — it is the hunt for facts with which to solve problems.[8]

* * * * * * *

One specific problem faced Whitaker that engineering research could do little to solve — McKinley Air Transport. The problem was, however, ameliorated by a new accounting system, in addition to new and more competent personnel and the spin-off effects from Roosevelt's "arsenal of democracy" speech. Financial records at MAT were kept haphazardly at best. Part of the problem was that MAT, since its inception, stated its tax returns on a cash rather than on an accrual basis, thereby avoiding the more complicated and time-consuming bookkeeping that accrual accounting procedures implied. Through his association with the Comptroller's Division at American Machine & Foundry Company, Whitaker had become friendly with one of its chief accountants, who took over Whitaker's personal and business accounting chores. It was he who advised the changeover to the accrual system, "in order to present a truer picture of the operations of the company."[9]

The new accounting approach was instituted in January, 1941. Whitaker advised Lou Ritzman and Earl Kail that for the time being MAT accounting would be transferred to New York. He explained to them, in an untypically lengthy letter, the purpose of all the new forms that had to be filled out monthly. Ritzman was learning the new procedures, and the financial records of MAT were effectively becoming rationalized, when, sometime in May, she suffered a stroke. She was unable to work, and Whitaker and Kail had to let her go. Then, a month later, Kail reported to Whitaker that Ritzman would never return to work at MAT. She "had another stroke in front of the Onesta [Hotel] and . . . has since been taken to a hospital in Cleveland. . . . Just one of those life's tragedies," Kail concluded.[10] (Ironically, a year later Earl Kail too became one of those life's tragedies. The plane he was ferrying to Africa for the Army Air Force crashed somewhere en route.)

With Lou Ritzman gone from MAT, George Swayze, trained as a pilot by MAT, was made a vice-president and took over the general supervision of company business affairs. Soon a new office girl and an auditor joined the staff. Earl Kail, now freed from office supervisory chores, could devote his full efforts to bringing in more business. In June, 1941, Whitaker commended Kail for his work in getting advanced rating approval for MAT and urged him to go after more government business vigorously. Kail, however, did not immediately undertake a vigorous campaign, for new student-training business just seemed to walk in the front door as the demand for experienced pilots escalated in 1941.[11]

Whitaker was pleased with the increase in business and the efficient manner in which Swayze and Kail were running the operation and he told them so. "It sounds like you fellows are getting ready to go to town [and] I appreciate fully the amount of work necessary to get the books in order." Whitaker was intensely concerned about the books. Like many Americans, he was feeling the effects of tax surcharges, defense taxes, and the heavy hand of a growing government bureaucracy, which was developing an increasingly more complicated reporting system. At tax time in 1941, Whitaker was already in battle with internal revenue officials over some of his farm deductions. He implored his father to send him receipts, cancelled checks, records of any kind so that he could defend those legal deductions before tax officials. He also urged Swayze and Kail to do the same. "There is nothing more important. . . . It is absolutely essential to have at least reasonably good records in these times of high government taxes and numerous reports."[12] Whitaker's experience with government was only just beginning; in the next several years he would become an expert in dealing with the bureaucracy, but he would never learn to like it.

* * * * * * *

In June, 1941, Whitaker was in the mood for some recreation; he had traded in his 1937 Dodge Coupe for a 1940 Buick Sedan; he had bought himself several new suits at Rogers Peet Clothes (his favorite haberdasher); he had sent in for and received a $2.00 book entitled *Relaxation in Everyday Life*, and he had made plans to put the book's theories into practice by spending the Fourth of July weekend with a Westinghouse Air Brake Company friend, George Misner, at the latter's cabin in Pennsylvania.[13] But that brief vacation eluded him, as would many others in the years to come. On July 2, 1941, he sent a night letter to Misner:

> WOULD LIKE VERY MUCH TO BE WITH YOU OVER THE FOURTH BUT AM TIED UP ON BUSINESS STOP SEEMS THAT BUSINESS MORE AND MORE INTERFERES WITH THE REAL WORTHWHILE THINGS IN LIFE.

In fact, Whitaker flew to Canton to hop passengers that weekend and attend to MAT affairs. But the real business that was on his mind was the investigation of what appeared to be a very attractive business proposition. Carl Hamilton had arranged for Whitaker to meet Stephen M. Buchanan, a part-owner in Industrial Manufacturers Inc. of Elizabeth, New Jersey. Buchanan had a small business with considerable potential; he was looking for new financial backing, a new "partnership". Hamilton had come up with the attractive proposition, and now it was up to Whitaker to do his job. Vacations remained out of the question all summer. Even a Labor Day weekend with George Misner was an impossibility. As Whitaker put it, with a characteristic western touch, "I am in the midst of a big deal that will either make me somewhere around a $1,000,000 or lose all I got, possibly the latter."[14]

During the week when Franklin D. Roosevelt delivered his "arsenal of democracy" fireside chat, the first B-26 medium attack bombers were rolling off the assembly lines at the Glenn L. Martin Company in Baltimore, Maryland. Glenn L. Martin had landed a $131,000,000 contract to produce 1,000 B-26's and with the testing phase over, the aircraft manufacturing company was gearing up its production lines.[15] Sometime in mid-1940, Industrial Manufacturers Inc. of Elizabeth, New Jersey, not yet a year old, began furnishing the Glenn L. Martin Company solderless electrical terminals and copper and aluminum bonding jumpers in large volume. In its first month of operation, Industrial Manufacturers Inc. had billed only $115, but sales rose rapidly and by the end of 1940 billings totaled approximately $38,000. From February to June, 1941, Industrial Manufacturers Inc. managed sales between $21,000 and $37,000 a month. With increased defense production, the company's potential was very strong.

Industrial Manufacturers Inc. was founded by Stephen N. Buchanan, a man in his mid-fifties, in collaboration with two associates, Charles Shoemaker and Trigve Skyberg. Shoemaker and Skyberg were associates as well in four related companies — Industrial Electric Inc. ("electrical contracting for businesses in high tension wiring"), Industrial Consultants, Inc.("consulting business in high tension electrical wiring problems"), Industrial Constructors, Inc. ("construction business in the electrical line"), and Industrial Realtors, Inc. ("incorporated to hold the real estate of the various other corporations"). Industrial Manufacturers Inc. was Buchanan's brainchild. It was established to manufacture and market his electrical terminals and related products.

Buchanan "had no formal education beyond high school" but in his work experience had developed his considerable inventive skills. He started out at DuPont, became a master electrician with the Baltimore Dry Dock Company during World War I, and then spent five years in a general electrical contracting business in Baltimore.

In 1925, Buchanan joined Thomas & Betts, in Elizabeth, New Jersey. In his fifteen years with Thomas & Betts he "claimed to have contributed ninety per cent of the ideas upon which the company's solderless terminals business was built." Between 1927 and 1939, the U. S. Patent Office issued thirty patents in Buchanan's name.[16] In Whitaker's view, Buchanan "probably knows as much about solderless terminals as anyone in this country." As a result of Buchanan's work, Thomas & Betts was one of the first, and by 1940, the largest concern to go into this relatively new field. At the time Whitaker came on the terminal scene, it had been in business for nearly forty years. As a potential competitor, Thomas & Betts was formidable.[17]

Buchanan left Thomas & Betts in 1940 and subsequently formed his own company to market his ideas in the field. Not surprisingly, the introduction of solderless connections, in place of the more conventional soldered electrical connection, met a good deal of resistance from users. Soldered connections had been the rule for so many years that many manufacturers were reluctant to change over to the new crimped-style connection that used no solder at all. Since the old style connection had worked so well in the past, many saw no reason for changing a well-established production procedure. Overcoming this resistance was a major problem for anyone trying to sell the newer and as yet "unproven" solderless connection.[18]

Buchanan had made some progress, however, and rather quickly at that. Thanks to the need for more rapid production methods by those engaged in defense work, the military establishment was prepared to take a positive attitude toward new ideas. Buchanan, who lived mainly in Washington, D. C. , was in fact his own lobbyist. He made important contacts in various government bureaus, both civilian and military, and convinced a select number of people that his solderless terminal was a better idea. By June, 1941, therefore, Industrial Manufacturers Inc. received permission from the Air Corps Materiel Division at Wright Field in Dayton, Ohio, to sell its solderless terminals for use in the manufacture of aircraft. That is, the company could sell them if the aircraft manufacturer would use them. Glenn L. Martin was one company that was completely sold on Industrial's terminals. So was the Navy Bureau of Aeronautics. Its electrical division under the command of Lt. Vernon H. Grant had given Buchanan and his company the go-ahead to develop a combined shielding, bonding and connector unit. A handful of federal navy yards were also enthusiastic about the company's connectors.[19]

In his own attempts to get financial backing as well as manufacturing facilities for his inventions, Buchanan called on Harvey Hubbell, president of Harvey Hubbell, Inc., a manufacturer and jobber of engineering products. Hubbell was impressed with Buchanan and his new product and evidently brought news of it to R. Miles Warner, a director of Harvey Hubbell and vice-president of H. M. Byllesby, investment bankers. It was probably through R. Miles Warner, a business associate and friend of Carl Hamilton, that Booz, Fry, Allen and Hamilton got wind of Industrial Manufacturers Inc. and the solderless electrical terminal, and as a result arranged the meeting between Buchanan and Whitaker in June, 1941.[20]

Beside the need for fresh capital to encourage Industrial Manufacturers Inc.'s growth, Buchanan had another motive in seeking out new backing; he had reason to be unhappy with his two associates, Shoemaker and Skyberg. Shoemaker and Skyberg had agreed to provide all the necessary capital for the new business. In fact, Shoemaker invested $1,000 (receiving 100 shares of preferred stock), and Skyberg invested nothing. He, too, however, received 100 shares of stock, "through rendering a bill for services in like amount." Shoemaker and Skyberg had agreed further to handle management and office detail work; apparently they handled only some curious cash transfers, one for $16,000, to another of their four corporations. Meanwhile, without consulting Buchanan, they paid themselves $1,800 for services in 1940 and another $2,000 in June, 1941 — all the while collecting salaries, Shoemaker of $800 a month, Skyberg of $400. Clearly, Buchanan needed a new arrangement.

Whitaker was impressed with Buchanan and with the potential in Industrial Manufacturers Inc. It was now time to enlarge his investigations, and on July 11 he flew to Washington to make inquiries there. He made the rounds of the various army and navy officers and engineers who knew Buchanan in order to check on his reliability. From Lt. Vernon H. Grant and others he "found Buchanan's representations reasonably accurate." The way was now clear to sign option agreements, while getting down to serious discussions with Hamilton over financial arrangements. That weekend, Whitaker and his accountant continued to pore over the books of Industrial Manufacturers Inc. to be prepared for those discussions.[21]

Hamilton was leaving Chicago for a quick business trip to St. Louis but told Whitaker that he would be available for a trip East the following week if he could "bring things to a head with Buchanan by that time." Whitaker replied by letter on July 19, telling Hamilton that the signing of options was near at hand. The option agreement allowed Whitaker and his business associates until August 15 to make a decision and until September 15 to make the first payment. The arrangement was to buy out the interests of both Shoemaker and Skyberg and to keep Buchanan on as an officer and director of the new corporation. Shoemaker and Skyberg, however, made their own demands and the plan was to pay them $42,000 for their two-thirds interest and to provide each a limited employment contract — Shoemaker for three and a half years and Skyberg for six. The two contracts totalled about $58,000. The option agreement was signed, and now Whitaker had his work cut out for him. With the option deadline just a few weeks away, there was a great deal to be done. He and Hamilton worked out a division of labor and on the first of August, just two weeks before the option decision had to be made, Whitaker's list of assignments arrived by mail from Hamilton in Chicago. Along with Whitaker's list was another for the auditor from Arthur Andersen & Company, who would be arriving in several days to make a further investigation of the company. The auditor, among other things, was to prepare comparative profit and loss statements, balance sheets, payroll analyses, and lists of suppliers and customers. Whitaker was charged with fifteen separate tasks that included patent analysis, customer interviews, credit reports, competition assessment, price analysis, product growth potential, machinery requirements, an organization plan, a three-year sales projection, and a profit and loss budget showing capital needs at various volume levels.[22]

Whitaker already had people at work on some of these items. His friend George Hastings, patent counsel at American Machine & Foundry Company, was investigating the possibilities of patent infringement between Buchanan's ideas and those existing at Thomas & Betts. Since Buchanan had spent so many years with Thomas & Betts, it was possible that some of his more recent innovations had come from research work done with the firm. Hasting's report of August 8 indicated that this possibility was slim, or as he put it, the risk "may be classified as a reasonable one." Patentability, however, was another matter.

> It is believed that no reliance should be placed on obtaining any
> substantial patent protection on any of these products for the reason
> that the prior art is very close and the differences between
> Mr. Buchanan's ideas and previous ones are of a detailed nature
> relating more to neater, simpler and cheaper construction than to
> substantial differences of function.

More specific claims, Hastings allowed, were possible. Broad claims
were not.[23]

A field investigation of terminal manufacturers was undertaken by
William S. Watts of Angola, Indiana, an engineering teacher at
Tri-State College in Angola, who had a free-lance engineering
consulting business on the side. Watts was probably contacted by
Frank Wells, Whitaker's engineering associate at American Machine
& Foundry Company. Wells, whom Whitaker had already enlisted for
service in the new company, had a previous connection with Tri-State
and knew Watts at that time. The Tri-State "connection" is an
interesting one. It would soon produce several employees for the new
company in addition to Watts, whose semirural Indiana background
was similar to Whitaker's, and whose small town outlook and values
coincided closely with Whitaker's world view. Watts made the
rounds of terminal manfacturers in his vicinity and reported at length
to Whitaker during the first week in August. He listed and analyzed
the four current methods of electrical terminating: the elementary
type of soldering wire to wire; soldering wire to terminal and
attaching terminal to instruments by means of screws and lock
washers; soldering a terminal to the wire, then assembling the
terminal to a snap or clip receiver; and the completely solderless
system. Watts discovered that most of the firms in his area either
used some kind of soldering method or worked with solderless ones
manufactured by the H. A. Douglas Manufacturing Company in
Bronson, Michigan. The firm itself had been sold by its former
owner, H. A. Douglas, who told Watts that few companies other than
his own manufactured only solderless connectors. Most of those who
did, he indicated, were quite small and of little consequence. His own
firm, now a division of a larger corporation, had at one time applied
for aircraft approval but had dropped the idea as bureaucratic
procedures began to overwhelm it. Recently, however, several large
aircraft manufacturers — Lockheed, Bendix, and Douglas — had
become interested and as a result government approval was
anticipated in the near future.[24]

Meanwhile, Whitaker was reviewing information daily. A list of potential competitors arrived early in August, identifying some thirty firms manufacturing solderless connections. Thomas & Betts was the largest; all others were a good deal smaller. Buchanan and his chief engineer at Industrial Manufacturers Inc. submitted the results of tests they had been conducting on the approximate time it took to apply both solderless and soldered wire terminals. In addition to their own laboratory tests, they had reports from about fifteen shipyards on the same comparison. They told Whitaker that the solderless type could be installed twice as fast as the soldered type in the factory and six to seven times more rapidly in the field. This was welcome news, as was a Dun and Bradstreet report on Thomas & Betts, showing that the leading solderless termination manufacturing company in the field had, for at least the three previous years, made money.[25]

In all important ways, the proposition looked good to U. A. Whitaker, or as he put it in his twenty-eight-page report to Carl Hamilton, on August 12, "a far above average speculation." The report, which carefully detailed all aspects of the business and its future potential, concluded with lists of "Hazards" and "Opportunities." There were five hazards and, according to Whitaker, each could be met. First was the absence of patent protection, which Whitaker hoped to overcome by "the combination of army and navy specifications and carefully prepared though quite narrow claims . . . on the company's present products." The decreasing availability of raw materials was a second hazard; Whitaker planned to meet that by increasing the number of requisite parts manufactured by the company, thereby relying less on suppliers. Third came the danger of rapid expansion "and eventually rapid contraction and decline." O. B.'s son thought this could be minimized by effective controls, but — still his father's son on this subject — he added, "Even under shrewd management . . . this hazard is real and threatening." Increased competition, a fourth difficulty, could be met by an aggressive research policy, keeping the company far ahead in the field. Fifth and finally, came taxes and the expectation of increased tax rates, but as Whitaker noted, Industrial Manufacturers Inc. was already in the highest bracket.

Opportunities far outweighed hazards. First came "the opportunity to capitalize profitably on a rapidly expanding defense program." The second advantage, no doubt particularly attractive to Whitaker, was the chance "to become more and more intimately connected with the rapidly expanding aviation industry." Third, Whitaker anticipated that an active research program would broaden the scope of their activities in the defense area. Last, he saw the "broader long-range opportunity to build up in less time than is ordinarily required . . . a soundly organized, well financed business which, through adequately organized research and patent efforts, can continue to operate successfully after the present flurry of defense work is over."

With such high expectations, Whitaker was pleased to report to Hamilton that the option had finally been signed on the afternoon of August 16 and that they had until the following Monday to exercise it. A few extra days had been tacked onto the original August 15 deadline. The delay came as Whitaker discovered for himself that Shoemaker and Skyberg could be difficult to deal with. "You will note," he informed Hamilton, "that this option agreement calls for the additional payment of $40,000, making a total of $90,200. At the same time the contracts for the services of Mr. Shoemaker and Mr. Skyberg have been cancelled." Whitaker had learned something of the two from Buchanan, and their last minute refusal to allow the examination of the books of the other four companies they controlled settled the matter as far as he was concerned.[26]

By the middle of August, Whitaker was thinking about key employees he needed to hire and working on an employment contract for the new company. He decided to model his on one that had recently been developed at American Machine & Foundry Company, which, presumably, he had had a hand in shaping. Whitaker understood that tightly inhibiting employment contracts had their disadvantages. He explained this to Hamilton:

> This employment contract that I am suggesting is not as "tough" as the contracts now in general use, but there has been a tendency of the courts to consider contracts that are too broad as unenforceable because they limit the inventive talent of the employee too much for the public good.

Whitaker knew his law; moreover, he agreed with the courts on the undesirability of unduly limiting creative talent. He suggested to Hamilton that he and Buchanan sign a standard agreement and also a confidential supplemental agreement on salary, bonuses, and length of employment.[27]

As to the amount of salaries and bonuses, Whitaker accepted the recommendation submitted by Hamilton in his letter of August 19. Hamilton, with his lawyer and the Arthur Andersen & Company tax man, had agreed that for 1941 Buchanan and Whitaker should each receive a salary of $20,000. Hamilton believed that modest salaries were in order until the company began to make a profit, at which time a bonus arrangement could provide higher compensation. Hamilton and his associates suggested "a sliding scale of total compensation to range from $12,500 to $50,000," and they asked Whitaker to develop a proper formula to apply. He and Buchanan talked it over and both agreed to accept Hamilton's outline of the principles regarding salary and bonuses.

Whitaker came up with the formula. It provided each man with a base salary of $25,000, assuming sales billed of $500,000. It also provided for automatic salary cuts should billings drop. If, for example, yearly sales should fall to a low of $150,000, the salary base would be adjusted by 50 percent — that is, $150,000 in billings would gross each man $12,500 in salary. A bonus plan would likewise be based on percentage of salary. Whitaker's schedule indicated that bonuses, would vary with net profit before research, development, bonuses and income tax were deducted. He projected that, on a sales volume of $1,000,000, combined salary and bonus would come to about $50,000.[28]

For a company that in its entire eighteen-month existence had only billed $200,000, the idea of a volume of $1,000,000 a year might appear overly optimisitic. But a projection of this magnitude was not without basis. With Buchanan's contacts, and with the immediate prospect of a good number of aircraft manufacturers switching over to solderless terminations at a period of a very significant escalation in defense spending, the business potential was certainly promising. Industrial Manufacturers Inc. already had a product that was in increasing demand; the competitive situation, although formidable in view of Thomas & Betts' relative domination of the field, was not insurmountable. Whitaker's projections for gross profit were based on the company's present profit picture; furthermore, a core of solid customers with great growth potential was already in the fold. Most important of all, though, was the fact that those who either awarded or influenced the awarding of government contracts already looked on Whitaker and Buchanan as an unbeatable team. Lt. Vernon H. Grant, for example, an important man in the Navy Bureau of Aeronautics, liked both men individually but even more as a working team. He was quoted as saying about the prospect of Whitaker's association with the organization, that "the addition of technical engineering education and experience and management ability would make Industrial an ideal source for Navy Air Bureau developments." Harvey Hubbell considered the partnership of the two men, "a first class arrangement."[29]

Whitaker, however, had no intention of standing still and basing the future performance of the company solely on what existed in the present. Industrial had very limited manufacturing facilities, and by mid-August Whitaker was already looking around for equipment and space. Hamilton proposed that they acquire an ongoing company for this purpose; Whitaker agreed, but his business sense warned him that such a move could be expensive. On the twentieth he wrote Hamilton about two current possibilities; "I looked up two companies today that had been offered to the American Machine & Foundry Company for sale, but neither of them would suit our needs, and both are right now making good profits and therefore we would have to pay a high price." He concluded that he believed "a systematic search might bring to light an equipped factory suitable for our use at a reasonable price. "[30]

Whitaker was anxious to get going on all fronts. He was becoming impatient with the interminable details raised by auditors, tax experts, and legal counselors.

> "The more I get into this deal," the frustrated Whitaker wrote Hamilton, "the more I feel that it is of extreme importance to get underway from both sales and engineering viewpoints. The sales should be moving so as to get in first, and the engineering-research should be started so as to begin to build a fence around our product to prevent others from getting into our field."

Whitaker was eager to begin investing the fairly large figure of 5 percent of sales billed in research and development work. In his terms, he wanted to get far ahead of his competitors in engineering, so far, in fact, that they would have great difficulty catching up.[31]

One particular incident both encouraged Whitaker and increased his impatience. One day toward the end of August he was sitting in his office at American Machine & Foundry Company preoccupied with solderless electrical terminals, and he decided he wanted to take another look at those Thomas & Betts manufactured. He knew that American Machine & Foundry Company's electrical department always kept a few on hand, so he sent one of his engineeers down to get some. Whitaker left for lunch, and when he returned he received the following report from his engineer:

> They don't have any more Thomas & Betts in the shop but here's something that just came that's the swellest thing you ever saw. It's short and the only one that's as short as a soldered connection. It took us six months to get these but they're what we're going to use. The Pratt & Whitney man is crazy about them and wants us to put

> them on all the rest of his machines. The secret is in that little
> tube. The other connections open up when you squeeze them down
> but the tube keeps this one from doing it.

Whitaker, who reported this incident to Hamilton, added, "the
terminal he is talking about is, of course, Industrial Manufacturers'. I
thought this unsolicited opinion was quite interesting."[32]

During those hectic weeks in August, Whitaker found a little spare
time to correspond with his friends and, of course, his father. On
August 6, he told Earl Kail and George Swayze at MAT something
about his new activities. "Supposed to be on vacation but working
on a business deal. I have to make a decision within a week from
now." Under the circumstances, he told them, he would have to drop
his plan to buy a new Cessna for MAT. He wrote home that day,
too, giving O. B. his first inkling of Uncas' new project.

> In regard to your inquiry about putting livestock on the farms, while
> I think live stock will certainly be a good investment, I would rather
> hold off making any decision for a while as I am considering a
> business deal here that might require some money. Am thinking of
> buying an interest in a small company and possibly giving my full
> time to it rather than my present position. I have always had an idea
> that I would like to be a big part of a small company rather than a
> small part of a big company, and have an opportunity at the present
> time, but do not know for sure whether I will take it or not. Will
> make up my mind within the next month or six weeks.

O. B.'s response was brief and not particularly encouraging. "Just
received your letter of the 6th. Of course you are considering the
possiblity of a general depression following the war in your
consideration of buying a business." The message was clear, but the
younger Whitaker chose to ignore it, merely agreeing affably with his
father.

> You say I should keep in mind that there probably will be a bad
> business depression when this armament program is over. I have
> that distinctly in mind, only I would leave out the "probably." This
> deal I am considering will either make me rich fast or poor fast,
> probably the latter. Will let you know when I have it worked out.

Like his father, Uncas was reconciled to the inevitable economic
slump, but unlike O. B. , he had not as yet accepted the inevitability
of war, or rather, as he would continue to put it, the end of the
armament program. Meanwhile, he was sure his father would
understand and appreciate his statement about getting rich or poor
fast. O. B. Whitaker had said the same things a few times in his life.[33]

While negotiations, investigations, and projections were underway, the question of finance capital had still to be dealt with. The major funding was arranged by Carl Hamilton who interested a certain Robert Hixon in the project. Hixon had funds available from the Midland Investment Company. Hamilton had very likely worked with Hixon before, for the Midland Investment Company at that time had its offices in the same building as Booz, Fry, Allen and Hamilton, at 135 South LaSalle Street in Chicago. Robert Hixon, a graduate of Yale in 1901, managed the investment firm, which at that time held controlling stock in about fifteen companies, including rather large holdings in lumber and oil and gas. Four of the major companies had assets totalling over $30 million. He was apparently impressed enough with Whitaker and the prospects of Industrial Manufacturers Inc. to promise to supply the new venture as much capital as necessary for its purchase and development.[34]

By the middle of August, Hamilton felt that the deal had proceeded far enough to begin talking about specific proposals for capitalizing the new company. He suggested to Whitaker that it might be a good idea if he flew out the next weekend to talk about alternative ways of setting up the capital structure. Their ideas could then be presented to Hixon for his examination. Whitaker agreed to come the last weekend in August and along with Hamilton and Hamilton's lawyer, Anan Raymond, he worked out four alternative plans for distributing the stock in the company, now tentatively named Aero-Marine Products Inc.[35]

Whitaker returned to New York September 2. Hamilton informed him on the fourth that Hixon would meet with him the following Monday in Chicago to discuss the alternative financing plans. Hamilton was confident that things would work out well. "I anticipate no difficulty in getting everything straightened out between ourselves and Mr. Hixon in my Monday session," he told Whitaker. He added that if he needed Whitaker, he would send for him, but for the moment Hamilton preferred to meet Hixon alone before arranging a joint session. Hamilton also asked Whitaker's advice about whether R. Miles Warner should serve on the board of directors. Warner, who had recently been talking to Harvey Hubbell about Buchanan's connectors, had run into Hamilton the evening before. They discussed Hubbell's idea that his concern, Harvey Hubbell, Inc. , might manufacture the connector with Buchanan handling the sales end. Warner was on the Harvey Hubbell board of directors, and Hamilton was concerned that the close business connection between the two firms might make it problematic for Warner to serve on the Aero-Marine Products Inc. board.[36]

Whitaker dodged the matter of Warner's board seat in his reply. He reported that he had been in Washington a few days earlier and had spoken to Hubbell at length about the possible business connection. Whitaker was apparently not enthusiastic about the idea, and his reply was designed to buy him some time: "while I think they would be a very fine outfit to be associated with, we will want to be sure that the deal is mutually satisfactory. As soon as I get his ideas more in detail I will be in a position to judge whether such an arrangement can be made."[37] Whitaker liked to keep as much freedom of action as possible in his business connections, and he often used this approach for suggestions or propositions he little liked. Even more significant here is that Whitaker, as head of the new company, wanted to reserve decisions of this kind for himself and his working associates. As he told a promising young businessman a few years later, "A Board will not dictate to the President. They will advise, most politely, and only relieve him of responsibility when he is failing, and then he will be glad to be so relieved."[38]

Whitaker also informed Hamilton that during his Washington visit he had taken the time to call on Lt. Vernon H. Grant. Grant told Whitaker that he was completely satisfied with development progress to date and asked that models of the connector be submitted for testing. Development work was practically under way, for Frank Wells, who had already agreed to join Aero-Marine Products Inc., was going to take one week of his American Machine & Foundry Company vacation time to get started on the research program for the new company. Wells planned to go to New York and to MIT to hold conferences with experts on the technical side of the program. Then he would go to Washington to see Grant and talk with people at the Bureau of Standards and other government agencies dealing with electrical devices. From Washington, Wells was to proceed to Bendix Radio in Baltimore and finally to Wright Field to confer with the technical division there. On Wells' return, Whitaker concluded in his letter to Hamilton, "he will have a lot of information from which we can probably outline enough research to keep about ten times as many men busy as we will have available, but that will give us a chance to select the most desirable projects." What Whitaker did not tell Hamilton was that he had written Wells a personal check for $200 to cover his expenses. Whitaker had no intention of falling behind before he was able to take command of the new company.[39]

The patent situation also received Whitaker's attention during the first week of September, 1941. He told Hamilton that he had been thinking a good deal about it and he had come up with some new ideas that he had already discussed with George Hastings. Hastings had assured Whitaker that his ideas not only looked promising but that a considerable amount of patent protection would be entirely possible. What Whitaker needed now was his own patent attorney to get things started immediately, and with Hastings' help he was trying to line up someone in New York.[40]

Hamilton's five-hour conference with Hixon went well. Hixon accepted one of the four alternative plans for capitalization. It called for an investment of approximately $100,000 in the new company. Reporting on this meeting to Whitaker, Hamilton advised him that he and lawyer Anan Raymond were making tentative plans to come East later in the week to tie up the remaining details of the business deal. The stage was now set for Monday, September 15, 1941, and the official founding of Aero-Marine Products Inc. U. A. Whitaker was about to set out on his "far above average speculation."[41]

8. Aircraft-Marine Products Inc.

September 15, 1941, was set for the first meeting of the Board of Directors of Aero-Marine Products Inc.; on that Monday, final papers were to be signed. Sunday evening, the Newark airport mounted a spectacular air show — a fitting, if unconscious, tribute to U. A. Whitaker's new venture. Whitaker had just moved to Newark, taking a room at the Hotel Robert Treat. Considering his love for air shows, he may very well have been among the 400,000 who jammed the airport grounds that night.[1]

The next morning, the out-of-town Aero-Marine contingent arrived. Robert Hixon, Carl Hamilton, and R. Miles Warner met the local men at the law offices of Lindabury, Depue and Faulks, located on Broad Street in Newark, for the official ceremony. Among the principals was a new man, C. J. Fredricksen, recently hired by Whitaker to attend to the new company's books. Fredricksen, an accountant, had been discovered by American Machine & Foundry Company's comptroller, George Ingalls, working in a utility holding company in New York City, and Ingalls had recommended him to Whitaker for the job. Fredricksen, like Ingalls himself, was to have a role in the development of AMP Incorporated.[2]

The first meeting of the Board of Directors of Aero-Marine Products Inc., was called to order and the stockholders present proceeded with the business of nominating and electing the company's officers. Robert Hixon was chosen as the company's first president; S. N. Buchanan as vice-president; Uncas A. Whitaker as vice-president and treasurer; and C. J. Fredricksen as assistant treasurer. Then Hixon made an official offer to purchase specified shares of preferred and common stock for $100,200; and with Hixon's signing of that piece of paper, Aero-Marine Products Inc. and Uncas A. Whitaker were in business. The list of shareholders as of September 15 was as follows:

Midland Investment Company
2,000 shares of preferred stock
3,000 shares of common stock

U. A. Whitaker
1,998 shares of common stock

S. N. Buchanan
2,000 shares of common stock

Carl L. Hamilton
1 share of common stock

R. Miles Warner
1 share of common stock

In addition, Robert Hixon, Carl L. Hamilton, and R. Miles Warner held option warrants to purchase 1,000, 1,000, and 400 additional shares, respectively, at $10 per share on or before December 31, 1944. Officers elected and shares distributed, the first board meeting was adjourned.[3]

One preliminary matter of business remained unsettled — the name of the company. Whitaker was uneasy with Aero-Marine Products Inc. because of its close similarity to Aeromarine Insurance Company. He had, therefore, assembled a list of over one hundred other possibilities and eventually narrowed that list down to three: Aircraft-Marine Products Inc., Industrial-Aero Products Inc., and Marine-Air Products Inc. Ten days after the first meeting of the directors, Whitaker informed Hamilton that he preferred Aircraft-Marine Products Inc., and, after a search revealed no conflict with any other organization, that name was adopted. Friend George Misner was puzzled when he heard of the choice. "I can understand why you might be interested in aircraft," he wrote Whitaker, "but I can't see the marine end of it, unless you mean by that you are making fishing tackle of some kind. Possibly you will take the trouble to explain at your convenience."[4]

Actually George Misner was in the dark about the whole enterprise as were most of Whitaker's friends. Misner's request for information came to Whitaker as late as March, 1942. Ellery Fitch, another hunting and fishing buddy, who worked at Bendix-Westinghouse Air Brake Company in Elyria, Ohio, apparently knew even less than Misner. He wrote to Whitaker in April, 1942, that Booz, Fry, Allen and Hamilton had asked him to suggest someone for the job of chief product development engineer with a particular firm. Would Whitaker mind having his name submitted? Whitaker's reply was to the point but lacked detail: "In regard to the opening referred to, I am now with a little company that we organized several months ago which is certainly keeping me pretty busy, so I am not looking for anything else at the present time. Booz, Fry, Allen and Hamilton were responsible for putting me in this company and I guess I had better not look at any other jobs that they have in mind."[5]

Whitaker, however, did confide in his friend Nat Sage, placement director of the Division of Industrial Cooperation at MIT. Sage had been among those men Frank Wells talked to on his fact-finding tour earlier that month. Then, a few weeks before the final papers were signed at Aircraft-Marine Products Inc., Whitaker was corresponding with Sage about a possible liaison with the Division. Such a connection could bring the company good personnel and also make available to it the research facilities at MIT. On September 22, Whitaker told Sage the deal had been closed:

> Well, I have decided to make the move in taking a flyer on this little company that I mentioned to you the last time I saw you. It seems to have everything I believe I like and therefore have considered it best for me to make this move. I am intending to get up and talk to you about the old proposition just as soon as I can get a little time. I will need all the help I can get from my friends.

On October 3, Whitaker wrote again to Sage, telling him the company's new name and passing on some sense of his enthusiasm and excitement: "Whether I have made a good move or not will be determined in the next two or three years, I imagine. However, it develops that I am having a tremendous amount of fun and prospects certainly are good."[6]

Whitaker's letters to his family in Missouri were no more informative than they had been in the past. But O. B. was about to get details from Uncas first hand, for he and Nettie came East to visit their children. They traveled to Alliance, Ohio to see Portia and her family early in October, and in his recently purchased Cessna, Uncas flew in from New York. He invited his father to travel back to New York with him for the last game of the 1941 World Series between the Yankees and the Dodgers. O. B. was hesitant, worried about the expense, but Uncas persuaded him to go, suggesting that it would be a good time to have a discussion about the management of his properties in Missouri.

Father and son took the train to New York on Sunday, October 5. They spent the early part of Monday touring New York City. It was O. B.'s first trip to the city and he was overwhelmed with it and with his son's life-style as it was reflected in the day's activities: the ball game, then dinner, then a Broadway show. He was at once anxious about and impressed with the amount of money Uncas was spending on him and told the family back home that he estimated his trip to New York must have cost his son at least $75; things cost a lot in the big city:

> I sure spread it on when I was in New York. My ball game ticket (paid for by Uncas) cost $5. 25, I had dinner (paid for by Uncas) that cost $2. 75, I attended a Broadway Theatre (also paid for by Uncas) that cost $5. 50 for the ticket. Don't know what my room adjoining Uncas in the hotel cost as Uncas paid for it. Mamma is lying on the sofa listening to me dictate this letter and just now she said, "Poor Uncas."

The family letter continued with O. B.'s estimates of Uncas' expenses. He was impressed at the amount of money Uncas apparently had to spend, but by his standards son Uncas was living a bit high off the hog.

> Uncas has a fine room in the best hotel in Newark, costs $100 a month and his meals, I am sure, cost him another $100 a month. Then he has to keep up a big fine automobile and his airplane and I don't know what else. His expense is considerable. His income tax this year he told me will be about $25,000 about one-half of his salary for the year.

It is highly unlikely that Whitaker ever told his father his tax obligations would be that high. Probably O. B. misunderstood him on that score. But in his detailed description of Uncas' new undertaking, most of the facts he presented were accurate, indicating that Uncas withheld very little information from his father about Aircraft-Marine Products Inc. or, as O. B.'s son always referred to it, "the small company." All that information, of course, was retailed to the family, as nearly, that is, as O. B. understood it.

> He is now president of a small company, I do not remember the name, that handles some little metal devices used in connecting electrical wires as I understand it, at present in demand in war equipment. He has no investment in the business, one-fourth of the common stock is his. His salary is between ten and fifty thousand a year. A big businessman and financier, I do not remember his name, owns one-half or more, I think, of the preferred stock that for which cash has been paid. He also owns

one-half of the common stock. The other one-fourth of the common stock is owned by the man who patented the devices of the company that is now taken over by the new company.

With the details of ownership out of the way, O. B. next went on to discuss Uncas' role in the firm.

> He makes all the contracts with the federal government on the one hand and the manufacturing establishment that provides the materials on the other hand, studies the law that affects or may affect them. . . . He does a good deal of traveling and also has much supervisory work at home.

O. B. told the family that Uncas was optimistic, that if business continued at its present pace, he would surely receive his maximum salary of $50,000 for the year. He praised his son's educational preparation and observed that he "could not better have fitted himself for his present job." Concluding his report, O. B. let the family know once more that Uncas had been as closemouthed as always before his father's visit: "It was all news to me and quite surprising."[7]

Uncas Whitaker soon had an opportunity to prove how well education and experience had fitted him for his new job. A potential new customer appeared, and a big one — the Boeing Aircraft Company of Seattle, Washington. Boeing had been testing Buchanan's terminals and wanted to switch over to them, but it was totally uninformed about the firm that produced them. Was the company a dependable source of supply? Boeing asked W. K. Houston of the C&H Supply Company of Seattle, which had furnished Boeing with Buchanan's terminals. Houston sent a letter to Industrial Manufacturers Inc. requesting information:

> The Boeing Company has expressed a desire to give us their terminal business, but they have asked us the question, "Who is Industrial Manufacturers Inc."? Your firm is not listed in Dun & Bradstreet, so we were unable to give them much information about you.

Given the size of Boeing's business, the company could not afford to operate with an unreliable source of supply. Therefore, Houston wanted information about that source: the amount of machinery, the level of daily production, the size of the plant, the number of employees, its length of time in business, its financial stability, the names of present accounts, and the priority it was prepared to give Boeing.[8]

Whitaker replied to Houston on October 24, 1941. In an

uncharacteristically lengthy letter, he set forth all the pertinent details surrounding the history and current makeup of Industrial Manufacturers Inc., now called Aircraft-Marine Products Inc. Although Houston did not request it, Whitaker provided the names of the stockholders with brief biographical sketches of each, including educational background (Hixon, Yale '01; Warner, Princeton, '25; Whitaker, MIT, Carnegie Tech, and Cleveland Law School) and either financial assets (in the case of Hixon) or directorships held (as in the cases of Warner and Hamilton).

As far as production facilities were concerned, Whitaker admitted that outside sources did the bulk of the work for Aircraft-Marine Products Inc.:

> At the present time our manufacturing is being done under contract by several manufacturing companies who specialize in the particular product they manufacture for us. Our most important manufacturing connection is the Edwin B. Stimpson Company, Brooklyn. They manufacture all the stampings that go into the terminals and lugs. Every care has been taken to assure an adequate source of raw material and we have encountered no difficulty whatever in obtaining such material. The Stimpson Company has assured us that they can increase their production of our parts to ten times their present rate. . . . We intend to continue the policy of buying a large proportion of our stampings from such companies as the Stimpson Company as we consider this the safer policy. As added insurance, however, we are doing a certain amount of manufacturing ourselves and do all of the inspecting, packing and shipping as well as all the assembly operations.

Despite its dependence on outside suppliers, Whitaker assured Houston that Aircraft-Marine Products Inc. could easily meet the Boeing Company's needs and that prompt delivery of both the terminals and the hand tools for their application would be no problem. "We are entirely sure they will be pleased with our product, as well as our service," Whitaker concluded. Boeing was a big customer and Whitaker could not afford to lose this chance, although the perfection of product and service lay a good distance in the future. For the present, Aircraft-Marine Products Inc. was still an unformed organization, with a promising future as its most important asset.[9]

* * * * * * *

In May, 1941, the American freighter *Robin Moor* was torpedoed by a German submarine in the South Atlantic; it was the first sinking of an American ship by the Germans. The U-boat commander had allowed the ship's eight passengers and thirty-five crewmen thirty minutes to abandon ship, and all forty-three survivors were subsequently picked up alive. Since no lives were lost, there was relatively little public furor. Then in September, a German U-boat fired on a ship of the U. S. Navy. The destroyer, U. S. S. *Greer*, was reported to have been on a routine mail run to Iceland, but it was revealed later that the destroyer was cooperating with a British air patrol in looking for German U-boats. Fortunately, the *Greer* was not hit; however, this incident did provoke the nation and caused Roosevelt to warn the Nazi government that if fired upon, the U. S. Navy would retaliate. As *Time* assessed the situation, "the U. S. was at war — an undeclared war."[10]

O. B. Whitaker, on the other hand, was concluding almost a decade of declared war — against F. D. R. and the New Deal. Members of the family continued to receive frequent communiques from O. B.'s war room on the state of his campaign against the enemies in Washington, D. C. With the *Greer* incident, O. B.'s rhetorical bombardment intensified. "What do you think of the battle between our Destroyer and the German U-boat?" he asked his brother Syd Whitaker in a letter dated September 9, 1941.

> Which side is lying? . . . Why should a German submarine fire upon an American destroyer, when the only purpose that it could accomplish would be to help the President drag the most dangerous military power of the world into a war against Germany at a time like this? It would certainly have been the act of total insanity. On the other hand the event was exactly what Roosevelt has been hoping and praying for.[11]

O. B.'s obsession with F. D. R. and the New Deal was reaching new heights. He was certain of the detrimental effects of past and present New Deal outrages; he now grew concerned about the distortions of history; how would future generations learn the story of F. D. R.'s presidency?

> I hate to think of the record that will be written for the future school children of American to read — "The Great Humanitarian," "the champion of the laboring people," "the author of the more abundant life," "the discoverer of the forgotten men," etc., Bah! What a pity a true history cannot be handed to the future

generations of our country.[12]

About six weeks after the *Greer* incident, the recently commis-
sioned destroyer, U. S. S. *Kearny*, was torpedoed and the first
American casualties of World War II were reported. Roosevelt
termed this German action no accident. Rumors swept the nation
about encounters between the U. S. Navy and the German
submarine fleet. Roosevelt spoke of clearing the decks and taking
battle stations, and it all began to seem quite plausible. His late
October announcement that the United States would embark on a
$100 billion "Victory Program," and build, among other things,
125,000 airplanes by 1944, served to convince most of the
nonbelievers that the United States was indeed gearing up for a long
and costly struggle.[13]

Aircraft-Marine Products Inc. would contribute significantly to that
war effort, and U. A. Whitaker was hard at work engaged in his own
gearing-up process. He was looking for hard-to-get engineering
personnel and additional administrators as the new company prepared
to step up production on its solderless electrical terminations. When
Whitaker took over the assets of Industrial Manufacturers Inc. in
mid-September, he found about two dozen production employees and
a handful of salaried workers, including James O. Johnson, then head
of engineering, John H. Thompson, a draftsman, Frank G. Wehler,
Jr., sales manager, and a small staff of clerical people. Plans for
increased staff and increased production meant as well the need for
larger quarters. In the fall of 1941, Industrial's offices were located in
a converted stucco house at 470 Rahway Avenue in Elizabeth, while
its production operations, such as they were, were located in the
Bayway Terminal Building. A fair number of suitable buildings were
available for sale, but Whitaker was looking for one to rent. He
found a solution to his need for better office space in Elizabeth, at
286 N. Broad Street, in a building that housed a Greek restaurant.
Over time, people's recollections of the precise locations of
Aircraft-Marine Products Inc.'s offices and factory have been blurred.
Echoes of Horatio Alger and images of the typical young inventor
have helped place the new company in a one-room store or in a
garage up a narrow alley. O. B. Whitaker couldn't have written it
better.[14]

Compromises could be made with office facilities; they could not
be made with personnel. First-class engineers had been in short
supply in the late thirties; now with war coming close, the situation
grew much more difficult. Just one week after signing the corporate

papers, Whitaker wrote to Nat Sage at MIT asking his advice about getting a former Hoover engineer out of the army to work for Aircraft-Marine Products Inc. as a research engineer. Sage suggested an appeal process to Washington and added that he would be on the lookout for good men. Bill Watts at Tri-State was looking too, although even inexperienced engineers were at a premium, and his graduates had a choice of two or three jobs offered them by recruiters who regularly visited the campus. Watts himself, selected as Aircraft-Marine Products Inc.'s field engineer, was tied down at Tri-State until the beginning of the year, but Whitaker urged him to start work immediately from his Indiana base. Whitaker travelled to Indiana in the middle of October, and he and Watts worked out plans to gather samples and information on competitive terminal products. Watts was also to keep an eye out for local shops with small presses, which might be able to take care of part of Aircraft-Marine Products Inc.'s manufacturing output. Meanwhile, Watts did a little recruiting on his own. He persuaded Kenneth L. Neijstrom, a Tri-State graduate whom Watts had placed with Bendix, to join the firm and even before Neijstrom came East, Watts had him working on some terminal and bonding jumper ideas in an Indiana laboratory. Neijstrom would become a mainstay of the company.[15]

Whitaker particularly needed a director for experimental engineering The man he had in mind was Vern Carlson, another Hoover engineer from Whitaker's division, now with Eureka in Detroit. Whitaker went after him. By the end of October, Carlson had made up his mind, as Whitaker reported to Hamilton. "I have a tentative agreement with Carlson, now Chief Engineer of Eureka, to start work for me the 15th of next month and I am also taking three other engineers from Eureka. This will be the four best out of a group of about sixty." Whitaker did not typically raid companies, but in this case he felt justified, for he understood that Eureka, having lost a considerable amount of money in the preceding year, was going out of business.[16]

Hoover contacts, so valuable to Whitaker in assembling his staff, helped Whitaker with a second strategy for solving his current engineering problems. Gordon C. Curry was a friend and former associate of Whitaker's; he was now Manager of Defense Products Sales at Hoover. Through Curry, Whitaker worked out an arrangement whereby the Hoover Engineering Department would do some engineering development research for Aircraft-Marine Products Inc. on a connection box and electrical harness for the Navy Air

Corps. Curry and Whitaker discussed this arrangement in North Canton the last week in October, and Curry achnowledged the agreement in a letter dated October 27. "The engineering work will cost $4. 00 per hour plus travel" Curry informed Whitaker and noted that engineers G. P. Daiger and C. G. Troxler "will go to Washington after going over the job with you to talk to Lt. Grant, and the final details in regard to the work will be made with you on their return."[17]

Whitaker was careful not to overtax the generosity of Hoover engineering, but for the present his own research and testing facilities were too limited to do everything the new company needed. Hoover's help was crucial. In acknowledging Curry's letter, Whitaker said:

> I have no question at all as to the arrangements with the Hoover Company being entirely satisfactory providing the company feels it can fit this into the engineering program. As I discussed with you it will, of course, be necessary for this project to have active and continuous attention since it is considered by the Navy Air Corps as being very urgent. I am sure you all appreciate what this means.

Whitaker had a way of making his point without appearing too insistent. The implicit appeal to patriotism did not hurt his cause. Nor did the possibility that Hoover might eventually receive contracts for the manufacture of some of the equipment developed and tested by its engineering department.[18]

Curry began drawing up an official agreement between Hoover and Aircraft-Marine Products Inc. while Daiger and Troxler journeyed to Washington and Elizabeth to study the development program for a new type of wiring system for airplanes. Early in November, Daiger officially recommended that Hoover do the work. The project looked good technically, and it offered very good possibilities for Hoover's own business.

H. Earl Hoover, vice-president of the company, thought it looked good too. In fact, when he read the complicated agreement between Hoover and Aircraft-Marine Products Inc. worked out by Curry and Whitaker, it seemed to him excessively legalistic. Shortly before Thanksgiving, 1941, Hoover explained this to Whitaker.

> I am wondering if there is any need for a formal contract or if simply by an exchange of letters we can arrive at a mutually satisfactory solution without going to the trouble of drawing up a formal document.

Hoover trusted Whitaker, and informal agreements were a mark of his particular business style, in any event. On the other hand, the contract placed limits on the Hoover Company that H. Earl Hoover found too restrictive, particularly in the long run. While he was generous in allowing any patentable items resulting from information secured from Whitaker's company to be assigned to Aircraft-Marine Products Inc. and in promising that Hoover would not go into competition with them in the specific area of the projected research, he did insist on protecting Hoover's longer range interests in "electrically connected devices."

> For patriotic reasons and to help a friend, we entered into this arrangement with you and for our services were to receive some $4.00 per hour and other charges. . . . My own thought when approving the project for the Engineering Department was quite naturally that if and when something satisfactory was developed, that having worked with you in its development, we might be in a favorable situation to bid on the production work. . . . In this connection it is understood, of course, that the development work did not guarantee to us any production work, but certainly we expected to be in a favorable position as a consequence.

The Hoover Company was, as H. Earl Hoover put it, undertaking this deal "on a personal friendship basis." They were doing Whitaker a favor, and, to Hoover, a formal contract did not look like a dialogue between friends.

Whitaker quickly agreed to an informal agreement and sketched out a scheme for a regular patent procedure. As for Hoover entering the production field, that was fine with Whitaker, too. As he told Hoover, if the project was successful, it would turn out to be a multimillion dollar contract. "There will be more business than we can handle and we would be more than glad to offer part of it to the Hoover Company, either by sub-contract or, if it would seem best, by direct contract with the Government." Success, moreover, seemed pretty likely; in Whitaker's words, "it is a pretty good gamble."

> A new development such as this offers the best opportunity to get defense work that is of a profitable nature due to the fact that it is much less apt to get into the competitive class with the run of the [mill] defense work.

Whitaker's philosophy of "don't do something that other people can do well" was already at work here.[19]

In these early months, Whitaker faced a staggering number of details in the daily running of Aircraft-Marine Products Inc. Nevertheless, he remained alert for any opportunity to enlarge the company's market regardless of limited production facilities. Once again, it was his association with the Hoover Company that offered him an interesting prospect along this line. While conferring with Daiger and Troxler about the contract with Hoover engineering, Whitaker learned that C. B. Colson, in charge of Hoover's foreign operations, was interested in Aircraft-Marine Products Inc.'s solderless terminal. Whitaker saw the possibilities of getting into the British market through Hoover Ltd., and he pursued the matter in earnest through the balance of 1941. He wrote Colson about the development work then underway and pointed out that if successful "these developments . . . will pretty much revolutionize the wiring practice for airplanes in this country." Whitaker was well aware of the large British market created by wartime needs and suggested to Colson that the two firms could easily work together on the project. Although nothing came of this possible liaison with Hoover's overseas operations, Whitaker continued, during the early war years, to investigate Aircraft-Marine Products Inc.'s entry into the British market through other avenues. For the time being, however, the company was busy enough trying to obtain a substantial share of the domestic market.[20]

Bill Watts, meanwhile, was hustling around the midwest investigating competitive products, looking for new ideas, searching for manufacturing facilities, designing new terminals and switching jacks, and testing terminal product samples made up by Ken Neijstrom under his supervision. He also served Aircraft-Marine Products Inc. as a kind of public relations man, going to this plant and that to talk to production engineers and convince them of the superiority of solderless terminals over the old-fashioned soldered type. Watts somtimes found a receptive audience, as at Zenith in Detroit; a key engineer there told him that Zenith was "very much in favor of eliminating all solder from radio if possible." Some visits produced skepticism, but in a good number of cases potential users of the solderless terminal were at least open to having samples submitted for testing purposes. Watts' work here would pay handsome dividends later.[21]

Pressures on Whitaker and his people came from all sides. Even the members of the board of directors got in the act. Early in November, Carl Hamilton wrote to Robert Hixon asking him to suggest that Whitaker furnish them a monthly balance sheet, operating statement, and even a weekly memorandum on the current state of business affairs. Hixon apparently did so, for, beginning in

November, Whitaker made his first formal comments on past business, current problems, and future prospects. Issued monthly, rather than weekly, they provide an excellent view of the early problems of the developing business venture and Whitaker's reactions to them. At the time, the reports served to keep the directors informed about and, more significantly, involved in, the activities of the company; as a result, their advice, which Whitaker sought, was useful to him as he implemented larger company policies.[22]

The first of the monthly reports was dictated by Whitaker on November 18, 1941. Sales for the month of October were the highest in the young business' history — a little over $54,000. Based on information he received from his associate, S. N. Buchanan, Whitaker reported optimistically that "prospects are still spectacular and we have concrete evidence that Chrysler, Ford and General Motors are standardizing on our terminals." He told the two directors that November looked like a $60,000 month and that such problems as personnel and the acquisition of raw materials would soon be solved as he anticipated a much better and more efficient organizational structure by the first of the year. But by the time Whitaker was ready to prepare the following month's report, the situation was not so rosy. The November billing figures declined by about $7,000 from October, with December shaping up as an even worse month. Whitaker guessed that December would be down to about half of November's billing; in fact, it dropped to slightly over $16,000, closer to a third than a half of the November figure of approximately $47,000.[23]

The decline in orders notwithstanding, Whitaker had been making plans to expand production facilities, anticipating correctly that things would pick up soon after the first of the year. The Stimpson Company, its major supplier of stampings and screw machine parts, promised Whitaker that it was prepared to do as much as five time the present volume of business for the company if need be. At the same time, it was necessary to find a second plant. Recalling from his days at American Machine & Foundry Company, how favorable conditions were at Glen Rock, Pennsylvania, Whitaker looked for another manufacturing facility in that town. He found what he wanted in a plant owned by Paul Shepperd, and Whitaker set up a contractual relationship with Shepperd for the use of the factory. That plant, he explained to Hixon and Hamilton "can easily be expanded to take care of two or three times our last quarter's business and our plant here can handle about twice our last quarter's business by working overtime and without adding further personnel." The attractiveness of Glen Rock was enforced for Whitaker when it became time to sign a labor contract with the local union in Elizabeth. Whitaker anticipated that the contract would prevent any trouble for at least a year, but he was neither pleased with the contract nor altogether secure about the eventualies of the labor situation.   By contrast, "The labor situation in Glen Rock is excellent," he informed his directors, "as all employees are residents of that town and there never has been any labor trouble of any kind." The inhabitants of this small town were the kind of people O. B. Whitaker's son understood and trusted. As he told a long-time associate on numerous occasions, "given some honest and God-fearing people, enterprise can succeed."[24]

The December business decline was severe but it looked to be short-lived. The entry of the United States into World War II on December 7, 1941, encouraged a flurry of inquiries: How soon could vital parts be manufactured and delivered? At first this deluge of requests for information resulted in few orders.   As Whitaker explained it, "Everyone is asking just how quickly we could ship materials but as yet they do not seem to know just what they want shipped."[25] Assured that business would pick up substantially after the first of the year, as American war production moved into high gear, Whitaker welcomed the temporary respite, as he told his father on the very day the Japanese attacked Pearl Harbor:

> My business is going at a quite satisfactory rate. I would just as soon
> it would not expand further for another month or two until I get
> things a little better organized. Have been feeling fine and enjoying
> the work, but will appreciate having a little time to myself when I
> get an adequate force hired and accustomed to the business. Right
> now I am a little too busy to suit me.[26]

Whitaker was so busy that he had not flown his plane for nearly a month. Immediately following the outbreak of war, he could not have flown had he wanted to. All pilot certificates were revoked as of December 8, and an elaborate system of reinstatement was necessary to get one's flying license back in order. One had to verify citizenship with letters, a birth certificate, and fingerprints. New flight plans would be necessary, and security measures at airports were to be tightened.   It took Earl Kail a good week to get his license reinstated. In the meantime business at MAT, already slow, ground to a halt. The training program lost ground when the draft began to take a considerable number of eligible students from it. For several months Kail had been between government contracts. With no students to train and no passengers to hop, MAT was effectively out of business. Like Whitaker, Kail anticipated a spectacular increase in business after the first of the year; MAT, unlike Aircraft-Marine Products Inc., would wait in vain.[27]

A few days after Pearl Harbor, Whitaker wrote home and commented on America's grim new situation.

> It certainly looks like our navy was caught asleep in Hawaii. Maybe this will shock both the army and the navy into getting a little efficiency. My impression was that the navy was in fair shape and that the army was about as bad as an army could be at the present time. The affair at Hawaii would indicate that the navy is lacking a lot of efficiency also. I imagine we will get going now, but I think it will be at least a year to a year and a half before our preparedness program is brought up to even fair efficiency.

The thrust of the letter fairly represents Whitaker's own preoccupations, especially in the thrice-repeated "efficiency." Whitaker had spent a number of months now in a business directly connected to the question of speedy and efficient preparedness.[28]

Although Aircraft-Marine Products Inc.'s solderless terminals were to become one of many essential items in America's program for wartime production, business problems remained complex for Whitaker. Contrary to popular wisdom on the subject, competition in America was not suspended for the duration, and in 1942 Aircraft-Marine Products Inc. faced tough competition. There were, first of all, rival companies producing solderless terminals; there was also the problem of continued resistance to the new method itself. That resistence had to be overcome by Aircraft-Marine Products Inc. people out in the field. Furthermore, interservice rivalry and bureaucratic infighting had to be contended with. Added to these external problems were internal tensions, natural enough in a new and yet unformed organization. At Aircraft-Marine Products Inc. those tensions came to a head with the establishment of a full-blown sales division, headed by a brilliantly aggressive sales manager. Between competition outside and conflict within, Whitaker had his hands full with the growth and early development of his firm (see Chapter 9).

Although Uncas Whitaker was essentially sure of his own entrepreneurial talents and of his ability to make Aircraft-Marine Products Inc. succeed, there was a corner of his mind reserved for doubts and ambivalences. In that part of his mind he remained convinced that a significant business crash would follow the war. Encouraged by his father to think about this eventuality, Whitaker may occasonally have allowed those doubts to color his business judgments, if only to make him more cautious at the first signs of any business letdown. Certainly, caution infused Whitaker's attitude toward government at all times. While he clearly understood Aircraft-Marine Products Inc.'s dependency on government war production, he was never altogether pleased with the conditions of that relationship. At times, the "damned if you do and damned if you don't" situation particularly irked him, as he wrote to Uncle Syd:

> Running or trying to run a business these days certainly has its complications. If you should, by some accident, make money, the government takes it all away in taxes and accuses you of being unpatriotic and a few other things, for profiteering. On the other hand, if you work day and night and lose money, the government probably takes your business over and so there is not too much compensation either way.

Whitaker was, of course, working under the wartime excess profit taxing system, and although he understood its purpose, felt its general application was somewhat unfair. Still, he admitted to Syd, things could be worse.

> The situation is not quite as bad as that, though the amount of routine required in running a business is tremendous and the chances of making a really substantial profit are quite low in spite of all that we read in the newspapers to the contrary. I am having plenty of worries in this business but there is a lot of interest in it too so I guess I shouldn't complain. We are about breaking even at the present time and the prospects are that we will make a fair profit this year [1942], probably 4% after taxes.

Whitaker was wrong in his projection. The 1942 profit was barely 1 percent after taxes, and in the succeeding four years the profit picture was equally dismal. Had he known that in 1941, Whitaker might have been less sanguine. As it was, he remained essentially optimistic, telling Syd that "if we do win the war and get everything straightened out after it is all over, it will be worth the effort however."[29]

O. B., on the other hand, now approaching seventy-two and in failing health, was nowhere near so optimistic about the state of the world or America's postwar prospects. As a lifelong opponent of capital punishment and killing in general, he feared and hated war. A very large measure of his opposition to United States entry into the war had been based upon his essentially pacifist philosophy. Perhaps he might have grown convinced of the importance of defeating Nazi Germany, but he was not given the time.

Christmas, 1941, was O. B. Whitaker's last. His annual Christmas letter was entirely personal; he made no mention of the war or politics. In the letter he reminisced about his earliest remembered Christmas, celebrated on the bleak plains of Iowa sometime in the late 1870s. The tone of the letter was both maudlin and pathetic; his opening sentences, blankly depressing. "How can one know," he began, "whether he is welcome as a visitor — even among his friends? Whether they tire of him and wish he would go? How can one know whether his letters or articles are cared for by those to whom he sends them? You answer those questions," O. B. commanded to no one member of his family in particular, "I have tried and failed." A little over four months later, on May 4, 1942, O. B. Whitaker died, perhaps convinced that his trial on earth had been a personal failure.[30]

Others thought differently. The Reverend Frederick Cooper, one of O. B.'s former pupils, delivered the funeral sermon in the Weaubleau Christian Church. He summed up O. B.'s life and expressed the sentiments of most who knew him. Cooper's remarks touched on all phases of O. B.'s personal and professional life and on the intertwining nature of the public and private man — the teacher, businessman, statesman, minister, moralist, husband, father, and friend.

The Reverend Cooper began: "I like to think of him first as a teacher preeminently, because, like the Divine Master whom he loved and followed, he reached men through teaching." He went on to talk of O. B. the man of honor in business and of faithfulness in political office. He was, the Reverend recalled, a liberal, hating "bigotry and sham of all kinds," and he was guided by deep convictions. Cooper spoke most fully of O. B. :

> As husband, father, and friend, his real feelings were best expressed. I can see him yet when his children, Portia, Minnie, and Uncas were small children. He was never too busy, even in the middle of a class, to turn aside to any message they might wish to bring him. He sought comforts, not luxuries, for his home, and always maintained the highest spiritual and moral tone in his home. As a friend I can testify that he was loyal and true when most needed. . . .Death entered our home taking three members . . . inside of three weeks. . . . Upon returning from the

cemetery. . . he extended his hand and said, "Brother Cooper, go on." I found they were not empty words when I learned that funeral expenses had been paid out of his own income.

O. B. Whitaker, was, the minister concluded, "preeminently a Christian gentleman.[31]

O. B. Whitaker's death was not only a matter of local concern. One of the leading newspapers of the state, the Kansas City *Star*, devoted a long editorial to O. B., lamenting the passing of "Old Hickory," whose legislative career the editorial characterized as the "impossible ideal" because of his selfless devotion to service.

> He believed in the kind of lawmaking visualized by the framers of the state constitution. He hated the caucus system and refused to consider himself bound by Repubican caucuses. He was the expert on legislative procedure, a weapon he used effectively in many battles on the floor of the House of Representatives.

The editorial noted O. B. Whitaker's numerous successes, emphasizing especially his educational reform legislation and his contributions to the Centennial Road bill which created the fine highway system that existed in Missouri. "For more than a quarter of a century," the writer continued, "he took an active part, for or against almost every important bill before the legislature. His practical experience was rooted in his life as a banker and farmer as well as an educator." But even more important than any of his specific accomplishments, according to the *Star*, was O. B.'s courage and convictions that led him to oppose "corruption and the self-seeking machine influences." O. B. Whitaker served his state, first and foremost:

> Sometimes he seemed to be an anachronism in a machine-dominated legislature. Men who went along with the sleek games of the partisan politicians smiled condescendingly at the mention of "Old Hickory." But the representative of Hickory County lived to see their power politics discredited before the state of Missouri and their favorite projects in ruins.

Indeed, O. B. Whitaker had been one of the leaders in the long-term fight against the Missouri Pendergast political machine.[32]

Had O. B. Whitaker been around to read this editorial about himself, he would no doubt have quoted sections of it in a newsletter to his family. But, in the final analysis, O. B.'s personal bravado was not unfounded. The people of his state, as well as his family, did, after all, appreciate him. He need not have worried about that. Speaking for his father, Uncas Whitaker wrote a letter to the editor of the *Star*, thanking him for "one of the finest eulogies that I have seen in the editorial columns of a great paper." He told the editor that his father had always admired the *Star* despite the frequent disagreements they had over state policies of one kind or another. As generous as his father, Uncas Whitaker gave the paper the credit it was due. "The fact that you could write such an editorial of one who had many times opposed your view is one of the reasons the *Star* is a great paper."[33]

Years later, U. A. Whitaker confided to a close associate and friend that O. B. had guided and advised him well and that he was thankful he had taken his advice. Except in one important instance, son Uncas was correct. O. B. had originally counseled him not to pursue an engineering career. He came to be thankful that Uncas had disregarded that particular piece of advice. But O. B., after all, could not have been surprised that his son had followed his own mind — he had spent a lifetime teaching him to do just that.[34]

9. The Organization

The turmoil of the first few months of business behind him, U. A. Whitaker settled down to cope with the problem of creating some organizational order for the recently born Aircraft-Marine Products Inc. company. After a ten-day trip to Los Angeles at the beginning of February, 1942, to investigate potential aircraft customers and their needs, Whitaker returned to his office determined to take the necessary action to get his company running smoothly.[1] He identified seven major tasks to accomplish at the outset:

1. Establish a modern sales organization with qualified personnel having definite ideas and territories, properly controlled, and each with suitable incentive compensation plans.

2. Establish a definite sales policy as to prices, deliveries, jobber representation. . . and see that this is followed out uniformly.

3. Establish a scientific survey of the sales possibilities of the country by territories and make proper plans accordingly.

4. Provide production drawings for all parts manufactured, showing dimensions, tolerances, materials and other specifications.

5. Inaugurate the test program covering all items sold and manufactured to determine their suitability for the service intended, whether they meet government or customer specifications, and comparative performance with competitive items.

6. Provide accurate, up-to-date records on all phases of the business so as to permit continuous analyses of this business situation.

7. Provide an organization chart.

Whitaker judged that a good number of months would be required to accomplish the bulk of this program. The first order of business was to devise an organization plan within which these important needs and tasks could be attacked and implemented. By March, 1942, a draft organization plan and chart were in existence, and on paper, at least, the situation looked orderly.[2]

U. A. Whitaker, as vice-president and general manager of Aircraft-Marine Products Inc., would bear two responsiblities, according to the organization plan. The six major divisions of the company — Financial, Sales, Engineering, Patent and Legal, Production, and Inspection — reported to General Manager Whitaker. In addition to these administrative duties, Whitaker headed the Engineering Division, itself composed of three departments — Production Engineering, Experimental Engineering, and Research. Production Engineering, headed by J. O. Johnson, an original Industrial Manufacturers Inc. employee, was responsible for furnishing drawings, specifications, engineering purchasing, blue prints and photostats. Experimental Engineering was run by V. E. Carlson, a former Hoover engineer recruited by Whitaker from Eureka Vacuum; he was responsible for the development of new items and the refinement of old ones, as well as for furnishing test data according to customer requirements. The Research Department had no specific head but was staffed by three part-time people, each of whom worked in his own environment — Dr. Frank Sowa, who ran his own chemical company in New York; Associate Professor J. S. Balsbaugh in Electrical Engineering at MIT; and G. P. Daiger (listed as Dr. Daiger), an electrical engineer at Hoover.

The original draft of the organization document defined the Engineering Division: "The departments of the Engineering Division will work according to work programs, the items and orders of which will be determined from time to time by the General Manager, and no new assignments may be undertaken except those on the work program unless approved by the General Manager." Whitaker's associate, S. N. Buchanan, a vice-president of the company, was also to contribute to the work of the engineering division, according to the draft organization plan. Buchanan was charged with exercising "his inventive ability in the production of ideas to be submitted for the purpose of patent protection and for such future development as decided by the General Manager." Whitaker, in effect, controlled the entire engineering mission of the company, including the efforts of his associate Buchanan.

The organization plan spelled out succinctly the duties and responsibilities of the other divisions of the company. The sales manager, G. Earle Walker, recently hired, was responsible for sales planning, sales control, direction of field salesmen, representatives, jobbers, control of prices, discounts and terms; however, all quoted prices had to be approved by the general manager — that is, U. A. Whitaker. Walker's division had four departments — General Sales, Sales Engineering, Advertising and Statistical, and Office. The Financial Division, at that time run mainly by C. J. Fredricksen holding the title of assistant treasurer, was similarly described, as was the Patent and Legal Division under R. J. Szukala, a protege of one of director R. Miles Warner's relatives. The organization plan and chart, simple but comprehensive, had a specific objective: "to avoid confusion and duplication by defining the duties and responsibilities of all officers and personnel of the company; to indicate the lanes of authority by which instructions are issued and duties outlined and controlled."[3]

If well-constructed organization plans and charts are an index to a well-run, efficiently-adminstered business firm, Aircraft-Marine Products Inc. appears to have had its problems well in hand. But plans on paper often differ considerably from realities in business life and in the case of Aircraft-Marine Products Inc., the realities were indeed something else. In truth, the situation Whitaker faced was terrible. It was, as he explained to Carl Hamilton on March 12, 1942, the lowest of low points:

> Since the last time I saw you in December, we have gone through a period which I hope can be described later as the darkest period of our history. About the time you were here I could see the storm clouds approaching and the storm broke shortly thereafter. We naturally had all kinds of troubles and worries due to the fact that there was scarcely any organization or system, we had no production drawings of parts, no specifications as to materials, no tests as to what our stuff would do. This was all very bad and caused us no end of difficulties due to having material rejected and not being in a position to make corrections because of lack of information. All this, however, was somewhat as I had figured, tho, frankly, a great deal worse than I expected.[4]

While Whitaker was merely dismayed over the shortcomings of his engineering division, he was profoundly distressed over his sales division. Whitaker had understood that a sales division was essential, but he would never really be happy with the need to have one. He admitted to Hamilton that he had made a monumental mistake in assuming that sales "could be run in a haphazard, unbusinesslike way and still be reasonably successful." What Whitaker early learned was that solderless electrical terminations, despite their excellence, did not sell themselves.

The mistake, however, carried more complications than this simple observation implies. S. N. Buchanan, who was determined to maintain a very active role in the new organization, convinced Whitaker that sales were his thing. Actually, Whitaker knew better; rather, he suspected that Buchanan could not do an adequate job in the sales area because from Whitaker's point of view the man had no business sense. What Buchanan did as "Sales Engineer" in the first few months of Aircraft-Marine Products Inc. was a disaster. "It's a long story," Whitaker told Hamilton, "but briefly, the set-up he made over the country was completely hopeless. It not only didn't get sales but the way it was set up, had it gotten sales, would have been so costly that it could not have been continued."[5] In fact, Whitaker had spent so much time trying to straighten out the sales problem that he had been forced to slight his other responsibilities, which in turn suffered accordingly.

If S. N. Buchanan was Whitaker's problem in sales, G. Earle Walker appeared to be his solution. In December he had informed Hixon and Hamilton that Walker had been employed on a three-month trial basis to review the situation and make appropriate recommendations. After Whitaker had looked Walker over, and vice versa, perhaps a permanent position with the company would be discussed. In fact, this December report on G. Earle Walker slightly masked the facts. Whitaker admitted to Hamilton in March that he had to bring Walker in as an office manager because Buchanan was opposed to hiring a sales manager, presumably believing that was one of the positions he himself was filling. It was Walker who had suggested the three-month evaluation period, but he found after less than a month at Aircraft-Marine Products Inc. that sales problems needed treatment immediately. As Whitaker put it, "it became evident that if we waited three months to take action, there wouldn't be anything to take action on so I persuaded Buchanan to take an extended sales trip in the South and gave Walker authority to do what was necessary."[6]

G. Earle Walker had come to Aircraft-Marine Products Inc. from the Crosley Company via Eureka Vacuum Cleaner. In a sense, Walker was between jobs. He had worked for a good number of years in Philadelphia, always in sales, before joining Eureka as sales manager. When Vern Carlson came to Eureka from Hoover Company, he met Walker and was impressed with his sales ability. It was Carlson, subsequently, who recommended that Whitaker get in touch with Walker for the Aircraft-Marine Products Inc. job. When Walker saw that the approaching war would slow the appliance business down, he went to Crosley, where for a brief time he handled some of their defense contracts. He considered next the possibility of going to Washington where he had made some contacts, notably one with future Secretary of State Edward R. Stettinius, at that time in charge of materiel control. Carlson knew that Walker was considering another job change and asked him to come to Elizabeth to talk to Whitaker about the Aircraft-Marine Products Inc. opportunity. According to Walker, he arrived in Elizabeth and met Whitaker in his office over a Greek restaurant. Whitaker had become an avid camera bug, and he owned an early model miniature Minox. During a good portion of the interview Whitaker snapped pictures of Walker. The two men discussed the job of reorganizing Aircraft-Marine Products Inc.'s sales department, and Walker was puzzled — both about the picture-taking which he thought "odd" and about the reorganization job, for he could see nothing to reorganize.

Walker, however, agreed to consider the job offer, mainly because he had no other interesting offers to consider. He went back to his home in Detroit, and a few days later Whitaker called to tell him that he wanted Walker to meet "Buck" Buchanan who would be in Detroit on company business. Walker's meeting with Buchanan turned out to be stranger than the one with Whitaker and his camera. They met in Buchanan's hotel room, and all Walker can remember of the interview was being shown one practical joke after another as Buchanan kept pulling them from his coat pocket. Walker telephoned Whitaker immediately and told him about his strange experience with Buchanan. Whitaker advised him not to be bothered by it but to come down and take the job on the three-month trial basis the two men had discussed in Elizabeth. The offer Whitaker made him was good, and Walker decided that cameras and practical jokes aside, he might as well take the short-term position. In late December, 1941, he joined the firm and by March, 1942, at the time of Whitaker's pessimistic report to Hamilton, was just beginning to institute his sales plan of action. Whitaker was relieved. He predicted that Walker would do an excellent job and as things turned out he was not disappointed. Walker, who in his own way could be termed a "character," would build a powerful and successful sales organization and become a key member of the firm.[7]

In March, 1942, Whitaker might well have felt his back up against the wall, but his pessimism did not grow into defeatism. He knew he was on the way to answering the company's problems even though it would take very long hours and much hard work "to get the company on a good business basis in all departments." The one really major problem that remained unsolved was that of S. N. "Buck" Buchanan. Walker, among others, could see that Whitaker and Buchanan were not a good match. Perhaps Whitaker always suspected that working with Buchanan would be difficult, partly, no doubt, for personal reasons and partly because Buchanan as a nuts-and-bolts type engineer had an entirely different way of looking at engineering problems than the more professionally trained Whitaker. In any event, by March, Whitaker saw the problem clearly and knew that when he had to tell Buchanan that G. Earle Walker was, in fact, the only sales manager of the firm, the sparks would fly. He confided in Hamilton:

> The one really great unsolved problem and headache is our mutual friend Buchanan. I thought I had encountered personnel problems before in my career and also had a little conceit that I could handle them. This old fellow would require a whole staff of personnel experts to control or at least I haven't hit the answer yet. I still have a few more tricks to try so haven't given up. I may have to request a more positive definition of the organization set-up by the directors, especially as to control of sales activities.

The newly created organization plan and chart were, in part, an attempt to provide that means of "control of sales activities." Meanwhile, Walker went ahead with his program as if no conflict existed at all.[8]

If Whitaker intended to force Buchanan's hand in this matter, he succeeded. In mid-June, S. N. Buchanan threw in the sponge and asked Whitaker if he would buy his interest in the company. Whitaker was not surprised at this development; no doubt, it was exactly what he wanted. His June 21 memo to the board of directors suggests this:

> Friday, Buchanan asked me if we would buy his interest in the company. For some time I have been of the opinion that we would sooner or later have to make some kind of arrangement by which Buchanan could be removed from any active participation in the affairs of the company, and I believe that the present time is probably as favorable a time as we will encounter. We have now pretty well completed our reorganization of the sales department, and he definitely does not fit in this new set-up.

The Buchanan dilemma could be solved only in this way, from Whitaker's point of view. He had originally believed that Buchanan would be most valuable to the organization as an "idea man," but as Whitaker now saw it, Buchanan's ideas were not very interesting. Buchanan, on the other hand, wanted to take an active part in the running of the company, but Whitaker saw this as, in the long run, "fatal to the business." No doubt, Whitaker felt that Buchanan had served his purpose, that his leaving would not affect the company, and that once he was gone the entire organization would operate more efficiently.

Whitaker, who had anticipated the coming of this day, was ready to work out a payment plan. He expected that Buchanan would demand more for his interest than it was worth, and he was right insofar as Buchanan did ask for a considerable sum — $65,000. Whitaker told him this was out of the question. But he promised Buchanan he would make a counteroffer after conferring with the directors. Buchanan still had a little over two years remaining on his employment contract with Aircraft-Marine Products Inc., and Whitaker estimated that over that period he would receive about $70,000 in salary if he remained with the company. In view of this, Whitaker recommended that Buchanan be paid $40,000 in settlement of his contract and $5,000 for his 2,000 shares of common stock (valued very low at that time.)[9]

Buchanan was in the mood to sell, and Whitaker wanted approval of his plan before his associate changed his mind.[10] He got that authority quickly. Robert Hixon wired two days later approving the plan. Whitaker met with Buchanan the next day to talk over his proposal and, shortly after that meeting, Fredricksen prepared a draft agreement based on their conversation. Fredricksen's draft agreement memo indicated that Whitaker got an even better settlement than he had hoped for. $21,000 was to be paid for Buchanan's contract, $3,500 for his stock (to be bought by Whitaker personally and later disposed of), and Buchanan's salary for May and June, amounting to $8,333.32. Better still, the $21,000 could be paid monthly in amounts equal to Buchanan's salary payments. No large cash outlay was necessary, thereby protecting the company's rather weak cash position. That same afternoon, June 24, Whitaker and Buchanan met with their respective lawyers, and the final details were worked out. By July 1, 1942, Buchanan had sold out and resigned from the company. Midland Investment picked up 810 shares of the stock, Whitaker 540, Hamilton 270, Warner 110, and three daughters of

Robert Hixon 90 shares each. S. N. Buchanan's short-lived tenure with Aircraft-Marine Products Inc. was at an end.[11]

* * * * * * *

U. A. Whitaker had a shorthand formula for improving the condition of Aircraft-Marine Products Inc. — patience and a lot of work. The sales volume recorded by the company in the first quarter of 1942 was unremarkable and unprofitable. Whitaker and his associates estimated that sales of $60,000 a month were needed to break even. Since the average figure for each of the first three months was under $40,000, Aircraft-Marine Products Inc. was obviously operating at a not inconsiderable loss. Whitaker did not anticipate that his newly reorganized sales division would produce significant results for at least three months and felt sure that it would take nearly a year before its sales representatives would be operating at maximum efficiency. The sales goals he set for the remainder of the year, therefore, were very conservative, all well under $60,000 until October. As it turned out, Whitaker's estimates were wrong, but no one cared. The $60,000 figure was reached the very next month, and the average for all the succeeding months of the year was even better. Better yet was the increasing sales backlog, which grew from $100,000 in April to $500,000 in December. As Whitaker told his friend L. E. Jermy, editor of *Machine Design* magazine, "We furnish electrical solderless terminals for a pretty fair share of all the aircraft and shipbuilding companies of the United States and are rapidly increasing our list of customers as more companies swing into war work."[12]

The war, of course, was what the sales increase was all about. Not that the company had any choice in the matter. Because of the scarcity of the materials they used — mostly copper and tin — in the manufacture of the solderless terminal and bonding jumpers, they were allowed to supply their product only to those concerns engaged in high-priority work, and that meant war production. Each month the list of important new accounts grew as such familiar names as Consolidated Aircraft, International Business Machine, Vought-Sikorsky, and Douglas Aircraft switched over to Aircraft-Marine Products Inc. But none of this happened overnight. It took, as Whitaker put it, patience and a lot of hard work.[13]

Out in the field, Sales Engineer Bill Watts was setting an example of a hard-working Aircraft-Marine Products Inc. employee. His weekly field trip reports sent back to the home office revealed a monumental effort on his part to spread the word about the company's new products. Watts made scores of calls during the year in an attempt to make friends for and converts to Aircraft-Marine Products Inc. In the process, Watts encountered a variety of reactions, problems, attitudes, and on occasions a stone wall. Without attempting to chronicle all of Watts' experiences, it is illustrative to describe several of his more interesting and important calls to demonstrate the general situation facing Aircraft-Marine Products Inc. in the competitive world of terminal users and suppliers.[14]

PRODUCT FAILURE

Philadelphia Naval Yard, January 13, 1942

It has been recommended by one of the officers of the Naval Aircraft factory that we substitute aluminum alloys for the copper and beryllium copper now specified in our quick disconnect bonding jumper as it is believed by the test engineers there that this will eliminate the troubles from corrosion which cause disapproval of our bonding jumper.

SALES RESISTANCE

Essex Wire Corporation, January 19, 1942

An unsatisfactory call . . . antagonistic because they still do not seem to know just what they want. . . . Mr. _____ stated that they have been clamping insulation supports for more years than we have been in existence, and, therefore, they would let us specify that part of the die for wire clamp only and would take care of the insulation clamp to suit themselves. Mr. _____ also stated that they expect to solder every terminal regardless of swedging for the entire production. He claims that this soldering is required in the specification.

COMPETITION

Wright Field, Week of Januay 14 - 22, 1942

Cold reception with respect to our terminals. . . very much Thomas & Betts minded.

Curtiss Wright, Week of February 26 - March 3, 1942

I find that they are now using Thomas & Betts terminals . . . probably Thomas & Betts jumpers.

Goodyear Aircraft Factory, Week of February 26 - March 3, 1942

Using Thomas & Betts jumpers on tanks.

Boeing Aircraft Company, April 24, 1942

I found the usual evidence of having been preceded into the plant by a Thomas & Betts man.

EDUCATIONAL NEEDS

Crosley Corporation, January 21, 1942

Any calls made by salesmen on the trade, radio or otherwise . . . should be accompanied by an engineering representative. There is no doubt in my mind that [the salesmen] have some excellent contacts through personal friends in the radio industry. However, these men they know would invariably call in the engineers interested in our equipment and when this happens we should have an engineer present to represent our material and answer technical questions which are bound to be asked.

Textile Machine, April 10, 1942

With regard to the tools for installing our terminals. It seems that they had not been told how to put the terminals on, how to use the tools, or anything else, as they were worried about how to "solder" such a terminal. Mr. _____ was well pleased with our terminals after the use of the hand tool was demonstrated to him. I told him that where large quantities of terminals were used, a foot press or a power press of some kind was usually employed to install the terminal.

Sales Manager G. Earle Walker faced the same problems in the company offices in Elizabeth that Watts encountered in the field. The number one question to be answered was, how do you market the product? Walker, who was first, last, and always a marketing man, had to discover a way to get the name of his virtually unknown company known to consumers of its products while at the same time convincing them that Aircraft-Marine Products Inc.'s devices for terminating electrical connections were not only better than its competitors' but superior to the "old-fashioned" soldering techniques. His experience in the appliance industry had taught him that marketing your products through distributors was ineffective because, after you sold it to the distributor, you still faced the prospect of having to sell it to the dealer. Unlike users of more traditional electrical hardware products, an electrical conduit for example, consumers of solderless electrical connections would not respond to a typical salesman's call by saying, "I'll take some of those and some of those, etc." Walker knew they had to be convinced of the product's worth, and distributors could not adequately perform that difficult task. By the same token, placing the company's devices in the hands of manufacturer agents would prove only slightly less ineffective. Walker reasoned correctly that while Aircraft-Marine Products Inc. remained unknown, the average manufacturer's agent would be disinclined to push its products over any of the other items he sold.

Walker knew that he needed a sales force that could penetrate the market, one that could reach the accounts. But when he began working for Aircraft-Marine Products Inc., Walker had no sales force; nor had he money to hire one. There was no money for catalogues, for specification sheets, for broadsides, for brochures or flyers. What Walker had was an idea and a contact from his old days in Philadelphia and these he turned into a plan of action. Without a sales force, Walker was temporarily forced into using manufacturers' agents; his plan was to make them effective. Those agents, he figured, had to go into the field equipped with the best information available to sell the products. He needed, therefore, a piece of literature superior to anything a jobber could turn out.

He also needed a printer who would extend him credit. Walker called upon his old friends at Central Printing in Philadelphia, convinced them that Aircraft-Marine Products Inc. was a firm on the move, one that would someday make it big, and persuaded them to wait five or six months for their money. From Central Printing, Walker also got the name of an artist, someone who could design a brochure to make the products readily recognized in those areas where they would be used — in testing, electrical and mechanical engineering departments, and in the shop. The artist was Richard Renner of Renner Advertisers, Inc., and Walker, in engaging him to do the work, began what would become a long association with that firm.[15]

Walker planned to send the advertising piece to presidents of companies and their engineering heads with a cover letter setting forth the philosophy behind Aircraft-Marine Products Inc.'s termination program. In this letter, Walker explained to prospective purchasers that due to material shortages they had no alternative but to consider Aircraft-Marine Products Inc.'s method of electrical termination, and that he had statistical evidence attesting to its superior quality and to the results it brought the user. Even more important to Walker's sales program was the idea that Aircraft-Marine Products Inc., was not selling simply a product at a certain price; rather, it was selling a product and the installed cost of that product. In other words, the cost of the terminal itself was not the issue. What mattered was the final installed cost and because Aircraft-Marine Products Inc.'s system required less labor and material use, that final installed cost would be lower. That was what "precision engineering applied to the end of a wire" was all about.[16]

In addition to the direct mail campaign, Walker also began an extensive program of advertising in the leading publications in the aircraft, marine, communications, and commercial fields. He retained Renner Advertisers on a monthly basis to help develop a rational merchandising plan through advertising. Walker requested a modest $3,000 for publication advertising for the year 1942 and explained his strategy to Whitaker as the best, and perhaps only, means of dealing with Aircraft-Marine Products Inc.'s competition at that time: "I believe that the best way to effectively overcome Thomas & Betts' preponderance of sales-manpower is by direct mail advertising supplemented by a carefully worked out and comparatively inexpensive national advertising program." Walker's first direct appeal brought such a sizeable response that he was able to hire his first salesman. F. E. "Bud" Howell, whom Walker knew at Eureka, came to Aircraft-Marine Products Inc. to begin the follow-up on the new and valuable leads.[17]

But Walker's problems as sales manager did not end with the production of brochures and the hiring of salesmen. He needed a continual flow of information from the Engineering Division to equip his sales force with the technical data it needed to compete successfully. This became particularly urgent as a second competitor, the Burndy Company, came into prominence along with Thomas & Betts. Walker needed information, and he needed it daily. If, for example, one of his salesmen walked into a potential account and was asked whether Aircraft-Marine Products Inc. terminals were more resistant to corrosion than another brand, he had to be able to produce uncontestable scientific evidence substantiating his product's superiority in that area. And he had to produce it on the spot. Or, to take another example, if the customer wanted to know which one of Aircraft-Marine Products Inc.'s terminals was the equivalent of a competitor's terminal, the salesman was required to exhibit a chart indicating information of that nature. Then, of course, there was the matter of samples. A particular customer would want to see the final product and perhaps do his own testing in order to see if the claims made for the company's terminals were valid. Samples had to be available when the salesman needed them. And finally, after the order was placed, any problems with delivery and service became the headache of the sales department.

What Walker soon learned in those early years was that Aircraft-Marine Products Inc. was a company oriented to engineering and that the sales division was considered, at best, a necessary evil. That, at least, was how Walker perceived things, and it sometimes drove him mad. For want of a piece of information, a sale could be lost — permanently. Walker's memos on these problems crossed Whitaker's desk daily, sometimes several times a day. Whitaker, then head of engineering, had to respond or take action, or just cool his sales manager down a few degrees. A few examples provide the flavor of Walker's pleas.[18]

*MEMO: GEW to UAW, May 23, 1942

Mr. [Tom] Welsby spent the entire day Friday at the Glenn L. Martin plant, and the Purchasing Department is still 100% on our side. However, Mr. _____, and I think Mr. _____, are very much put out by the fact that they have not yet received samples of the terminals with insulation support and tools for application. T&B [Thomas & Betts] have been following them very closely, and both Mr. _____ and Mr. _____ indicated that unless these samples are made available next week, they intend to disregard our product entirely and go to T&B. This situation is quite serious, according to Mr. Welsby, and they seemed quite incensed by what they claim were numerous promises which we did not fulfill.

I believe this matter should receive your personal attention.

MEMO: GEW to UAW, May 30, 1942

I am receiving repeated requests for corrosion and resistance test data from new contacts where we are making an endeavor to develop new accounts in new fields of application for our product. I am informed that such data is not yet available but I believe you told me some tests were being made either at Hoover or MIT. Do you expect to have them in the near future?

MEMO: GEW to UAW, July 27, 1942

Need comparison charts [to Thomas & Betts and Burndy] . . . field organization is considerably handicapped by lack of comparison charts of Thomas & Betts and Burndy equivalents.

---

*For an explanation of the memo abbreviations see page 273.

MEMO: GEW to UAW, September 4, 1942

To date this month I have received three cancellations, reasons for cancellations customers could not wait for material and secured same elsewhere.

MEMO   GEW to UAW, October 19, 1942

I dislike very much to again disturb you about problems of delivery and service, but here are two instances which indicate a condition which certainly should be corrected.

Walker was obsessed with competition from Thomas & Betts and Burndy, a point he hammered home in memo after memo. With the war on overseas, Walker often adopted the rhetoric of battle when posing his problems to his boss. He told Whitaker in August, "As you know, our sales organization works under tremendous odds in respect to manpower and seniority of our largest competitor, so we need every possible weapon in the hands of our organization to help us in our activities." In 1942, Aircraft-Marine Products Inc., like the United States military establishment, was still the underdog in Walker's view of the situation.[19]

Whitaker, in his engineer's capacity, was neither idle nor unresponsive nor complacent about the matters continually on Walker's mind. Understaffed and overworked, engineering had to respond first to immediate needs and, as a result of those pressures, had great difficulty developing the new products demanded by customer requirements. Through his salesmen Walker learned that this account or that one wanted some variation on a connector or hand tool and wanted it yesterday. The realities of business decision making sometimes caused Whitaker to reacquaint his sales manager with the facts of productive, profit-making life. The matter of producing two- and three-way connectors is a good case. "Due to the pressure of other work," he told Walker early in April, 1942, "it has not been put into production. If substantial orders were received for this, we would be willing to go ahead with the idea, but with the present materials and labor situation, we should not promise deliveries earlier than approximately three months from date of receipt of order, with priorities."[20] Whitaker always believed that the exigencies of wartime business set research and development work back several years. He liked the situation no better than Walker but he knew that a decision to develop and produce an item like the two- and three-way connector had to be guided by marketplace demands. Only with a significant demand could he afford to go ahead.

New products that were in demand were being developed and manufactured by Aircraft-Marine Products Inc. For example, one, called the Diamond Grip Insulation Support Terminal, became available in midyear, 1942, and immediately turned into a best seller. In a detailed memo to Walker, Whitaker described the terminal in a manner useful for sales information purposes.

> This terminal is a scientifically engineered and tested product throughout, precision built, and tools are to be supplied which will insure the precision application of the terminal to the wire. This terminal, in general, will give the best electrical and mechanical properties of any terminal so far developed. Its electrical and mechanical properties surpass every government specification. At the same time, it is the lightest and most compact of any insulation support terminal that has come to our attention.[21]

With this newly developed termination device, Aircraft-Marine Products Inc. became a real factor in the competitive field, and its better financed and more experienced competition began to take notice of the new situation in the solderless connectors field. Their immediate response to the new market condition was predictable: price cutting as a means of holding on to their share of the existing market.

Aircraft-Marine Products Inc. had to follow suit. By the beginning of June, 1942, price cutting was already well underway. Whitaker told his directors about it and described his method of dealing with the problem. "Price cutting is still being encountered from our competitors but the cost reduction program that was started two or three months ago is beginning to show results and, so far, manufacturing costs have been reduced so as to maintain our profit in spite of reduced prices." One method of reducing manufacturing costs was to find another supplier who could handle the increasing volume of orders from Aircraft-Marine Products Inc. at a lower price. The Gaynor Electric Company of Bridgeport, Connecticut, was the beneficiary in this instance, and Whitaker looked forward to making it his principal manufacturing firm.[22]

A major reason for Aircraft-Marine Products Inc.'s considerable impact on the market was its ability to gain government approval of its products. Considerable time and effort were required to convince the necessary agencies to look at a product, test it, approve it and finally place the company name on the list of approved sources. Whitaker and his associates made frequent trips to Washington all through the year to meet with people like Lt. Vernon H. Grant and discuss their latest innovations, the state of their development work, their ability to design and then produce devices to meet the needs of the large manufacturers, and their intense desire to get on approved lists. Aircraft-Marine Products Inc.'s growing success along these lines provided another source of worry for competitors. In June, for example, the company was placed on the approved list for solderless connectors for all army tanks. Previously, the only name on the list was Thomas & Betts.[23]

A fair portion of Aircraft-Marine Products Inc.'s success can also be attributed to the needs of the aircraft manufacturers. In their effort to meet F.D.R.'s goal of 125,000 aircraft by 1943-44, they sought every means available to step up production methods in their plants. Any new, workable technology that could cut production time served their own interest. Particularly crucial were more standardized products from their subcontractors in order to facilitate their own production procedures. As they turned more and more to solderless type connectors, they needed to assure themselves of adequate sources of supply and, even more important, of uniform parts numbers as well as application tools that would work on all types of competitive terminals. Shop foremen scrounging for the proper tool to apply one terminal or another grew frustrated in their efforts to keep things running smoothly. Managements wanted something to unplug that kind of bottleneck.

Procedures for air materiel procurement, including a more standardized approach to the production of aircraft and their accessories, had been in effect for some years before the war and with the war became only more sophisticated in detail and administration. The history of government industry partnership in these matters need not concern us here except to remark that during the war procurement and standardization procedures came to affect every product used in the construction of warplanes. Electrical accessories were no exception. The National Aircraft Standards Committee was just one of literally hundreds of similar groups that met periodically to make policy applicable to the production and use of aircraft material.[24]

One subgroup of this committee was the Electrical, Radio and Instrument Installation SubCommittee, which by May, 1942, was meeting for the sixth time on matters of common concern; it was the subcommittee that most affected the businesses of those engaged in solderless terminal manufacturing. Representatives from Douglas, Hughes, North American, Vultee, Lockheed, and Glenn L. Martin met on May 21, 1942, to wrestle with the problem of a more standardized terminal and application tool.   The major aircraft manufacturing concerns at the meeting concentrated mainly on the tool problem and directed their major suppliers to work it out among themselves:

> It is the considered opinion of the committee that the first action to be taken with respect to universal tooling should be an attempt to get the terminal manufacturers to come to an agreement within themselves. It was accordingly agreed that copies of these minutes should be sent to the Thomas & Betts Company, the Aircraft-Marine Products Company Inc. and Burndy Engineering Company, Inc. , and their comments requested. In the event that they wish to confer directly with the subcommittee, a meeting will be called for this purpose.

The aircraft manufacturers were impatient for this problem to be solved quickly. In the past, their pleas for industry participation in decision making of this kind had gone unheeded. Now, the subcommittee insisted that the three companies named reply with their comments immediately, asking with heavy handed irony that they "inconvenience themselves to the extent of responding promptly."[25]

Aircraft-Marine Products Inc.'s West Coast representative, Don Porter, was fully aware of the aircraft industry's wishes about standardized terminals and tools. For some weeks he had been hearing all about it. The standards engineer at Lockheed, he wrote Walker,

> wants me to convey a message to you to the effect that, in the interest of National Defense, that our company, as well as T&B and Burndy, should get together and standardize on some tool that could be used on all three types of terminals. His claim is that every one of us would benefit. He even went so far as to say that he was going to take this up with the National Aircraft Standards Committee.[26]

Obviously, he had.

But the promise of mutual benefit was not that clear in U. A. Whitaker's mind. "The question would immediately arise," he told Walker in response to Don Porter's story, "as to whose tool would be used as standard." He was doubtful that Aircraft-Marine Products Inc.'s new double crimp tool with the insulation support crimping arrangement would work on the Thomas & Betts terminal. He suggested that tests be made on the T&B terminal with the

Aircraft-Marine Products Inc. tool. If standardization was to be, Whitaker was anxious that it be accomplished on their hand tool. "This new tool," he added, "has several features which we believe will get quite good patent protection so that if it should be used as standard, it might react to our advantage."[27]

About a month later, at the end of June, Thomas & Betts and Burndy had both written letters expressing their views on the tool standardization matter, but Aircraft-Marine Products Inc. had not. Neither of Aircraft-Marine Products Inc.'s two major competitors had responded favorably to the subcommittee's "cause of defense" approach. Independently or not, both warned that antitrust laws might make it inadvisable for the three terminal manufacturers to get together. The chairman of the subcommittee was outraged. According to Walker, he told the two reporting firms that "the aircraft manufacturers had given the automobile manufacturers all their secrets for the cause of defense and he can see no reason why the terminal manufacturers cannot do likewise among themselves." Aircraft-Marine Products Inc.'s failure to respond also irritated the subcommittee chairman and he hinted, not very gently, that if the company did not reply soon it would find itself out of the picture. Adding threats to chastisement, the chairman spread the word that if the terminal manufacturers did not come to some agreement, a new committee in cooperation with the army and navy would just go ahead and do their work for them.[28]

Whitaker was not unconcerned about the legal ramifications raised by tool standardization, but he was bothered more by the subcommittee chairman's judgment about the company's hand tool, which he did not favor. Walker learned, probably through Porter, that the chairman believed the hand tool used on the now popular Diamond Grip Terminal would not work on any others and was, therefore, not "a step forward to the idea of standardization." Aircraft-Marine Products Inc., having designed and produced a better device for the aircraft industry, now found itself trapped, paradoxically in the dilemma of standardization, which might in the end endanger the continued production of this new, profitable item, and perhaps the continued existence of the company itself.[29]

"The battle is on," Walker informed Whitaker on July 17. The subcommittee had indeed gone to Washington on the tool problem and now the Army-Navy Board was beginning the process of testing possible devices. Walker tried to get a commitment from Whitaker to take part in the hand tool derby by getting a sample off for testing purposes. Don Porter informed Walker enthusiastically, though not necessarily accurately, that Lockheed was using the Diamond Grip tools on T&B terminals. Vern Carlson, in engineering, read this report and penciled a note at the bottom: "Looks like a good stride toward standardization on our tool??" Walker forwarded the Porter note and the Carlson comment on to Whitaker. The excited Porter was convinced that the aircraft people meant business now and urged Walker, who in turn urged Whitaker, to get on the bandwagon while there was still time.[30]

As things developed, there proved to be plenty of time. Meeting after meeting was called in Washington, with all the participants appearing for interminable conversations and arguments. The Bureau of Aeronautics, from experiences they had gone through, believed that standardization on any one tool was improbable. A three-week testing program at Wright Field was underway by September, but the results were not as yet in. Other governmental research facilities were making the same kind of tests and holding the same kinds of conferences. At one meeting in Washington, an officer from the Navy Department Ordinance Bureau announced that in at least one of its programs employing terminals, tool standardization procedures would be dropped for the present. One of his associates stated that in the event of tool standardization directives, they would do what they had always done in the past, order a certain manufacturer's terminals and tools and assign them to a specific ship, thereby assuring that no problem would arise.[31]

Bill Watts, as Aircraft-Marine Products Inc.'s field representative, was forced to attend a considerable number of these meetings, and now began to get the message, or rather the moral, appropriate to all this hubbub over tooling. After a particularly long and fruitless meeting, he reported to Whitaker and Walker that "there is a great deal of confusion in this whole standardization program because none of the Government Bureaus keep in close enough contact with one another to prevent duplication of effort and we, in turn, are forced to attend all of these meetings and go through the same rigamarole at each meeting." And if all this was not senseless enough, Watts was learning that none of it would matter in the last analysis. More and more engineers from the aircraft manufacturing companies were telling him that although they had no objection to a standardized tool, "they all seem to feel that it would be much better if they used the tool recommended by the terminal manufacturer on their own production assembly lines."[32] After 1942 there is no further mention of tool standardization in the company's files.

As so often happens, while high-level deliberations of the tool-standardization variety were absorbing the energies of the managers, the people at or near the bottom of the organization chart were busy affecting the changes. What the engineers and production people wanted was a product that was efficient to handle and one, above all, that did the job for which it was intended. They seemed to be finding it in Aircraft-Marine Products Inc.'s Diamond Grip Terminal. The whole question of tool standardization was merely an academic one to them. With the November results in, Whitaker proudly announced to his directors that the company's backlog of orders was now the highest in its history — $500,000 — and that over half the orders for November were for the Diamond Grip Terminal. But even more important, these Diamond Grip orders came from a variety of new accounts, most notably several who were among the most insistent on the standardized tool question. Douglas placed a big order. Vega, a subsidiary of Lockheed, came over to Diamond Grip Terminals exclusively.[33]

Vega in making the decision, Whitaker told the directors, became the first major West Coast aircraft-manufacturer to adopt completely the company's terminal. And, although Aircraft-Marine Products Inc. had done some volume of business with Douglas before, it had had to sell the terminal at much lower prices than it wished in order to compete successfully with Thomas & Betts. Now good news! So satisfied were both Vega and Douglas with the Diamond Grip Terminal, that they were now willing to pay $3. 00 to $4. 00 more per thousand for the company's product over the price they could pay for a competitive device. The year-long pricewar was over Aircraft-Marine Products Inc. was now established and rolling forward. Sales for the year would equal about $830,000, an increase of half a million dollars over 1941. As Whitaker had noted earlier in the year, "The war program is really beginning to speed up." In 1943, it would be speeding even faster.[34]

10. The War Years

A week after the Japanese attack on Pearl Harbor, Earl Kail heard a rumor that the government was considering setting up an antiaircraft detachment at the McKinley Airport to protect Republic Steel and the Timken Roller Bearing Company in the event the Axis powers bombed the area. In the shock waves that struck America in the wake of the Japanese bombardment of our Pacific military installations, even such unlikely possibilities seemed reasonable and frightening. Measures like the re-registration of all licensed flyers, certainly an irritating inconvenience, did not seem illogical or excessive to those affected by the ruling. However, while a ruling in itself might appear necessary and therefore reasonable, the bureaucratic process for putting the regulation into effect often seemed to be irrationality itself.[1]

Early in 1942, George Swayze at McKinley Air Transport met just such a set of irrational procedures; not surpisingly it cost him money, or rather, it cost U. A. Whitaker money. The Civil Aeronautics Administration (CAA) issued a regulation under which only its agency could determine those airfields that could be designated as landing areas. What this meant in practice was that each airport wishing to be certified as a landing field had to file complicated applications with the CAA and then await the arrival of its inspectors. Meanwhile, no business could be conducted at the airfield. Swayze waited day after day, until the last of Whitaker's most recent loan of $700 was used up. An additional $300 was requested to tide the operation over until its planes could fly again; Whitaker sent it along with a note expressing his sympathy and full understanding of what such a problem posed for a business enterprise like MAT.[2]

McKinley Airport eventually received CAA approval as a landing field, and then Swayze encountered his next difficulty with the agency, now over MAT's certification to train advanced flyers. MAT officials had thought Earl Kail had received that certification some months earlier, but Swayze discovered this was not the case. The description of MAT's flying course was quite precisely stated, and the application was rejected. Then it was rejected again, and again, and again — four times, in fact — for the same reason. As delay followed delay, more money was requested from Whitaker to keep things afloat. Swayze was so dejected over the situation that he asked

Whitaker if he might be interested in selling the operation, for several people recently had indicated an interest in buying it.[3]

Whitaker, certainly justified by now in throwing in the MAT sponge, said no. He gave Swayze a vote of confidence and the financial support he needed to carry on until business picked up. It was, coincidentally, at this time, March 1942, that Whitaker's other business venture appeared to be on the rocks. In response to his "darkest hour" letter to his directors, Whitaker received a similar vote of confidence and the promise that all the money he needed to stay afloat would be forthcoming. He must have reasoned that he could do no less for Swayze at MAT.[4]

Earl Kail was no longer with MAT; he had taken a job ferrying military aircraft for Pan American Airways. It seemed, therefore, to Whitaker that this was the time to reorganize the management of MAT and establish a corporate structure complete with a board of directors. He asked Swayze to hold a meeting and elect officers, much as had been done some months earlier when Aircraft-Marine Products Inc. was born. Swayze was amused with the new formality but dutifully reported that the meeting of the directors had been held (Swayze and MAT's attorney Frederic Wilkins were in attendance) and that the following list of officers had been elected: President, U. A. Whitaker; Vice-President and Secretary, Frederic Wilkins; Vice-President and Treasurer, George Swayze. "Aren't you thrilled?" Swayze joked.[5]

Whitaker soon won another election as president. At the July, 1942, meeting of Aircraft-Marine Products Inc.'s board of directors, Robert Hixon resigned to take over the newly created post of chairman of the board. With the departure of S.N. Buchanan, it was decided to bestow the presidential title on the person who was actually running the company. Whitaker, now in name as well as fact, became president. Moreover, as the company began to hold its own, it was possible for the Midland interests to become somewhat less visible, at least as far as the public was concerned.[6]

As Aircraft-Marine Products Inc. became more directly involved in government contract work, it like McKinley Air Transport, had necessarily more contact with federal bureaucracies and federal regulations. The National Aircraft Standards Committee's attempt at standardization (see Chapter 9) was only one interesting example. What had begun as a perfectly reasonable approach to the problems of war production ended with a bureaucratic maze of overlapping and repetitious investigations. Other such instances would follow.

Take, for example, the matter of minimum wage requirements. Late in 1942, with the prospect of larger direct government contracts in sight, Aircraft-Marine Products Inc. was forced to think about minimum wage and maximum hour laws as they were embodied in the Walsh-Healy Public Contracts Act passed in 1936. This legislation and the regulations that followed had a proper and reasonable intent: to allow the secretary of labor to regulate hours and wages for those working in manufacturing or shipping operations for firms holding government contracts in excess of $10,000. The secretary of labor had the authority, in this broadly written bill, to adjust the hours and wages of those workers to conform to the hours and wages of persons employed in similar work in the same locality.

Aircraft-Marine Products Inc.'s in-house legal adviser, R. J. Szukala, investigated the problem and issued a six-page opinion regarding the effect of the Walsh-Healy Act on the company's manufacturing operations. Szukala concluded, among other things, that the provisions of this act did cover the products manufactured by the company. Francis W. Thomas, the company's lawyer from the firm of Lindabury, Depue and Faulks, agreed but posed the further question of whether aircraft products used in shipbuilding were included in the scope of the ruling. He suggested that Aircraft-Marine Products Inc. write the Labor department to get a further ruling. On January 23, 1943, the letter went out to Secretary of Labor Frances L. Perkins. Five days later, one of the Department's administrators replied:

> The minimum wage determination for the aircraft manufacturing industry would be applicable to items sold for uses other than aircraft ONLY if the primary design and construction of the items fitted them especially for use on aircraft, with their application to other than aircraft use being incidentally convenient. If the material being used, let us say, on ships differs in design and construction from items for use on aircraft or if the items for use on ships are regular commercial electrical items, there is no minimum wage determination applicable to their manufacture.

In other words, employees working on terminals to be used in aircraft were subject to minimum wage determinations; employees working on terminals for ships were not, as long as the design and construction of their terminals are different from the ones being manufactured for aircraft. Since minimum wage rates could vary from product to product, it was possible for a company to have more than one rate applicable at the same time in the same factory. The

Labor Department, however, had worked out an answer for this problem.

> If employees are engaged within the same work week on products subject to two or more minimum rates of pay, they must be paid the appropriate rate of pay for each hour so worked if your payroll records clearly indicate the time spent on each type of work.

The language is clear and straightforward; the ruling made sense on paper. But in practice it proved, at best, complex and unwieldy.[7]

A second example of government-business relationships in 1943 illustrates the kinds of difficulties encountered by relatively small firms like Aircraft-Marine Products Inc. One of the company's customers questioned the price of a particular bonding tab. The customer in question was making the finished product for the Air Corps Materiel Division, which quite properly became involved in the negotiations. Its representative considered the price of the bonding tab excessive and properly asked Aircraft-Marine Products Inc. for an explanation. Then, not quite so properly, it requested that Aircraft-Marine Products Inc. "submit a break-down showing the method of operation on this part, time required to manufacture one unit and your hourly quoting rate." Since few if any business concerns sell anything strictly on the basis of the manufacturing cost of a particular item, the request presented real difficulties.

The request first came to G. Earle Walker who forwarded it to C.J. Fredricksen. Fredricksen responded by explaining the pricing structure in terms that made no reference to the cost breakdown requested:

> Evidently you have not taken into account the fact that considerable money was spent for engineering work, developing work, and for tools in connection with the bonding tab before it could be manufactured. Also, up to this time our production and sales of bonding tabs have been very low and we have no indication that they will greatly increase in the future, therefore, the preliminary cost of engineering, development and tools has been spread over a very thin volume.

Fredricksen suggested that if the volume went up, the price would go down. Fredricksen was telling the truth about Aircraft-Marine Products Inc.'s volume in bonding tabs; in 1943, bonding tabs represented an infinitesimal . 003 percent of total sales. In further support of his contention that the price of the bonding tabs was not excessive, Fredricksen pointed to the low profits of the company during 1942 — 4. 8 percent of sales before income taxes and 2. 1 percent after income taxes.[8]

If the Air Corps Materiel Division did not find Fredricksen's arguments convincing, he had a further suggestion. It could, if it wished, seek another source for the bonding tabs; furthermore, he added, "we will gladly authorize you to do so without any license or royalty charge if you will advise us accordingly." In other words, Fredricksen was telling the government agency they could buy from another manufacturer and Aircraft-Marine Products Inc. would donate their innovation, free of charge, with all the accompanying engineering and development work, to the cause of national defense. Aircraft-Marine Products Inc., like AMP Incorporated later, never took any government funds for research, always using their own resources for that purpose. They also always offered the government the benefits of any of their independent research at no cost. The engineering business philosphy behind this policy was the one the company adhered to: if a customer (government or other) wanted to buy a shelf item, AMP Incorporated would be glad to sell it to them and show them that the installed cost would be lower than its competitor's, regardless of the selling price of the shelf item in question. That is what "engineering the hell out of a product" meant.[9]

During wartime, however, Americans anticipated and accepted the government's need to control most aspects of civilian life. For Americans on the home front, such control seldom meant more than inconvenience caused by rationing, regulations, and restrictions. Patriotism was the order of the day and winning the war the number one priority. Like millions of Americans, Whitaker understood that priority. When the Office of Strategic Services (OSS) requisitioned his registered Minox camera for its intelligence work, he immediately complied by sending it off to Washington. These inconveniences were part of the exigencies of war, and a small price to pay for living in a country unscarred by battle or bombings.[10]

On the other hand, all of these minor encounters with government — from MAT to Minox cameras — only reinforced Whitaker's distaste for doing business with Washington. "The big problem these days," he wrote his Hoover friend W. C. Davidson, "is not manufacturing but sales, government regulation, taxes, priorities and all that sort of thing." Sales during the war, of course, meant sales to or for the government. "When and if this war ever ends," he told field engineer Bill Watts, "I certainly want to get into a business where I would never be required to sell the government anything." In the meantime, Whitaker had to settle for what was possible; the postwar period was only something to be dreamed about in 1943.[11]

If government-related business was irritating and not particularly profitable for Aircraft-Marine Products Inc., it certainly was improving its sales picture. The first quarter of 1943 produced a sales volume of over $500,000 and the second quarter looked just as promising. The company was rapidly outgrowing its current production facilities, and some kind of move appeared to be in order. For a short period, Whitaker had considered building a plant in Union, New Jersey, but that idea, never altogether to Whitaker's taste, had major disadvantages, as a professional plant location survey, authorized by the board of directors in 1942, revealed. The preponderance of war-related industries in northern New Jersey was a major negative factor: suitable buildings were impossible to find, material shortages and government restrictions largely precluded new construction, and the labor pool was not extensive. Aircraft-Marine Products Inc. needed a location where there was not too much war-related industry, but where there was adequate industry to assure a reasonable labor pool and a choice of buildings to house production facilities. The survey results pointed to central Pennsylvania as the most attractive possibility, and R. J. Szukala, early in 1943, was charged with the task of following up on the plan for relocation.[12]

At this juncture, Aircraft-Marine Products Inc. was already pretty far along toward decentralization, a situation that had undoubtedly developed out of Whitaker's philosophy that a company should not attempt to do something that others can do well or better. Thus, the company had left its terminal manufacturing requirements in the hands of Stimpson in Brooklyn, later adding Gaynor Electric in Bridgeport to take care of its growing needs. The small operation in Glen Rock, under contract to Aircraft-Marine Products Inc. since late in 1941, was yet another source of terminal supply. The production facilities in Elizabeth took care of the assembling, packing, and shipment of the completed terminals and manufactured a fair portion of the aluminum and copper bonding jumpers that were still being used in the manufacture of aircraft. Decentralization had become a fact, but just when it became an institutional goal is not entirely clear. Two unrelated incidents, however, in the winter and spring of 1943 evidently convinced Whitaker that decentralized operatons were not only desirable but necessary.

In February, 1943, the employees of the giant Phelps Dodge manufacturing operation, directly across the street from tiny Aircraft-Marine Products Inc., went out on a wildcat strike. Phelps Dodge's 17,000 unionized employees were joined by Aircraft-Marine

Products Inc.'s 17 affiliated production workers. Although the strike was brief, Phelps Dodge lost its Army-Navy "E" for efficiency, and Whitaker gained some insight into the problems of being shut down due to labor disputes. The strike helped convince Whitaker of the value of being decentralized. It probably also convinced him that staying on in Elizabeth was impossible.[13]

Whitaker, certainly, had no intention of expanding his facilities in Elizabeth, preferring to subcontract with Stimpson, Gaynor, and Shepperd Industries, his own outlet in Glen Rock. The Glen Rock location looked particularly attractive to Whitaker in the face of labor unrest. The nearly 200 people who worked in the Glen Rock facility were longtime natives of the area. They were dependable, family oriented and adhered to older American values, among them, giving an employer "a day's work for a day's pay."

In mid-1943 the second of two incidents occurred to reinforce Whitaker's decentralization theory. In May, lightning struck the Glen Rock production building; the ensuing fire totally destroyed the building as well as most of the machinery and equipment. The losses were minimal; no one was hurt, and the building was over forty years old. Nonetheless, Whitaker was worried about the fire's impact on production. "The greatest possible danger is the possibility of loss of customers due to failure to meet deliveries," he wrote his directors. Meanwhile, the resourceful Shepperd had presses set up in every available vacant building, including an empty grange hall in Seven Valleys and in Shepperd's own nonoperating gas station in Glen Rock. By the Monday following the fire, production was back to about 75 percent of normal, and Whitaker predicted that in about ten days in would be running at or near 100 percent. Whitaker believed the loss would be substantial but that it would not materially affect the year's overall volume. Yet, the lesson was clear. Accidents of nature could be as destructive in cutting back production as strikes. Multiple production units to guard against either eventuality became the goal of Aircraft-Marine Products Inc. for the future.[14]

When Whitaker sent Szukala out on his plant location trip early in March, 1943, the fire at Glen Rock was still two months in the future. Both men were, of course, thinking about labor problems and the survey's first choice for a new location proved to be out of the question for that reason. Reading, Pennsylvania had looked promising because of the large number of unemployed, but Szukala struck it off the list after a short visit. Reading, he wrote, is "not desirable in view of its socialistic municipal government and very

troublesome union." Scranton, also in eastern Pennsylvania, failed as
well to impress Szukala. Scranton, he reported, "is generally
depressed economically, ugly, railroad service poor, housing difficult,
social activities limited, public education below average." But in his
visits to several Scranton manufacturing plants, Szukala noted that
union organizing campaigns appeared to have little impact on small
operations employing between fifty and one hundred people, at least
in the Scranton area.[15]

A second choice of the location survey had been the area around
York, Pennsylvania, just below Harrisburg, in the south-central part
of the state. Whitaker, as well as Vern Carlson and Ken Neijstrom,
had spent some days in the York area looking for available factories.
Whitaker particularly liked the countryside south of York; it
reminded him of Missouri and looked like a good place to raise
mules. But what might have been productive mule-raising country
did not prove equally appropriate for fabricating terminals and hand
tools. No buildings were available and the search had to be moved
elsewhere.[16]

While the Aircraft-Marine Products Inc. people were looking the
York area over, they learned that Harrisburg itself might be a
possibility. A good number of skilled tool and die makers lived in
the area; they had been previously employed by a firm that was no
longer in business. Harrisburg had not turned up on the survey's list
of possible locations, and before Szukala left on his own survey trip,
he was instructed to write the Chamber of Commerce in Harrisburg
for information. Through his correspondence he learned why
Harrisburg had not been included. The Chamber told Szukala that
"the town had no housing available and would not desire any new
enterprise in the community." Despite this negative reply, Szukala
put Harrisburg on his itinerary and after his unpleasant Scranton visit
made his way there.[17]

Szukala's meeting with Harrisburg Chamber of Commerce officials
was fruitful. At first they continued to insist that housing problems
presented a major problem for new industry, but by the end of the
long afternoon meeting their attitude had changed. Szukala
speculated that perhaps the Chamber was dominated by some of the
larger industries in Harrisburg and, as he put it, "was instructed to
keep out new industries [in order to assure] an adequate labor
supply." At any rate, the Chamber became cooperative and Szukala
was pleased with what he saw — two fine hotels, the Harrisburger
and the Penn-Harris; attractive shops, clean stores and modern office

buildings; the state governmental complex; well-paved streets — in all, a pleasant community in which to locate a new industry.

Szukala left Harrisburg on March 12 to make a quick tour of Lancaster and Lewistown before returning to the capitol for further negotiations. Apparently the Chamber was now fully convinced that Aircraft-Marine Products Inc.'s labor requirements would not threaten any other businesses in Harrisburg. A Sunday morning meeting was arranged, and after lunch Szukala was shown a number of possible location sites. An automobile agency building at 1521-31 North Fourth Street looked perfect. He described its features in great detail, commented favorably on its rental cost, noted it could be either leased or purchased, and pointed out that its location in the city was ideal. Another feature that pleased Szukala was that the building was set on a high section of the town, therefore reasonably safe from flooding. "I was told that Harrisburg suffers extraordinary floods every fifty years, which do a great amount of damage," he reported. And he added, "the last sizeable flood in the area was in 1936." Szukala seemed to be convinced that Harrisburg was the right spot. Motoring through the small Pennsylvania communities and the farmland around the capitol, he was impressed with the beauty of the area and with the possibility of setting up satellite plants outside of town.[18]

During the week following Szukala's March 18 report on plant locations, he began negotiations for the building on North Fourth Street, and an arrangement was soon agreed upon with a local bank, which provided an option to purchase the property after a reasonable period of time. By mid-June the proper government agencies had given permission for the necessary repair work and the board approved contracts for remodeling the building.[19]

By the end of June, the state Chamber of Commerce became interested in Aircraft-Marine Products Inc. and began to request information from the Harrisburg Chamber. Szukala noted that "the curiosity in town about our company was reaching great heights." Szukala assured the Harrisburg Chamber that on the day the lease was signed he would give the local papers all the information they needed about the company and its plans for Harrisburg. He also promised Chamber officials that Whitaker would provide a statement for publication "about the cooperation and self-sacrifice of time and effort by the members of the Chamber in informing us of the desirability of locating in Harrisburg and aiding us in details of settling in the town." The once reluctant Harrisburg Chamber of

Commerce now wanted some credit, which they had, after their
initial false start, earned. The Chamber's Annual Report for 1942-43
emphasized the key role it played in bringing Aircraft-Marine
Products Inc. to Harrisburg. By the end of 1943, that move was
complete.[20] Despite strike, fire, and moving, Aircraft-Marine
Products Inc.'s sales for 1943 were better than double the 1942
figures. Approximately $2. 2 million was recorded for the year, but
profits were just as meager as in 1942 due to high excess profit taxes
and the expenses of the move to Harrisburg. Business prospects for
1944 looked good to Whitaker although the firm was beginning to
feel the effects of government cancellation orders as early as
November 1943. Whitaker reported to his directors just before the
end of 1943 that the company was getting a "large number of
cancellations on account of the government terminating prime
contracts." Fortunately, the impact of the cancellatons had in part
been offset by an increase in new business, but Whitaker warned his
associates to look for more and more cancellations as the war drew to
a close.[21]

A fair portion of the new business was the result of research and
development work leading to new products. A new splicing terminal
was ready for the market at the beginning of 1944, and Whitaker was
cautiously optimistic about its chances: "The new splicing terminal
looks very good. But like a show on Broadway, however, the only
way to determine whether it will be a real hit or not is to see what
happens."[22] Through the first half of the year, Whitaker noted a great
deal of interest and enthusiasm for this and other new items, but
bookings were not as good as might have been expected. Part of the
reason for the lag in bookings was that production on new airplanes,
such as the B-29 was behind schedule, and new items like the
preinsulated terminal and the disconnect splice to be used on the
aircraft promised prospective, but not immediate, sales. In a letter
accompanying the firm's April financial statement, Whitaker noted
that these prospects were good but added realistically that "prospects
do not improve the profit picture."[23]

The spring of 1944 was a crucial period for Aircraft-Marine
Products Inc. A good number of separate but related problems had to
be juggled at one time. The increasing number of wartime contract
cancellations suggested that the company had better begin quickly to
think about peacetime business and to make plans for the postwar
period. G. Earle Walker, for example, prepared a long memo in
April, 1944, entitled A Consideration of Post War Marketing

Practices as They Relate to A-MP Products Currently Available. Walker's purpose was to identify the postwar market and suggest the best means for penetrating it. The major market problem in Walker's mind was overcoming the great advantages held by Aircraft-Marine Products Inc.'s competitors due to long years of marketing experience complete with a network of long-established distributors. Although the main point of the memorandum was to suggest that the company hook up with already established distributors rather than attempt to go through the long and costly process of creating new ones, Walker's analysis encompassed a very broad marketing organization structure.

Walker identified four major marketing areas and then ranked them in importance. Number one was the "bread and butter" category — the multiple market that, according to Walker, consisted of "a multiplicity of small and large manufacturers, public utilities, transportation companies . . . municipal and state agencies, federal government agencies, building contractors and all other outlets using terminals for maintenance or for other purposes than consumer goods." Second on his priority list was the service market, which would be furnished a variety of kits for electrical and automotive dealers, service stations, and consumer goods manufacturers. Third was the consumer goods market per se. Finally, in fourth position, was the export market. About this latter market, Walker suggested that already established export agencies be used because of the great expense involved in maintaining a separate department within the present company structure.[24]

Although the export market held a low postwar priority for Walker, overseas sales possibilities were not neglected even during the war. After Whitaker's initial attempts to make a liaison with Hoover Ltd., other outlets were considered. Aircraft-Marine Products Inc. was still vitally interested in getting into the British war market and attempted to arrange for a technical man from the company to go to England to advise the British on how to use the solderless terminals. Whitaker even considered going himself, perhaps because the adventure associated with such a trip in wartime appealed to him. Priorities for such travel were hard to come by, however. First one had to go through a distributor, who in turn had to convince the British Ministry of Aircraft Production that English manufacturers needed such a device. Whitaker's planned trip never did materialize, wartime conditions making it impossible. Whitaker explained the situation to Lt. Vernon H. Grant late in October. "I didn't get to

England as about the time I was ready to go the robots were a little too thick and they would not give me permission to go." Aircraft-Marine Products Inc. was, in fact, represented in England but it would be some years before the company made any real impression on that market. Nevertheless, before the end of the war, the company established an export office in Chicago to handle all foreign transactions.[25]

One very major consideration in terms of postwar planning was that pesky problem of contract cancellations. The real danger was that if cancellations came in large bunches, their settlement might involve such a considerable period of time that a small company like Aircraft-Marine Products Inc. could suffer fatal financial effects. To offset this possibility, Whitaker and his financial advisers determined that the firm needed additional financing to carry it through the transition period. They decided to apply for what was called a Victory Loan (V Loan for short), but applying for one and getting it were two different things. It was that familiar business problem — you had to have money in order to borrow more.

Whitaker explained the complicated problem and process to director Robert Hixon early in May, 1944.

> In order for our company to meet the formula to permit a 90% guaranteed V Loan, our current position will have to be improved by $130,000. Without this additional capital we would have to apply for a 100% government guaranteed loan. Such a loan if granted, which is extemely doubtful, places numerous restrictions on the operation of the business.

> It is my belief that securing of a V Loan is of extreme importance to the company in order to insure against the possibility of getting involved in endless discussion and possible litigation at the end of the war when contract cancellations will not be settled in the matter of a few months but may take several years, and, therefore, any company that is not covered by a V Loan may easily be put out of business before settlement of claims can be obtained.

The matter of being able to discount the company's receivables at a bank while cancellation contracts were being settled was, in Whitaker's opinion, crucial. In the meantime, additional capital requirements were necessary even to apply for the loan. Whitaker suggested to Hixon that additional funds might be raised by selling common stock. Specifically, he wanted to increase the stock holdings of the present stockholders by requesting that all warrants be exercised now and that each stockholder increase his holdings approximately 50 percent, to increase working capital by $75,000. He noted, in closing, that in conversations he had had with Carl Hamilton on this subject, Hamilton had voiced approval of the plan, provided that he and the others could raise the additional capital necessary to participate in the stock-holding increase idea.

Whitaker acquired the balance of the $130,000 of working capital needed by suggesting that Midland purchase an Aircraft-Marine Products Inc. note in the amount of $55,000, later to be converted into 1,100 shares of preferred stock. This note was then discounted by $11,000, which in turn was used to purchase an additional 1,100 shares of the company's common stock at $10.00 a share. Thus, the total of these three transactions — the exercising of warrants, the purchase of an additional 50 percent of common stock, and the sale of the Aircraft-Marine Products Inc. note, plus the 1,100 shares of Aircraft-Marine Products Inc. common stock — added the necessary $130,000 of working capital to the company.[26]

Whitaker succeeded in getting this plan adopted by the directors, and the records indicate that at the end of July the amount of common stock had been increased from 7,000 shares to over 16,000. In addition to the main participants, Robert Hixon's three daughters increased their holdings, while three members of Carl L. Hamilton's family and several key Aircraft-Marine Products Inc. employees joined the list of stockholders as well. None of this, however, made securing the loan any easier. The New York bank that was considering the company's application was encouraging for some months, but as summer turned into early autumn, the prospect of the war's quick end caused it "to lose interest," as Whitaker put it.[27]

Aircraft-Marine Products Inc. next turned to a Philadelphia bank to secure the needed V Loan, and like its New York counterpart, it exhibited a good deal of initial enthusiasm. But soon another stalemate developed as it began to understand that the large number of the company's accounts (which stayed open an average of two months) meant that collection expenses might very well eat up any interest the Philadelphia bank could gain from the loan. At that point, Aircraft-Marine Products Inc. had to appeal to Washington to see if a lump-sum deal could be arranged on its war contract cancellation settlements. Negotiations dragged on for the remainder of the year before the loan was finally granted with a number of restrictions that were not particularly pleasing to Whitaker and the board. Probably most annoying was the amount of detailed and personal information that had to be furnished to bank officials. The pressure by the bank on Midland Investment for an examination of its books was especially displeasing to Robert Hixon, who believed that the financial affairs of the investment company were of no concern to banking officials in far-off Philadelphia. Other conditions for securing the loan included the need for the company to petition the bank for any salary increases for executives during the term of the loan agreement and the subordination of loan repayment to Midland Investment until the Federal Reserve loan was repaid. Nevertheless, from Whitaker's perspective, it was the best deal that could have been made.[28]

As Aircraft-Marine Products Inc.'s newly created Termination Department wrestled with the problem of contract cancellation, postwar planning went on. In August, 1944, a Special Products Division was established to develop products for immediate introduction to the market, but geared particularly toward postwar sales. Tom Berger, one of Walker's key salesmen, was placed in charge of this division, working under Walker's supervision. A new hand tool, a special terminal kit, and a splicing device system were already being offered as important postwar sales attractions.[29]

Even before the war ended, major changes began to take effect at Aircraft-Marine Products Inc. New products, innovative and complex in design, demanded an increase in quality control. Furthermore, prompt delivery was crucial to assure rapid penetration of the potential postwar market. Now, with the move to Harrisburg, company headquarters was at a greater distance from its manufacturing suppliers, requiring better systems of coordination. It became clear that the company philosophy of subcontracting the kind of work others could do better had to be modified in the interest of speedy delivery. When one supplier fell behind in the production of a new product, it was decided to use the stamping machines in Harrisburg to take up the slack and fill in the backlog of orders. The proper dies were quickly brought in and in less than a week, production in Harrisburg was underway. Allied operations such as plating and heat treating were soon added, assuring not only quality control but production control. Time study projects confirmed that the decision was a good one. Additional production capabilities in Harrisburg also improved the company's ability to handle an increasing sales volume.[30]

As these changes took place at Aircraft-Marine Products Inc., they pointed up the need for some revamping of the organizational structure to bring it into balance with the needs of the company. Had U. A. Whitaker been unaware of this situation, he had his sales manager, G. Earle Walker, around to remind him of any organizational shortcomings, especially in regard to production and delivery. Walker's job was to sell the company's products; Whitaker's job, from Walker's point of view, was to see that the products once sold arrived quickly in the hands of the buyers. When this did not happen, Walker heard about it from his salesmen in the field. Walker passed the information along to Whitaker. Walker's personal style allowed for the pulling of no punches. His memos on the subject of production control and delivery could not be called deferential.

A particularly colorful example is Walker's "crying wolf" memo, dated June 12, 1945. Walker's approach to the problem of postwar sales is explicitly stated in the memo — as is his irritation.

> This is another memorandum which may be considered as "crying wolf." I am simply dropping the entire subject in your lap, and I do not intend to follow it further. I want the "wolf" to bite you boys in the trousers at the point where it will hurt the most — namely, in your pocketbook — then you will recognize that the things we are doing, or not doing, are steadily hurting our sales and will continue to have a more serious effect on us.

Walker went on to outline the specifics of his complaint — in this case, the unavailability of an adequate number of tool and terminal kits, fast becoming a best selling company item. Aircraft-Marine Products Inc. distributors, Walker pointed out by quoting from one of his salesmen, were getting so disgusted with the delivery situation that some were seriously thinking of quitting and selling somebody else's products. Walker then went on to explain, or rather, reiterate what he had already said:

> If a distributor is sold a bill of goods on kits and becomes enthused, and then has to wait for kits, and then waits still longer for the terminals even when the kits are delivered, his interest is dulled, and the salesman has a much harder selling job to re-sell him and to re-enthuse him to the point that he will go out and sell the kits and re-order. . . . You can't build a sales organization on this kind of program, and you can't keep distributors happy. We will be in the kit business when we have 10,000 kits in stock and can ship at once.

Now, warmed to his subject, Walker got to the final point of his "crying wolf" memo: "I am not going to bring the subject up again, and I am not going to look foolish by pushing for kit sales. If you want kit sales, do something about it. Otherwise, I can assure you, you will have a very serious reflection in your sales in the next sixty days. . . . I am not going to bring this up again." But G. Earle

Walker, just beginning to build a direct sales organization, found many future occasions to bring it up again, and again, and again.[31]

Walker, of course, was a marketing man, and as a marketing man he waged a continual campaign at Aircraft-Marine Products Inc. to get his associates in engineering, including U. A. Whitaker, to understand his point of view. Walker believed that a sale lost today was a sale lost forever. Whitaker, as we shall see in more detail, came at the problem of engineering and sales from an entirely different perspective, believing that a customer lost today will be replaced by a customer gained tomorrow. If you had a good enough product, if you out-engineered your competition, the potential customer would beat a path to your door. But Walker insisted that sales should take precedence over engineering. In yet another production-bottleneck memo he laid out his approach for Whitaker: "I think a manufacturing organization which has products to sell is, in its entirety, a sales organization and should have that philosophy; and by sales organization I mean that its attitude should be that the customers' interest — our own profit situation taken into consideration of course — should be paramount." In brief, Walker's message to Whitaker was that "you need a little sales consciousness in production control." Despite Whitaker's different orientation, he understood the message and if he did not always appear to respond directly, he certainly did so indirectly by allowing Walker virtually a free hand in matters of sales development.[32]

Whitaker was not at all unaware of the problems that Walker raised at the time the company stood ready to enter the post-World War II world. Recognizing growing pains when he saw them, he knew that organizational modifications were in order, and to that end he engaged management consultant K. B. White to assess the matter and recommend some changes. That decision was made on the first of June, 1945, and White's strategy, which he announced a week later, seemed to indicate, at least implicitly, that Walker's complaints were not unjustified. Addressing his remarks to Whitaker, White wrote:

> Your company has an enviable record of distinguished service during the war period. Its phenomenally rapid expansion and brilliant engineering achievement must be a real and legitimate source of pride to you and your associates.
>
> The results have amply justified your policy of concentrating on engineering and on getting enough of your products on the aircraft on time. I believe that you are equally wise and timely in

embarking now upon a program which will bring the complete circle of your management methods up to the same high level of effectiveness as your engineering.

It would not be long before White began to make specific references to the problems of production. After attending a production meeting in August, 1945, White came away with the feeling that the matter of production controls was, "more urgent than I had realized." By the first of the year, White and members of Aircraft-Marine Products Inc.'s management were hard at work trying to correct the situation. More sophisticated cost and budgeting procedures would soon follow.[33]

If production, sales, and deliveries were problems, so were profits. By the end of the war, Aircraft-Marine Products Inc. had at least nine separate manufacturing operations of its own, as well as tie-ins to manufacturing subcontractors, mainly Stimpson and Gaynor. Whitaker's goal for his in-house manufacturing operation was to produce approximately 50 percent of the company's terminal requirements. The program was a costly one, calling for the purchase of additional machinery, dies, and tools. The capital investments, plus the large federal tax obligation, caused net profit to slump even further. In 1944, on sales of approximately $2.6 million (up about $450,000 over 1943), Aircraft-Marine Products Inc. earned approximately 1 percent after federal taxes. The even higher volume of 1945, $3.4 million, showed no improvement, the final result being less than 1/4 of 1 percent profit after federal taxes.[34]

In addition to all of the internal concerns affecting the company's operations in the immediate postwar market, future planning was filled with uncertainty about the impact of the war's end on the firm. To a former engineering associate who wrote Whitaker about a job just days before the end of the European phase of World War II, Whitaker expressed this uncertainty: "We have nothing definite to propose that we think would suit you. Like everyone else, we are somewhat undecided as to what the imminent end of the war might do."[35]

All through the summer of 1945, Aircraft-Marine Products Inc., like many other production facilities, began to cut back, but even that decision was done with uncertainty. Nor did the end of the war with Japan produce a clearer picture. Whitaker explained the dilemma to his friend Vernon H. Grant, on September 21, 1945:

> In regard to A-MP, our whole setup at present, like many others, is in considerable turmoil. The atom bomb not only ended the Jap war

suddenly, but upset various business plans just as suddenly. When
we get dug out from under the debris we will know more where we
are, but our operations will be very much less than they were
during the war, 'though it looks like our prospects are good for a
nice small business.[36]

By this time, Aircraft-Marine Products Inc. was almost totally
converted to peacetime, postwar production, but the problem of how
quickly their customers could convert remained an unanswered
question. The company had survived the contract cancellation impact
nicely and despite heavy war production requirements towards the
end of the war had been able to move its engineering people in the
direction of postwar thinking. All Whitaker knew for certain was that
the immediate future, that is, the final quarter of 1945, would
produce red ink on the company's books. The decision of whether to
expand or to contract further would only be solved with the passage
of time.   Whitaker, of course, had not forgotten the specter of
postwar recession that his father had warned him about four years
earlier, just days before Aircraft-Marine Products Inc. was born.[37]

11. The Whitaker Style

While Aircraft-Marine Products Inc. had its headquarters in Elizabeth, New Jersey, the small staff of development engineers, headed by Vern Carlson, did its research over in Westfield, a short auto trip away. U. A. Whitaker made it a point to drop in on his engineering group once or twice a week to see what was going on. He would ask each man what he was doing, how things were going, and what he thought about his own work. Ken Neijstrom — one of the original group of talented engineers who came to the company via Tri-State College, Bendix, and Bill Watts — recalled that Whitaker cared little for business protocol, preferring to let people run things without watching over the details of an engineering project. According to Neijstrom, Whitaker had learned that important lesson while at the Hoover Company some years earlier.

> Old man Hoover, who Whitaker apparently knew very well, insisted that his tool and die makers have their names put on the back of their stools at their benches [to make it] easy for him to go up to a man and say, "Charley, how are you doing?" One day he did this and it wasn't Charley sitting in the chair at the time. The system went to hell right there.

Whitaker always made it a point to allow his personnel the widest possible latitude in their work. Neijstrom recalled that Whitaker gave a man a responsibility or an assignment and then let him carry it out for better or for worse. Whitaker did not interfere; he allowed people to perform. For such a system to work, it was necessary to have good men, and Whitaker always made it a point to find such men. As Neijstrom explained it, "not only did he gather a number of good people around him but he apparently knew people throughout the industry who were talented. He made every attempt to bring that talent first to Industrial Manufacturers Inc., then to Aircraft-Marine Products Inc. and in later years to AMP Incorporated."[1]

Whitaker's policy of finding the best men and then giving them a free hand to carry out their responsibilities was one he applied not only to key management personnel and engineers but also to those who sat on the board of directors of the company. He insisted, right from the start, that his directors receive a reasonable remuneration for their services.[2]

The word "incentive" applied equally well to Whitaker's patent policy. To Whitaker's way of thinking, the primary purpose of patents was to create in his engineers the spirit of competition, to spur them on to "engineer the hell out of a product." Those frequent visits to Westfield were sometimes used for patent meetings at which all the engineers came together to describe their work. If several engineers were working on a project, Whitaker would ask the man most active in the work to talk about what they were doing. Whitaker would occasionally interrupt to ask a question or make a suggestion. There they would be — the president of the company, his patent attorney Truman Safford, who came in from New York City for the meeting, and the various engineers, each telling what they had accomplished, what they had done, what it was good for — and, in the process, getting the encouragement they needed. Safford would take notes on the sessions and write up those ideas that he thought might be patentable. But the important thing about the patent meetings was the conversation. Whitaker's role was that of moderator. As Ken Neijstrom described him in this role, he was "an outstanding encouragement man."

Later, Whitaker and Safford would go over the patent suggestions and decide which, if any, should be filed. When Safford first joined forces with Whitaker in 1942, he was at a loss to see what could be patented in the first place. What was there, he asked Whitaker, "in a field as old as metal stamping and electrical connections?" Whitaker replied in terms of the necessity for protection, an important problem in a field where anybody with a machine could go into business by copying what was already there. As the two men began to work together, Safford gained considerable respect for Whitaker's approach to patent problems. "We went over his new products and picked out the innovations which could be patented. He was enthusiastic that I could see the possibilities and I was enthusiastic that he could see the advantage of patenting new developments and could appreciate the difference between just filing and getting patents as compared with selecting the critical innovations and getting control of them by valid patents."

Patents not only provided an arena for competition among Whitaker's engineers, they also allowed him to give credit where it was due. The patent meetings at Westfield served both functions, and Whitaker exploited them fully. Safford's recollection of those meetings reveals something of Whitaker's thinking and something of his management style.

[Whit] always wanted to sit in on our patent conferences. This, I think, was done partly because he felt that it emphasized the value he placed on ingenious solutions to the problems, partly because it made all who attended the conference get to the essence of the practical problems and recognize the importance of solutions which were more than routine — which had that unexpected advantage which not only made it patentable, but gave it great commercial advantage.

Whit usually knew pretty well what the men were doing and the value of their accomplishments before we gathered in such a meeting; but he didn't tell me. He got the man who had given birth to the idea to bring it out and tell how it had come into being. It also gave me an opportunity to add whatever suggestions occurred to me from my experience in related fields.

We all enjoyed these conferences as we would a "bull session," and it kept the engineers alert to what was going on in the company's development program. Often suggestions turned up which helped the engineer on a particular project to see ways in which the development could be hastened or improved. Whit, as the man who was buying the program, would draw out the suggestions from the various points of view and, as the boss whose opinion was the most important, would encourage the men who were working on the project. A considerable part of my function in the conference was to recognize and rejoice over what was a "stroke of genius" whether great or small. To some extent I was an expression of him in his position as head of the company. The men who were reporting to me on the patentable developments in their work were also giving him the report and getting from him the approval and guidance of seeing how it fitted into the patent program.

Marshall Holcombe, Safford's partner and another active Aircraft-Marine Products Inc. patent lawyer for some years, also saw the effectiveness of Whitaker's style. "It seemed to Whitaker. . . that he could get his guys to think over a wider area by asking them a few questions than by telling them what to do." According to Holcombe, Whitaker never, in any of their dealings, issued him a specific order.[3]

For Albert Curtis, one of the original members of the company, Whitaker's hallmark was his willingness to delegate responsibility, and then to provide an individual the freedom to work out the best methods, solutions, attacks. Curtis once had an experience with Whitaker that drove home the point that — at Aircraft-Marine Products Inc. — a man was responsible for his actions. During the war, Curtis filled a government order with Aircraft-Marine Products Inc. tools when a competitor's tool was specified. When the tools were shipped back, Curtis was baffled until he pulled out the order and discovered he had misread it, that it had not called for an equivalent tool, as he had believed. Curtis was in trouble; the order amounted to about $3,000 and now, in addition to the money loss involved, Curtis had to fill the order with the correct tool. As Curtis tells the story, he went downstairs and found Whitaker in conversation with Sales Manager G. Earle Walker, Curtis' immediate boss. He broke in and told them the story of his mistake and then asked Whitaker what "we" should do about it. Whitaker's reply shook Curtis: "What do you mean WE? I didn't quote them. Walker didn't quote them. You quoted them. You have to get those tools and get them to the customer." Curtis did.[4]

Whitaker's theories about incentives carried over to the competitive world outside the walls of the company. If there was anything he did not want, it was a monopoly in his field. Without competition, Whitaker believed, no progress was possible in terms of company growth and expansion. During his time at American Machine & Foundry, he saw the effects of the lack of competition on several of that company's divisions — little innovation, little development, and ultimately sterility. He viewed the challenge from Aircraft-Marine Products Inc.'s competitors as beneficial to his own engineers. His confidence that the company could out-engineer the competition led him to establish the policy that no one should be driven out of business on account of any overt act by Aircraft-Marine Products Inc. The success of the company during the war convinced him that this was the proper approach. As Holcombe described it, "Whitaker. . . wanted Aircraft-Marine to grow because each year it offered more new products at an attractive price. . . . He wanted to grow that way," not by forcing the competition out of business.[5]

In building Aircraft-Marine Products Inc., Whitaker was able to put into practice his ideas about the relationship between engineering innovations and business profits. Unlike his sales manager, G. Earle Walker, he did not conceive of the company as one large selling organization. He believed that engineers functioned best as engineers, not as an arm of the sales division. The engineer's job was to apply his knowledge to creating products to meet market needs; moreover, the sales department, in addition to soliciting orders for those products, was to help identify market needs.

The market had been a major factor in Whitaker's decision to go into the termination business. His previous work experience had long ago convinced him that there must be a better way than the time-consuming process of soldering. Once acquainted with an alternate and more economical method, he quickly saw that significant improvements were possible — given the right people and an abundance of energy. The special requirements of war production — faster and more reliable applications and products — only substantiated what he already knew. His faith in engineering problem solving preceded the necessities of war by a considerable period of time.

Whitaker's experience with the 1936 Hoover vacuum cleaner model is a good example of such problem solving in a business context. Whitaker understood the demands and constraints of a depression market and through engineering problem solving helped produce the kind of machine that would sell in that market. When he began his work at Aircraft-Marine Products Inc., he applied the same approach. In this case, it was the war market, and the products he and his associates designed met the needs of defense. On the other hand, the basic product itself, the electrical termination, was not one limited to a war market. Whitaker's wisdom in choosing the engineering field he did played no small part in his business survival following the war. The electronics takeoff period was still a short distance in the future, but Whitaker's judgment that it would soon be a growth industry was altogether sound.[6]

One additional illustration of Whitaker's understanding of the engineering-business relationship provides a coda to these general remarks about the first years of his company's existence. Just before Christmas, 1945, his friend Carl Hamilton wrote asking if he would mind going up to Niles, Michigan, to look over a new bowling pinsetting machine. Hamilton wanted Whitaker to give Jim Allen, now a partner in Booz, [Fry] Allen and Hamilton, an opinion on the feasibility of this particular machine. At American Machine & Foundry, Whitaker had had an opportunity to learn something of that company's version of the pinsetter, and Hamilton wanted to know if the firm in Niles had one as good or even better. Whitaker agreed to go, as busy as he was with the affairs of Aircraft-Marine Products Inc. and on the first day of February, 1946, he made his visit and sent his report to Hamilton two weeks later.

Whitaker's report, nearly three single-spaced typewritten sheets, is remarkable in its depth of understanding of the problem as well as in its detail. What is more, the report was the result of a single day's visit. What Whitaker described as a "more or less offhand statement of my thoughts on the matter," reveals a substantial amount of analysis leading to the conclusions he presented to Hamilton and Allen. Among other things, Whitaker addressed the differences between American Machine & Foundry's pinsetter and the one he was reporting on; costs of production and possible profits; the best means for testing the machine; the problems of servicing; and the headaches of going into the rental-machine field. Whitaker concluded that the pinsetter represented too much of a gamble for the small engineering firm in Niles — the amount of profit possible over the current cost of building the machine was much too low.

But Whitaker's critique, although conservative in its conclusions, was decidely radical at its core, if by radical we mean going back to the root of the engineering-business problem he was called on to evaluate. He explained the situation to Hamilton this way:

> In talking to Mr. _____, and to the Executive Vice President, and from looking at their shop and business, in general, I would feel extremely nervous if I were associated with the Company and thinking of going into this business. My impression is that they have a mighty fine business of their own and that it is probably very well run and it probably has a fine future, but they certainly don't appear to have the background, or experience, for the development and sale of automatic machines, especially for running a rental business. As I pointed out to Mr. _____, the automatic machine business is just as tough as any business. It requires a special type of engineering, manufacturing, service and sales.

Whitaker was, by this time, well aware of the problems involved in getting automatic machines on the market since Aircraft-Marine Products Inc. at that time was struggling to get its own automatic terminal production machines in the field. Whitaker, however, saw something even more fundamentally wrong with the situation than inexperienced personnel. It was the company's basic approach to an engineering business problem that struck Whitaker as all wrong. "The first thing that impressed me," he told Hamilton, "was a statement by Mr._____ that, if the machine could be made to operate satisfactorily, there would be little doubt that it would be a profitable business. I told Mr. _____ that my impression was the exact opposite, that is, if it could be figured out that the business would be highly profitable, there would be little problem, given time and money, to develop a satisfactory machine." For this bit of sound analysis, Whitaker submitted Booz, [Fry] Allen and Hamilton a bill for $95.93. His time, experience, and intellectual effort were "on the house."[7]

* * * * * * *

"This will be the victory year," read the first sentence of the editor's page in U. A. Whitaker's appointment book for 1945. This year, the editor went on to say, will be "perhaps one of the most eventful years in your business experience. . . . It will be the year when business will turn from making the tools of war to supplying the pent-up needs of our civilian population. It will be the year of reconversion — new ideas, new products, new plans, new achievements." On July 23, 1945, G. Earle Walker and Frank Pierce met in Whitaker's office to talk about new ideas, new plans, new products, and new achievements. Frank Pierce had recently joined Aircraft-Marine Products Inc. as a consulting engineer. He had come from Eureka in Detroit, having replaced Vern Carlson there as chief engineer in 1942 through Whitaker's recommendation, and Whitaker now offered him unlimited expenditures for the development of new products.[8] Whitaker had compiled a long list of such products — new terminal sizes, several assorted kits, plugs, applicators, disconnect devices, etc. — many of which Whitaker optimistically promised would be available for the market by the first of the year. Aircraft-Marine Products Inc. appeared ready to plunge into the postwar civilian market with a vengeance.

The meeting as reported by Sales Manager Walker appeared to be lighthearted, if not a bit wacky. For example, Whitaker's offer to Pierce was not unqualified. Pierce could have unlimited funds with which to work if he could promise $200,000 worth of business per month on any or all of the items contained on the list "up to the first of the year." Walker, commenting on this offer, noted that "it is my recollection that in an off-guarded moment, Mr. Whitaker went much further than this." Then, when Frank Pierce indicated that by January a minimum of 25 automatic terminal crimping machines would be available for rental, Walker got into the spirit of the meeting and, as he put it, "went completely nuts and talked in terms of 15,000 rental machines." According to Walker, Whitaker received this idea skeptically and "very modestly agreed to accept about 250 the first of the year and 750 the second." In gratitude Walker, representing the Sales Department, promised they would arrange their quotas around Whitaker's suggested goals.[9]

By April, 1946, Aircraft-Marine Products Inc. had missed Whitaker's tongue-in-cheek goal of 1,000 automatic machines for the first two days of January by something in the neighborhood of 995. All three men knew, of course, that automatic machines, only about a year out of the final development stages, would take some time and effort to sell to their customers. Aircraft-Marine Products Inc. was new to the rental-machine business and as Whitaker had told the pin-setting company officials, the automatic machine business was a tough one. The need, however, was there. Large mass-production manufacturers should have welcomed the advantage of automatically applying electrical terminals to the ends of wires, but as we have noted, not all of the prewar trained engineers were ready to accept the newfangled idea of solderless terminals, much less an automatic machine for their application, despite the solderless terminal's wartime successes. In addition to trying to place the machines, the company's salesmen had continually to sell the basic concept itself. For some time after the war's end, the company had to make available test results on the solderless terminal to prove its value and reliability to many "old-timers."[10]

The development of the automatic machine was a logical one. Given Whitaker's judgment that the electrical termination business would be profitable, it was inevitable, according to his engineering business philosophy, that something would be developed capable of mass-producing terminal connections to meet the needs of the general mass-production consumer market. The exigencies of wartime production only accelerated the development of an automatic method of attaching terminals to wires.[11]

Another war-induced innovation that Whitaker judged would have broad peacetime application was a new electrical insulating film called Alsifilm, under development at MIT. With the fear that the Japanese conquest of Southeast Asia would cut the Western world off from supplies of mica, used as a major insulator in electrical devices, research on the mica substitute was stepped up at MIT. As a member of the visiting committee for the Division of Industrial Cooperation, Whitaker probably learned of the new development on one of his early trips to MIT in that capacity. Professor Ernst A. Hauser, a chemical engineer at MIT, had invented Alsifilm, and Whitaker saw its use in electrical condensers as holding possibilities for the future. After the war began, Professor J. S. Balsbaugh, an electrical engineer at MIT, took over that aspect of the project that had as its goal the improvement of the electrical properties in the film. Balsbaugh, as we have seen, was also a part-time research engineer for Aircraft-Marine Products Inc. and worked extensively on perfecting the solderless terminal.[12]

In late 1942, Aircraft-Marine Products Inc.'s directors authorized the company to enter into an informal agreement with MIT's Division of Industrial Cooperation for further development work on the Alsifilm idea at a cost of about $3,000 per month for a period of several months, or until some indication that the research work was leading somewhere. Then, if its commercial use in electrical condensers appeared to be practical, a long-term formal agreement would be drawn up between the division and Aircraft-Marine Products Inc. The leading characteristic of Alsifilm was its stability at very high temperatures, a feature that was not inherent in its organic counterpart.[13]

Like Aircraft-Marine Products Inc. , MIT's Division of Industrial Cooperation went to war. In 1940, the visiting committee recommended that the division more actively seek research contracts with industry. At that time contracts amounted only to $100,000 to $200,000 in annual dollar volume. Then, like other large universities with extensive research facilities, it undertook defense commitments just prior to United States entry into the war. As a result, its dollar volume leaped to a yearly $3.8 million. By the end of the war, through its Division of Industrial Cooperation, MIT zoomed to approximately $40 millions in dollar volume. In the first twenty years of its existence, the division, organized in 1920 to carry out the fund-raising goals of MIT's Technology Plan, had, by the standards of the time, grown considerably. But, by 1940, research and development work at MIT, propelled forward by American defense needs, was beginning to become a big business.[14]

By spring 1943, the Alsifilm project was going better than expected. With Frank Wells of Aircraft-Marine Products Inc. working closely with J. S. Balsbaugh at MIT, and with the company's chemical research consultant, Frank Sowa, the Alsifilm condenser project was off the ground and some small orders were already being placed. But a year later, few condensers had been produced and sold. Then, General Electric placed an order for 500 condensers ($87,000) to be delivered early in 1945, and although Whitaker was disappointed that the order was not larger, he saw it as a chance to break even on the condenser project. Acknowledging to his directors that future prospects were "mixed," Whitaker could still report on the bright side that "both the Army and Navy advise us that they will want us to stay in business and that there will be substantial orders for condensers after the German and Jap war is over due to the fact that they are expecting to modernize all equipment with radar." The Alsifilm project itself was later described by MIT's John Burchard as producing "one of the few new electrical insulating materials developed during the war." Very early on, U. A. Whitaker saw its potential, and took a chance on it. Eventually the Aircraft-Marine Products Inc.'s interest in Alsifilm for condensers paid large dividends.[15]

For the present, however, the months immediately following the end of the war reflected most clearly that postwar uncertainty Whitaker had predicted. Aircraft-Marine Products Inc. closed out 1945 with the highest sales volume in its brief history — $3.4 million. But its profit percentage after federal taxes — one-fourth of 1 percent — was as low as it had been in the past. In 1946 Aircraft-Marine Products Inc.'s volume was cut almost in half and in that year the company recorded a profit of $755. Only a decision to cut expenses dramatically prevented a significant loss. By the end of the first quarter of 1946, the company's sales engineering department had been drastically reduced, and Whitaker promised the directors even more cutbacks if volume did not improve. Whitaker also took the opportunity to explain why business had deteriorated so markedly.

> The reason . . . is material shortages in our own plant to a small degree and in the plants of our customers to a large degree. A very large percentage of our small customers have run out of material in some one item so that they cannot further operate and none of them wish to build up inventories. Most of the big fellows are on strike or are trying to clean up the mess from their last strike.

Although Whitaker did not believe that the material shortages would continue much longer, it was his intention to continue cutting back to maintain a breakeven level.[16]

The cutbacks Whitaker promised did, in fact, become necessary as the year wore on. Roughly 70 percent of Aircraft-Marine Products Inc.'s sales staff and 30 percent of its engineering department were laid off. Layoffs only made it more difficult to increase sales. The impact of a reduced sales organization is obvious. A small engineering corps created an even more profound problem, though, because the electrical industry, now deeply involved in its own reconversion problems, needed more engineering work than ever. So great were wiring problems in the industry that on numerous occasions representatives from major electrical firms traveled to Harrisburg to seek help in answering their most pressing questions. The company's files from those days are filled with memos and reports describing in detail hundreds of industry problems that had to be solved and long lists of development projects that needed attention.[17]

While postwar planning at Aircraft-Marine Products Inc. had anticipated problems related to conversion from war to peace, both for themselves and for their customers, that planning had not anticipated those material shortages that Whitaker commented on to his board. Material shortages, however, plagued all industry for most of 1946. After V-J Day, government regulations on the use of steel, for example, were no longer enforced. Like most other concerns, Aircraft-Marine Products Inc. loaded up, believing that the situation would continue along the same lines. But with the threat of large-scale steel strikes in early 1946, the Civilian Production Administration notified steel users that wartime regulations would soon be re-enforced, thus drastically affecting company plans for increased production. Other crucial materials, like copper, also developed very short supplies. By now Aircraft-Marine Products Inc. manufactured about 3,000 different items and its inability to build up inventories, even at the lower level required by a lower business demand, endangered its chances of holding on to the customers it was currently supplying. The alternative to solderless electrical terminals, of course, was the old soldering method and the company feared that the unavailability of some of their products might cause some customers to return to their former method of terminal application.[18]

At midyear, 1946, business conditions worsened. Aircraft-Marine Products Inc.'s smaller customers were running out of wire; some were forced out of business. Bigger customers, because of strikes, were not yet back to full production. Whitaker reported to the directors in late June that large firms like General Electric, Westinghouse, and Western Electric had placed orders, but delivery was to be sometime in the future. For the present, Whitaker told them business would continue to be very slow, and until the copper situation righted itself, little improvement would be forthcoming. Aircraft-Marine Products Inc.'s sales for May were behind those of May, 1945, but Whitaker's cost-cutting measures prevented any loss being incurred. In fact, Whitaker reported that without the expenses of the automatic machine project, a profit of about $7,500 would have been posted.[19]

The Automatic Machine Division had great potential for increasing sales markedly. The difficulty was that the machines were expensive to build and costly to service. The market was certainly there, as surveys indicated. The problem Whitaker faced in getting the program off the ground was that the company did not have the capital it needed to go into production in a big way. Without sufficient capital, Whitaker was wary of any large expansion plan. He feared the possibilitiy of a depression, which he believed could wipe the company out unless there were adequate reserves to see them through an extended period of business turndown. For a time, he and his financial advisers considered setting up a separate Automatic Machine Company if they could somehow get their hands on about $750,000 with which to finance the idea. Alternatively, Whitaker suggested to the board of directors that Aircraft-Marine Products Inc. step up its sales of semiautomatic machines, each of which would cost relatively little — about $300 — and was much less complicated than its fully automatic counterpart. Royalties on each 1,000 terminals would amount to approximately $500 every six months. Whitaker thought the semiautomatic machine would be at least self-sustaining.[20]

But even the semiautomatic machine plan required additional capital, at least $100,000 to get it to the point where it could support itself — assuming business improved at a moderate rate. Whitaker was forced once again to approach the Federal Reserve System for operating capital. For most of the balance of the year negotiations were carried on to secure a loan from local sources based on a mortgage on the Fourth Street building, while at the same time work continued to complete a loan with the Philadelphia Federal Reserve Bank. The mortgage idea fell through, but the Federal Reserve Loan was completed by the end of the year. Even with a $350,000 credit line, Whitaker continued to worry about the possibility of depression. In his mind, if the depression did not ensue through natural causes, government actions would certainly bring it about. At election time, 1946, he expressed this point of view to Uncle Syd Whitaker back home. "Looks like the Republicans might get their chance to get in this time," he wrote. "I think about nine-tenths of the present business troubles are due to the OPA [Office of Price Adminstration] and other meddling, and if something isn't done pretty soon, we are surely headed for a depresssion."[21]

By this time, if depression had not hit, the company was certainly experiencing a bona fide recesson. Approximately 250 employees had been dropped from the payroll, which now averaged slightly under 350 people for the year. The Harrisburg plant and office employed about 250 people with the remaining 100 split between the facilities in Glen Rock and Seven Valleys. Whether Aircraft-Marine Products Inc. was working with a full or a reduced labor force, Whitaker tried to maintain the same kind of flexibility in this area that he had achieved through his decentralized production program. For one thing, flexibility within the labor force made it easier to introduce automated equipment, and since Whitaker believed firmly that the purpose of automation and mechanization was to make work easier, this was an important consideration for him. Moreover, since Aircraft-Marine Products Inc. was actually in the business of producing automatic machines for the market, Whitaker's sensitivity about this philosophy lay fairly near the surface.[22]

Whitaker's general philosophy toward labor was progressive and company policies followed that philosophy. Almost from its beginning, the company tried to provide adequately for its workers. In 1944, Aircraft-Marine Products Inc. workers were offered group accident and sickness insurance, for which the employee paid, as his share, between eighteen and eighty-one cents per week, depending on salary. Four years later all employees received six paid holidays per year, and shortly thereafter a company pension plan was adopted. Incentive plans and grievance procedures were also added in this early period of the company's development, and the personnel department, headed then by R. J. Szukala, worked long and hard to keep labor-management relations on an even keel. With the small number of employees associated with each operating unit, it was possible for the immediate superviser to know his employees intimately and thus be able to deal with personal as well as work problems — advice Szukala had received on his 1943 visits to possible plant location sites. In short, the idea was to provide employees with benefits equal to or better than they might have received under a union contract. The kind of flexible balance Whitaker wanted in labor matters was achieved by this approach.[23]

Flexibility and balance were particularly important to Whitaker in the period immediately following World War II, but they were not always obtainable goals. As we have seen, Whitaker's wartime dependence on direct or indirect government military contracts convinced him that in the future the company could not afford to become so reliant on the military segment of its business. Unfortunately, from Whitaker's perspective, it was not long after the war that the problem had to be faced again. With the advent of the Cold War, the United States stepped up its military preparedness program and Sales Manager G. Earle Walker quite understandably saw a potential market there. Early in 1948, Walker informed Whitaker by memo that his department was increasing its efforts to obtain business from the army and navy as well as from their subcontractors. Walker's man in Washington, T. Odon Mathews, was busy making the appropriate contacts while Walker was reestablishing his relations with the people at Wright Field in Dayton. Walker's final comment in his memo of February 4, 1948, suggests that perhaps Whitaker was dragging his feet. "I would like very much to have a statement from management as to their attitude on this matter. If our opinion is that we do not care to work with the Services, then we may as well stop contacts, save this time and money, and figure that business is out so far as we are concerned."[24]

In March, Walker increased his pressure on management. He had now given the matter of contacting government agencies a title — Preparation for War Projects — hammering home his point in this manner; "From items in *The Wall Street Journal*, trade bulletins, and other general news issues, it is obvious the entire military program has been stepped up. This has been made more obvious to me by the fact that we have been requested to have FBI approval for any new contracts for the Atomic Program and the Guided Missile Program. I am very much afraid our competitors will steal a march on us." Further communications from Walker followed during the summer and fall of 1948.[25]

Whitaker reported to his directors in August that prospects for business remained unchanged and that there was "very little, if any, increase due to war business." By December, however, Walker's efforts were beginning to pay off, and Aircraft-Marine Products Inc. was obtaining some government business. Whitaker may not have been enthusiastic about it, but as long as a proper balance was maintained between defense and civilian work, he was satisfied. An incident in spring, 1949, though, probably made Whitaker wonder whether he had done the correct thing in having sales push forward for government business. One of the company's aircraft manufacturing customers had contracted for terminals to be used in the construction of new military aircraft. The vicissitudes of big business and big government relations entered the picture, changing the focus of the situation. As Walker explained it to Whitaker, "I suppose you know that the recent Boeing order for 44 B-54 planes was cancelled and the order placed with Consolidated for 44 of their equivalent to this plane." Then Walker went on to explain how it all happened, or rather how he supposed it happened:

> Looking behind the scenes, this seems pretty obvious since [Louis]
> Johnson, the new Secretary of Defense, was formerly a director of

Consolidated Vultee. Floyd Odlum, who is President of Atlas Corporation, the holding company for Consolidated Vultee, as you may have noticed from the newspapers, spent considerable time in Washington recently. I suppose, by putting 2 and 2 together, we can presume that Consolidated is now the fair-haired boy.

Walker's suggestion that Boeing's contract cancellation would have an impact on Aircraft-Marine Products Inc. no doubt had an additional sobering effect on Whitaker's already very sober attitude about dependency on government contracts. He would not let things get out of balance if he could help it.[26]

In addition to the external problems caused by America's postwar recession, Aircraft-Marine Products Inc. had not yet solved all of its internal organizational difficulties. All through the late 1940s, the tensions between sales and engineering continued, and with Walker's department, like all the rest, working with a lower budget, the problems were only exacerbated. The battle for good customers was intense, as usual, and Walker complained constantly about deliveries that were not met, tools that were defective, orders that were returned because of production mistakes, foul-ups in a disorganized order department, and the general disarray in production control.

Walker to C. J. Fredricksen, August 4, 1947 (cc to Whitaker)

Leave us Face Facts [on how much money the Sales Department has saved, even to the point of handicapping its efforts].

The Sales Department doubts that the total organization followed along those lines . . . the Sales Department now absorbing the task of preparing a new catalogue and is gathering together engineering data and such other data, work formerly done in the Engineering Department.

Walker to UAW, August 5, 1947

I noticed in Management Meetings you get glowing reports on the delivery situation, but in the last few days I have seen some glaring discrepancies.

Walker to UAW, March 19, 1948

When are we going to put a competent man in charge of production control? We have muddled up our production program to the point it has so seriously affected the morale of our business here that each time [two salesmen] visit here, I find it necessary to dissuade them from doing, what sooner or later they will do — resign and take their men with them. Management may think this is funny — I don't.

Walker's memos on orders lost because of failures in delivery and production control are numerous, and his enumeration of internal foul-ups even larger.[27]

By the end of 1949, Walker was resigned to the situation he faced in production control. He was now convinced that engineering would never develop a sales point of view. As he told one of his key salesman some months earlier, "I have discovered . . . that this is a condition with which we have to live, just as we have to live with women and mice in this cockeyed world." Walker's final 1949 sally to his boss U. A. Whitaker explained his concern more precisely:

> Our biggest complaint about Production Control concerns their attitude — not toward the Sales Department but toward the orders which, in effect, meant toward the customers. Proper judgment is not used, probably because orders are regarded as so many pieces of paper and not as customers or as a factor in customer relations. In our opinion, the Production Control Department should view orders from the customer's viewpoint and not merely as a bookkeeping or recording transaction. They should not accept a rule as being irrevocable where obviously it is hurting the customer but should consult the Sales Department, or whoever has made the rule, to obtain authority to break it.

This was the memo in which Walker pleaded with Whitaker to instill "a little sales consciousness in Production Control." Walker's major bone of contention at this time was that engineering controlled the product being marketed from its earliest stages to its final manufacture. Quality control was also in its hands. Walker felt that the customer knew what he wanted better than the boys in engineering did, and he argued from this basis. Whitaker remained convinced of his own view of sales, firmly believing that the selling had to be done by technical men, that is, those responsible for "engineering the hell out of a product." In his thinking, the sales manager should act as a buffer between the technical person and the customer wishing to purchase the product; beyond that, his main job was "to pressure people to sign on the line." It was what patent man Marshall Holcombe called "soliciting offers to buy."[28]

****

No better illustration of Whitaker's management style existed at Aircraft-Marine Products Inc. than what went on in the Automachine Division. In 1949, nineteen people worked in the division, which was assigned the responsibility of developing automatic equipment for the production of terminals and other electrical devices in large quantities. Dick Leuba, an Antioch College engineering student working at the company through the college's co-op program described the atmosphere in Automachine at the end of 1949:

> There's not much formality or class consciousness in this group; the work is interesting enough and free from possible stagnation, so as to keep us occupied and not concerned with who's in charge of whom. Actually the placing of responsibility is constantly juggled about in keeping with the irregular nature of the work, and the distribution of authority is in effect slip-shod. So at the expense of occasional confusion over what or whose project a person will work on, and over who shall decide what, there is a wonderful preservation of individual dignity and self-importance, and an encouragement for the individual to assume responsibility.

To Leuba, the whole operation in Automachine was clearly a team affair:

> In Automachine on the 2nd floor "back," the objects are to keep production going at Carlisle, and to whip along a number of concurrent development projects for new and improved terminals and ways of making them. This is everybody's object ...It's a purely "group-dynamics" situation, and our solution so far is a myriad of unplanned, informal, verbal exchanges between two, three, and four people. The result is that the more we become familiar with what each of the rest is doing, the easier it is to use good judgment in planning one's own work.

Although Leuba recommended that perhaps the physical clutter and the disorganization might be tidied up a bit, he seemed to be echoing Whitaker's philosophy when he said that "the most important thing of all is that we suppress system and regulation enough to retain the freedom that is necessary for the varied work we have to do." The Automachine Division, he concluded was a place where ideas counted. It was, in Leuba's opinion, an exciting place to work.

The Automachine Division was also a small community, perhaps a successful reflection of Whitaker's management goal of establishing such a community concept among the various units comprising the company. Essential to that success, and to the freedom from restraint was the personnel in each unit. In the Automachine Division, as elsewhere, Whitaker had worked to attract the best people available. As a result, informality and individualism, the fundamental aspects of Whitaker's own personality, were nourished, as can be seen in Leuba's description of the "live wires" working in the Automachine

Division:

> Briefly, there is [Frank] Pierce, who's Chief Engineer, and who
> instead of enclosing himself in one of the . . . offices, sits plunk in
> the middle of the middle office and is surrounded by seven other
> people in the same room! , and as a result knows seven times better
> what goes on. . . . [Quentin] Berg is next, and has an enormous
> assortment of talents. He has a four dimensional mind: He invents
> ingenious Rube Goldberg machines in three dimensions, and with
> the fourth keeps so conscious of the passage of time that 24 hours a
> day and two hands on a man never seem to be enough to satisfy
> him. He has a deep respect for the individual; it is to him that the
> co-ops in automachine are technically responsible. Bill Pollock
> (already we are down to first names) does special projects; Joe
> Brenner is in charge of the multi-terminal [automatic machine]
> production and four secretaries, who drink coffee in our coffee club,
> complete the middle-office roll call.

It should be noted that two of these "livewires" later became leading
executives of AMP Incorporated: S. W. Pollock, vice-president for
Engineering and Research; J. D. Brenner, president and chief
executive officer.[29]

Whitaker knew a lot about community; he had learned it first from
his Missouri origins, and it was enforced in his previous work
experience, especially at Westinghouse Air Brake and at the Hoover
Company. For Whitaker, work was as much a home as it was a place
to earn a living and be productive. In the early days in Harrisburg,
Whitaker often showed up at May's Tea Room around the corner
from the Fourth Street plant to eat lunch with some of the
production men at a long table. He also could be found at the corner
drug store eating lunch with "the boys" — Fredricksen, Carlson,
Walker, Wells, Pierce, etc. Later, lunch with the boys became an
established routine for Whitaker. It provided an informal atmosphere
for the exchange of ideas and information and worked to supplement
the management commitee system beginning to emerge after the
war. Although Aircraft- Marine Products Inc. was fast becoming an
established company, responsible for a growing list of industry firsts,
it would always remain for Whitaker his "little company."[30]

Whitaker always wanted to be a big part of a small company rather
than a small cog in a large operation. Having achieved that goal along
with the promise of reasonable financial security, he began to think
seriously about changing his private life in significant ways. First,
there was the matter of Helen Fisher to be settled.

Whitaker had met Helen Fisher in 1930 when he first came to the

Hoover Company. She was employed in the Hoover Central Stenographic as assistant manager, and a mutual friend arranged a blind date. It was on the first date that Helen Fisher learned what a private person U. A. Whitaker was. Returning home after a Saturday evening dinner, Helen asked Whitaker to bank the fire in her furnace. With Whitaker thus engaged in gallant service, Helen attempted to find out something about her escort's life. According to Helen, Whitaker gave her quite a line and tried to convince her that his family had come from Germany and settled in New Jersey. Since his Missouri accent made the story particularly improbable, Helen Fisher decided to look up Whitaker's personnel record. Several days later, she greeted him with the question, "how's everything in Weaubleau?" At that moment, Whitaker must have known he had met his match.

The two of them dated on and off during Whitaker's years in North Canton, and Helen occasionally did some clerical work for McKinley Air Transport for which she received payment in plane rides around the area. Helen, however, was dubious about anything serious developing between them because of Whitaker's well-known views on marriage. As she put it, "At thirty he was already a confirmed bachelor with great compassion for those men friends who were tied down to marriage." Consequently, Helen Fisher was not too sure that she wanted to continue the relationship, and she did not confine her dating activities exclusively to Whitaker. They remained friends and saw each other occasionally either for dinner or late evening snacks after Whitaker's law classes and Helen's evening art classes.

In 1943, family problems took Helen Fisher to California. After Whitaker left North Canton for New York in 1939, the two of them kept in frequent touch by telephone. Helen returned to North Canton briefly in 1943, but missing the relatives and climate in southern California, she returned West. News of her decision to leave Canton was greeted by a long phone silence from Whitaker. At the end of that year, Whitaker wrote her that he was taking a business trip to the coast and made plans to spend the holidays with Helen. He arrived, hinted around about marriage, and told Helen a little bit about his new company. He made it clear he was now making enough money to support a wife, a consideration of much importance to him. Remembering what she called his "dim view" of the state of marriage in the past, Helen felt that substantial thought must be given Whitaker's offer. As she amusingly puts it, "His views on the wedded state had covered a wide area."[31]

Indeed they had. Everyone of Whitaker's friends and business associates had at one time or another been exposed to Whitaker's views on the subject, especially those who had put up with his good-humored ribbing about their being married. Whitaker's stock answer to the question of why he had not married was that the cost of maintaining an airplane was just about the same as that of keeping a wife in good condition, and that a man could afford either one or the other, but not both. Years of such evasiveness about marriage probably established Whitaker so firmly as a lifelong bachelor in the minds of his friends, that when he finally gained Helen Fisher's consent in the autumn of 1944, he viewed secrecy about the coming ceremony as his best policy. He and Helen were married secretly in Baltimore, Maryland on September 26, 1944. It would be some weeks, in some cases, months, before his best friends, except George Ingalls, would learn about Whitaker's changed state. He did not even tell his family in Missouri![32]

Incredibly, it was nearly two years later when the family back home learned of the marriage. In April, 1946, Whitaker went back to Missouri. His sister Minnie was gravely ill with cancer, and he had arranged for her to come East to Canton to see if radiation treatment could be of any help. But even back home, Whitaker made no mention of his marriage, for it was three months later when his Uncle Syd Whitaker, having received a letter from Minnie now in a Canton hospital, wrote his nephew Uncas about learning of the news. "Minnie wrote about meeting Helen and liking her so, and and all of us heartily welcome into the family our new relative. That does not remove, however, the slight grudge we hold against you for not telling us sooner." Syd Whitaker's reaction was one matter; one can only imagine what O.B.'s epistolary response would have been.[33]

Minnie, unfortunately, did not recover, and her death occurred during the late summer of 1946. Ironically, like her aunt, also named Minnie, she died leaving young children to be taken care of. Privacy notwithstanding, U. A. Whitaker's family ties were strong; he offered to, and did, adopt his late sister's two teenage daughters and have them come to Harrisburg as his and Helen's children. It was an indescribably generous act at his age — he was then 46 years old — and a tribute not only to his character and sense of responsibility but to the generosity of his wife of two years.[34]

There were other changes as well in U. A. Whitaker's life in these years, a result of his marriage and partly because of the increasing demands of building his business. Early in 1945 he began his first

serious attempt to dispose of all his Missouri farm property. As he
told Uncle Syd, he felt it was the best thing to do since he was so far
away from the Missouri scene. By the end of 1948, almost all of the
farm property had been disposed of and Whitaker was finally relieved
of the responsibility his father had given him over a generation
before. At the same time, Whitaker also got rid of his interest in
McKinley Air Transport, and, perhaps in a metaphoric sense, the end
of this adventurous episode in his life officially marked the end of his
bachelorhood. Although Whitaker continued his flying, he never
again set down at McKinley Airport.[35]

Friends reported that Whitaker seemed to mellow somewhat as a
result of his marriage and family routine, and in part this may have
been a correct assessment. But Whitaker, who approached everything
he did with gusto if not passion, had found a new outlet for his
excess energies. His new enthusiasm was now in sailing, and every
spare moment he could steal from his business was devoted to the
sport. During the 1940s he owned a series of sailing boats, each
succeeding one larger and more technically sophisticated than the one
it replaced. Patent attorney Truman Safford remembers the first of
Whitaker's boats he saw — a 17.5-foot open cockpit catboat, which
Whitaker kept at Red Bank, New Jersey in 1942. Whitaker sold that
boat to his friend and business associate George Ingalls in 1944 and
bought himself a 30-foot Alden yawl called *Retriever*, which he kept
on the Sassafras River in Maryland. In 1946 and 1947, Whitaker was
looking for still a larger boat and found one called *Gallivant*, a 38-foot
Rhodes cutter. By 1949, he had a 42-footer on his mind, and so it
went. Truman Safford, a fine sailor in his own right, helped get
Whitaker into the exclusive New York City Yacht Club in 1949, and
Whitaker joined several others as well. After moving to Harrisburg in
1943, Whitaker spent many weekends on Chesapeake Bay with his
wife Helen and his sailing buddies — Safford, Ingalls, Berg, Bill
Broske, and others. He taught Helen the art of navigation, and the
two of them sailed the larger boats from port to port. Whitaker, not
unexpectedly, became a boating expert.[36]

Whitaker had thought at several times of retiring and devoting his
attention to the important things — hunting, fishing, boating, and
flying. He looked into that possibility again in 1948. Whether or not
he was completely serious about retiring at that time is problematic,
but he did send away for a book about retirement in Florida.
Whitaker, who sent in for anything that interested him at a particular
time, received the book, entitled *How To Retire in Florida* and was

dissatisfied either with the book or the idea itself. He returned it to the publisher with the comment that it did "not meet my expectations." No doubt the book portrayed retirement as a time for lazy basking in the Florida sun, with card games and social events programmed for older citizens. For Whitaker, however, retirement called for as much energy and activity as work. For the time being, he decided to stick to business interspersed with his kind of meaningful play. There was, after all, still a good deal to be done with Aircraft-Marine Products Inc.[37]

U. A. Whitaker was generally pleased with his business situation by the end of the 1940s even though he wished more progress might have been made in the company's first eight full years. In a note accompanying Aircraft-Marine Products Inc.'s final payment to the Federal Reserve Bank, he expressed his sense of accomplishment and added his typically optimistic comment on future prospects.

> Compared to the statements which we submitted to you in our first negotiations, we have made a great deal of progress and we credit your organization with a very large share in that progress. Certainly the Federal Reserve of Philadelphia showed an interest and consideration beyond that warranted by the size of our business and the financial help given us enabled us to make a sizeable contribution to the war effort and to make the transition back to peacetime business. There is, of course, a great deal more to do in the way of improving our financial position, but the prospects look good to do this.

Aircraft-Marine Products Inc.'s prospects must have looked good to others as well. In 1946 Whitaker received the first of what later would become many offers to purchase his company. He politely refused this one and all the others that followed in the years ahead.[38]

The years 1946 through 1949 could not be called boom years. Aircraft-Marine Products Inc. managed to keep its sales fairly steady, averaging slightly under $2.5 million annually for those years, while the annual average profit after taxes improved, edging up to about 4 percent in the last three business years of the decade.[39] The next half-dozen years, however, would prove that Whitaker's optimism about future prospects for the electrical termination business was correct. His "little company" would become part of a major growth industry.

12. Foreign Trade Activities

Three years after Winston Churchill delivered his historic "Iron Curtain" speech in Fulton, Missouri, he returned to the United States to speak at an MIT convocation on the subject of "The Social Implications of Scientific Progress — an Appraisal at Mid-Century." The question was humanity, man's ability to control the future, and intellectual and political leaders from all over the world assembled in Boston to discuss the intelligent use of the scientific knowledge that had been accumulated over the years. Beneath the rational discussion of the betterment of mankind, lingered the equally rational fear of atomic holocaust as it might result from the divided world Churchill had defined in 1946. In March, 1949, Churchill recalled that day and reiterated his position.

> Three years ago I made a speech at Fulton. . . . Many people here and in my own country were startled and even shocked by what I said. . . . Today there is a very different climate of opinion. . . . We have the famous Mashall aid, the new unity in Western Europe, and now the Atlantic Pact. . . . No one could have brought about these immense changes . . . but for the astounding policy of the Russian Soviet government.

According to Churchill, Soviet policy had been engendered "because they fear the friendship of the West more than its hositility. They cannot afford to allow free and friendly intercourse to grow up between the vast areas they control and the civilizations of the West." Once again, Churchill had chosen an American forum to express the now widely accepted explanation of the origins of the cold war.[1]

U. A. Whitaker, MIT class of 1923, was in the audience that day in late March, 1949, listening to Winston Churchill's remarks and no doubt worrying about their implications. As a quietly patriotic American, Whitaker was sincerely concerned about the future of American society and in the years ahead would work in a variety of ways to ensure its preservation. Unlike his father, O. B. Whitaker, the now forty-nine-year-old business executive was not a flag waver. He was, however, a deeply conservative man politically, and like his father, supported conservative causes and conservative solutions to the nation's problems. Certainly he understood the complexity of political issues. As an experienced engineer, he struggled daily with complicated problems whose solutions did not come easily. As an experienced businessman, he had learned that corporate decision making was not based on simple explanations of the problems which had to be confronted. As both a businessman and an engineer, U. A. Whitaker lived in a world which, in the late 1940s and early 1950s, found itself embattled globally as well as nationally. That world of business and industry had created its own environment, one that was complex enough, indeed. Now that world perceived itself threatened from both the inside and the outside, and its response to those threats only compounded the problems and multiplied the complexity.

Professional management organizations, such as the National Industrial Conference Board, provided business executives with a wealth of information on business trends, management procedures, and social problems of a national and international nature. Founded in 1915 "to broaden the industrial viewpoint" of its members, the NICB was, in fact, an interesting example of the progressive movement in its obsession with industrial as well as societal efficiency. Its concern with what it termed "industrial unrest" marked the conservative direction of the Board's philosophy. In the sense that it wished to create a new generation of enlightened business and industrial leaders, it was reformist in nature. Recognizing that the uninhibited bootstrapping days of the so-called robber barons were now at an end, the NICB was committed to creating an atmosphere of industrial peace and progress.[2]

U. A. Whitaker belonged to the National Industrial Conference Board as well as to the management section of the American Society of Mechanical Engineers, whose goals paralleled those of the former organization. As a man committed to efficient management policies, Whitaker often attended conferences of both groups and benefited greatly from both the formal and informal discussions of the problems facing business managers. Whitaker's association with the NICB dated back to his Hoover and American Machine & Foundry days, when on various occasions he represented those companies at the NICB meetings usually held at the Waldorf-Astoria in New York City. Beginning in 1947, each year he faithfully attended the management conferences sponsored by the ASME and held at Skytop, a mountain retreat in the Pennsylvania Pocono Mountains.

These conferences also addressed themselves to large social issues. The 1947 ASME management conference was called "The Manager and the Forces He Contends with Today." The 1951 NICB meeting labeled the major evening session "Social Responsibilities of Business." Straightforward managerial topics such as plant expansion, productivity, and capital requirements were debated and discussed, but usually in the smaller panel sessions. The interest in social questions began as early as 1948, when both management organizations became increasingly concerned with employee problems generally termed human relations, and with the problem of keeping the peace in a world threatened by socialism and communism. As the cold war made its impact on the programs of these groups, the issue of domestic industrial peace and progress became intertwined with the fight for international tranquillity.[3]

The 1948 meeting of the NICB, which Whitaker attended, held a general session called "The Fight for Peace: America's Contribution." The major speaker at that meeting was General William ("Wild Bill") Joseph Donovan, head of the Office of Strategic Services (OSS) during the war and now head of a powerful Wall Street law firm. At that time Donovan was chairman of the American Committee on United Europe, which had as its goal the integration of Western Europe to provide a bulwark against the expansionary tendencies of the Soviet Union. The 1949 NICB meeting, which Whitaker did not attend, addressed itself primarily to a program for "averting socialism" and for warding off "the process of creeping collectivism" in the American economy. One session, for example, was devoted to the question of "how much social security can we afford?"[4]

The ASME Skytop conferences, which Whitaker attended with regularity in the early postwar years, began to include with more frequency antisocialist and pro-American panels. The 1951 Skytop program lists no fewer than three of seven group meetings devoted to the problems of preserving the American economic system. One, entitled "Understanding America's Miracles," received U. A. Whitaker's enthusiastic approval, as far as his penciled marginal notes reveal. The keynote speaker at the session received high marks from Whitaker as he discussed the responsibility of businessmen for maintaining their faith in the system and continually working to sell that system to the rest of America. The message was clear — the American free enterprise system was in competition with the unfree system of the Soviet Union.[5]

Combatting "isms" became a primary concern of these management organizations, and the improvement of industrial relations was seen as an essential means of shoring up the existing American system. Almost daily during these years, literature asking support for one or another organization committed to upholding and extending the promise of the American free enterprise system crossed Whitaker's desk. The insecurity of the business community was reflected in such statements as the following, printed over the signature of a president of a large steel company; in this instance the goal was to provide information to the confused young people of America:

> As you know, the newspapers, radio and general atmosphere are filled with all kinds of talk about the failure of America's capitalist business system — the very system whereby you and we are in business at all. . . . It is up to someone to give American youth an understanding of how this nation makes its living and has developed the greatest standard of living in the world.

Messages like this one soon became tied into the issue of national security, especially just before and immediately after the outbreak of the Korean War. In addition, fears first of depression and then of inflation further clouded the business picture. The preservation of the profit system seemed ultimately to be at stake as American business settled down to fight collectivist tendencies.[6]

The years before the outbreak of the Korean War in June, 1950, make up a curious period in American history. Companies like Aircraft-Marine Products Inc. were caught in a double dilemma — an unstable economic climate (essentially recessionary) and increasing engineering needs. Sales Manager G. Earle Walker, for example, just a year before the Korean hostilities began, informed ace salesman W. H. Mavity that the company could not give him more than a one-year contract because of business uncertainties. Mavity, largely responsible for cultivating the IBM account, was told by Walker that "management is determined to make a reasonable profit and survive." On the other hand, six months or so later, in early January, 1950, Automachine Division head F. L. Pierce wrote Sage at MIT pleading for leads to some experienced engineers because the "business was growing fast." Eighteen months later Aircraft-Marine Products Inc.'s engineering needs had tripled.[7]

In the meantime the growing imperatives of national defense began, quite naturally, to become mixed with the notion of industrial expansion. Along with a rapidly developing consumer market, the need for a much increased industrial output was obvious to most economic observers. Beginning early in 1950 and continuing on for some years, literature about opportunities for expansion came to Whitaker's desk and entered his files from a variety of sources.

Offers to locate came from chambers of commerce as far away as Duluth and several Canadian provinces. As the idea of industrial expansion became infused with a kind of patriotic fervor and linked with the concept of national defense ("in view of the world situation," as one such advertising piece put it), manufacturing growth came to seem a response to a national emergency.[8]

Whitaker, of course, was aware of the growing market for his products as a result of increasing defense requirements. Shortly after the Korean War began, he reported to his investors that "we are in a good position to change to war work since generally we will be dealing with the same customers and selling the same type of goods."[9] Whitaker, however, was not entirely pleased with the prospect of doing business with the government on a large scale again. His remembrance of those relationships during World War II could not have dimmed much, and in any case the daily mail brought him numerous reminders. One management planning group in Washington, D. C., looking for new clients, made the point directly in a letter that arrived in mid-August, 1950.

> It's quite probable that your company's profits will be affected more by what happens in Washington during the next few years than by any other single factor. Whether the war spreads or not, you will have to deal with the government on almost every move you make. In the extreme, this could mean that you will be told what to make, how much to make, what raw materials you may buy, whom you may hire, what wages you may pay, what prices you may charge, and what profits you may keep.

Whitaker, as we have seen, had strong views on this kind of government meddling in business. He must have shuddered when he read these words. In fact, by October, 1950, Aircraft-Marine Products Inc. was already feeling the effects of copper shortages, the existing supply being administered by Washington bureaucrats.[10]

Throughout the early 1950s, a multitude of conflicting realities and images forced themselves into the considerations of businessmen. The cold war and its attendant pressures on industry to expand for purposes of national security reached down to the lowest levels of business boosterism, including both state and local departments and chambers of commerce. Anticipating increased defense contracts in the state of Pennsylvania, for example, that state's Department of Commerce contacted such companies as Aircraft-Marine Products Inc. in an effort to help them identify qualified subcontractors for their defense contracts. Regional defense production committees were set up by the department "in order to help meet the present challenge to America." Similar help, of course, was received from Washington. One pertinent example was Washington's attempt to attract private industrial investment in Puerto Rico, nominally in the interest of national defense. The Office of Emergency Planning, working with the Economic Development Administration of Puerto Rico, began actively looking for continental-based firms to expand in that United States territory. Early in May, 1951, Aircraft-Marine Products Inc. received information encouraging it to expand in Puerto Rico and a year later, as we shall see, the company created a manufacturing operation on the island.[11]

But it was not, strictly speaking, the national defense needs of the 1950s that led U. A. Whitaker and his associates to consider foreign markets. Whitaker had for some years known about the potential of foreign outlets for American products. His work experience prior to Aircraft-Marine Products Inc. had been with companies that either had foreign operations or held patents in foreign countries. Furthermore, during the Second World War, Whitaker had briefly investigated the possibility of selling solderless terminations in Great Britain to meet the demands of that nation's aircraft manufacturing needs. In March, 1945, the possibility of setting up a postwar arrangement with the British was still receiving the company's attention.[12]

Plagued by the problems of postwar reconversion, and even of survival, Whitaker had his attention momentarily deflected from notions of selling and manufacturing worldwide in significant volume. But company postwar planning did not exclude that possibility. With the European Recovery Plan in full operation by 1949, Western Europe once again began to look like a promising market for U. S. products. With the decision to allow West Germany to rebuild, the prospect of Western European political and economic unity no longer looked like a pipedream. At the end of September, 1949, Whitaker received a letter from his longtime friend George Hastings, still patent counsel at American Machine & Foundry, informing him that his company had filed a patent application in Germany on one of Whitaker's inventions, the cigarette-detecting and -correcting apparatus. Underscoring America's policy of rehabilitating West Germany, Hastings wrote: "The fact is that the U. S. wants to re-establish an effective German patent system. France is very much against re-establishing the German patent system with French logic, namely that a patent system is very helpful to a country's industrial success and efficiency, and France does not want that for Germany." It would not be long before Aircraft-Marine Products Inc. would be doing its own business in Germany. In the meantime, Whitaker was pleased with this report from Hastings and he wished American Machine & Foundry well in the new venture, but indicated in his typically humorous manner that he did not intend "to rush out and buy American Machine & Foundry stock on the prospects." (Whitaker apparently changed his mind, for less than two months later he did, in fact, purchase 100 shares of American Machine & Foundry stock.)[13]

Just a day or two before receiving Hastings' letter about the future business potential of the German market, Whitaker received a copy of a memo from his own Export Division on the future of the export market, especially as it applied to England. Although the current British shortage of dollars effectively prohibited British manufacturing operations from purchasing outside the sterling area in large quantities, R. C. Conangla, then head of Aircraft-Marine Products Inc.'s Export Division, pointed out that this would not always be the case, for the British in the near future would begin to increase their dollar reserves. But more important than this observation was Conagla's recognition of one significant fact that he believed was of considerable importance to the company's export future: neither Great Britain, nor any other country for that matter, manufactured solderless terminals in such quantity (if at all) to permit them to export large quantities. For the present, the shortage of dollars around the world impeded the growth of Aircraft-Marine Products Inc.'s export market, but the potential market was most assuredly there as the need for the company's system of electrical termination was recognized around the globe. A vacuum was waiting to be filled.[14]

Shortly after the beginning of August 1951, Sales Manager G. Earle Walker received a confidential memo on foreign trade activities from R. C. Campbell, Aircraft-Marine Products Inc.'s representative in France. Marshall Holcombe, the company's patent lawyer, remembers "dumping" Campbell on a boat for France with instructions to evaluate the desirability of establishing a manufacturing operation in that country. Campbell did so and reported affirmatively to Walker. "It appears that a wholly owned subsidiary in France is eminently feasible at the present time. IBM has given us as much assurance as they possibly can that they will purchase from us in Europe for all their European plants. If we cannot supply them in

Europe, they will be forced to manufacture terminals themselves." In fact, IBM did not want to undertake terminal manufacturing in its own plants because of other urgent production needs. The head of IBM World Trade Corporation in New York had already informed Campbell that he had ordered the suspension of terminal manufacturing in IBM overseas plants and was, therefore, very eager for Aircraft-Marine Products Inc. to get its operation going as soon as possible.[15]

IBM first became a customer of Aircraft-Marine Products Inc. in 1942. IBM orders in those days were modest — under $1,500 in 1942 and under $500 in 1943. After the war, when Bill Mavity took over the account, IBM business became a more significant factor in the company's sales strategy. By the late 1940s, Aircraft-Marine Products Inc. was "more and more a part of IBM's supply picture," as S. W. Pollock put it.[16]

In 1951, as things developed, Aircraft-Marine Products Inc. also was faced with a business decision of considerable magnitude. Despite Whitaker's long-term interest in overseas expansion, the question remained as to whether or not the time was right for a commitment to a European manufacturing operation. Alternative approaches to foreign trade were possible. Exporting products was an obvious solution. There was as well the possibility of licensing someone else to manufacture Aircraft-Marine Products Inc.'s system. Finally, there was the option of the company setting up its own manufacturing facilities overseas. Now, with IBM's increasing domestic dependence on Aircraft-Marine Products Inc. as its supplier of essential electrial termination devices, the possibility of a European operation became very attractive. As the company's engineering and development staff got deeper and deeper into satisfying IBM's electrical engineering needs, the relationship of the two companies became more symbiotic than problematic, despite the fact that not all business done with IBM was particularly profitable in those early years. The most compelling argument in support of a foreign operation in France was that the IBM offer itself, a virtual guaranteed volume of business, assured Aircraft-Marine Products Inc. a foot in the European market.[17]

Campbell's confidential memo to Walker paid considerable attention to the details of setting up a profitable operation in France. He had made the rounds of the various French governmental agencies, both in the United States and abroad, in an effort to gain approval for a wholly owned subsidiary in France, and he had discovered no significant impediments to the plan, at least from the

French point of view. "If we comply with the provisions of a certain notice #419 of the Office des Changes of the French government," he informed Walker, "we are assured by France of the convertibility of dividends as well as of the proceeds from liquidation of capital investment." Other equally significant indications of cooperation and essential guarantees were also forthcoming.

> There is no statutory limit in France on the amount of dividends which can be converted annually and in some cases 20% to 30% of the capital invested can be transferred annually. In addition to the guarantees of the French government we can get a twelve-year insurance contract from the United States Government, through the Export-Import Bank and the ECA Industrial Guarantee Division, which will guarantee our investment against expropriation and will furthermore guarantee the transfer of dividends.

Campbell listed a series of other advantages, such as the tax picture in France, which he described as "not totally unfavorable," and the fact that France had no excess profits tax. Finally, the shipping of equipment to the French subsidiary posed no problem; in fact, machinery, dies, parts, and other goods could become part of the capital paid in and the subsidiary would be allowed to pay for the equipment in American dollars. In this way the parent company could sell those needed items at a profit rather than at cost.[18]

By the fall of 1951, the decision to open in France had virtually been made, virtually but not officially. Walker, as sales manager, was impatient for action by Aicraft-Marine Products Inc.'s management group because he wanted to get on with the work of formulating a sales program. His irritation showed through in an early November memo to C. J. Fredricksen, the company's assistant treasurer, and one of the members of the management group: "It is my opinion from conversation which we have had that we have pretty much determined to go ahead with the Paris Factory. As a matter of fact, Mr. Campbell has acquired an apartment in France on the basis of our preliminary conversations; most particularly on the basis of my promises as a result of my conversations." In late January, 1952, at a directors' meeting held at the New York Yacht Club, the decision to operate in France was approved. Only the details remained to be worked out.[19]

In February, 1952, S. W. Pollock, now in charge of getting the French operation off the ground, was in frequent mail communication with Campbell in Paris. Campbell, who was deeply involved in setting up the formal corporation — Societe AMP de France —

maintained his contacts with IBM officials in France, keeping them up to date on Aircraft-Marine Products Inc.'s progress. Since three to six months were usually required for the filing of corporate papers, things seemed to be dragging on, but in fact Campbell was accomplishing a great deal given the vicissitudes of French bureaucracy. Early in June, Campbell lunched with Pailloux of IBM and reported on his progress to date. Pailloux was more than pleased. "He was amazed at the progress we have made," Campbell informed Pollock, "and said it was better than his most optimistic expectations. He is going to send me within the next few days firm orders for the rest of the year for France, Germany and Italy. He is hoping to begin using our terminals in these countries September 1. I am hoping so too."[20]

So cooperative was IBM, that Pailloux promised Campbell all the brass he needed while he awaited his own supply from the States. By mid-July, Campbell had his IBM orders in hand, and by August 1 the necessary machinery and dies were shipped from Harrisburg through the French port of Le Havre. Production began almost immediately and on August 25, 1952, AMP de France shipped its first order of terminals to IBM's French operation. Campbell must have hurried to his typewriter to report the news to Pollock in Harrisburg. "The first shipment of 800,000 terminals just went out the door." AMP de France was officially in business. IBM, Campbell happily noted, was "amazed and delighted by our progress." By the first of September, IBM in Italy, Germany, Scotland, and Holland had sent in orders for terminals, and the future looked bright, at least as R. C. Campbell peered into it. At that point his major problem seemed to be the complaints of neighbors living in an adjoining apartment house who were feeling the effects of vibrations from the manufacturing presses. Campbell apologized to the tenants and padded the presses.[21]

It was the fall of 1952 before Campbell encountered his first real problem. IBM orders, although generous, did not begin to require the available manufacturing capacity and, therefore, the need for additional customers quickly became apparent. On October 1, he told Pollock, "we have decided that we must find other customers as soon as possible" and indicated that he was beginning to make the necessary contacts. The very next day Campbell was at the headquarters of Simca, the auto manufacturer, and a few days later he approached Compagnie Bull, a large manufacturer of business machines in France. Later in the month, while on a trip to supervise the installation of automatic machines in various IBM plants, he noted a beginning flurry of European activity in the manufacture of their own terminals. "We are none too soon in commencing our production in Europe," he informed Pollock, while advising him that perhaps Aircraft-Marine Products Inc. ought to move rapidly to establish its patent position in all Western European countries. He foresaw eventual competition from European sources who, like Aircraft-Marine Products Inc., were beginning to recognize the growing needs of manufacturers for effective termination devices. The major advantage that the company had over these newer arrivals was one that Campbell and other Aircraft-Marine Products Inc. observers emphasized on many occasions — European manufactured solderless terminals were very crude compared to Aircraft-Marine Products Inc.'s system. Campbell was able to convince his customers that although European models were cheaper, "the difference in quality and reliability of ours was worth the extra cost."[22]

In November, Campbell was traveling the continent and the British Isles looking for orders to supplement the company's IBM business. In England he contacted British Tabulating Machines, Ltd., a longtime builder of IBM equipment until the two firms went their separate ways in the late 1940s. BTM was interested and the way was cleared for that corporation to buy from Aircraft-Marine Products Inc. when IBM in England agreed that the termination it was buying from Aircraft-Marine Products Inc. was not, as Campbell put it, "exclusively theirs." The real problem, as Campbell quickly discovered, was how to get into the British market from France. Import duties made the prospect very unlikely. Another solution had to be found.[23]

One possibility was the licensing route, that is, the granting of licenses to manufacture and to sell the company's terminals, specifically loose piece terminals, those not applied by automatic machines. There was, however, a difference of opinion developing between Campbell in Europe and Aircraft-Marine Products Inc. headquarters in Harrisburg. During the war, Aircraft-Marine Products Inc. had begun negotiating an agreement with a company in England called Erma Ltd., headed by E. Marx. Although nothing substantial developed during that period or immediately after the war, the relationship was maintained, and Marx even traveled to the United States to look over Aircraft-Marine Products Inc.'s operation and pursue a formal agreement more seriously. This possibility, therefore, remained a real alternative as the concept of the English market came closer to being a fact. The difference of opinion came about as a

result of Campbell's trip to England. In his conversations with the
British Board of Trade, the ultimate arbitrator of British industrial
requirements, Campbell learned what he believed to be some
disquieting information about Marx's manner of doing business —
nothing illegal, to be sure, but in Campbell's opinion not entirely
straightforward.[24]

Campbell believed, furthermore, that Marx would never be
successful in convincing the Board of Trade to approve the licensing
agreement because the result of the agreement would produce fewer
rather than more dollars for the starved British dollar balance. In
addition to this, Campbell asserted that Marx had not succeeded in
selling the proper industries and ministries on the essential need for
Aircraft-Marine Products Inc.'s termination system, a basic requirement before the British government would allow new manufacturing
into the country. A product had to be essential to the prosperity of
the country and had to promise that more dollars would be brought
in than would be sent out. Campbell doubted that Marx had done or
was prepared to do the necessarily "tremendous amount of intensive
and specialized missionary and sales activity" that was needed.[25]

Harrisburg had another view of the situation. Aircraft-Marine
Products Inc. had very little capital to expend in new ventures like
the one in France and the one now being contemplated for Great
Britain. The problem of available management personnel also plagued
the relatively small organization. There were barely enough good
people to go around. In fact, the decision to operate a manufacturing
unit in France placed severe strains on the already strained
management pool. Overextension, therefore, both in terms of capital
and personnel, was on management's collective mind when, in
November, 1952, they were seriously considering a licensing
agreement with Erma Ltd. as a way to conserve both of these scarce
resources. Pollock explained Harrisburg's thinking to Campbell:

> During last week Mr. Marx was in our office for several days at
> which time his proposal for an initial operation in England by A-MP
> was thoroughly discussed. . . . A few of the reasons behind such a
> move [licensing Erma Ltd.] at the time should be brought out so
> that you can entertain them in your thinking, along with the reasons
> and arguments you have advanced through Walker, for not going
> into such an agreement based on your previous contact with Erma.
> First, for the foreseeable future, the American company will be very
> much limited as to any capital expenditure it would be able to make
> in a foreign operation such as France or England. This is due to
> several factors, among them being a continued growth of our

American operation in the face of severe taxation, as well as the contemplated establishment of a manufacturing subsidiary in Puerto Rico which will become fact the early part of next year.

Additionally, we are setting up a selling organization to better serve Western Hemisphere countries, particularly Canada. There is also in the negotiation process, a formation of manufacturing and sales facilities in Brazil. All these factors make us inevitably come to the conclusion that we would not be able to set up any operation, particularly for loose piece work in England, in the foreseeable future of perhaps several years.

Pollock concluded with the management judgment that nonexclusive manufacturing and selling licensing agreements with Erma Ltd. was the best possible arrangement for at least the following five-year period; in lieu of that, setting up some means of manufacturing and selling either from France or the United States was a possibility. Pollock did advise Campbell that the agreement with Marx and Erma was extremely tentative pending further negotiations.[26]

The debate went on throughout the late winter and early spring of 1953, and by that time another licensing possibility emerged to complicate the picture. While the British market languished, as far as Aircraft-Marine Products Inc. was concerned, a well-established manufacturing firm called Hellerman Ltd. was briefly considered as a licensee. Harrisburg sent another man to England, Ricki de Laet, to report on the termination climate, and in his first report to Walker, de Laet underscored the urgency of the situation by telling him that "A-MP must either start or get off the pot. . . . There are a number of companies seriously thinking of entering into solderless terminals." De Laet's tour of the north of England in April, 1953, revealed two interesting things, both of which supported Campbell's observations on the same matters. The first was that England's method of electrical termination was still mainly old-fashioned and in some instances quite crude, and the second was that he had discovered practically no evidence that Mr. Marx of Erma Ltd. had ever been seen in the industrial north of England. On this latter point, de Laet wrote, "my trip up country has convinced me that if Marx has shown anyone our lugs, they certainly don't act like it and secondly had he pushed them, he could have gotten more import licenses." De Laet, like Campbell, supported the notion of a wholly owned Aircraft-Marine Products Inc. manufacturing and selling organization. At any rate, the problem of breaking into the British market was placed on a back-burner for the time being, although sporadic attention was given to the licensing arrangement with Hellerman Ltd.[27]

Meanwhile, in February, 1953, Aircraft-Marine Products Inc. established a wholly owned subsidiary called American Pamcor Inc., to market products manufactured by its newly created Puerto Rican operation. Although electrical termination manufacturing was not labor intensive, it was hoped that Puerto Rican production would make possible some price advantages on a variety of items. American Pamcor Inc. was conceived as a complement to Aircraft-Marine Products Inc., intended to go after kinds of business not normally handled by the parent firm; yet, at the same time a spirited competition between the two selling organizations was envisioned. O. W. Holmes, who had worked for four years in Aircraft-Marine Products Inc.'s sales division under G. Earle Walker, was named to head the new subsidiary. Right at the outset Walker warned Holmes against adopting a policy of competition on the basis of price, first, because American Pamcor Inc. would come off second best in such a campaign, and, second, because price as a sales strategy had never been the company's way of doing business.[28]

Walker pointed out to Holmes that limited capital would be one of his major problems. "A-MP had similar problems in its beginning," Walker noted, "but yours are somewhat more acute. Aircraft-Marine Products Inc. was fortunate in one respect; it did not have Aircraft-Marine Products Inc. with which to compete. You do." And then the warning about price-cutting: "As an important member of A-MP's Sales Department for over four years, you are aware I presume, that I can either unleash the wolves or hold them back." Walker promised Holmes he would hold the wolves in check for the time being. Some few months later, Holmes presented his policy for the newly established American Pamcor Inc. operation. That presentation stressed price more than any other factor and Holmes got some more advice from Walker on that subject:

> As Herman Haas has pointed out, we arrived at our present position in the Aircraft Industry and, as a matter of fact, in the solderless terminal field through the literal application of our slogan "Precision Engineering Applied to the End of a Wire." We never have been price manufacturers in the sense that we have been lower in the initial cost and, as a matter of fact, we constantly have been able to face competition lower in price and overcome this competition either with a lower installed cost or a better engineered product, or both, and, of course, selling has had something to do with it.

Walker urged Holmes to come up with a more innovative approach to selling and made a number of specific suggestions that might be followed up. The point was, however, that in a price-competition approach to selling, Holmes and American Pamcor Inc. would not only lose but would also be guilty of violating established company ideals.[29]

As we have seen, a good number of G. Earle Walker's memos often had a moral, seldom hidden and directed generally towards "management" and indirectly towards the person receiving the memo. The moral, at present, had to do with innovativeness in sales thinking. Walker gave Holmes that message, and he had the same advice for the parent company's engineering segment. For several years now, Walker had been issuing warnings about the lack of product diversification and development work, which he believed was essential to moving the company forward. Just after the first of the year, in January, 1950, he directed a memo to U. A. Whitaker, entitled "Humpty-Dumpty." In that particular memo, Walker warned Whitaker about companies that "tumble from the wall of prosperity and crack [their heads] on a stone called bankruptcy by neglecting to diversify. . . activities."[30]

A Walker memo to Holmes (with a blind copy to Whitaker) in April, 1953, reiterated this viewpoint — the lack of product improvement at Aircraft-Marine Products Inc. could have serious consequences. "We have lost not only our pioneering position but, apparently, our pioneering zeal. Competition has caught up with us in quantity and that is not the fault of the competition — that is our fault. If we are unable or unwilling to expedite our program of product improvement. . . then I say we must consider price as our next competitive deterrent." This was, of course, a double-edge message, applicable both to American Pamcor Inc., and the parent firm. When Walker concluded his memo to Holmes by telling him to hold off on a selling strategy based on lower prices ("until we are certain we cannot consolidate our position through our traditional practices of product superiority.") he meant the message primarily for Whitaker. His list of suggested improvements included nylon-insulated terminals for the aircraft industry, miniature hand tools, large insulated terminals, and aluminum terminals, to name but a few. In the midst of both domestic and foreign expansion, Walker was insisting that new markets could only be conquered with new products. Walker's files were filled with requests from his sales personnel, who were attempting to enter profitable new fields. It was simply the case of the customer dictating his needs to the manufacturer, a business process in which Walker firmly believed.[31]

Whitaker, of course, was in total agreement with Walker about the relationship between company growth and the development of new products. Engineering, in fact, was constantly at work on most of the items contained in Walker's list. But as sales manager, Walker filled a job that required immediate gratification in the sense that new products had to be available for sale on a regular basis. As sales manager and as a man inclined more towards impetuosity than patience, Walker had a decided tendency to become irritated if things were not accomplished rapidly enough. Whitaker, while recognizing the absolute need for a continued outpouring of new products and new product lines, complemented his sales manager's impatient temperament by taking a rather more considered long-range approach, both to expansion and new knowledge produced through experimental research. Where Walker criticized engineering research for not devoting all of its efforts to the immediate solving of the problem of wire terminations and connectors, Whitaker emphasized not only this kind of immediate research need but also projects that would be attractive to customers a good number of years in the future.[32]

The divergent points of view of Whitaker and Walker, already important in the early years of Aircraft-Marine Products Inc.'s development, took on a new significance as the company began its overseas expansion. Behind all the debate and discussion about where and how to expand the company's operations, the assumption remained that new product development must play an integral part in the success of those expansion plays. The question at issue was how far in the future development work should aim. It should not be forgotten that Whitaker's experience during World War II convinced him of the absolute necessity of thinking continually about the years ahead. The cost of doing very little fundamental development research during the war was graphically revealed in Aircraft-Marine Products Inc.'s profit and loss statements in the early postwar years.

The survey of foreign market potentials continued under Whitaker's guidance at a regular pace in the years 1953-55. Opportunities for expansion in Asia were being investigated in the fall of 1953. John T. Burnite, Jr., who became a kind of traveling "troubleshooter" in this effort, was already checking on the possibility of gaining a foothold in the growing Japanese market. His reports to Whitaker and Walker indicated that a mainland operation, as opposed to an offshore manufacturing unit, would be a feasible approach to the Japanese market. The business potential in Japan, Burnite noted, was tremendous and the business atmosphere on the island, so much like that in the United States, was particularly conducive to operating there. Burnite later made similar surveys in Brazil and Australia and eventually Aircraft-Marine Products Inc. would locate operations in all three countries.[33]

Whitaker, who never allowed any interesting proposition to escape investigation, used the occasion of the 10th International Management Congress, held from February 12 to March 6, 1954, in Sao Paulo, Brazil, to spend some time in that country getting a feel for the business atmosphere. After the conference was concluded, Whitaker was asked by its directors to comment on its value. Whitaker always preferred informality in his business associations as well as in his personal life, and his report reflects that preference. He noted that at a social event, when he had an opportunity to speak with several executives from General Motors' Sao Paulo plant, he learned more than he did at the more formal roundtable discussions, which were, as he put it, "dominated by the professional experts [who] spent most of the time talking to themselves on subjects we already heard at various meetings we have attended." On the other hand, the engagement he had with the General Motors' executives was "one of the most constructive things I did at Sao Paulo in that I could talk directly and informally with the management people at the General Motors' plant in Sao Paulo and find out just what they were doing in all the types of cases that came to mind."[34]

Although Aircraft-Marine Products Inc.'s primary overseas interest in the early 1950s lay in Europe, investigations went on all over the globe. For example, in replying to an unsolicited summary of economic opportunity in Turkey, Whitaker noted that possible expansion in that area had already been assessed:

> We have considered opening in Turkey and other parts of Europe, in fact have had two people in Europe for over a year making general surveys. We do have a little [always "a little"] plant in France, as you probably know, and are planning to open another in England which is about all we feel we could do at the present time. Possibly next year we will consider further expansion at which time we might want to consider Turkey and may want to make use of some of your advice.[35]

Even by 1954, Whitaker's statement about "planning to open" a British operation was slightly premature. S. W. Pollock, some two

months later, noted in a letter to the Hellerman company in England
that Aircraft-Marine Products Inc. had "not as yet reached a
satisfactory solution" on the matter. In fact, as Pollock informed the
British manufacturing concern, "at the present time we are thinking
of opening a little plant in Holland." Pollock did point out, however,
that some sort of English operation would come eventually, since the
company's management did not believe that either France or Holland
could effectively serve the British market. He suggested that because
of the large investment necessary for the opening of an English
manufacturing plant, more detailed market surveys would be in order
under the direction of Sales Manager Walker. The important matter
here was that Aircraft-Marine Products Inc. had by this time totally
given up the idea of licensing anybody and had now decided to jump
feet first into the English market with its own manufacturing and
sales operation.[36]

In the fall of 1954, S. W. Pollock, as director of the Foreign Trade
Division, traveled to Europe to get a firsthand view of the French
operation, to choose a location for the new plant in the Netherlands,
and to see what could be done about opening in England. Like AMP
de France, the manufacturing unit in the Netherlands would begin
modestly with an investment of about $20,000 and the prospect of
approximately $13,000 per month in sales. And again, it would be
IBM business that would account for the major share of
AMP-Holland's bookings. Pollock's first reports from Europe were
cautiously optimistic about sales potential for 1955. He estimated that
perhaps the European operation might do $1 million during the year.
In the Netherlands, Pollock looked over a number of possible sites,
including Amsterdam, Leiden, and Rotterdam, but saw as the best
possibility the little town of 's-Hertogenbosch. He reported that
's-Hertogenbosch had the best looking building available for
occupancy and the presence of other large corporations there, such as
Remington Rand, convinced him that Aircraft-Marine Products Inc.'s
decision to settle there would be a wise one. Generally, Pollock was
pleased with what he saw. "I believe A-MP is doing the right thing in
coming to Holland," he told Harrisburg. "The country, the people,
the American plants already here contribute to that feeling." By late
October, 1954, the final arrangements to open a subsidiary in the
town of 's-Hertogenbosch in the Netherlands were completed, and
the process of getting the plant in operation began. The Dutch
government, along with the Netherlands Industrial Institute and the
local officials, had been extremely cooperative and Aircraft-Marine

Products Inc. management encountered very few obstacles in setting up the new firm.[37]

Pollock's experience in Great Britain was another matter. He termed his efforts there "one of the most frustrating jobs I have ever undertaken in my life." Pollock quickly discovered his path strewn with bureaucratic obstacles that he had continually to struggle over. In the preparation of an application for an investment permit, for example, one official interview followed another, with no apparent end in sight. Finally, with the application filed in March, 1955, and knowing that some days, if not weeks, would pass before any official action would be taken, Pollock set off to look for a proper plant location.[38]

Pollock found his choices limited. His first desire to set up outside of London was rejected by the government, telling Pollock that if Aircraft-Marine Products Inc. wanted to do business in Great Britain, it would have to settle in some economically distressed area such as Ireland, Wales, or Scotland. Pollock rejected Ireland because of the problem of shipping across water to England and was unimpressed with Wales. In the end he chose Scotland, noting that the Scots appeared to "be hard working and diligent." With the decline of traditional jobs in such industries as coal mining and shipbuilding, the Scottish Industrial Estates were working hard to attract new industry. By 1955 they had succeeded in drawing several American-based firms into the Glasgow area — IBM, National Cash Register, and Burroughs, to name but three. But the industrial parks in Glasgow were unsatisfactory from Pollock's point of view, for no proper building was available. The only feasible alternative was to take over a building in the Port of Glasgow, some 15 to 20 miles west of the city. Pollock learned that a building there would soon be available because the firm then occupying the premises was about to go bankrupt, and eventually that site was chosen.[39]

When Pollock returned to London from Glasgow early in March, 1955, however, the reality of opening in Great Britain did not seem near at hand. He still faced the long process of convincing the British government that Aircraft-Marine Products Inc. would both contribute to the improvement of the nation's dollar balance and provide a valuable commodity not presently available for industrial use. Pollock was not so certain about his ability to argue convincingly about the dollar balance, but he was unusually optimistic about selling the British on the second point. There was no doubt in his mind that Aircraft-Marine Products Inc.'s termination system would prove vital to the British economy.

S. W. Pollock's nine-page, single-spaced memo to U. A. Whitaker, dated March 18, 1955, is an intelligent, informed report on the total Western European market picture as he perceived it during his several months' stay in France, the Netherlands, and Great Britain. In addition to Pollock's microscopic analysis of the problems of living and working in the European environment at that time, the report also presented information on the long-range problems that the parent company might face in its international operations. Pollock was certain, for example, that more money would be needed to see the young operations through the early period of growth. But perhaps even more significant was his observation that "the biggest single problem in Europe at the moment is to produce sales." Like other Aircraft-Marine Products Inc. people on the European scene, Pollock saw that the company's current production facilities on the continent were consistently able to produce well beyond the IBM requirements, which had gotten them started in the first place. "I think that . . . the sales force is certainly going to have to be built up to provide to at least some degree the same hard driving type of selling which has been largely responsible for the growth of the American company." This task, Pollock suggested, could best be accomplished by G. Earle Walker was there, "shaking things up," as Pollock put it. The sales force we need so badly at this time."

As Pollock knew, Walker was already on his way to Europe to do just that. When Pollock returned to Europe in the fall of 1955, Walker was there, " shaking things up," as Pollock put it. The outlook for the Netherlands and France, Pollock was able to report to U. A. Whitaker early in October of that year, "never [looked] brighter." He noted that Walker's quotas for the following year — $500,000 for the Netherlands and $800,000 for France — would probably be met. Whitaker arrived in Europe on his own tour later that month and he was able to see this progress for himself. By the end of 1956, Aircraft-Marine Products Inc.'s European subsidiaries accounted for $1.3 million of the company's total sales of approximately $33. 5 million. Each year thereafter the percentage of foreign sales would rise with the addition of new subsidiaries in Europe and other parts of the world. Aircraft-Marine Products Inc.'s representatives would travel the world over looking for new opportunities and new markets, and eventually over twenty wholly owned subsidiaries would comprise the multinational operation.[40]

Meanwhile, at home, sales quadrupled between 1950 and 1955. The problems accompanying that growth presented new challenges and forced complex decisions for Aircraft-Marine Products Inc.'s management — among them, the question of going public in 1956. During the next ten-year period, sales would increase over five times again, and by 1965 the company would become one of the 500 largest corporations in the United States. Aircraft-Marine Products Inc. would no longer be U. A. Whitaker's "little company." Consequently, Whitaker's policy of "engineering the hell out of a product" would meet its severest test, for in the prosperity of the present, well-intentioned men have a tendency to overlook the future. Whitaker's major role in the years ahead would be to remind his associates that, indeed, there would be a tomorrow.

13. Expansion in the 1950's

Evidence for the increasing success of U. A. Whitaker and for the growing importance of his company began to pile up steadily in the early 1950's. Late in 1953, Whitaker received a letter from the editors of *American Biographies*, requesting an account of his career for the next edition (1954). In the spring of 1954, U. A. Whitaker was awarded an honorary Doctor of Science degree by Elizabethtown College for his contributions to engineering and to business. By this time, Whitaker was a member of a number of professional organizations, including the prestigious American Association for the Advancement of Science.[1]

As Aircraft-Marine Products Inc. (now frequently referred to as A-MP) steadily increased its share of the electrical termination market between 1950 and 1955, management began to reflect, somewhat self-consciously, an awareness that future growth had become a certainty. In the spring of 1954, management formed a new committee, chaired by U. A. Whitaker and including G. Earle Walker, C. J. Fredricksen, V. E. Carlson and S. W. Pollock, to project a five-year sales plan for the company. Marshall Holcombe, the company's patent lawyer, further impressed the notion of significant growth on management in a memo concerning the intricacies of existing antitrust legislation. "The company is a substantially larger factor in the nation's economic system today than it was ten years ago," he told the Executive Committee. "The larger A-MP becomes the more likely it will be that antitrust enforcement will review our methods of doing business looking for questionable practices to which to attribute our success." As Holcombe explained it later, the Justice Department believed that if one company did consistently better than its competitors, it must be violating the law somewhere. According to Holcombe, officials at the Justice Department did not operate on the premise that any one company in a particular area could possibly be better managed than any other company against which it competed.[2]

U. A. Whitaker, however, did operate on the premise that with superior products, developed through superior engineering and sold and serviced through a superior sales organization, one company, namely his, should and could outstrip the competition. With the challenge of maintaining superiority always before them, the people in Aircraft-Marine Products Inc. could, Whitaker believed, continually meet the competition. As the company's chief patent lawyer, Holcombe was charged by Whitaker with seeing that members of the organization observe all antitrust laws. Whitaker sincerely felt that the company's personnel were better than those in any competing firm, and he was more than willing to play the game within the existing rules. Although the opportunity existed, for example, to operate in Europe under somewhat less restrictive antitrust legislation, Whitaker chose to follow the rules and regulations of American laws, believing again that Aircraft-Marine Products Inc. could win even under that considerable handicap.[3]

An interesting illustration of this point of view was the question of selling application tools (automatic machines or hand-tools) to European customers and then requiring them to use those application devices only on Aircraft-Marine Products Inc. terminals. Holcombe, who spent some time and effort investigating this possibility, discovered that most of the European antitrust laws indicated a premise that a European user of Aircraft-Marine Products Inc.'s hand tools and machines could be legally compelled to restrict his use of those hand tools and machines to applying the company's terminals. It should be pointed out that there was nothing in American antitrust law to keep a company from following a foreign nation's law in this area. That issue was continually examined by antitrust experts in the United States, but it was never altogether resolved. Whitaker, however, despite occasional pressure from his sales personnel elected to proceed under the more restrictive American laws. His method for sales reflected this general attitude toward meeting competition: let sales convince a potential customer that by using Aircraft-Marine Products Inc. application tools and terminals, he would have a final installed product better than that offered by competition and one that would be trouble free. That approach was implemented, and with outstanding results. A good number of Aircraft-Marine Products Inc.'s foreign customers were convinced that it was safer to use only the full line of Aircraft-Marine Products Inc.'s products on the application tools furnished by the company.[4]

In addition to external evidence of growth, such as increased sales volume and the penetration of foreign markets, internal company policies and procedures also reflected a changing and expanding situation in the early years of the 1950s. The relationship between information and decision making and the search for new business opportunities were acknowledged with the creation of a staff analysis department under Leon V. Whipple, brought to the company for that purpose. Whipple, who had been employed by Aircraft-Marine Products Inc. some years earlier, was urged by S. W. Pollock to return in late 1954 to establish the new department. "The type of position we have in mind," he wrote Whipple, "would deal with analyses and statistics with the broad objective of presenting factual information which would guide this company toward future investments and which would bring the greatest overall benefit to the Company." Whipple soon defined his role in these terms, explaining to management that the primary purpose of a staff analyst is to "provide data that would help management determine a course of action which would be most likely to promote continued company growth and prosperity."[5]

There were a number of approaches available to achieve that goal as Whipple described it, the more important of which could generally be classified under the umbrella heading of diversification. A company might, for example, diversify by attempting to move into markets not presently being exploited, such as public utilities (a field Aircraft-Marine Products Inc. had great difficulty entering) or into another service area, such as the building trades, to supplement business gained through manufactured goods. There was, of course, always the prospect of diversification through merger, a frequent solution to the problems accompanying growth in the mid-1950s. Although a good deal of material on attractive merger opportunities was collected in these years, it was never Whitaker's intention to expand or diversify in that manner. Through Whitaker's leadership over the years, a company policy had developed based on the philosophy that the company's engineering people could produce new ideas and new product lines which would be as good as, or superior to, any that might be purchased on the market through acquiring the rights to a new product or to a company already marketing that product. Whitaker's extraordinary thoroughness in everything he undertook provided the impetus for the compilation of statistics about possible acquisitions, but after all the rocks had been turned over, as Marshall Holcombe described the process, any money available for investment always went to finance an idea that originated at Aircraft-Marine Products Inc. Someone always seemed to come up with that better idea, and consequently the company's growth continued to be anchored to the notion of internal new-product development.[6]

However, diversification and growth through new technological developments, which in turn led to the development of new profitable product lines, was an approach more easily asserted than accomplished. Various members of management, in addition to U. A. Whitaker, voiced frequent concern about the state of research and development work, and Sales Manager G. Earle Walker's view of the problem was perhaps typical. In the late summer of 1955, he sent a memo to Whitaker directed to the problem of diversification in general and to the specific issue of R & D emphasis within the company: "Technological developments in the field of electronics and nuclear developments tend to increase the obsolesence of many processes," he warned Whitaker, "and it is certainly within the realm of reason that our method of wire termination may some day become obsolete or represent restricted usage because of new methods of fabrication or electronic development."[7]

A little over a year later, in a Planning Committee meeting held in the late fall of 1956, Whitaker described the matter of development work as "one of the most critical problems of the company at present." He told the members of the committee "that the basic problem is that since a large part of the Company's growth comes from new products, there must be a corresponding increase in creative development engineering with each increase in size in order to maintain a satisfactory percentage growth in the future." Whitaker expressed his concern that unless creative engineering people were given the proper working environment in which to carry on their development projects, the possibility of "obtaining maximum creative results in the field of development engineering" would be lessened. As an added suggestion, he proposed that perhaps development personnel "should be removed from the production organization, and possibly more small groups should be created." Whitaker's eye was constantly on the future, the long-range project. As he put it, "the importance of long-range projects with large potentials must be kept in mind."[8]

Whitaker continued to focus his attention on the problem of creative development work in the next few years. In Planning Committee meetings he raised the issue on various occasions, emphasizing the need for putting the creative minds in the organization to work on important development projects. In the context of a general discussion on the communication of technical information throughout the company, Whitaker warned his associates that procedures for improved reporting should be accomplished "without forcing productive, technical minds to the task of report writing." A Technical Evaluation Department was proposed and implemented in the summer of 1957, with the purpose of reviewing projects and recommending to the president those which might be undertaken. The objective of the department was to uncover new ideas and inventions through a continual review of engineering's research activities and then bring those new ideas and projects to the attention of the appropriate department heads.[9]

By the mid-1950s the success of Whitaker's "little company" was further enhanced by the growth of the electronics industry. Electronics had taken off at the beginning of the decade at such a rate that by 1960 it was the nation's fifth largest industry, topped only by autos, steel, aircraft, and chemicals. While the overall industry's growth rate of 15 percent per year meant a fourfold increase in sales for the 1950's, Aircraft-Marine Products Inc. had increased its sales by more than eight times, doubling the growth rate of the electronic industry. Within the context of the national atmosphere of business growth, diversification, and a period of intensified merger activity, Aircraft-Marine Products Inc. itself now had to think seriously about its future financial needs as they related to projected growth. The question of merging with someone larger or of going it alone with a public offering of company stock emerged as the two alternatives Whitaker and his associates faced in 1956.[10]

Various recapitalization plans had been under consideration for several years by Whitaker and his board of directors, with significant concomitant in estigation of tax and legal implications. Whitaker and his financial advisers, George Ingalls and C. J. Fredricksen, had spent considerable time in New York discussing the matter of recapitalization with experts both on and off Wall Street. By early 1956, when the alternatives of going public or merging with another firm were clearly delivered as viable alternatives, Whitaker had engaged in conversations with a number of leading investment banking houses in New York. He was particularly attracted to Kidder, Peabody & Co. and to its president, A. H. Gordon, a dynamic and straightforward individual. Although Whitaker could fit in with all types of people in a variety of social situations, he was never comfortable with the so-called Eastern Establishment. As Whitaker admitted later, "have found that there are a lot of 'ins' and 'outs' in doing business on Wall Street other than the straight matter of selling stocks and bonds." The old western rural prejudices about the East remained a prominent part of Whitaker's personality all of his life, as they had in his father's.[11]

In the spring of 1956, at about the same time that Aircraft-Marine Products Inc. was beginning seriously to think about expanding its U. S. manufacturing operations outside the Pennsylvania area, Gordon, of Kidder, Peabody & Co., wrote Whitaker about a possible merger opportunity he believed worth considering. When Whitaker, who was then touring the company's European installations, returned, he found Gordon's letter with an enticing come-on. "Yesterday," Gordon began, "I had a very intriguing talk with Mr. Buetow, President of Minnesota Mining and Manufacturing Company about which I am very anxious to tell you as soon as conveniently possible for you." The upshot was that Minnesota Mining and Manufacturing (3M) was interested in acquiring Aircraft-Marine Products Inc. as part of its own diversification planning and Whitaker, as usual, was willing to listen. He authorized Gordon to talk to 3M officials about an offer to buy and meanwhile set his own staff to work analyzing the long-range impact of such a decision on the future of his company.[12]

The offer from 3M was well worth considering. It appeared certain, when Whitaker and his associates finally rejected the merger alternative in favor of going public, that 3M was willing to pay nearly $30 a share. In spite of that attractive possibility, 307,700 shares of Aircraft-Marine Products Inc. stock were publically offered at $16.25 per share. After underwriting discounts and commissions, and after compensating stockholders who had released agreed-upon amounts of their stock, the company netted approximately $1.5 million. Whitaker had to make his judgment on the basis of what might be in the best interests of the stockholders, and part of that decision was, in fact, a gamble on the company's growth rate possibilities, as part of the 3M organization or on its own. Whitaker determined that a decision to go public was in the best long-term interests of his stockholders, and although a number of years would pass before all the evidence was in, Whitaker's gamble proved to be a wise one. By the end of the 1960s, the company's growth rate began to exceed that of the 3M Corporation.[13]

At the time that Aircraft-Marine Products Inc. went public in the fall of 1956 and changed its name to AMP Incorporated, the company employed approximately 2,400 people who produced nearly 10,000 different types and sizes of solderless electrical terminals and connectors in plants located in the United States, Puerto Rico, and Western Europe. With annual sales approaching the $30,000,000 mark in 1956, the company's customers numbered more than 16,000;

approximately 200 of the largest of these purchased nearly 50 percent of the company's output. In addition to its extensive line of terminals, AMP Incorporated produced and sold a complete line of application tools and machines for attaching terminals to wires. It had, by this stage of development, entered headlong into the rapidly growing fields of business machines and computers and had made its own contributions toward programming systems, from their design through their production and installation. Furthermore, the Chemicals and Dielectrics Division, soon renamed the Capitron Division, manufactured those capacitor products necessary for use in radar-guided missiles and similar devices. Whitaker's continued emphasis on research and development work, calling for an expenditure of about 15 percent of each sales dollar, was paying off.[14]

Sales in 1956 represented an increase of almost 50 percent over 1955, and net income doubled from the previous year. Expansion was on management's mind as plans were laid to add to existing facilties in Pennsylvania and open new ones in North Carolina. The decision was made to begin marketing operations in Japan, and now a thorough investigation of the Australian market was undertaken to assess potential growth possibilites in that area. In his first annual report to new investors after the company went public in November 1956, Whitaker catalogued all of these encouraging gains, but sounded as well his usual note of honest caution: "While we expect the company to continue to grow at a favorable rate as compared with industry in the United States generally, the usual improvement in earnings for 1956 should not be regarded as indicating the rate to be anticipated for future periods." As things developed, Whitaker's warning was not an idle one. The recession of 1957-58 was just around the corner and AMP Incorporated like a large number of American industries and businesses, soon began to feel its effects.[15]

Early warnings indicating that bookings for 1957 would fall behind previous estimates came to the members of AMP Incorporated's Planning Committee from Sales Manager G. Earle Walker on May 9, 1957. Noting "softness in certain market areas," Walker pointed specifically to those markets associated with the appliance and power fields. Part of the problem, he told his associates, was "the tendency toward corporate mergers with the consequent change in buying attitudes on the part of the big, new corporate giants, manifested either in a demand for better prices or a trend to acquire their own manufacturing facilties for the products we supply them." Walker appeared fully informed about the merger mania in American business; smaller producers in such areas as appliances were being gobbled up by larger ones, bringing about the pressures on suppliers that Walker outlined. IBM, one of AMP Incorporated's major clients, was already engaged in this process, and as Walker noted in a follow-up memo to Whitaker later in the month "IBM is moving ahead with a program for making their own [plug wires and jumpers] having rejected prices that were over 40% under AMP present prices."[16]

Whitaker, an astute businessman, kept up with business trends and was well aware of signs forecasting the problems Walker warned of. In November 1956, for example, he lunched with an acquaintance who indicated interest in investing in AMP Incorporated's stock, and the two men had a conversation about the survival chances of small businesses in the ten years ahead. Whitaker's luncheon companion, fearing for the future of small businesses, indicated to Whitaker in a letter a few days later that he believed "that only a small number of very outstanding small businesses will be able to survive in certain lines of business." Because he felt AMP Incorporated would be one of them, he was planning to buy a significant amount of the company's stock. Nevertheless, it remained his contention that big businesses' growth would, in the long run, have an adverse effect on the nation's economy.

Whitaker's reply about these matters is instructive, for it reveals his own reading of the then current business situation as well as his own point of view about the problems under discussion. It also reveals just how well informed Whitaker was.

> I agree the next ten years only a small percentage of the present small businesses will be in business, as statistically over many years only about 1 in 10 survives for ten years, but I believe this is one of the hard facts of competitive business and not too much a matter of bigness.

In addressing one potential solution to the problems of small businesses — tax advantages to help them survive — Whitaker turned that coin over and stated the counter argument: tax advantages would "simply induce more people to go into business and therefore makes more [businesses] liable to elimination."[17]

Whitaker, in fact, believed so strongly in the idea of competition and the associated notion that the business that did things better than its competitors would survive, that he had little patience with government-sponsored remedies to aid the free enterprise system. In 1967, in a letter to then Senator Robert F. Kennedy, who was seeking the support of business leaders for a bill he was sponsoring in the Senate, Whitaker explained his position on government subsidies to business while expressing his own business philosophy:

Dear Senator Kennedy:

Since I am a right-wing, ultra-conservative Republican, I naturally look with considerable skepticism on anything the Government does in the way of tax incentives, low-interest loans and so forth.

As a matter of fact, though our company has never taken advantage of any such incentives in this country we have taken advantage of tax incentives in Puerto Rico and other places in the world.

However, it must be kept in mind that the success of a business venture depends much more on the intelligence, ability and drive of its employees than on low taxes, low-interest rates, or low-labor rates. For instance, the wages in our plants in the United States are the highest of any in the world, yet we produce most of our products at a lower cost in the United States than anywhere else.[18]

For Whitaker, the "Washington Crowd," like the "Wall Street Crowd," could be wrong more often than right. To succeed in business, Whitaker continued to believe, being better than the other guy was what mattered. In the case of AMP Incorporated this meant, of course, "engineering the hell out of a product," which implied that by always being a step ahead of your competition, business success would be assured.

The importance of engineering research and competition received strong support from G. Earle Walker in Sales. In the period of business "softness" beginning early in 1957, Walker was not hesitant to point out those internal factors he believed contributed to the problem of decreased bookings and a lower yearend sales volume. The culprit, according to Walker, was Engineering, which was failing to produce new product lines for his salesmen to market. "The fat [must be] removed from initiative grown flabby through complacency and the acceptance of perhaps too good times as something due rather than as a reward for industriousness, and individuals [must be] motivated to acceptance of challenges rather than the avoidance of them," he told Whitaker and the members of the Planning Committee. "There is nothing wrong with our business but ourselves," he announced in a later memo on the same subject. For G. Earle Walker, what went up might, without proper vigilance, just as easily come down. The "Humpty-Dumpty" syndrome was constantly on his mind.[19]

But despite Walker's perception of its activites, the Engineering

Department was not idle. In early August, 1957, S. W. Pollock submitted to the Planning Committee a long list of new products, which he stated would be available for marketing in the months immediately ahead. Three months later, Marshall Holcombe's Patent Department submitted an equally long list of suggestions for future investigation, indicating that others beside Whitaker were thinking about the long-range growth of the company. Walker, of course, understood the implications of a business slowdown as it would affect his sales division. Inevitably, it was Sales, in times of recession, that suffered the first effects of retrenchment measures, and Walker, anticipating this prospect in August, 1957, himself proposed a cutback of $50,000 in his sales budget for the final quarter of the year. The question remained, however, of just how far sales expense could be reduced before existing sales levels would be affected adversely.[20]

It may well have been the ever-undaunted Whitaker's question to Leon Whipple about how to get AMP Incorporated back on a twenty-percent per year growth pattern that moved Walker to offer the more conservative approach of a ten-percent growth rate. In late September, 1957, Whitaker had asked Whipple to come up with some suggestions for achieving the twenty-percent figure, and soon thereafter Walker submitted his own views on the subject. His approach was, as has been noted, more conservative, even modest compared to Whitaker's goal, but Walker did agree that growth per se was essential. Company-wide retrenchment was necessary, he observed, to bring costs into line with the reality of existing sales figures. Drastic cuts were essential to assure investors that earnings per share could be maintained at current levels. "Again I urge, get the cutbacks over all the business at once. We are in business to make a profit and to attain a yearly growth record of the hypothetical minimum standard of 10%. In my opinion, the failure of the company to produce such a growth record this year will cause more harm than all of our cutbacks; for the repercussions of such a failure become public property as well as customer-employee property and through it much faith in AMP will be lost." Ten percent yes; twenty percent no: Walker seemed to be saying.[21]

As the recession deepened in the latter half of 1957, AMP Incorporated's competition appeared more frequently as a source of irritation to management. The Burndy Company and Thomas & Betts (AMP Incorporated's major competitors) stepped up sales activities to increase their share of the market in areas presently dominated by AMP Incorporated. Walker, of course, had always kept himself and the organization up-to-date on the activities of all of competitors to be able to offset or prevent losses in one area or another. Now, however, especially with Burndy on the move, Walker's reacton took on the characteristics of a military skirmish if not an open field battle. As the issue developed within the ranks of AMP Incorporated's management, Walker again pointed his finger at engineering inertia as the root of the problem. In calling for an updated technical handbook on the company's solderless wiring devices in the spring of 1957, Walker had noted in a memo to S. W. Pollock that his people who were working on the project were "experiencing difficulty in obtaining adequate data from various sections of our Engineering Department." According to Walker, Burndy had moved well ahead of AMP Incorporated in this kind of project, for its version of the technical handbook was currently being used as a basic textbook in engineering schools. Although Walker believed that the initiative lay with engineering people at AMP Incorporated, he told Pollock that he had to authorize the production of a small brochure on the subject, what he termed "a counter-agent," to offset Burndy's claims to preeminence in this area.[22]

In fall 1957, a chance remark by U. A. Whitaker about the large number of "expensive catalogues or brochures" that seemed to be proliferating from the Sales Department set Walker off again on this subject. Walker fired off an acerbic memo to Whitaker along with a copy of an earlier technical data handbook recommendation, noting that these publications "were inaugurated in a kind of hold the line position on our part and in an endeavor to counteract Burndy propaganda that we have lost our initiative in this field." Competition from Burndy in other areas only seemed to exacerbate AMP Incorporated's deficiencies in the technical handbook controversy as Walker viewed the overall situation.[23]

Burndy's competitive presence also seemed to aggravate the perennial problems of new-product development and old-product improvement. More controversy between Sales and Engineering was engendered by a sales hassle on the West Coast. Some of AMP Incorporated's customers were experiencing difficulty with certain of the company's application tools, and a few, at least, turned to Burndy's products as a solution to their problems. Then came the threat of Burndy's emergence as a possible competitor for IBM's business. In mid-October, Bill Lange, in charge of the IBM account, reported that future booking with the large electronic firm would be on the down side as IBM management issued orders to its manufacturing units to cut inventories due to declining orders. If this wasn't enough to contend with, Lange reported that one type of application machine furnished by AMP Incorporated was causing IBM vendors difficulty, and he predicted Burndy and perhaps others might move in on AMP Incorporated's most lucrative items by furnishing an improved version of the machine. Although Lange had requested AMP Incorporated engineering to get to work on the problem of improving the machine's design, he knew that this kind of development would take over a year or a year and a half to accomplish. In the meantime, Lange hoped that some small improvements would enable the company to "hold the line" with IBM until something better would come along.[24]

Successive articles about the Burndy Corporation appeared in late October and early November, 1957, in the influential trade journal *Electronic News*, which further irritated both Walker and the situation. One article announced that Burndy, through new product development hoped to increase its sales to a volume of $40 million by the early 1960s, about a thirty-three percent increase over their 1956 sales volumes — only $5 or $6 million less than AMP Incorporated's sales for that year. The second article on Burndy followed a week later and indicated that one new development, a taper pin assembly for missile launchers, was already in the works and was to be displayed at an electronics convention that very month. Both articles and a memo from Walker soon arrived on U. A. Whitaker's desk with Walker's comment that AMP Incorporated had been outdone again.[25]

As sales manager, Walker contended that the only way to increase sales in a declining business period was, as he put it, "to separate accounts from competitors" by introducing new products into those areas where AMP Incorporated had no particular comparative advantage at that moment. One such area was the public utility field, where Burndy controlled a good share of the market. According to Walker, about half of Burndy's volume came from its activities in the utility market. One great advantage to exploiting the public utility market, in addition to its large volume potential, was its stability — even in recessionary times service was a continuing requirement. For the time being, Walker reasoned, AMP Incorporated could get into the service area while awaiting new-product development, which would allow the company a more extensive opportunity to exploit the field as a whole. The problem at hand was to break into the more limited service market by finding a way to offer products at a price competitive with the Burndy Corporation. Quantity pricing, Walker argued, was a reasonable means to this end and, as he pointed out, some few favored AMP Incorporated customers were already receiving quantity discounts. Why not broaden the policy to apply to areas like the servicing segment of the public utilities market?[26]

In fact, AMP Incorporated already had an organizational unit in existence to cover the repair and service market. American Pamcor Inc. (API) had been set up in 1953 for the purpose of servicing the maintenance and repair market. During that recessionary period, extra business volume in the servicing of old equipment helped offset the effects of cutbacks in new equipment purchases. The creation of API as a hedge against recessionary periods was part of Whitaker's overall policy of flexibility and balance in the total organization. It was also Whitaker's belief that the institutionalization of such a concept would lead to healthy competition between the parent company and the subsidiary organization as each would vie for new customers in fields not yet cultivated by the corporation. In the public utility field, therefore, API seemed to be a natural avenue to increased sales volume in a relatively wide-open, and as yet untapped, area.[27]

Such a solution to the problem of falling sales volume, however, brought with it a number of complexities. S. W. Pollock was disturbed about the decision to allow API full coverage of the utility field, and he expressed his reservations to the members of the Planning Committee early in January 1958. As vice-president, Pollock was under the impression that AMP Incorporated would be the selling organization, not API. When the switch was made, Pollock stated his reservations. Considering the terms of the agreement between API and AMP Incorporated, Pollock could not see how the parent company could make any profit. He reminded his colleagues of this historical relationship.

> You will recall that the 30 percent discount we give to API from the quantity price is based on the general theory that: 1) no AMP Incorporated Sales Department costs are incurred in an API sale and 2) no engineering or other costs are required for the sale of API merchandise. In the case of the utility program, however, these fundamental rules do not apply. We have been and are continuing to expend substantial sums in research and engineering for the development of terminals intended exclusively for the utility program.

To cover research and development costs incurred by the parent firm, namely the General Products Division of AMP Incorporated, Pollock recommended that the discount be cut to 15 percent.[28]

Walker, as a vice president and director of sales, had reason to make his own distinction between API and AMP Incorporated, in this case in relation to proposed budget restraints on sales due to the continuing recession. Walker took pains to point out, in a lengthy January, 1958, memo, that the sales mission of the two organizations were entirely different, and as a result of that difference API could not be expected fully to pick up the slack and, so to speak, carry the parent organization. Therefore, any further cutbacks in the sales budget at AMP Incorporated would be disastrous. The difference lay in the actual selling approach, as Walker explained. API's selling technique, which he called closed selling, involved over-the-counter purchases of familiar replacement products, a system demanding little expertise on the part of the sales staff. On the other hand, AMP Incorporated's selling mission, which he termed "presentation selling," involved a great deal more skill and complexity, for potential customers had to be convinced of the worth of new products and new product lines before they would commit themselves to using them. After a decade of experience, Walker told his colleagues, he had learned that investment in the sales organization was analogous to investment in the operations segments of the company; that is, a sales machine had to be built and developed just as capital equipment had to be built and developed. Often the time between the marketing of a new product and the consequent return on the sales investment could be as long as one or two years. In view of all the new products that Whitaker, Pollock, and others were promising for 1958, any further cutback in Sales would be senseless. To underscore his position, Walker quoted himself on the subject, as he had written about it for the company newsletter *The Terminator.*

> The economic value of products or ideas is determined by the ability to convince individuals, corporations, or society of the specific value to them of those products or ideas. The degree of that ability is the measure of a salesman.

And, he might have added, to determine the measure of that salesman took a great deal of time and money.[29]

L. B. Paules in engineering was delivering a similar message to management in the face of declining business volume and the consequent threat of additional cutbacks in his area. Paules, like Walker, argued that further reduction in the engineering staff would have adverse effects on future research and development work with the return of normal business operations. "We have gone through some pretty rough experiences in attempting to find the right type of engineering personnel," he informed the members of the Executive Committee, "and with our present force of people, we have a tremendous investment. It is not the type of individual that, if he is laid off in a recession, would sit around and wait to be called back." Pressures from AMP Incorporated's sales department and from the company's competitors convinced Paules that the employment line had to be held. The final paragraph of his first-of-the-year memo underscored the pressures he was feeling:

> Even at this writing, we are being called upon by our Sales Department to crash development programs which are urgently needed to meet the expanding business of the newer aircraft, the missiles, and the advancement of electronics. The reason for these crash programs is that our competitors are breathing down our necks and I feel irreparable damage will be done to the future of a company such as ours, if we hastily reduce the very means for creating future expansion of our company.[30]

Recession, competition, and the impetus given the American defense program by the Soviet launching of Sputnik in 1957 led AMP Incorporated management into a consideration of more active involvement in government-related work. An ad hoc management committee met in early January, 1958, to consider "whether or not it would be in the best interests of the company to enter into a development contract with North American Aviation Company as it concerns high temperature terminals and splices." The committee recommended acceptance of the contract for competitive reasons and to improve AMP Incorporated's relationship not only with North American but also with the entire airframe industry in the likely event that future defense needs would benefit that industry. The missile field as a whole appeared to have considerable potential in the years ahead; an AMP Incorporated staff report on the subject revealed that at least 150 different types of missiles were in various stages of design, development, and production.[31]

AMP Incorporated, of course, was already furnishing products to a number of its regular customers for use in missile production. The question now being raised was what further portion of research and development work should be devoted to new products for missiles and related defense items. U. A. Whitaker, who became alarmed when too many of the company's eggs fell into one or two baskets (whether those baskets were held by IBM or by the Defense

Department or its subcontractors), argued, as he usually did, for balance in all of the company's efforts. In a July, 1958, meeting of AMP Incorporated's Research Committee Whitaker emphatically made his point:

> Whitaker called the attention of the Committee to the fact that approximately 80 percent of our efforts were directed towards a war economy and that it would be desirable and would introduce more flexibility into the divisions if an effort were made to seek more peace economy applications of our products. He observed that such measures should be taken to continue consistent business. As an example he cited the forming of the API subsidiary as a hedge against depression and noted that current performance by that subsidiary in the present recession has justified the action.

Whitaker, it should be pointed out, was not opposed to taking on defense-related work but felt that its relationship to the overall development and sales picture must be held in proper perspective. Asked directly by one of his research people whether the company would be interested in a particular project associated with a war economy, Whitaker replied that "there was no policy against such activity."[32]

Whitaker's sense of balance and flexibility continued to have an impact on AMP Incorporated decision making in a variety of areas. His unaltering policy of planning for the future, and making sure there would be one kept certain members of the management staff busy seeking out alternative solutions and directions for the company. In mid-1958 L. B. Paules was chosen to head a new company function called New Product Planning, whose broad purpose was to examine the best means for "promoting AMP Incorporated's growth either by the acquisition of related companies or by the development of new product lines." Paules' job largely involved information gathering and processing to uncover new ideas outside the company that might prove useful in the development of new products. By the time Paules issued his first report, some three months after taking over this function, he had accumulated a mass of information for evaluation.

Inevitably, Paules' search for new-product ideas led him to the prospect of acquiring other companies as a means for dealing with future expansion. Most of the questions he raised for the purpose of discussion centered around the method of acquiring companies with potentially interesting electronic products. One important related consideration for Paules was that of marketing products that were developed by persons or companies not yet affiliated with AMP Incorporated. In some notable cases, moving into a new area, like the construction industry, called for new merchandising approaches, such as working exclusively through distributors and jobbers. Since AMP Incorporated's Sales Department and its management had considered and rejected that approach some years before, it would be necessary from Paules' point of view to receive some clear policy directions so that he could proceed with his task in a more efficient manner. As the questions at the end of Paules' report implied, there was little sense in moving in some of the directions he suggested if in fact certain basic company objectives or methods of operation were not to be changed or altered.[33]

Paules' report, with a cover memo from S. W. Pollock, was sent to Whitaker, C. J. Fredricksen, and George Ingalls, the latter since February, 1957, an AMP Incorporated vice-president and comptroller. Pollock urged the members of the Planning Committee to read the report prior to their next meeting so that some reasonable guidelines could be given to Paules.

> I think we should air these questions [Pollock told the members of the Planning Committee] so that we, as well as Blair [Paules], may have a better understanding as to the probable best route the Company should take in its quest for future growth. I think the Planning Committee needs to hammer out some fundamental ground rules as may concern consideration for possible future acquisitions of other companies by purchase, future merger with other companies by exchange of stock, acquisition of major products involving expenditures of considerable magnitude, etc.[34]

Paules' report was discussed thoroughly at the next meeting of the Planning Committee, on October 21, 1958. The guidelines Paules subsequently received were yet another indication that management in general, and Whitaker in particular, remained open-minded to a variety of approaches to growth, while at the same time maintaining traditional company patterns. It was the Whitaker style to look into every opportunity, regardless of whether he favored or opposed the specific approach. Acquisition by merger or purchase, for example, was fine as long as such a deal would be beneficial to AMP Incorporated, but management concluded that "we are not actively looking for any such situations." The same was true in the matter of buying a product manufactured by another company if that product promised to be profitable to the company in the long haul. For the present, however, AMP Incorporated's slogan, "engineering the hell out of a product," would remain the basis for future expansion and growth. Pollock, speaking for himself as well as Whitaker, concluded that "AMP's most profitable expansion was through products developed from within the company," and with Whitaker's kind of balance he added, "however, 'outside' companies, products, organizations etc., should not be ignored." As Patent Counsel Marshall Holcombe put it years later, "every time you would find something that looked like a good investment opportunity, there would be some guy in the company that would have a better one and who wanted to spend the money. And we spent it in the company." That had always been the Whitaker style.[35]

14. The American Genius

U. A. Whitaker was one of those practical men of business affairs typical of a legion of entrepreneurs who had come before him in the American business experience. No doubt, despite his outward modesty, Whitaker associated himself with those successful entrepreneurs of the past. Whitaker, even in the context of the technologically advanced society of the twentieth century, seemed in many ways to fit the description of "The American Genius," described by *The* [London] *Economist* in the mid-nineteenth century.

> The Americans . . . seem to be an eminently practical race. Their numerous inventions all tend to the common and general advantage, to bring about equally beneficial results for all by less labor. Their intellect is exerted for the benefit of all. It is not warped to consult the gratification of the few. They look Nature in the face, attend to her minutest signs, learn to read quickly her directions, and they are inventive, skilful, and prosperous. . . . More than any existing people . . . they are free to use all their faculties to promote their worldly success, and they are eminently successful.

Although U. A. Whitaker would never have admitted it publicly, he might very well, in private, have defined himself and his career in these terms. In any event, a copy of the 1853 *Economist*, with its article on "The American Genius," can be found in Whitaker's files for 1958.

As an engineering businessman, Whitaker had always believed that applied research was the only strategy for a company of his to follow. Although scientific or basic research and development appealed to him intellectually, it was in the area of applied research that he staked his future. As a business manager as well as an experienced inventor, the romance of pure scientific research held little attraction for him. Whitaker's response to a plea from New Product Director L. B. Paules for more attention to purely scientific research at AMP Incorporated in 1958 was typical of his approach both to business and to engineering. As S. W. Pollock explained Whitaker's reaction to Paules' proposal:

> Mr. Whitaker never did warm up to this idea. Being a practical businessman, he felt — and I most certainly agree with him — that we should confine our research activities to what is more commonly

known as *applied* research. . . . . It did not seem to make any
practical business sense to try to do work in the nebulous area of
basic research. . . .The odds against bringing to the company and its
shareholders any meaningful results are formidable.

According to Pollock, Whitaker believed that scientific research
and development had to be carefully defined so that it might "in all
probability . . . be incorporated in our broad area of product activity
and knowledge."[1]

After a visit to AMP Incorporated's Harrisburg facilities, an
associate of Whitaker's from his American Machine & Foundry days
in Brooklyn wrote his old friend a letter emphasizing not only
Whitaker's engineering business philosophy but also his consistency
in carrying it out. The recent visit to Harrisburg in September, 1958,
had impressed the visitor with both the general progress of the
company and with "the many developments [in] engineering and
research. . . that are so vital and so great a contribution to
transportation and communication as well as manufacturing
activities." In recalling Whitaker's plans for the future as he
remembered them from his American Machine & Foundry days
nearly a generation earlier, Whitaker's friend noted that "you have
followed through as you indicated would have been your purpose if
you had stayed with the Foundry Company." And, in an attempt to
sum up Whitaker's career in the years following the American
Machine & Foundry experience, he added:

> Little did I expect to find upon my visit the old adage so well
> demonstrated by your own efforts, namely, he who makes the best
> mouse trap will find a beaten path to his door, etc., because you
> have made the finest mouse trap in the world, which has captured
> the finest and most profitable business, just through your own
> intelligent initiative.[2]

In the crucial two-year period, 1958-60, AMP Incorporated under
U. A. Whitaker's leadership, came out of the recession and began
making its way towards the select circle of America's top 500
corporations. Whitaker's continued insistence that AMP Incorporated
keep research and development fixed firmly on the future played no
small part in the company's growth plans. Like his Sales Manager
G. Earle Walker, Whitaker believed that in prosperous times the
company should remain as vigilant in implementing its policies of
growth as it was protective of its position in periods of business
downturn. Staying ahead in the game was crucial. He told the
members of the Research Committee in spring, 1959, that he

"deplored the tendency in the company to spend less and less on new products as the company became more and more prosperous, and then to work frantically on new products during a recession period." Rather, he suggested, "we should be continually working on products which we will be selling 5 to 10 years from now." The message was a familiar one: Whitaker's concern for the future was a major aspect of his philosophy.[3]

Whitaker's foresight, which, along with the IBM presence, had gotten AMP Incorporated into overseas markets early in the 1950s, continued to direct management's attention towards expanded foreign operations. By the end of 1958, plans for the establishment of new facilities in Spain and Italy were already underway; at the same time AMP Incorporated's Japanese operation was being rearranged, and the possibility of opening in Australia was under investigation. Whitaker always insisted on two major requirements before any overseas facilities could be approved. The first criterion was that entry into a new area had to be accomplished with as little investment by the parent company as possible; the other was that initial agreements with foreign countries be negotiated so as to allow the company a maximum amount of flexibility in future dealings with those countries. The latter point was a most important one to Whitaker. In absolutely no circumstances would Whitaker consider expansion in a country that insisted on shared ownership. India, for example, appeared to Marshall Holcombe as an ideal country to develop as a market because, as he put it, "there are an awful lot of people in India [and] if you could get 5 percent of them to have a toaster on their table, an electric coffee pot, etc., for which AMP supplied the parts, you could get rich." Unfortunately for Holcombe and AMP Incorporated, there was no legal way to start a company there without sharing ownership with someone in India. According to Holcombe, Whitaker was never willing to be placed in a position where, under the Sherman Antitrust Act, he could be accused of conspiring with anyone else. Ownership had to be 100 percent in AMP Incorporated's hands from his point of view.[4]

AMP Incorporated's establishment of a base of operations in Australia is an interesting example of decision making and of U. A. Whitaker's general approach to future expansion overseas. The discussion about gaining a foothold in the Australian market began early in 1957, shortly after AMP Incorporated had set up a distributorship in Japan. Preliminary economic surveys conducted by Sales Manager G. Earle Walker indicated the existence of what

Walker termed "a substantial Australian market." Several Australian
manufacturers, among them the Westinghouse Corporation, appeared
to be enthusiastic about accepting AMP Incorporated's terminating
products and, with the information that the company's two major
competitors — Thomas & Betts and Burndy — were already licensed
to manufacture and sell in Australia, Walker recommended that
further market surveys be undertaken. Walker informed the
Planning Committee that he was sending John Burnite to Australia
"to explore and endeavor to develop the new market and to
determine its potential." Burnite had done exactly this thing in Japan
in 1956 prior to AMP Incorporated's decision to set up a distributing
group in that nation. Apparently, not every one on the Planning
Committee was favorably inclined towards the Australian venture,
and Walker appealed to Whitaker, early in June, 1957, to discover
whether it was worth the additional effort to continue with the
Australian surveys. "Since there seems to be some doubt in some
quarters as to whether or not we should try this development of the
Australian market," Walker asked Whitaker, "I would like to know
your opinion in the matter inasmuch as you have probably been
more interested than anyone in foreign trade. I certainly do not want
to send Jack Burnite to Australia and have him laboring against
odds."[5]

Whitaker evidently gave Walker the support he needed, authorizing AMP Incorporated's Comptroller, George Ingalls, to prepare a
study on the profitability of setting up a manufacturing subsidiary in
Australia. Ingall's report indicated that after four years such a
manufacturing operation would produce a profit yield of nearly
twenty-five percent on an investment of about $166,000. In the fall
of 1958, the company sent Burt Hendricks, who had gotten its Dutch
operation off the ground, to Australia to investigate that country's
market and determine whether or not manufacturing there was a
feasible idea. Hendricks' trip substantiated the view that the
establishment of a manufacturing operation in Australia would be an
appropriate decision. Final approval awaited Hendricks' return to
Harrisburg, at which time he could present the final results of his
on-the-spot survey.[6]

The Australian question was discussed at some length at the
meeting of the Planning Committee on November 18, 1958, and all
estimates indicated that both sales and profits, at least for the first
several years, would be modest. George Ingalls indicated his support
for the new operation by pointing out that a manufacturing unit could

be established in Australia without fear of loss since, as was the case with AMP Incorporated's original overseas venture in France, IBM business alone could support a small operation. In a special meeting on AMP-Australia, called a few days after Burt Hendricks' return to Harrisburg, it was tentatively agreed to go ahead with the Australian operation, based on IBM's letter of intent to purchase a guaranteed minimum of AMP Incorporated termination devices over a four-year period. There was a problem, however; management's decision was being forced by IBM, which stipulated AMP Incorporated's first delivery to IBM-Australia be made by July, 1959, or the contract would be terminated. A final decision was delayed until the next regularly scheduled Planning Committee meeting, December 16, 1958.[7]

At the December meeting, Whitaker revealed that early projections about the Australian market had been overly optimistic; that, in fact, much less business could be counted on than originally expected. The modest profit anticipated during the first year now turned into a projected loss, but Whitaker demonstrated that an intelligent exercise of financial control could, very soon, produce a profitable operation. Whitaker, who believed in establishing firm footholds in all promising markets, defended his position vis-a-vis Australia by stating that "this would be an interesting experiment as to possible use of similar small manufacturing units in other parts of the world." Typically, Whitaker dealt with AMP Incorporated and its subsidiaries by conceiving of each new operation as one of a series of "little companies." The vote in favor of forming a wholly owned subsidiary in Australia was three to two, indicating some uncertainty despite Whitaker's assessment.[8]

Expansion and growth brought organizational problems to the attention of AMP Incorporated management, and, with the increased emphasis on new overseas markets, new forms of organization had necessarily to be considered. The year 1959-60 was crucial for the company in this respect. The first meeting of the Planning Committee in the new year, January 20, 1959, met the issue head-on. In the context of a discussion of another subsidiary, this one to be established in Italy to service Fiat, AMP Incorporated's largest Italian customer, C. J. Fredricksen reported that plans were underway to set up a permanent Foreign Trade Division, complete with its own director and a variety of managers heading up sales, manufacturing, engineering, and accounting departments. All of AMP Incorporated's foreign trade, it was agreed, should come under the direction of such a division. U. A. Whitaker, as the minutes of the meeting note, not only endorsed this organizational change but "observed that the organizational problems of Foreign Trade are a part of the overall need for some organizational changes in the entire company." He urged, further, that something be done about the general problem during the ensuing year.[9]

In fact, changes were already further along than the minutes of the January meeting reveal, for at a special meeting of the Planning Committee called on February 11, 1959, significant organizational shifts were announced. Herman Haas, who had been general sales manager for AMP Incorporated, under G. Earle Walker, was appointed director of the Domestic Subsidiaries Division. This new division oversaw the operations of American Pamcor Inc. (API), AMP-Canada, and Pamcor Inc. in Puerto Rico. Bill Lange, long active in foreign trade, was named director of the Foreign Trade Division of AMP Incorporated with responsibility for both the European and Southeast Asian subsidiaries.[10]

Meanwhile, Leon Whipple in his position as staff analyst had submitted a report filled with recommended organizational changes. As Whipple wrote in his 1958 annual report to Whitaker, "the most significant change made at AMP during 1958 was the increased awareness of the need for developing an adequate supply of future leaders." Recognizing that Whitaker always stressed the importance of this need, Whipple offered a complex approach for identifying those potential leaders whom he referred to as the "stars of the future." In addition to this specific aspect of organization needs, Whipple also reacted to another problem recognized by management as becoming more troublesome as AMP Incorporated grew in size — the matter of contact between middle management and top management. Whipple's investigation of this issue produced evidence that fewer than twenty-five members of AMP Incorporated had contact with Whitaker in regularly scheduled meetings. It was Whipple's opinion that improved communications between middle- and top-management people were necessary not only for morale reasons but also so that "more people at AMP Incorporated [could] become exposed to the policies, philosophy and personality of top management representatives."[11]

Whipple's plan, discussed at a Planning Committee session in mid-February, 1959, involved a radical restructuring of the committee system. The minutes of the meeting describe the Whipple plan as follows:

Basically it would involve the use of each member of the Planning
Committee operating as a team captain, selecting members of the
Executive Committee to meet with first line supervisors in the
various plant locations approximately five times annually. Adoption
of this proposal would probably reduce the current number of
Operating and Executive Committee meetings.

AMP Incorporated, like many business organizations, had so
proliferated the number of regular committees that virtually every
week of the month had a full calendar of permanent committee
meetings of one sort or another. Whipple's goal, therefore, was not
only to improve communications among management of different
levels but to reduce the number of meetings. Although Whitaker
approved of the idea, he did not in the final analysis approve of the
plan, which would have required each designated team to hold nine
meetings per year. Whitaker's management style was, in fact, not
particularly adaptable to meetings of this nature. Albert Curtis, a
longtime AMP Incorporated employee, underscores Whitaker's
attitude about meetings in an anecdote from the company's earlier
years. One day Whitaker happened to pass Curtis' office and saw
seven or eight people crowded into it. Later he asked Curtis if he was
holding a meeting. Curtis said no, he was not holding a meeting, but
that some customers had dropped in to chat. Whitaker appeared
relieved at Curtis' explanation, and he told him that that number of
people never could come to a decision. Furthermore, he instructed
Curtis that a meeting should be restricted to two or three people; to
arrive at any decision, Whitaker added, two people were preferable.[12]

Behind the organizational changes that were effected, and some of
the proposed changes that were not, was Whitaker's concern with the
eventual prospect of what is termed the transition "from a founding
management to professional management not representing such large
blocks of stock." Although Whitaker had made certain, almost from
the company's outset, that key employees could participate in owning
stock along the way, he was nonetheless thinking seriously about a
future transition of management authority. At any rate, since it was
his manner to investigate a variety of alternatives in all aspects of his
business career, he set Whipple to work on this important question.
Whipple met with Harold Stieglitz of the Division of Personnel
Administration of the National Industrial Conference Board in
February, 1959, and the two men reviewed the changes at AMP
Incorporated to date, concluding that what had been accomplished
had provided the company with a more efficient organization.[13]

In the spring of 1959, Whipple visited a number of firms to investigate the best means of developing an executive cadre for key positions in the company's organization in future years. In addition to the problems of executive training and communication between top and middle management, Whipple paid some attention to the vital question of the transfer of management power from one generation to the next. In early September, Whipple followed up a request from Whitaker to attempt to get an up-to-date General Electric organization chart. No doubt an admirer of then Chairman of the Board and Chief Executive Officer Ralph Cordiner, Whitaker was apparently interested in understanding the organizational details of the highly successful electrical firm. Whipple's report on GE revealed that the company had not had an organized and functioning committee system since Cordiner took over in 1951 because, as Whipple put it, "Mr. Cordiner believes a decision must be made by an individual who has the responsibility for carrying out such a decision." According to Whipple, it was Cordiner's belief that committees tend to "usurp this decision-making process [and that] by eliminating committees it now becomes mandatory for the operating head to make the decision." What did remain at GE, Whipple recorded, was an Executive Office, which functioned essentially as a discussion group to deal with broad policy matters. Whipple concluded his report by indicating that although GE was a much larger corporation than AMP Incorporated, some of its "policies and philosophies could very well be considered at AMP ."[14]

Despite Whipple's efforts and all of his work on the reorganization problem, nothing fundamentally changed in the company's approach to management. The Planning Committee made up of Whitaker, Fredricksen, Ingalls, Pollock, and Walker continued to debate the company's broad policy concerns and settle matters both large and small. In fact, ever since the inception of the firm back in 1941 the policy and decision making group at AMP Incorporated, whatever it was called, was comprised of most of these same men. Decisions and policies, very largely, always had been made by committee, with Whitaker acting as the group leader, prodding here and there where needed. When necessary, votes were taken on crucial policy matters and, except on very rare occasions when Whitaker was absolutely determined to have his way, the majority opinion prevailed.[15]

As the firm's leader, Whitaker, of course, set the tone and direction. From his perspective, the matter of executive development and the transfer of authority from one generation to the next were problems whose solutions were inherent in the philosophy of the organization itself, namely that those people charged with responsibility were expected to be left alone to make their own decisions, good or bad. They were, in short, expected to take the ball and run with it. Whitaker's role was primarily to keep the firm on the right track while allowing his associates and employees the fullest freedom possible within the constraints of production and profit goals. Balance and flexibility as always were the two cornerstones of Whitaker's approach to engineering and business management, with new-product development as the keystone.

Several examples from Planning Committee meetings held during the spring of 1959 serve as illustrations of Whitaker's management leadership and policy-making role:

Planning Committee Meeting Minutes, March 17, 1959

Whitaker stated that any major expansion in the Sales Department should be equaled in engineering if the Company is to maintain the necessary balance in these areas. Whitaker again emphasized the need for having additional engineering teams working on development of products which we can profitably market several years from now.

Planning Committee Meeting Minutes, April 22, 1959

Whitaker stated it was very necessary to seriously consider methods of making patentable improvements to certain of our patented products which patents will expire in a few years. Whitaker suggested such improvements be preferably of a type which will not require any heavy investment in dies and tooling.

Planning Committee Meeting Minutes, May 19, 1959

Whitaker stated we must continue making every effort to get additional engineering groups started on new-product development.

Although Whitaker, from time to time, could appear satisfied with progress in new-product development during one specific period, his constant monitoring of the situation allowed him to tighten the screw when slackening effort became evident. In June, 1959, for example, he was pleased; in November of the same year he was not. "Whitaker stated that in spite of the apparently increased rate of expenditure requested for 1960 by the various divisions, he does not believe the Company is spending enough money in engineering to start new projects that will produce the growth that is needed and anticipated in future years."[16]

Two final examples from 1959 further illustrate Whitaker's policy-making role and his continuing attempts to prevent the company from becoming mired in situations that might inhibit its freedom of action. One, involving development work on programming systems for eventual use by the government, called for cost information to be revealed, something Whitaker and AMP Incorporated management would never allow. Whitaker's firmness on this matter is recorded as follows:

> Whitaker stated that as far as so-called development business is concerned and the divulging of cost and granting of exclusives, our policy should be that we should not accept such business. Whitaker stated that you are always better off to invest your own money for development and own all resulting patents and marketing rights outright. Whitaker also suggested that the matter be reviewed with the Legal Department to be reasonably sure that we do not inadvertently commit ourselves to revealing any of our cost data.

So firmly did AMP Incorporated hold to this policy that patent attorney Marshall Holcombe recalls being criticized by members of the United States Senate committee before whom he was called to testify on the company's refusal either to license another producer to manufacture one of its products or to reveal cost information. Holcombe explained AMP Incorporated's refusal to divulge such information in the face of a good deal of ranting and raving from the senators about the company's lack of cooperation in assuring the government more than one source of supply. It was AMP Incorporated's position, Holcombe told the committee, that the company was entitled to the profit stemming from its own development work and that if the government or any of its contractors wanted to buy the particular item AMP Incorporated would be happy to sell it to them and show them how its installed cost would be cheaper in the finished product. AMP Incorporated, according to Holcombe, was always hard-nosed about this sort of thing and since the company never took any government money for research, preferring to spend its own, it never incurred the obligations usually accompanying government subsidy of that kind. Moreover, it had always been Whitaker's policy that if the government needed information stemming from AMP Incorporated's research, the company would gladly provide it at no cost to the taxpayers.[17]

Whitaker's policy on licensing AMP Incorporated's ideas to other manufacturing firms was equally hard-nosed and was related intimately to his overall engineering business philosophy. Much to the frustration of the Sales Department, Whitaker would sometimes rather lose an order than grant a license to a customer who wanted to secure another source of supply for a product AMP Incorporated had developed. It was Whitaker's belief that everything his company developed and produced for its customers would save them money in the long run on account of the labor saving inherent in the final assembly — whether in the automobile, the aircraft, or the appliance. AMP Incorporated was selling a system rather than a product, he reasoned, and the relatively high markup on the part itself was in fact a minor expenditure when the entire process of manufacturing was considered. To keep ahead of the competition by any manufacturing operation that could easily copy and produce an AMP Incorporated device, Whitaker insisted that his development engineers constantly figure out ways to make something new and unique that would save the user even more money in the final assembly. For Whitaker, the company's investment in this kind of research had to be reflected in the profit received from selling the device itself, regardless of how simple it might be. AMP Incorporated's automatic machine application process assured both consistent quality and lower costs per unit. Since AMP Incorporated took the responsibility of installing and servicing these machines, the customer had no need to maintain his own staff of machinists, and on a three-shift basis that amounted to a considerable saving in labor expense.[18]

The AMP Incorporated system, therefore, contained a dynamism of its own, which in Whitaker's mind involved an endless quest for an even better mousetrap. The relationship between scientific/technological improvements and profit growth and expansion was an organic one for Whitaker. Now, in 1959, with evidence that the brief recession was on the wane, Whitaker looked forward to the promise of the 1960s with typical enthusiasm. In June, 1959, he wrote Bill Lange, AMP Incorporated's director of the Foreign Trade Division, about his feelings. "We are in the throes of setting budgets for 1960 as you know. There is a startling wave of optimism going around this country and it has affected AMP Incorporated and API sales departments so that there are figures coming up that would have seemed fantastic a few months ago." AMP Incorporated's recovery from the recession must have seemed just as fantastic to Whitaker, as sales figures for 1959 scored more than a 33-1/3 percent increase over those recorded for 1958. In his annual letter to AMP Incorporated shareholders Whitaker noted the firm's progress.

In a decade of growth from sales of less than $3,000,000 in 1949 to over $43,000,000 in 1959, product development was a most important factor. The year 1959 saw AMP further broaden the scope of its research and development activities beyond electrical terminations and contact fields and into the basic components used in a variety of electronic equipment. AMP Incorporated shift registers, memory units and electronic counters should have favorable impact on the electronic market and through diversification provide new avenues of growth.

Whitaker, along with a good number of marketing specialists, already anticipated what would come to be called "the golden 60's of marketing."[19]

AMP Incorporated prepared for this expected surge in business by dusting off its pre-1957-58 overall plan for company growth, temporarily laid aside during the recessionary period. Whitaker had urged this plan in a Planning Committee meeting towards the end of 1958, and, as a result, Leon Whipple's extensive facility surveys were there in the files to be acted upon. New location studies were also under consideration at the time when Wall Street was recognizing AMP Incorporated's importance by approving the listing of its stock on the "Big Board" of the New York Stock Exchange late in October, 1959.[20] Finally, as if to punctuate the reality of success, AMP Incorporated had produced for public consumption an industrial film *The End is the Beginning* narrated by TV news personality Chet Huntley at, one could say, great expense to the management. Notwithstanding G. Earle Walker's objections to this particular promotion piece ("I submit that the leading actors and heroes in such a film would be AMP and its PRODUCTS; neither television personalities nor pretty girls are in the case"), AMP Incorporated management had to respond to potential investor interest with promotional material of this kind.[21]

By the beginning of the 1960s, as Whitaker's "little company" appeared on the path towards becoming one of America's largest 500 corporations, AMP Incorporated had attained "the rank of leadership" in its industry. In 1961, AMP Incorporated stock split three for one and the corporation received the 1960 Growth Company Award from the National Association of Investment Clubs and its 75,000 members. AMP Incorporated's earnings, which had grown from $104,000 in 1949 to $5,000,000 in 1959, more than qualified the company for this award. U. A. Whitaker was present at the 10th Annual Convention of the National Association of Investment Clubs to receive the award and to talk about his company's accomplishments. Some excerpts from Whitaker's presentation reveal the specific process of development over a nearly twenty-year period:

> There are two basic reasons for AMP Incorporated's continued success and growth — accomplished, incidentally, without benefit of mergers or acquisitions. The first of these reasons — the engineering approach; the second — our direct sales method.

About the first, Whitaker had this to say:

> At the outset, AMP Incorporated adopted a very broad engineering approach and applied it to a confined product area. This approach was applied to the wire termination field and to this day is very appropriately described as 'Precision Engineering Applied to the End of a Wire.' This field has been the backbone of the company, our bread and butter items, and will continue to be so during the next few years. As a result of this precision engineering, AMP produces complete terminations that usually reduce termination costs through speed, simplicity and uniform quality of application.

> An engineering approach such as this is no small task as evidenced by our present customer list which numbers in the thousands, by our 15,000 product items, and by some 2,000 patents issued both here and abroad. It requires spending some 13 or 14% of our sales dollars to maintain a staff of over 500 persons in research, development and engineering activities, the majority of whom are graduate scientists or graduate engineers or engineers specially trained in the areas of physics, electronics, chemistry, electro-mechanics, atomic energy or other related fields.

Whitaker then turned to the second primary reason for AMP Incorporated's growth — the company's sales methods, what he called a direct selling program.

> The foundation of this program is a force of highly trained District Sales Engineers exceptionally qualified to work with the customer's own engineering and other technical personnel. At staff level we have both industry sales sections concentrating on individual industries and their changing technology and product sales managers promoting our newer lines of products.

Behind these groups, Whitaker described the functions of AMP Incorporated's Field Service Engineers who, acting as "troubleshooters," were prepared to move anywhere in the country to install or service the company's automatic equipment. Finally, Whitaker explained, AMP Incorporated's sales methods provided customers with the service of creative teams of analysts available for consultation on any manufacturing operation in need of expert assistance in the area of electronic problem solving, and, Whitaker hastened to add, "without charge to the customer."

Whitaker then noted how AMP Incorporated, "as far back as 1952," had begun, before many other American industries, its expansion into international markets with the establishment of its first wholly owned subsidiary overseas. Finally, Whitaker concluded his talk by noting the general context for future growth prospects:

> The rapid expansion of the electrical and electronic fields provides AMP with an ever-greater market for its products. The trend of today's world toward a mechanized, automated way of life demands more and more complex and sensitive electrical and electronic devices and moreover demands them in smaller and smaller sizes. As a leader in this field, AMP is in a strategic position not only here but abroad where foreign markets, comprised of so many fast-growing economies, offer a dynamic potential for both expansion and penetration.

Within the next five years, U. A. Whitaker's belief in the future growth of AMP was more than realized. With sales topping $100 million in 1965, AMP Incorporated, found itself included on the list of the nation's 500 largest industrial companies.[22]

15. Businessman in the Community

Like many American businessmen, U. A. Whitaker accepted his role as a citizen in a community, and in that role he contributed responsibly to a variety of organizations and causes. Each year Whitaker recorded those contributions in the back of his personal appointment book. Typically, in his early years in Harrisburg, he made donations ranging from three to fifty dollars to the Community Chest, the YMCA, the Red Cross, the Salvation Army, the League of Women Voters, the Boys' Club, the Boy Scouts and the alumni funds of the Massachusetts Institute of Technology and Carnegie Institute of Technology. Similarly, like many successful local businessmen, Whitaker joined his hometown Rotary organization, was elected to serve on the board of the Chamber of Commerce and was an active member of the board of one of the Harrisburg hospitals. Traditionally, these are the services American businessmen perform for their communities, and no doubt U. A. Whitaker contributed his time and money for those traditional reasons that have come to be associated with service to the community. When Whitaker became a director of the Harrisburg Chamber of Commerce in 1951, the publisher of the evening newspaper sent him his congratulations and an expression of the rationale for service: "The Good Lord made it possible for all of us to earn a living by working, but to a select group of worthy souls he has given us an opportunity to earn a life by giving and serving. You have accepted the challenge. Good luck to your task."[1]

Although Whitaker might have agreed with the sentiment of this congratulatory message, he would never have described his own charitable and philanthropic activities in precisely that manner. Whitaker did appreciate the advantages he had been given in his lifetime and consequently chose to devote a considerable amount of time and money to helping individuals, groups and institutions achieve a variety of personal and collective goals. As AMP Incorporated began to prosper in the 1950 , more money became available for charitable and philanthropic purposes under the then current tax laws regulating corporate giving. In 1955, for example, Whitaker pledged $10,000 to the Harrisburg Hospital building fund, and two years later he and his wife Helen established a fund with the New York Community Trust for selected distribution of AMP

Incorporated stock and, on occasion, the proceeds from the sale of some of that stock. Early recipients were Hood College, where Whitaker's two daughters were educated, the Women's Medical College in Philadelphia, the Sloan-Kettering Institute for Cancer Research, the Cleveland Clinic for cardiovascular research, and a good number of struggling college students identified by the rector of the Episcopal Church in Hershey, Pennsylvania.[2]

Not surprisingly, behind most of U. A. Whitaker's serious giving lay a plan. Whitaker engaged himself in philanthropy in much the same way he applied himself to business, and with similar purposes in mind — total involvement, total commitment, with the goal of improving the quality of life for a larger number of people. In this sense, U. A. Whitaker was like his father O. B. , for both devoted a considerable portion of their lives to public service in the broadest sense. In the political arena, O. B. Whitaker fought a consistent battle to improve the conditions of life for his constituents, those less affluent Missourians who populated the rural areas and small towns of the state. In an effort to preserve traditional American individualism as he understood, O. B. used the public political forum to support those measures which he believed would most benefit the largest number of his fellow Missourians.

U. A. Whitaker, on the other hand, working largely behind the scenes and outside any specific geographical boundaries, chose to improve the lot of mankind: first, through the intelligent utilization of the products his company developed and produced; and second, through the intelligent application of a portion of the profits subsequently earned to a variety of related projects in the field of medical technology and health care. While O. B. Whitaker, as a lifelong minister and educator, constantly stressed the moral regeneration of the American people and their institutions, U. A. Whitaker, as a man committed to problem solving through engineering and business techniques, stressed the technological and profit-oriented approach. As deeply committed conservatives, both men worked toward the same end — the preservation of the integrity, health, and welfare of the individual in a free society, a goal they believed should, and could, be achieved with a minimum of government aid and interference.

U. A. Whitaker's longtime connection with the Massachusetts Institute of Technology provided him with an initial base for the development of his interests in health care and health sciences. Since Whitaker was a man who worked best among men he knew and trusted, his active association with people at MIT, dating from 1940 with his first appointment as a member of the Visiting Committee of the Division of Industrial Development, provided him with an opportunity to build those intimate relationships. It was exactly a year after the end of World War II when Whitaker made his first formal offer of aid to some ongoing cancer medical research at MIT. A very short time had elapsed since his sister Minnie Frost had died of cancer, and it may have been that loss that prompted Whitaker to write Nat Sage, his old friend at MIT, expressing his interest in contributing something towards the research program. Optimistic, as usual, Whitaker told Sage that he felt "certain that the new developments at MIT and other places will make the cure of cancer possible, even in advanced cases." And he added, also characteristically that "there certainly would be no greater contribution to humanity than the cure, or prevention, of this disease." When Whitaker learned that scientists and technicians at MIT had developed a practical means for using X rays in the treatment of cancer but were having difficulty in interesting some large manufacturers in taking on the project for commercial purposes, Whitaker offered MIT not only his considerable technical expertise but also his services in finding some additional monies to help develop the device.[3]

Whitaker's company, of course, which for some years — over a decade by the mid-1950s — contributed directly to the support of research at MIT through its membership in the Division of Industrial Cooperation, continued that support when the program was reorganized in 1955 and retitled the MIT Industrial Liaison Program. James R. Killian, then president of MIT, wrote Whitaker personally asking him to join the new program, emphasizing the importance of large-company participation in the university's research endeavors. Killian underscored the need for major gifts from private industry and touched a sensitive chord in Whitaker's personality by implicitly noting the value of private over government contribution. "We feel that this solicitation of support by industry is necessary," he told Whitaker, "in order to maintain our strength and independence." This was an argument Whitaker could seldom resist, given his strong negative views about governmental participation in areas where he believed it did not belong. As he told his friend and former patent counsel, Truman Safford, some years later, "I feel the same as you do about the Government moving into everything, especially medical research, but I can see no sign of this situation improving. In fact, I

would suspect it will get worse before it gets better." AMP
Incorporated, renewed its formal connection with MIT early in 1956
by joining the new Industrial Liaison Program.[4]

Characteristically, Whitaker did not always wait to be asked. On
occasion he would come up with a research project of his own, find
the proper person at MIT to carry it out, and then contribute the
funds to support the work. For example, late in 1957, he submitted
an idea which, as he put it, "would attempt to utilize the most recent
mathematical and statistical methods in the study of some basic
problems of medicine." Within a period of less than two months,
Whitaker had found his man, committed the money, and instructed
the officials of the New York Bankers Trust to transfer the
appropriate number of AMP Incorporated shares to MIT to cover the
costs of the project.[5]

U. A. Whitaker's longtime association with MIT is a fascinating
story in that it reveals a number of facets of his personality as well as
the intellectual breadth and richness of his mind. From the late 1950s
until his death in 1975, Whitaker was a frequent visitor to the MIT
campus, involving himself in both the technical and political functions
of the university. As a man possessed of seemingly limitless physical
and intellectual energy, Whitaker found in his commitment to and
association with MIT a new challenge and a new outlet for those
energies in the later years of his life. Whitaker's visits to MIT,
according to one of his intimate colleagues on campus, served to
recharge his mind, leaving him refreshed after a demanding period
of work in Harrisburg. Perhaps of equal importance was the
comfortable feeling he had with the group of people he associated
with at MIT. Whitaker liked President James R. Killian as an
individual and for his progressive view of engineering. He was
impressed with Killian's broad educational perspective and was
especially pleased when Killian added a strong humanities segment to
the MIT curriculum in the 1940s. In fact, Whitaker's high opinion of
Killian led him to ask the MIT president to serve on the board of
directors of AMP Incorporated Inc., a request Killian had to turn
down on account of other commitments. The offer, it should be
noted, was hardly gratuitous — Whitaker always insisted that AMP
Incorporated directors be close to the organization; Killian's prestige
had little, if anything, to do with Whitaker's proposal.[6]

As a man who believed strongly in the application of knowledge to
practical and ameliorative ends, Whitaker fitted perfectly the MIT
intellectual atmosphere under Killian's and later Jerome Wiesner's

leadership. When Vannevar Bush and others at MIT began to work toward bringing biology into the modern era by combining it with engineering to deal with the problem of human organisms, Whitaker became excitedly involved in this new approach. Whitaker had long been interested in medicine. So curious was he about the mysteries of medicine, that he had seriously considered attending medical school after he completed his law degree back in 1935. When the opportunity to contribute significantly to the developments in the field of health sciences came along, Whitaker was prepared to offer his energy and knowledge. As the project developed, however, Whitaker found himself drawn into it far more deeply than he might once have intended.

In late October, 1959, Whitaker received a brochure from MIT announcing the university's "Second Century" fund-raising campaign. Among the needs and proposals listed in the brochure was a Life Science Center. Shortly after the beginning of 1961, Killian and an associate visited Whitaker in Harrisburg to explain the general purpose of the Second Century Program and especially to present the details for the proposed Center for the Life Sciences. In thanking Whitaker for the opportunity to speak with him at some length about MIT's needs, Killian noted that in the near future he hoped that Whitaker and Professor Irwin W. Sizer, the head of MIT's Biology Department, could meet in order to discuss the matter in even more detail. Whitaker's relationship with Dr. Sizer proved to be crucial for MIT's life science plans and for U. A. Whitaker's future relationship with his original alma mater.[7]

Six months passed before Whitaker received any further communication about the project. In June, 1961, Walter J. Beadle, an aide to President Killian, wrote to Whitaker about the project and enclosed an article from *The New York Times*, summarizing a paper delivered by a member of the MIT Biology Department reporting "intriguing progress in the field of Life Sciences." Noting the university's particular advantage in this area, Beadle commented that "this is a field in which MIT has an opportunity to make real progress — an opportunity which is almost unique because of the interdisciplinary research opportunities at MIT." An appealing argument to a businessman like Whitaker, whose corporate philosophy had always been based on his own company's ability to move into those areas of engineering technology that most complemented the existing strengths of his organization.[8]

But perhaps the more significant piece of news in Beadle's letter was the announcement that U. A. Whitaker had been nominated by the members of the MIT Corporation for a Term Membership on the Corporation. By mid-June, 1961, Whitaker was accepted as a member of the governing board and duly informed of his acceptance by President Killian, who expressed his great pleasure over the decision and spoke of the importance of serving the corporation at what Killian described as a crucial period in the history of the institution. Whitaker accepted the appointment immediately, feeling it a great honor and opportunity to serve on the board, as he wrote Killian: "It is one of the most important periods in the Institute's history in view of the tremendous changes and advancements in science and education in general."[9]

A few days after Whitaker first learned of his nomination to the MIT governing board, he received additional good news from Killian about the proposed Life Sciences Center at the Institute. The National Institute of Health, Killian reported, had indicated its intention to fund aproximately forty percent of the cost of constructing the new center, estimated at nearly $5 million, provided that MIT undertook a campaign to raise the additional amount from private sources. Killian proposed that he and Whitaker sit down and discuss the matter further, and Whitaker agreed to do so in the not too distant future. He did, however, caution Killian that he still had some thinking to do about his own role in such a large project. "I have not yet clarified my own thinking in the matter of charities," he replied to Killian, "so that I doubt that I would want to put a large amount into any one project at this time."[10]

Any further consideration about the Life Sciences Center project was delayed temporarily when U. A. Whitaker suffered a heart attack early in July, 1961. Actually, it was not his first; earlier in the year, while vacationing at his Florida home in Fort Lauderdale, Whitaker had been hospitalized over a weekend for what appeared to be a heart attack, but was released on Monday morning since nothing showed up on an electrocardiogram test. Although Whitaker had been instructed to rest following this first incident, he neglected (purposely) to tell his wife Helen about the orders he received from his doctor, and, when he returned home, he carried on his activities as usual. A compulsive cleaner and organizer, Whitaker immediately went out to clean his garage on an especially hot Florida day and by evening had to admit to his wife that he didn't feel well. Another hospital visit clearly revealed the heart problem, and Whitaker was forced to rest for some weeks. It was early spring before he returned to Harrisburg, where despite a barrage of admonitions to take it easy, Whitaker resumed his normal pace. His attack in July also failed to convince him that restraint was necessary. By late summer, 1961, it was again work as usual.[11]

In mid-August, Whitaker's attention again was directed to matters at MIT. He received information about the work being done in the Biology Department as well as his committee assignment for the following year, which found him on the biology and electrical engineering Visiting Committees. A meeting of the Department of Biology Visiting Committee was set for early March of the following year, and that meeting marked the beginning of Whitaker's significant relationship with Dr. Irwin W. Sizer, then head of the department.[12]

Sizer, who had joined MIT as a young biologist in 1935, was a man who spoke Whitaker's language. Like a good number of his colleagues at MIT, Sizer, very early on, had come to reject the traditional approaches to his discipline, involving the classical categories of botany, zoology, taxonomy, public health, and education. Like Vannevar Bush, Sizer wanted to bring biology into the modern era by applying the discipline to the life sciences in a synthesis with engineering, thereby creating a new field called biological engineering. The first practical use of this new sythesis was the application of a biochemical point of view to the problem of nutrition and food science, that is, the matter of food preservation, especially in canning. By the time Whitaker arrived on the scene, Sizer and his colleagues had already shifted their attention towards the health sciences and the application of molecular biology to the problems of medicine. Since Whitaker had also become interested in cardiac research and had funded separate projects in both Boston and Cleveland, his relationship with MIT and Dr. Sizer was a natural one. Sizer, in fact, would soon become Whitaker's "window on MIT," as he called him, the man on whom Whitaker depended for information and advice about various activities at the institute.[13]

In the years immediately following his appointment to the board of the MIT corporation, Whitaker had a good deal of contact with a variety of people at the university and because of his growing involvement in the life sciences project, made periodic trips to Cambridge. Partly due to his increasing commitment to this project and related matters at MIT and partly as a result of his heart attacks, Whitaker relinquished his position as president of AMP Incorporated in October 1962, moving up to the post of chairman of the board. His longtime financial adviser and friend, George Ingalls, who had joined AMP Incorporated in 1957 after retiring from American Machine & Foundry, became the company's third president, following Robert Hixon and Whitaker. Although he continued to remain active in the company, Whitaker was now freed from the details of its day-to-day operations and thus able to concentrate more fully on the new challenges presented by the now-flourishing field of biomedical engineering.

By the middle of 1963, Whitaker's financial commitment to the construction of the new Life Sciences Building at MIT had grown to a total of $1. 7 million. A little over a year later plans were already underway for the dedication ceremonies to be held in December, 1965, and the final transfer of funds to meet Whitaker's $2. 1 million original pledge were completed. The Uncas A. and Helen F. Whitaker Building for the Center of Life Sciences was dedicated on December 3, 1965. Late in the fall of that year, a special assistant assigned to Whitaker sent him a draft of a suggested short speech, which he was expected to deliver at the dedication ceremonies. Characteristically, Whitaker altered the rather formal text in keeping with his more informal personality; references to "Mrs. Whitaker and me" were pencilled out on the draft and replaced with "Helen and me."[14]

Also characteristically, Whitaker's interest in the life sciences did not end with the dedication of a building. Because of his intellectual involvement in the project, Whitaker understood that to apply the research derived from biomedical engineering, some kind of meaningful liaison between engineers and medical people had to be effected. The costs of establishing a medical school at MIT were prohibitive by the mid-1960s; moreover, the existing facilities at Harvard and in the Boston area were superlative. Therefore, the idea of combining MIT's technical expertise in biomedical engineering with the facilities available at Harvard was both practical and appealing. The linkage between the two institutions was created in 1967, and the result was a new division of Health, Science, and Technology which allowed a medical student from Harvard to earn a Medical Engineering degree at MIT. It was U. A. Whitaker who made this liaison possible in 1967 by endowing a Biomedical Engineering Chair at MIT.[15]

But Whitaker was not content to rest with these accomplishments alone. The next development concerned a slightly different kind of involvement and was Whitaker's own idea. Demonstrating a remarkable astuteness about education itself and drawing on his own experiences in research and development work, Whitaker suggested a unique approach to further research in the area of biomedical engineering. His proposal, which in 1974 became The Health Sciences Fund at MIT, (now known as the Whitaker Health Sciences Fund), was a plan to support research for graduate students and for faculty beginning new projects or changing career directions. For Whitaker, who had always done the same thing for his bright young engineers at AMP Incorporated, this appeared a logical and a productive approach to the matter of creating new knowledge and new innovative devices. Engineering for profit and engineering for public service were one and the same for U. A. Whitaker.[16]

By the mid-1960s, U. A. Whitaker had become a familiar figure on the MIT campus. As a major contributor and as a Life Member of the Corporation, Whitaker involved himself in both the projects and the politics of the university. In the summer of 1965, for example, Vannevar Bush asked for Whitaker's recommendation for the posts of president and chairman of the board of MIT. Whitaker replied with a letter supporting Dr. Charles A. Townes for president and Dr. J. R. Killian for chairman. A year later, on learning of Dr. Jerome B. Wiesner's promotion from dean of the sciences to provost at MIT, Whitaker wrote Wiesner "getting in a 'plug'" for his associate and friend Dr. Irwin Sizer to fill the dean's position vacated by Wiesner. (Later, U. A. Whitaker would serve on the search committee that selected Dr. Wiesner as president of MIT.) Meanwhile Whitaker's involvement and visibility at MIT had apparently become significant enough to convince at least one outside agency that he belonged at the Institute. In 1969, the National Research Council in Washington, D. C. , seeking appraisals of a particular proposal, sought Whitaker's opinion and directed its correspondence to Dr. Uncas A. Whitaker, AMP Incorporated, Cambridge, Massachusetts. Whitaker, his humor showing through, replied: "I have just received your letter of June 19th since it was misdirected to Cambridge, Massachusetts. However since I do not consider myself qualified to judge the merits of the research proposal entitled 'Feedback Control of Gyroscopic Systems,' this wrong address is of no moment."[17]

Whitaker's prominence, of course, was understandable by this time. In addition to receiving a host of professional, educational, and business awards, Whitaker now found his name beginning to appear in a variety of "Who's Who" categories. *Town and Country* magazine, for example, in a 1968 listing of the "names that count in the Big Business Establishment," included Whitaker's name in the category Men of Electricity and Electronics. In the same list with Whitaker, appeared such familiar names as Thomas J. Watson, Jr. (IBM), Robert Sarnoff (RCA), and David Packard (Hewlett-Packard).[18]

Like most business chief executives of his generation, Whitaker preferred to remain out of the public limelight, letting recognition come to the corporate name and the AMP Incorporated organization. When, therefore, an extremely congratulatory feature article on U. A. Whitaker and AMP Incorporated appeared in *Forbes* magazine in 1969, Whitaker was at a loss as to its origins. Although he should have been flattered at the article, which pictured Whitaker as a man who had "built a better mousetrap" and made millions for himself and others in the process, Whitaker, was, in fact, a little irritated about the exposure. To make matters worse, from Whitaker's point of view, the magazine had transposed his name with that of AMP Incorporated's current president, Sam Auchincloss, under the photograph set in the article. Whitaker made his positon about this sort of publicity quite clear in a letter to his longtime friend Sam Williams.

> The article in *Forbes*, though not unfavorable was quite inaccurate as all such articles are to the best of my knowledge. They called about correcting the picture-name situation and I told them to leave it alone because they probably would get both the picture and the name wrong the next time. We do not advertise in *Forbes* to the best of my knowledge so I don't know just why they decided to write the article. I personally try to avoid being interviewed by any of these magazine people and refused in this case, so I don't know just where they did get the information.

Whitaker must have known, however, that interest in him and his company was not unwarranted. According to *Fortune*, in the ten years from 1957 to 1969, Whitaker had guided his company into the top twenty firms in the nation in increased earnings over the decade.[19]

Informal, modest, and virtually invisible as he traveled the country in his gray flannel business suit, Whitaker was constantly reminded of his prominence. For a successful business leader, heading one of America's larger corporations, anonymity was possible only up to a point. A man of Whitaker's business and professional stature was well known to those people who, for a variety of reasons, made it their business to seek out influential types like Whitaker. And in some instances, Whitaker was willing to use his prestige. Like nearly all of his acquaintances, friends, and business associates, he was a conservative. Therefore, conservative causes and conservative politics attracted him and although his political involvement was minimal, he was not loathe to use his influence, upon occasion, to lend support to certain personalities, ideas, and organizations that he believed best represented his and the nation's interests.

Whitaker's political profile is interesting and instructive, not because he was an influential and powerful activist, but because what he thought, believed, and actually did was typical of an important segment of the business world. In fact, Whitaker behaved politically like most ordinary middle-class Americans, writing an occasional letter to his senator or representative and making fairly regular contributions to a political party. The major difference between Whitaker's participation and that of the ordinary American was that Whitaker's position in the business and professional world carried considerable clout. When he fired off telegrams and letters to his congressmen urging them, for example, to oppose further restrictions on the use of firearms, those legislators knew who that constituent was and, as a result, took more seriously the position he asked them to consider.[20]

Whitaker's contributions to the local, state and national Republican Party organizations were modest by any measure. Amounts of $500 or $1,000 for the state Republican Campaign Committee were his limit and on the national level his largest single contribution in any one year was $4,000 — to help Richard Nixon through the primaries and general election campaign of 1968. In nonpresidential years, he usually sent a check for $1,000 to the Republican National Finance Committee. Whitaker's identification with the Republican Party stretched over the whole of his life. Like many supporters of that party at his economic and professional level, he saw the Republicans as the more fiscally responsible party. In this sense, he certainly was his father's son.[21]

Whitaker seldom made more than a passing comment about politics in his correspondence and as a topic of general conversation it seldom occupied a great deal of his attention, except perhaps in those areas where individual freedoms were affected. He did, however, have definite views on general current political issues and once, in the latter part of the 1960s, he expressed some of those views in a letter to his sister Portia. During a visit with his sister in the summer of 1968, Whitaker was apparently asked about his opinions on Vietnam, the American economy, and Richard Nixon and his attitudes toward the problems of health care, crime, and race relations. Portia probably sought the information in order to be better informed about the upcoming presidential election. Whitaker returned to Harrisburg, thought about the questions he was asked, and dictated his answers. If not politically sophisticated, they do reveal Whitaker's common sense approach to life, as well as his ability to remain reasonable and hopeful about the possible outcomes of current situations.

June 20, 1968

Dear Portia:

On the specific questions that you ask I will give my opinion, but don't think it would be better than your ideas.

On Vietnam, I don't think we should have gone in there in the first place, but now that we are in there it is hard for me to believe that it would be right to just pull out and let the communists take the country over. The idea of trying to build up a good army of South Vietnamese so that they can take over their defense themselves would sound to me the best plan, but that will take a long time. There is some chance, of course, that the meetings in Paris will reach some kind of solution.

On the American economy, the country has been running a deficit for a great many years and eventually this, of course, catches up. Right at the present time some very positive things have to be done, or the country will have to go off the gold standard, or have violent inflation, both of which are very harmful for our people in general and do the most harm to people in the lowest income bracket. I think there are considerable signs, however, that some corrections will be made. Taxes certainly should be raised and spending has to be cut. Along this line, as to who I would vote for for President, I would vote for the Republican candidate and would prefer Nixon for the reason that I have just discussed in relation to the economy. What is needed now is a President and a Congress that will cut spending and increase taxes so as to balance the budget and get things back in order. Otherwise, we could have a violent depression several years from now. When this is done, however, it will hurt business and probably some people will lose jobs, so undoubtedly there will be more people out of work. This is a very unpopular thing to do, but must be done.

As far as accomplishments along the lines of human health, especially related to science, there is a lot of progress being made and certainly over the next generation or two most of the ills that people have now will be solved. Unfortunately these things take a long time.

As to crime and race problems, I think the matter of crime can be fairly easily solved by simply enforcing the laws as they are now written. This will require more police and better grade police.

The race problem is going to be extremely difficult, I think, and will undoubtedly take several generations to solve, if indeed it can ever be solved, but the Negroes have made a lot of progress over the last ten years and undoubtedly will make more progress in the future. Certainly in the long run riots and burning buildings etc. , is not the way to solve this problem.

Whitaker's essential optimism was reflected here and elsewhere in a tendency to discount the underlying importance of the traumas of the 1960s. At the beginning of 1969 he had observed, "I don't believe that our country is as badly mixed-up as we are led to believe from watching the television scenes and listening to the radio and even reading the magazines. At least the people that I know personally seem to be about as sensible as they ever were."[22]

Perhaps highest on his list of sensible people were Whitaker's old time school, Westinghouse Air Brake, and hunting and fishing friends, George Misner and Sam Williams. The continuity of those relationships added immeasurably to Whitaker's confidence that sanity and rationality ultimately ruled the world in which he lived. For Whitaker, the swapping of tall tales with these two men in letters and on an occasional hunting or fishing weekend at George Misner's camp was proof enough that his circle of associates were carrying on their affairs in an orderly and comprehensible manner. Following an October, 1968, hunting weekend, Whitaker underscored those feelings by summing up the issues the men had debated during the long evenings before the fire:

I have spent all the time since I got back investigating the coloring of the common red fox and after all this research I find that they all have a white tip on their tail, also I investigated the speed at which a fox runs and find a fox, a rabbit and a horse run at the same speed approximately but are capable of speeds for a few seconds up to 40 miles an hour. I believe those were the two major questions we were discussing in the three days we were at camp.

More than an escape from the affairs of business, these outings in the country gave Whitaker the chance to exchange stories, information, and ideas with his old friends. Along with sailing, these weekends with old friends provided Whitaker his most pleasant relaxation.[23]

Whitaker, as one of his friends put it, "did not suffer fools gladly," and consequently spent as little time as possible in their company. He found puttering alone in his garage or on his boat a use of time far superior to hours spent listening to pompous monologues from pretentious individuals in either social or professional settings. Nor was he easily cowed by expertise. Although Whitaker necessarily spent a great deal of time with experts of all sorts, he never believed he had to take them seriously. His own judgments, he felt, were just as often correct as were those of others whose claim to expertise was greater than his own. Financial people, for example, amused Whitaker and, like his father, he was less than tolerant of the so-called Eastern Establishment. He found the forecasting ability of the "Wall Street Crowd," as he often referred to the eastern financial experts, somewhat less than perfect. In 1974, a year before his death, he wrote:

> I spend a considerable time with the Wizards of Wall Street about once a month or so. The only difference between last year and this year is that they now admit they don't know what is going on.

Unlike his father, however U. A. Whitaker never claimed to have the answers to complex questions involving the country's frequent economic ups and downs. What he did have was faith in the system, partly because things had always worked out in the past and partly because he cared so much about his country. As he explained it in 1974: "I suspect . . . that we will come out of this recession . . . in due time as we always have and . . . we will eventually solve the inflation problem without a major recession, but will have to admit that I don't know much about it either."[24]

Despite U. A. Whitaker's claim to modesty he did, in fact, know a great deal about a good many things both important and trivial. What he knew best, of course, was how to be successful in the engineering business, as he demonstrated during the nearly thirty-five years he devoted to the founding, development, and growth of AMP Incorporated. As the management authority Peter Drucker once put it, "all kinds of people built American business and very few of them were 'tycoons.'"[25] U. A. Whitaker was decidedly not a tycoon. He was, however, a superb organizer, an even better engineer, and, perhaps most important of all, a consummate manager of men. He asked for and received a measure of loyalty from his associates and from the working personnel who knew him, and that loyalty continues today, even after his death.

Whitaker himself would never have admitted that he possessed any simple formula for his success, but he probably would not disagree with the notion that the basis for this success was the spirit of community which, over the years, developed within the corporation. In the synthesis between engineering problem solving and private enterprise profit making, a reasonably balanced community of purpose emerged. One employee understood that sense of community in this way: "Frequently. . . I have found myself thinking about the influence the organization that you have built has had on my life. The AMP Incorporated environment has offered us the opportunities, the challenges and the rewards to make our lives richer and more meaningful."[26]

For U. A. Whitaker, the AMP Incorporated environment, the AMP community, revolved around the problem solving engineer working to provide solutions for the company's customers. All of his working life, Whitaker was obsessed with establishing the proper environment for his engineering personnel. This theme, as we have seen, appeared again and again in his conversation and in the context of executive decision making. As the company grew and as the AMP Incorporated environment became more difficult to control, Whitaker worried even more about the problem. At the age of 71, now effectively semiretired, he still concerned himself with that all-important matter:

> Unfortunately as a company gets the size of this one a lot of routine controls have to be put in and this is just the kind of atmosphere that the creative engineer doesn't like and in which he doesn't function properly. Creative people not only need to be protected, they also have to be supervised in a manner that will keep them reasonably happy.

Whitaker understood the need to be particularly careful in managing his engineering talent, both in protecting them from distraction and in supervising their activities to mitigate excess frustration. Additionally, he knew that creativity had to be nurtured as well as watched over. "Most of them [engineers] need to be shifted occasionally to a completely new project [because] some of them only come up with a good idea every few years." Whitaker believed it worth the cost to shift men from project to project, because patience of this kind very often paid handsome dividends in new ideas and innovations and, subsequently, new products. "Not only should we protect the creative people that we have," he concluded "we should try to employ additional people."[27] Whitaker, at age 71, continued to fight the battle of creativity and new-product development, which he had waged all of his professional and business career. "Engineering the hell out of a product" had created the AMP Incorporated community in the first instance; in the long run it was necessary to sustain it.

* * * * * * *

U. A. Whitaker died in September, 1975, while vacationing at his summer place on Swan's Island just off the coast of Maine. That May, at the commencement ceremony at Carnegie-Mellon University he had received an honorary degree, the last in a long series of awards and distinctions recognizing his many accomplishments. The citation, accompanying the degree of Honorary Doctor of Engineering, enumerated a number of those accomplishments, fittingly concluding with this sentence: "Through his significant contributions in Industry, his valued service to Research, and his inspiring entrepreneurship, U. A. Whitaker is a magnificent symbol of individual achievement."

In its Annual Report for 1975, AMP Incorporated honored its late founder, president, and chairman of the board. The brevity, the succinctness, and the absence of sentimentality in that statement would have pleased Whitaker. A paragraph reviewed his career with AMP Incorporated; a second paragraph stated confidence in AMP Incorporated's future. A small photograph of Whitaker, placed beside these paragraphs, shows him smiling wryly — perhaps amused by the company's final tribute:

It started with a terminal

Notes

The following abbreviations are used throughout the notes for names
frequently referred to.

UAW	U. A. Whitaker
OBW	O. B. Whitaker
OBWNL	O. B. Whitaker's family newsletters
SWW	S. W. (Sid) Whitaker
CLH	Carl L. Hamilton
CJF	C. J. Fredricksen
VEC	V. E. Carlson
GEW	G. E. Walker
SWP	S. W. Pollock
RJS	R. J. Szukala
WHC	William H. Cohn

Notes: Chapter One

(1) Information about U. A. Whitaker's family background was pieced together from
a variety of sources, both official and unofficial. Among the most important are: *Index
to the 1860 and 1870 Census for Hickory County, Missouri*; *The 1880 Soundex for
Missouri*, Missouri Division of Health, Bureau of Vital Records, State of Missouri,
County of Hickory; Warranty Deed Records, State of Missouri, County of Hickory;
State Almanac and Official Directory of Missouri for 1879; *Official Manual of the State of
Missouri for Years 1905-06 and 1919-20*; *History of Hickory, Polk, Cedar, Dade and
Borton Counties, Missouri* (Chicago, 1889); catalogues from Weaubleau Christian
Institute 1887 to 1913; Docia Whitaker Wilcox, *From Covered Wagon to Jet Plane, My
Life Journey* (Woodburn, Oregon, 1967); F. Marion Wilson, *History of Hickory County*
(Hermitage, Missouri, 1907); B. B. Ihrig, *History of Hickory County, Missouri*
(Warsaw-Clinton, Missouri, 1970).

The weekly newspaper, *The Index* was useful for the years 1885-1900 as were a
series of articles about Weaubleau and The Weaubleau Christian Institute and College
by Eugene Harryman published in a Springfield, Missouri, newspaper in 1953 and 1955.
Mr. Harryman, a lifelong resident of the area, kindly furnished me copies of these
invaluable articles. As clerk of the Whitaker-founded church in Weaubleau for over
forty years, Mr. Harryman also provided me with records of the Whitaker family, who
are buried in the small cemetery plot adjoining the church grounds. Finally, I am
grateful to members of the Whitaker family and friends of the family living in
Missouri, who generously took the time to speak with me about life in and around

Weaubleau many years ago. Their recollections proved to be an invaluable source of information.

(2) Wilcox, *From Covered Wagon*, p. 12.

(3) O. B. Whitaker's 1941 Christmas letter to his family. O. B. Whitaker generally made it a practice to send copies of his letters to members of his family; usually up to seven copies of each letter were produced.

(4) SWW to UAW, September 27, 1946; *The Index*, September 8, 1887, and March 1, 1888.

(5) *The Index*, July 24, 1885.

(6) *The Index*, February 25, 1897. Old-timers remember the muddy roads and sidewalks vividly. During the winter and early spring articles about Weaubleau similar to this one frequently commented on the conditions. Paul Vanderford, a Weaubleau resident since 1911, recalls that the place, even then, resembled a western frontier town.   The Weaubleau Christian College Catalogue, 1912-13, indicates that Weaubleau's population was about 1,000. The college by that time had enrolled nearly 3000 students over the years since its first class of six had graduated in 1877. Old-timers recall the importance of the college to the town for both economic and educational reasons. Also see *The Index*, June 10, 1886, and June 16, 1887, for contemporary praise of the college.

(7) *The Index*, April 8, 1886.

(8) *The Index Supplement*, June 17, 1886.

(9) OBWNL, January 19, 1923; *The Index*, March 30, 1893, and July 27, 1893.

(10) OBWNL, July 20, 1941.

(11) Kansas City *Star*, March 2, 1935. Docia Whitaker Wilcox, as a very young cousin of O. B. Whitaker, attended Kansas Christian College for several years during the mid-1890s. She described O. B. as a strict disciplinarian just like his father John Whitaker. The rules were strict: mandatory evening work, no dating except on weekends, and enforced evening study hours. Wilcox, *From Covered Wagon*, p. 36.

(12) OBWNL, September 13, 1939.

(13) Weaubleau Christian College Catalogue, for 1895-96; *The Index*, April 3, 1890, for reprint of an address delivered by John Whitaker before the Southwest Missouri Teachers' Association, December 26, 1889, in Springfield, Missouri. An advertisement for the Institute which ran regularly in *The Index* in 1885 listed a curriculum which included five programs of study: Academic, Collegiate, Commercial, Normal, and Music.

(14) Weaubleau Christian College Catalogue, for 1895-96, p. 20.

(15) Weaubleau Christian College Catalogue, for 1895-96, p. 15.

(16) *The Index*, August 6, 1896, recorded the usual enthusiastic response to this lecture in a brief note.

(17) OBW to UAW, May 8, 1941; Kansas City *Star*, March 2, 1935.

(18) *The Index*, November 25, 1897, and May 26, 1898; Wilson, *History of Hickory County*, pp. 73-74.

(19) *The Index*, November 23, 1899, February 22, 1900, and March 9, 1900.

(20) Drury College, Springfield, Missouri, *Record of Students*.

(21) Drury College, *Record of Students*, Book 3, p. 57.   United States Army Discharge Papers.

(22) Missouri School of Mines and Metallurgy, Rolla, Missouri, *Grade Record* and appropriate pages from the general catalogue covering the period when Whitaker was enrolled as a student.

(23) UAW to Roger Burnell, January 4, 1949.

(24) UAW to Harry Demaree, January 15, 1957.

(25) OBWNL, undated letter fragment.

Notes: Chapter Two

(1) SWW to OBW, January 2, 1925.

(2) *MIT, Directory of Officers and Students, 1920-21* (Cambridge, Mass: Massachusetts Institute of Technology, 1920), p. 32; Eric Hodgins, *Trolley to the Moon* (New York, 1973), p. 142. Hodgins called the tuition of over $300 a "huge sum."

(3) Hodgins, *Trolley to the Moon*, pp. 140-41.

(4) *MIT, Directory of Officers and Students, 1920-21*, p. 64.

(5) Hodgins, *Trolley to the Moon*, p. 151. Also see Francis E. Wylie, *MIT in Perspective* (Boston, 1975), pp. 17-21.

(6) Official Transcript, Office of the Registrar, MIT, dated March 4, 1977.

(7) Hodgins, *Trolley to the Moon*, pp. 159-60.

(8) *MIT Catalogue, 1924-25* (Cambridge, Mass: Massachusetts Institute of Technology, 1924), p. 143. In Whitaker's senior year he elected a business and patent law course, described by the catalogue as "a general course in business law with five or six exercises devoted to the principles of patent law." Also see *MIT Directory of Officers and Students, 1922-23* (Cambridge, Mass: Massachusetts Institute of Technology, 1922).

(9) S.D. Heath to UAW, May 3, 1961; UAW to S.D. Heath, May 10, 1961. For the academic year 1920-21, Whitaker is listed as living at 503 Beacon Street with eight other MIT students. *MIT Directory of Officers and Students, 1920-21.*

(10) Samuel L. Williams to WHC, July 11, 1977.

(11) U. A. Whitaker, "The Design of a Rubber Heel Testing Machine," MIT Senior Thesis, June, 1923, p. 2.

(12) Wylie, *MIT in Perspective*, p. 21.

(13) Hodgins, *Trolley to the Moon*, pp. 144-45.

(14) *Reports of the President and Treasurer 1919-20* (Cambridge, Mass: Massachusetts Institute of Technology, 1921), p. 15.

(15) *Reports of the President and Treasurer 1919-20*, pp. 18-22.

(16) *President's Report, January, 1922* (Cambridge, Mass: Massachusetts Institute of Technology, 1922), p. 19.

(17) For a summary of Professor Harrison W. Hayward's career, see his obituary in *Technology Review* (December, 1932).

(18) On faculty opposition to the Technology Plan, see Hodgins, *Trolley to the Moon*, pp. 145-46 and Wylie, *MIT in Perspective*, p. 70. According to Wylie, MIT professors feared that this liaison with business and industry would be made at the sacrifice of pure research; Hodgins, in addition to describing this same fear, indicates that MIT was attempting to provide some outside source of extra income for their poorly paid faculty, who regularly left university employment for better paying jobs in industry. In fact, MIT had been offering research services for industry for some years, and the Division of Industrial Cooperation and Research merely provided a rational organization for whatever existed in haphazard form. See *President's Report, January, 1922*, p. 20.

(19) *Reports of the President and Treasurer 1919-20*, p. 11.

(20) Wylie, *MIT in Perspective,* p. 73, shows a picture of the 1923 graduation class, and the caption indicates that seniors wore caps and gowns for the first time that year. Another picture shows Ted Edison receiving his degree "while father Thomas snoozed in audience."

(21) This account of the 1923 MIT graduation appeared in *The Technology Review* (July, 1923), pp. 424-25. Although the article is unsigned, it is unmistakably written in Eric Hodgins' style.

(22) *The Technology Review* (July, 1923), p. 442.

(23) *The Technology Review* (July, 1923), p. 425; U. A. Whitaker was one of 106 graduating seniors receiving a degree in mechanical engineering. By comparison, only 82 and 86 mechanical engineering degrees were granted in 1924 and 1925 respectively. *President's Report, October, 1925* (Cambridge, Mass: Massachusetts Institute of Technology, 1925), p. 62.

Notes: Chapter Three

(1) OBWNL, February 21, January 14 and 26, and February 4, March 18, 1923.

(2) OBWNL, February 1, and January 26, 1923.

(3) OBWNL, February 21, 1923.

(4) OBW to his children, November 20, 1924.

(5) SWW to OBW, January 2, 1925. Approximately 560 acres of Missouri farmland were involved in this transfer to U. A. Whitaker; see OBW to UAW, October 1, 1927.

(6) Samuel L. Williams to WHC, July 11, 1977.

(7) OBW to UAW, October 1, 1927. At this time, Whitaker's father estimated that his son's land might bring as much $14,000 if sold. Uncle Syd Whitaker thought otherwise. See SWW to UAW, December 27, 1927. A year later, however, Syd Whitaker was saying just the opposite; and so it went. SWW to UAW, December 29, 1928.

(8) SWW to OBW, January 2, 1925.

(9) SWW to UAW, December 29, 1928.

(10) *Golden Echoes. Official Publication Commemorating Wilmerding's 50th Anniversary Celebration, 1890-1940* (Wilmerding, Pa. , 1940), pps. 9, 11, 43, 93.

(11) Henry P. Prout, *A Life of George Westinghouse* (New York, 1921), pp. 24-28. For a detailed description of Westinghouse's contribution to air brake technology see Prout, pp. 341-49. John Morton Blum, "The Entrepreneurs," in Stefan Lorant, *Pittsburgh, The Story of an American City* (New York, 1964), pp. 243, 246.

(12) Prout, *A Life,* p. 62.

(13) All of this information about life in Wilmerding was supplied by Samuel L. Williams; Williams to WHC, July 11, 1977. WAB employment records indicate that Whitaker did indeed begin work on June 14, 1923, as a special apprentice. On December 16, 1923, he was transferred to salary status.

(14) For an excellent discussion of the professionalization of mechanical engineering in America see Monte A. Calvert, *The Mechanical Engineer in America 1830-1910* (Baltimore, Md.; 1967). By Whitaker's time, Westinghouse Electric had been recruiting directly from engineering schools for over twenty-five years. According to Calvert, by

1925, "engineering offered a sure route into desirable executive positions." (p. 232) WAB, however, began somewhat later than Westinghouse Electric, perhaps following World War I. Earl O'Connell, who has been with WAB since 1937, recalls that the process was started about 1920. Interview, with Earl O'Connell, June 20, 1977.

(15) Samuel L. Williams to WHC, July 11, 1977.

(16) Interview with George Misner, September 17, 1976.

(17) According to WAB officials, the rubber parts operation was established in 1919. Whitaker entered the department as an assistant foreman and worked his way up to assistant supervisor. Interview with Earl O'Connell, June 20, 1977.

(18) Samuel L. Williams to WHC, July 11, 1977.

(19) UAW to James Olson, July 8, 1940.

(20) During this prolific inventive period of Whitaker's career, he was wholly or partly responsible for twenty-five separate domestic patents related to air brake technology.

(21) Prout, A Life, pp. 294-300. WAB was established in Britain and France before 1890. Mira Wilkins, The Emergence of Multinational Enterprise: American Business Abroad from the Colonial Era to 1914 (Cambridge, Mass., 1970), p. 213.

(22) All of the material on The Carnegie Institute of Technology during this period is taken from Arthur Wilson Tarbell, The Story of Carnegie-Tech 1900-1935 (Pittsburgh, Pa., 1937), Chapter VII, pp. 152-67.

(23) Bulletin of the Carnegie Institute of Technology, 1928-29 (Pittsburgh, Pa., Carnegie Institute of Technology, 1928), p. 73.

(24) Official Transcript, Carnegie Institute of Technology, covering period of Whitaker's enrollment at CIT, January, 1927 to May, 1929.

(25) UAW to OBW, September 30, 1927.

(26) 26th Annual Report of the President of CIT, 1929-30 (Pittsburgh, Pa., Carnegie Institute of Technology, 1930), p. 88.

(27) See Footnote (7).

(28) SWW to UAW, December 29, 1928.

(29) SWW to UAW, December 30, 1926, December 27, 1927; OBW to UAW, April 2, 1928. According to colleague George Misner, when Whitaker left WAB in August, 1929, he was earning approximately $275 per month.

(30) OBW to UAW, April 2, 1928.

(31) OBW to UAW, August 7, 1928. Several years later, O. B., in the midst of a legislative battle over a new liquor law for Missouri, told his family about his lifelong opposition to drinking: "Since I have been old enough to understand the matter I have been engaged more or less in opposition to the liquor traffic. When I left my home at Lincoln, Kansas, where I had lived thirteen years, the leading paper of that town gave me credit for closing the saloons of that city." OBWNL, December 5, 1933.

(32) OBW to UAW, February 9, 1929.

(33) OBW to his wife and children, February 15, 1929.

(34) OBW to his wife and children, February 16, 1929.

(35) OBW to his wife and children, February 15, 1929.

(36) OBW to his children, April 11, 1929; OBWNL, April 12, and May 10, 1929.

(37) UAW to James Olson, July 8, 1940; OBW to UAW, August 8, 1929. WAB employment records indicate that Whitaker "quit" on August 3, 1929.

Notes: Chapter Four

(1) Stefan Lorant, *Pittsburgh, The Story of an America City* (New York, 1964), pp. 478-81. As a longtime baseball fan, Whitaker might well have been among the thousands of baseball enthusiasts in attendance at one of the world series games the Pittsburgh Pirates played at Forbes Field in 1925 and 1927. It was also at Forbes Field in the fall of 1926 that Whitaker's new alma mater, CIT, upset Notre Dame before 45,000 people.

(2) Frank G. Hoover, *The Story of Hoover: The Fabulous Dustpan* (Cleveland, Ohio, 1955). *The Stark County Story* (Canton, Ohio, 1949, 1952, 1955), Vol I, 571-77; Vol. III, 123-37; Vol. IV, Part I, 108-34.

(3) UAW to James Olson, June 8, 1940.

(4) *The Stark County Story*, Vol. IV, Part I, 116-19.

(5) UAW to James Olson, June 8, 1940.

(6) Hoover, *The Story of Hoover*, p. 214.

(7) U. A. Whitaker, "Development and Engineering Procedure," *Product Engineering* (April, 1936), pp. 122-25.

(8) U. A. Whitaker, "Determining Results of Abuse in Advance," *Machine Design* (August, 1931), p. 31.

(9) U. A. Whitaker, "Determining Results of Abuse in Advance," *Machine Design* (August, 1931), p. 31.

(10) U. A. Whitaker, "Don't Limit New Design by Sticking to Tradition!" *Machine Design* (November, 1936), pp. 58.

(11) UAW to James Olson, June 8, 1940.

(12) *The Saturday Evening Post* (December 12, 1936), pp. 68-69. All during the 1930s, the Hoover Company placed similar pre-Christmas advertisements in the *Post* during the first or second week of December.

(13) Whitaker contributed or was involved in eight Hoover patents during his years with the company.

(14) UAW's income tax records for the years 1926-40.

(15) OBW to UAW, March 17, 1933; OBW to SWW, December 28, 1933.

(16) OBW to children, August 3, 1930.

(17) OBW to children, August 3, 1930.

(18) OBW to children, August 3, 1930; James Fenimore Cooper, *The Last of the Mohicans* (New York, 1962), pp. 32-33.

(19) OBW to children, August 17, 1930.

(20) Joseph Whitaker to OBW, September 7, 1930. (This Joseph Whitaker, OB's brother and UAW's uncle, is not to be confused with John Whitaker's brother of the same name.)

(21) *State Almanac and Official Directory of Missouri for 1879*, *The Index*, May 3, September 13, October 4, and November 15, 1888.

(22) OBW to children, March 13, 1932; OBW to UAW, March 27, 1932.

(23) OBWNL, January 13, 1931.

(24) OBWNL, November 5 and 9, 1932.

(25) O. B. Whitaker wrote extensive tracts on his various political and moral positions. He was most vehemently opposed to the undermining of the private school system through the use of the sales tax to subsidize public education.

(26) OBWNL, April 1, 1931.

(27) Minnie Frost to UAW, September 18, 1931; OBW to UAW, September 22, 1931.

(28) UAW to James Olson, June 8, 1940.

(29) OBW to UAW, September 22, 1931. As a young boy, Whitaker's eyes were considerably weakened after a bout with scarlet fever.

(30) OBW to UAW, September 22, 1931.

(31) In December 1931, O. B. received news that he had failed his law exam. Other failures would follow. OBWNL, December 19, 1931.

(32) OBW to UAW, June 22, 1931; OBWNL, July 4, 1931, and January 30, 1932.

(33) SWW to UAW, December 10, 1931.

(34) New Smyrna Investment and Loan Co. to UAW, March 10, 1932.

(35) OBW to UAW, April 30, 1930. In a postscript, O. B. wrote: "It is quite a pleasure to me to know that my reading law helps you. I greatly enjoy the reading of law – always did. Have very little hope of passing the exam however."

(36) OBW to children, February 18, and March 13, 1932.

(37) OBW to UAW, August 10, 1932; OBW to Portia Burnell, October 2, 1932; OBWNL, November 5 and 9, 1932.

(38) OBWNL, November 9, 1932.

(39) SWW to UAW, January 5, 1933.

(40) OBWNL, January 8, February 6 and 13, and March 17, 1933.

(41) A series of letters about cattle purchases were exchanged between the two men during the months of April and May 1933. After the eventual purchase of twenty-seven cows and one bull, O. B. wrote to his son Uncas: "Here's hoping the investment will prove profitable and that we are at last heading back towards prosperity and the road may not be long." OBW to UAW, May 4, 1933; UAW to OBW, May 9, 1933.

(42) OBWNL, May 14, 1932.

(43) OBW to children, July 24, 1933.

(44) UAW to SWW, December 28, 1933; SWW to UAW, January 3, 1934.

(45) OBWNL, December 31, 1933; February 1, 1934.

(46) OBW to UAW, May 18, 1934; OBWNL, June 10 and 17, 1934; OBW to SWW, August 10, 1934; OBW to children, August 26, 1934. O. B. bragged to his family that during his campaign he did not spend a penny.

(47) UAW to SWW, December 28, 1934; SWW to UAW, December 31, 1934.

Notes: Chapter Five

(1) OBW to UAW, September 25, 1932.

(2) OBWNL, July 10, 1935; OBW to UAW, March 20, 1935.

(3) UAW to OBW, August 7, 1935; OBWNL, August 10, 1935.

(4) Whitaker's flying logs indicate that he began taking flying lessons in August, 1935. Whitaker's mother, who on very rare occasions corresponded with her son, worried a great deal about his health, his work habits, his marital status (or lack of one) and his life style in general. Shortly after Whitaker had begun his job with The Hoover Company, his mother unilaterally decided that overwork would cause her son to become a nervous wreck. To this concern son Uncas replied: "No Mamma, I am in no danger of overworking, or falling down the stairs and breaking my neck, so please pick on someone else to worry about." OBWNL, March 7, 1931.

(5) OBWNL, January 5, 1934.

(6) OBWNL, February 17, and April 10, 1935. O. B. told his family that "Representatives of the State of Missouri from Hickory County and two members of the house have called me to run for governor on the Republican ticket, which said party elected 10 members out of 150 in the House at the last presidential election."

(7) OBWNL, February 1, and April 12, 1935; SWW to UAW, May 24, 1935; OBW to SWW, November 17, 1935.

(8) UAW to OBW, August 7, and September 27, 1935.

(9) OBW to UAW, September 23, 30; October 3,12,14,15,16,21,23, and 27 November 2,9, and 17 and December 24 and 31, 1935; UAW to OBW, October 10,16,23, and 29; November 14, and 26, and December 23, 1935.

(10) UAW to OBW, October 29, 1935. UAW to SWW, December 23, 1935.

(11) UAW's flying log, 1935-36.

(12) UAW to OBW, January 23, 1936.

(13) OBWNL, December 13, 1935.

(14) UAW to OBW, December 23, 1935.

(15) OBWNL, January 6 and 13, 1936; UAW to OBW, January 23, 1936.

(16) UAW to OBW, January 23, 1936.

(17) OBW to UAW, January 27, 1936.

(18) OBWNL, February 4, 1936; OBW to UAW, February 12, 1936; UAW to OBW, February 21, 1936.

(19) OBW to UAW, March 19, 1936; UAW to OBW, March 31, 1936. The previous year O. B. admitted he could not remember exactly in which year his son was born. OBW to UAW, March 20, 1935.

(20) UAW to OBW, March 31, 1936.

(21) The Hoover Company Earning Statements for 1935 and 1936; UAW's check register for 1936.

(22) OBW to UAW, April 3, 1936; OBWNL, April 12, 1936.

(23) OBW to UAW, April 3, 1936.

(24) OBWNL, April [?], 1936.

(25) OBWNL, June 14, and August 6, 1936; OBW to UAW April 2, 22, and October 7, 1936; UAW's check register for 1936.

(26) OBW to UAW, October 7, 1936.

(27) OBW to UAW, October 16, 1936.

(28) UAW's flying logs for 1937.

(29) Handbill entitled, "Why You Should Vote for O. B. Whitaker for Congress," O. B. Whitaker, Republican Candidate for Congress, Second Missouri District.

(30) Handbill, "Why You Should Vote for O. B. Whitaker for Congress."

(31) Marcia Magill to WHC, June 17, 1976.

(32) OBWNL, May 13, 1937.

(33) In all, UAW flew nearly thirty-five hours distributing handbills. See flying log for October and November, 1936. OBW to UAW, November 6, 1936.

(34) OBW to UAW, November 6, 1936.

(35) OBWNL, December 6, 1936.

(36) OBWNL, Christmas, 1936.

(37) SWW to UAW, July 28, 1937.

(38) OBWNL, June 10, 1937.

(39) UAW to OBW, July 2, 1937.

(40) OBW to UAW, June 9, 23, and 27, 1937; UAW to OBW, July 2, 1937.

(41) OBW to UAW, June 18, 1937; OBWNL, June 24, 1937.

(42) OBW to UAW, June 18, 1937.

(43) Whitaker sent his father sums of money all through 1937, sometimes for farm expenses but equally often because of O. B.'s poor financial situation. OBW to UAW, January 29, March 6, 19, and 24, May 2, August 10 and 31 and October 8, 1937.

(44) On MAT advances see UAW check register for 1937; mortgages held by UAW totalled $4,150.52, and total assets were listed as $6,500.

(45) SWW to UAW, December 30, 1937. UAW to OBW, December 29, 1937. OBW to UAW, January 3, 1938.

(46) Organization Chart, Engineering Department, The Hoover Company, North Canton, Ohio, September 7, 1938. Whitaker described his department in an engineering talk sometime after the New Model Hoover 150 went on the market in 1936.

(47) UAW, income tax records for the years 1926-40.

Notes: Chapter Six

(1) OBWNL, August 3, 1938. O. B. had let his subscription to the *Literary Digest* expire a year earlier. In a newsletter to his family, he said, "I have taken it ever since I was married and father took it while I was a boy . . . . I don't like it anything like I used to." OBWNL, June 10, 1937.

(2) OBW to UAW, September 30, 1938; OBWNL, November 4, 1938.

(3) OBW to UAW, October 28, 1938.

(4) OBWNL, December 18, 1938.

(5) OBWNL, December 18, 1938.

(6) Morehead Patterson to UAW, November 23, and December 1, 1938.

(7) OBWNL, December 18, 1938

(8) OBWNL, December 18, 1938.

(9) UAW to Morehead Patterson, December 26, 1938.

(10) UAW to Morehead Patterson, December 26, 1938.

(11) UAW to L. E. Jermy, February 13, 1939.

(12) Interview with George Hastings and Truman Safford, March 24, 1977; UAW to F. L. Pierce, June 16, 1939.

(13) UAW to SWW, January 1, 1939; UAW to OBW, February 6, 1939.

(14) Lou Ritzman to UAW, January 8, 1939.

(15) UAW to Lou Ritzman, January 12 and 30, 1939; Lou Ritzman to UAW, January 15, 1939.

(16) Lou Ritzman to UAW, March 2, 1939.

(17) UAW to Lou Ritzman, April 4, 1939.

(18) UAW to Earl Kail, April 4, 1939; Earl Kail to UAW, April 6, 1939.

(19) UAW to Earl Kail, April 4, 1939; Earl Kail to UAW, April 6, 1939.

(20) Earl Kail to UAW, April 6, 1939; UAW to Earl Kail, April 12, and May 11, 1939.

(21) Earl Kail to UAW, September 7, 1939; Lou Ritzman to UAW, September 7, 1939.

(22) UAW to Earl Kail, September 11, 1939; Earl Kail to UAW, October 19, 1939.

(23) OBW to UAW, June 28, and July 20, 1939; UAW to OBW, July 6, 1939.

(24) Earl Kail to UAW, October 27, 1939; UAW to Earl Kail, October 31, 1939.

(25) Earl Kail to UAW, December 1, 1939; UAW to Earl Kail, December 5, 1939.

(26) Earl Kail to UAW, January 25, 1940; Lou Ritzman to UAW, January [?], 1940.

(27) Earl Kail to UAW, January 25, and February 12, 1940; UAW to Earl Kail, February 2 and 16, 1940.

(28) OBW to UAW, January 27, and February 1, 1940; UAW to Lou Ritzman, February 27, 1940.

(29) UAW to Earl Kail, May 17, 1940; Earl Kail to UAW, May 23, 1940.

(30) Earl Kail to UAW, June 5, 1940; UAW to Earl Kail, June 18, 1940.

(31) Earl Kail to UAW, June 29, 1940; Lou Ritzman to UAW, July 26, 1940.

(32) UAW to Earl Kail and Lou Ritzman, August 13, 17, and 26, 1940; Lou Ritzman to UAW, August 29, 1940.

(33) Earl Kail to UAW, October 11, 1940; Lou Ritzman to UAW, October 26, 1940; UAW to Lou Ritzman, October 28, 1940.

(34) UAW to Earl Kail, December 3, 1940; Lou Ritzman to UAW, December 5, 1940; UAW to Lou Ritzman, December 10, 1940.

(35) UAW to SWW, December 30, 1940.

(36) OBW to SWW, November 1, 1940.

(37) G. Earle Walker to WHC, April 5, 1977.

(38) In 1940, Whitaker's total flying time exceeded his 1939 total by nearly fifty percent. See flying logs for the years 1939 and 1940.

(39) UAW to R. W. Rummel, Chief Engineer, Rearwin Aircraft and Engines, Inc., Kansas City, Missouri, March 10, 1941. There are a large number of letters in Whitaker's personal airplane files for the years 1939-43 which pertain to the buying and manufacture of this particular airplane.

(40) UAW to Jack J. Roemer, January 31, 1940.

(41) UAW to Mark Heaney, April 3, 1940.

(42) W. C. Davidson, an associate and friend of Whitaker at The Hoover Company reported that "there has been a pretty steady exodus of engineers in the past few months." W. C. Davidson to UAW, March 29, and June 18, 1940. Whitaker was joined at American Machine & Foundry Company by both F. L. Pierce and Frank Wells, two highly talented engineers, who would later play important roles in the development and growth of AMP Incorporated. Pierce followed Whitaker to American Machine & Foundry Company, from the Hoover Company. F. H. Wells to UAW, August 11, 1939.

(43) C. G. Troxler to UAW, June 2, 1940; UAW to C. G. Troxler, June 5, 1940.

(44) Interview with George Hastings and Truman Safford, March 24, 1977; W. C. Davidson to UAW, June 18, 1940; UAW to James C. Olson, June 8, 1940.

(45) N. McL. Sage to UAW, November 14, 1940; UAW to N. McL. Sage, December 20, 1940; Charles E. Locke, MIT Alumni Secretary, to UAW, April 11, 1940; UAW to Charles E. Locke, April 12, 1940; J. R. Killian to UAW as a member of the Visiting Committee for the Division of Industrial Cooperation, December 15, 1940.

(46) OBWNL, May 25, and July 3, 1940. UAW wrote his father early in June about a speech of Wendell Wilkie's that had impressed him. UAW to OBW, June 7, 1940.

(47) UAW to OBW, July 25, and August 26, 1940; OBW to UAW, August 20, September 21, and October 16, 1940.

(48) OBW to UAW, September 21, 1940; OBW to SWW, November 1, 1940.

(49) OBWNL, May 25, and November 17, 1940.

Notes: Chapter Seven

(1) *Time*, January 6, 1941.

(2) OBWNL, January 22, and May 28, 1941.

(3) OBWNL, April 9, May 2, June 7, and July 20, 1941. Although lonely, frustrated and tired, O. B. could conduct business as usual. He told son Uncas in one of his newsletters, "Uncas, I wish you could come back and look things over and talk over plans. If inflation comes and land values go up, is it your intention to sell?"

(4) Henry Dreyfuss to UAW, March 21, 1941; UAW to Henry Dreyfuss, March 27, 1941; Truman Safford and George Hastings to WHC, December 10, 1976; Samuel L. Williams to WHC, July 11, 1977. Whitaker's application for a Cigarette Detecting and Correcting Apparatus was filed April 2, 1941, and it was patented September 12, 1944.

(5) Interview with George Hastings and Truman Safford, March 24, 1977.

(6) Interview with George Hastings and Truman Safford, March 24, 1977.

(7) Promotional brochure published by the National Research Institute, October 1, 1939.

(8) Lewis W. Waters, "Industrial Research in Your Own Business," *Dun's Review* (September, 1940). This brochure was published as a supplement to Dun and Bradstreet's October, 1940, *Industrial Bulletin*. Whitaker's penciled marginal notes can be read alongside those suggestions that particularly interested him.

(9) I. L. Ingalls to UAW, August 24, 1944. Irving Ingalls (no relation to George Ingalls, Whitaker's friend, longtime financial advisor and later president of AMP Incorporated) handled Whitaker's accounts until the summer of 1944. In this letter, Ingalls summed up the various financial tasks he had done for Whitaker over the years, tasks which included UAW's personal, farm, and McKinley Air Transport accounts.

(10) UAW to Lou Ritzman, February 6, 1941; UAW to Earl Kail, February 14, 1941; Earl Kail to UAW, May 27, and June 14, 1941.

(11) Earl Kail to UAW, July 21, August 8, and 12, 1941; UAW to Earl Kail, June 18, 1941.

(12) UAW to Earl Kail and George Swayze, July 24, 1941; UAW to OBW, March 3,

April 16, and May 23, 1941. Whitaker's Missouri farm files are filled with account sheets, bills of sale, receipts, purchase orders, sales slips, and copies of letters to his father requesting (at times pleading) for information for income tax purposes. Consistently, what it all added up to was a lot of work and a small loss to be deducted from Whitaker's salaried income. In 1940, for example, Whitaker's farm losses saved him approximately $150 in federal income taxes. See UAW's Form 1040, US Individual Income and Defense Tax Return for the Calendar Year 1940.

(13) UAW, check register for 1941; UAW's automobile file for the years 1941 to 1958; UAW to Sherwood Press, Cleveland, Ohio, May 6, 1941; UAW to George Misner, July 2, 1941.

(14) UAW flying log for 1941; UAW to CLH, July 19, 1941; interview with George Hastings and Truman Safford, March 24, 1977; UAW to George Misner, August 19, 1941; UAW to CLH, August 12, 1941, "Report on Industrial Manufacturers, Inc." Unless otherwise indicated, all references to the history, personnel, and operations of Industrial Manufacturers Inc., come from this extensive report, apparently put together by Whitaker himself.

The background for the coming together of Whitaker's interests and those of the Hixon family is provided in a supplement to a 1944 V Loan application: "The Midland Investment Company, owner of all the preferred stock of Aircraft-Marine Products Inc. is a family banking company for the Hixon Family interests. For a period of time preceding the formation of Aircraft-Marine Products Inc., Mr. Robert Hixon was interested in investing for Midland Investment Company in one or two small companies that had engineering possibilities. He inquired of Carl Hamilton, a member of Booz, [Fry] Allen and Hamilton, nationally known firm of management engineering consultants, to inform him of any companies that might have good investments possibilities. Mr. Hamilton and Mr. Whitaker, now President of Aircraft-Marine Products Inc., advised Mr. Hixon to purchase Industrial Manufacturers Inc., of Elizabeth, New Jersey, as a company which would have some future based on its products and possibilities for engineering development. At that time the use of solderless terminals was not prevalent in American industry. The company had government approvals of its products in war equipment and had a small amount of business, chiefly with Glenn L. Martin Aircraft Company. In fact, Glenn L. Martin purchased, we believe, all of their necessary requirements in solderless terminals in sizes 22 to 14 inclusive, from Industrial Manufacturers. This business from the aircraft company seemed promising and held potentialities for sales to other aircraft companies." See Supplemental Statement, V Loan Application, December 16, 1944.

(15) *Time*, January 6, 1941.

(16) Whitaker's information on S. N. Buchanan's career and patent contributions came from a Buchanan letter dated August 11, 1941, to which was appended a listing of his patents by name, number, and date of issue.

(17) In his report to Carl L. Hamilton, Whitaker noted that there was only one major manufacturer of solderless electrical terminals, Thomas & Betts. The Thomas Register for 1940 listed thirty such companies but noted that all but Thomas & Betts were small concerns.

(18) Even after World War II there was a continuing resistance to the use of solderless terminations in some manufacturing areas. G. Earle Walker interview, March 31, 1977.

(19) War Department/Air Materiel Division, Wright Field, Dayton, Ohio, to Industrial Manufacturers Inc. Elizabeth, New Jersey, June 26, 1941.

(20) CLH to UAW, September 4, 1941. Buchanan's relationship with Harvey

Hubbel began with the Hubbel firm conducting a series of experiments on Buchanan's electrical devices.

(21) Invoices billed to UAW by American Machine & Foundry Company indicate that Whitaker flew to Washington, D.C. on July 11 and returned on July 13. Whitaker also received a bill for a series of long-distance calls he made to Elizabeth, New Jersey. See also UAW to CLH, July 19, 1941. The Hooper-Holmes Business Report on Industrial Manufacturers Inc. dated August 15, 1941 provides background on the net worth of Buchanan, Skyberg, and Shoemaker and their respective roles in the firm.

(22) CLH to UAW, July 16, and August 1, 1941; UAW to CLH, July 19, 1941.

(23) George Hastings to UAW, "Report on Electrical Connectors," August 8, 1941.

(24) William S. Watts, "Investigation of Wire Terminals and Connection Devices," submitted August 7, 1941. Whitaker used a good deal of Watts' report in his own report to Carl Hamilton on August 12, 1941.

(25) List of Manufacturers of Solderless Connections from Thomas Register, 1940; results of testing done by S. N. Buchanan and Chief Engineer James O. Johnson; Dun and Bradstreet Report on Thomas & Betts; also UAW to CLH, August 19, 1941.

(26) UAW to CLH, August 16, 1941.

(27) UAW to CLH, August 19 and 20, 1941.

(28) CLH to UAW, August 19, 1941; UAW to CLH, (two letters) August 27, 1941.

(29) Undated, unsigned interview about Industrial Manufacturers Inc. in Whitaker's personal correspondence file pertaining to Aircraft-Marine Products Inc.

(30) CLH to UAW, August 19, 1941; UAW to CLH, August 20, 1941.

(31) UAW to CLH, (two letters) August 27, 1941.

(32) UAW to CLH, August 27, 1941.

(33) UAW to Earl Kail and George Swayze, August 6, 1941; UAW to OBW, August 6 and August [?], 1941; OBW to UAW, August 8, 1941.

(34) In fall, 1941, Whitaker listed some of Midland's holdings in a letter identifying the officers and directors of Industrial Manufacturers Inc. He enumerated Midland's holdings in lumber, oil, and gas and estimated the total net worth of the Hixon family interests to be over $30 million. See UAW to W. K. Houston, C&H Supply Company, Seattle, Washington, October 24, 1941. Midland Investment, managed by Robert Hixon, was actually controlled by the family of his brother Joseph Hixon, then deceased.

(35) CLH to UAW, August 27, 1941; in a memorandum to Whitaker dated September 8, 1941, Hamilton outlined some alternative plans for distributing the common stock equity in Aero-Marine Products, Inc.

(36) CLH to UAW, September 4, 1941.

(37) UAW to CLH, September 7, 1941.

(38) Denis M. Robinson interview with UAW, September 11, 1946.

(39) UAW to CLH, September 7, 1941; UAW to Lt. Vernon H. Grant, September 7, 1941; UAW's check register for September, 1941.

(40) UAW to CLH, September 7, 1941; also interview with George Hastings and Truman Safford, March 24, 1977.

(41) CLH to UAW, September 8, 1941.

Notes: Chapter Eight

(1) The Hotel Robert Treat was the meeting place for many late night meetings in the early days.

(2) CLH to UAW, September 11, 1941. The law firm of Lindabury, Depue and Faulks, located in Newark, New Jersey, handled the initial legal work for Industrial Manufacturers Inc. See CJF to Lindabury, Depue and Faulks, November 19, 1941.

(3) Certified copy of Resolution of Aero-Marine Products, Inc., September 15, 1941; Board of Directors Minute Book 1, meeting held September 15, 1941; Resolution, Stock Warrants, September 15, 1941; Statement of Problems and Conclusions, Industrial Manufacturers Inc.; Aero-Marine Products Inc., Opening Balance Sheet, September 15, 1941; Aircraft-Marine Products Inc., List of Stockholders as of September 15, 1941.

(4) George Misner to UAW, March 13, 1942. The list of possible names was first narrowed down to nine—Aircraft-Marine Products Inc., Industrial-Aero Products, Inc., Marine-Aviation Products, Inc., Marine Aviation, Inc., Aviation-Marine Products, Inc., Aviation Marine Inc., Marine-Aero Products, Inc., Marine-Air Products and Marine Aero, Inc. Also see UAW to CLH, September 24, 1941.

(5) Ellery Fitch to UAW, April 11, 1942; UAW to Ellery Fitch, April 13, 1942.

(6) UAW to N. McL. Sage, September 22, and October 3, 1941; N. McL. Sage to UAW, September 27, 1941.

(7) OBWNL, October 10, 1941.

(8) W. K. Houston to S. N. Buchanan, October 17, 1941.

(9) UAW to W. K. Houston, October 24, 1941.

(10) *Time*, June 16, and September 15, 1941.

(11) OBW to SWW, September 9, 1941.

(12) OBWNL, November 9, 1941.

(13) *Time*, October 27, 1941.

(14) C. G. Troxler to UAW, September 28, 1941. Troxler at the Hoover Company sent Whitaker some names of engineers he believed were available. A list of Industrial Manufacturers Inc.'s employees included one engineer, two draftsmen, a sales manager, a bookkeeper, an invoice clerk, a file clerk and typist, and a switchboard operator, who also did stenographic work when not answering the phone. Production employees received hourly rates ranging from eighty cents down to forty-five cents. Engineer James O. Johnson was the highest paid salaried employee at $67.50 per week. The Hooper-Holmes Bureau Business Report on Industrial Manufacturers Inc., dated August 15, 1941, describes the building the company occupied. Albert Curtis, longtime AMP Incorporated employee, passed on his recollections of those early days in an interview on May 25, 1976.

(15) UAW to N. McL. Sage, September 27, 1941. The engineer serving in the U.S. Army Whitaker wanted was Quentin Berg. Berg later did join the company and played a key role in product development work. Also see UAW to W.S. Watts, October 3, 1941; W. S. Watts to UAW, October 15, and 21, and December 14, 1941. Interview with Kenneth L. Neijstrom, May 25, 1976.

(16) UAW to CLH, October 29, 1941. Whitaker was wrong about Eureka; the company did not go out of business.

(17) Gordon C. Curry to UAW, October 27, 1941; UAW to Gordon C. Curry, October 29, 1941. Whitaker told Carl L. Hamilton on October 29 that the personnel question remained his greatest problem. About the Hoover connection he wrote: "I have a tentative agreement with the Hoover Company to loan me engineers as needed with the understanding that we will allow the Hoover Company to subcontract some work that we need. This deal is not completed as yet but if it can be set up properly would put us in a position where we could expand rapidly should business require." UAW to CLH, October 29, 1941.

(18) UAW to Gordon C. Curry, October 29, 1941.

(19) On the Hoover Company arrangement see G. P. Daiger to UAW, November 3, 1941 and attached "Report on Visit to Aircraft-Marine Products Inc. in New York City Concerning Contemplated Development Contract," dated October 30, 1941. UAW to G. P. Daiger, November 5, 1941; H. Earl Hoover to UAW, November 21, 1941; UAW to H. Earl Hoover, November 27, 1941.

One of the first tasks Hoover engineers accomplished for Whitaker was a visit to the Navy Department Bureau of Standards and Naval Research Laboratory in Washington, D.C. "in order to obtain technical information to assist Industrial Manufacturers Inc., in fulfilling their development contract with the Navy Department on aircraft wiring equipment." G. P. Daiger to Lt. Vernon H. Grant, November 21, 1941. Daiger's report was completed on December 4, 1941. An associated report, dealing with the Navy development contract and other future work, was released on December 2, 1941. See C. G. Troxler, "Report on a Visit to Aircraft-Marine Products Company, Elizabeth, New Jersey, November 29, 1941."

(20) UAW to J. F. Hattersley, October 30, 1941; UAW to C. B. Colson, November 12, 1941; T. H. Welsby to UAW, February 23, 1942.

(21) W. S. Watts to UAW, October 28, and 30, November 1, 10, 12, 116, 22, and December 2, 4, and 10, 1941.

(22) CLH to UAW, November 5, 1941; UAW to CLH, November 10, 1941.

(23) In fact, Buchanan's information that Chrysler, Ford and General Motors were about to adopt Aircraft-Marine Products Inc.'s terminals was erroneous. See UAW to CLH, October 29, 1941; also see UAW to Robert Hixon, November 18, and December 15, 1941, and January 18, 1942. All Aircraft-Marine Products Inc. directors received Whitaker's monthly reports.

(24) UAW to Robert Hixon, December 15, 1941; R. Paul Mitchell to UAW, November 24, 1941 enclosing copies of proposed contract to be signed between Aircraft-Marine Products Inc. and Local No. 441 of the United Electrical, Radio and Machine Workers of America, affiliated with the CIO.

Whitaker got himself some hard-working directors in Hixon, Hamilton, and R. Miles Warner. Periodically, for the first several years of the company's existence, each of the men would write Whitaker with suggestions of all kinds, requests for information, and leads to new business accounts. All three men had valuable contacts in a variety of major manufacturing corporations and from time to time attempted to introduce Aircraft-Marine Products Inc. people to those contacts. Whitaker generally encouraged such activities believing firmly in the idea that a company's directors should be conscientious advisers. Occasionally, however, Whitaker had to politely decline a potential account explaining that the company's current production facilities could not handle the increased volume. For some typical examples from the directors see Robert Hixon to UAW, November 27, December 2, 12, and 18, 1941, and March 27, 1942; R. Miles Warner to UAW, June 5, 1942. Whitaker's responses can be seen as well. See UAW to Robert Hixon, December 2 and 23, 1941; March 20, and April 6, 1942; UAW to CLH, May 19, 1942; UAW to R. Miles Warner, May 28, 1942. It was, in fact, Robert Hixon who first suggested regular board meetings. On December 18, 1941, he posed the question for Whitaker's consideration: "Don't you believe that we should be thinking of having some periodical director's meetings so that we will not all be taking too much for granted?"

(25) UAW to Robert Hixon, December 15, 1941.

(26) UAW to OBW, December 7, 1941.

(27) Earl Kail to UAW, December 15, 1941. All flyers received this "Immediate Suspension of Airmen Certificates" notice shortly after its December 8, 1941 date of issue. General D. H. Connolly, who signed the notice instructed all airport managers "to prohibit Japanese or suspected Japanese from flying or riding as passengers in any airplane until further notice."

(28) OBWNL, December 12, 1941.

(29) UAW to SWW, April 7, 1942.

(30) OBWNL, Christmas, 1941.

(31) The funeral service for the Rev. and Honorable O. B. Whitaker on May 6, 1942 in the Weaubleau Christian Church was conducted by Rev. Frederick Cooper, who had been a student of O. B.'s. Cooper sent a copy of the sermon he delivered to U. A. Whitaker for his approval. Whitaker read and edited it and sent it along to his Uncle Syd Whitaker for his additions. See UAW to SWW, May 14, 1942.

(32) "Old Hickory," The Kansas City Star (May 7, 1942).

(33) UAW to Editor, The Kansas City Star (May 14, 1942).

(34) U. A Whitaker was always grateful for his father's guidance and advice all through his life, but fortunately he ignored his father's early opposition to an engineering career for his son.

Notes: Chapter Nine

(1) Whitaker's West Coast trip included visits to a number of aircraft plants, where he observed the production methods of applying electrical terminations. He was particularly struck by the time-consuming work involved in the "old-fashioned" soldering approach to termination tasks. He returned more convinced than ever that his solution to the problem –solderless electrical terminations–was the answer to improved production goals. Interview with GEW, March 31, 1977; also see UAW to GEW, April 27, 1942.

(2) Draft on the need for an organization plan and chart, [February-March], 1942.

(3) Draft on the need for an organization plan and chart, [February-March], 1942; Draft, "Organization Chart," March 20, 1942.

(4) UAW to CLH, March 12, 1942.

(5) UAW to CLH, March 12, 1942.

(6) UAW to Robert Hixon and CLH, December 15, 1941; UAW to CLH, March 12, 1942; interview with GEW, March 31, 1977.

(7) Interview with GEW, March 31, 1977.

(8) UAW to CLH, March 12, 1942.

(9) UAW to directors, June 21, 1942; UAW to R. Miles Warner, February 11, 1942.

In his letter to Warner, Whitaker suggested that one of Buchanan's "original" ideas had been on the market for many years.

(10) UAW to directors, June 21, 1942; also see UAW's *Deskaide* for Friday, June 19, 1942.

(11) Robert Hixon to UAW (Telegram), June 23, 1942; Draft letter written by CJF, June 24, 1942; Aircraft-Marine Products Inc. List of Stockholders, as of July 1, 1942; UAW to S. N. Buchanan, July 21 and 22, 1942.

(12) UAW to CLH, March 12 and 29, May 12, and December 21, 1942; UAW to L. E. Jermy, June 8, 1942. Jermy actually had written Whitaker asking about his new company. Jermy said he had heard by the grapevine (C. G. Troxler at the Hoover Company) that Whitaker had left American Machine & Foundry Company. He asked Whitaker if he could run an announcement about the employment change in *Machine Design*. Whitaker complied, and it appeared in the July issue. See *Machine Design* (July, 1942), pp. 102-103. Amusingly, Whitaker had his first, of several, experiences with journalistic imprecision. *Machine Design*, in its announcement, featured one of Aircraft-Marine Products Inc.'s new products and inadvertently ran the wrong photograph. The announcement appeared again in the September issue, this time with the correct illustration. In Whitaker's files are several examples of later press stories about his company on which he has circled those parts that he considered incorrect "factually" and labeled "wrong,"[signed] UAW.

(13) In his monthly reports to the directors, Whitaker would list the important new accounts gained since his last formal communication with them. "The new accounts," he wrote Carl L. Hamilton, "from the high grade companies are of great importance because of the opportunity for increased business as these companies swing over into full war production. UAW to CLH, May 12, 1942. In the first quarter of 1942, Aircraft-Marine Products Inc. added fifteen large accounts. Also see UAW to CLH, April 8, 1942. On the subject of the scarcity of materials, Whitaker told Jermy, "Since our material is made mostly of copper and tin, we can supply only those people engaged in higher priority work" UAW to L. E. Jermy, June 8, 1942.

(14) These examples are from a file labeled Watts, Correspondence and Reports, *Field Trips*, 1942.

(15) Interview with GEW, March 31, 1977.

(16) In a memo to Whitaker, Walker explained the rationale behind his direct mail campaign and sent along his cover letter and a copy of one of the printed brochures. GEW to UAW, March 2, 1942.

(17) GEW to UAW, March 3, and April 2, 1942. Attached to his March 3 memo was Aircraft-Marine Products Inc.'s first published advertisement, which appeared in the February, 1942, issue of *Marine Engineering and Shipping Review*. UAW to Sterling Tools Products Corp., April 28, 1942, explains the advertising arrangement with Renner Advertisers, Philadelphia, Pennsylvania. In July, Walker proudly announced that he had obtained over the past six months, forty-five inches of free press release publicity. He told Whitaker that it was "considerable more space than we have used in paid advertising." GEW to UAW, July 10, 1942.

(18) One thick file called Miscellaneous, Sales Department, 1942, is crammed full of Walker memos on virtually every problem which came across his desk.

(19) GEW to UAW, August 8, 1942.

(20) UAW to GEW, April 10, 1942.

(21) UAW to GEW, May 29, 1942.

(22) UAW to CLH, July 30, 1942.

(23) W. S. Watts to UAW, August 14, 1942; GEW to UAW, June 24, July 3 and

14, and August 31, 1942. Whitaker told Hamilton about the company's efforts to gain favor with government bureaus: "A great deal of time was spent during the month in bettering our position with various government agencies and this, we believe, has placed us in a more secure position. As a direct result, we have been placed on the approved list for solderless connectors for all tanks built for the army, whereas heretofore Thomas & Betts was the only source approved." UAW to CLH, June 10, 1942.

(24) For an overview on standardization procedures in effect in the aircraft industry before World War II, see Irving B. Holley, Jr., *United States in World War II, Special Studies. Buying Aircraft: Material Procurement for the Army Air Forces* (Washington D.C., 1964), pp. 26-33.

(25) National Aircraft Standards Committee, "Confirmed Minutes of the Sixth Meeting of the Electrical, Radio and Installation Sub-Committee" (May 21, 1942) at the Douglas Aircraft Company, Inc., Santa Monica, California.

(26) GEW to UAW, May 22, 1942. In this memo Walker quoted Porter's statement.

(27) UAW to GEW, May 29, 1942.

(28) GEW to UAW, June 29, 1942

(29) GEW to UAW, June 29, 1942; UAW to GEW, June 30, 1942.

(30) GEW to UAW, July 6, 17, and 31 and August 10 and 11, 1942.

(31) W. S. Watts to GEW (cc to UAW), September 16, 1942.

(32) Watts to GEW, September 16, 1942. Bill Watts also attended meetings in Detroit at which the Society of Automotive Engineers were engaged in similar standardization talks for their industry.

(33) UAW to Robert Hixon, December 21, 1942.

(34) UAW to Robert Hixon, December 21, 1942. Despite Whitaker's enthusiasm over war contracts, he remained frustrated with government contract work. As Bill Watts recalled near the end of the war: "Seldom a day goes by that I am not reminded of a remark you once made when you stated 'when and if this war ever ends I certainly want to get into a business where I would never be required to sell the government anything.' " W. S. Watts to UAW, August 2, 1945.

Notes: Chapter Ten

(1) Earl Kail to UAW, December 15, 1941.

(2) George Swayze to UAW, February 17 and 20, 1942; UAW to George Swayze, February 18 and 25, 1942.

(3) George Swayze to UAW, March 12 and 19, 1942; UAW to George Swayze, March 17, 1942.

(4) Robert Hixon to UAW, March 30, 1942. Hixon wrote: "I have at hand your letter of March 29th addressed to the three Chicago directors and it came just after my having a long talk with Miles Warner, so I am quite conversant with your problems. There has been through this office a considerable amount of money put up for this venture and you can be sure we will back to the limit any plan you think necessary to not only safeguard this investment, but to make it a good one. In fact we will not only back you up but we will probably be on your back until it's done."

(5) UAW to George Swayze, March 9, 1942; George Swayze to UAW, March 12, 1942.

(6) Board of Directors, Minute Book 2, Meeting held July 3, 1942.

(7) RJS to UAW, November 19, 1942; Francis W. Thomas to UAW, January 13, 1943; L. Metcalfe Walling, Administrator, Department of Labor, to UAW, January 28, 1943.

(8) W. H. Perks, War Department Air Corps Materiel Division to Aircraft-Marine Products Inc., June 26, 1943; GEW to CJF, June 28, 1943; CJF to War Department Air Corps Materiel Division, July 2, 1943. Fredricksen indicated that the 2.1 percent return after taxes was done on a sales volume two and half times as great as that of the previous year. Aircraft-Marine Products Inc.'s "Daily Order and Billing Report," dated December 31, 1943, clearly substantiates Fredricksen's claim that bonding tab sales were indeed but .003 percent of total sales.

(9) CJF to War Department Air Corps Materiel Division, July 2, 1943; interview with Marshall Holcombe, May 18, 1977.

(10) The government offered owners of recalled Minox cameras the original purchase price which, then, was $120. UAW to the Office of Strategic Services, April 6, 1943. Like many American civilians, Whitaker did his part for the war effort by joining a Civil Air Patrol Squadron attached to the airport at Lancaster, Pennsylvania, where he kept his own plane. He indicated to the commanding officer that business pressures would probably limit the amount of time he could give to the CAP. Whitaker's flying logs for the war years do not contain any entries which indicate he flew any hours as a member of the squadron. UAW to Lt. C. W. Rutzler, January 4, 1943.

(11) UAW to W. C. Davidson, February 3, 1944.

(12) UAW to CLH, April 21, 1943. A plant location survey, authorized by the directors in 1942, noted the undesirability of New Jersey as an area for expansion. An earlier location survey suggested that either western Pennsylvania or Ohio were the most desirable areas for locating a new factory, because they were near the geographical center of the aircraft, radio, and electrical machinery industries. Report from D. C. Witzke to UAW, October 7, 1941.

(13) *The New York Times* (March 16, 1943); interview with Albert F. Curtis, May 25, 1976; Francis W. Thomas to UAW, August 7, 1943.

In an advertisement placed in *The New York Times* on March 25, 1942, the United Electrical, Radio and Machine Workers of America (CIO) offered to work for straighttime wages on Saturdays, Sundays, and holidays and contribute the actual sum of overtime pay its members would have earned, to the United States Treasury, "to help our Government pay the Companies for whom we work for war products which we make." Although this offer appears to be exceedingly altruistic on the surface, it really was a not so subtle attack on the companies that union officials asserted were gouging the government in the first instance. What the union really wanted in exchange for foregoing time-and-a-half and double-time rates, was company assurance on job security, wage rates, job classifications, etc., after the war ended.

(14) Philadelphia *Evening Bulletin* (May 21, 1943); The York Pennsylvania *Gazette and Daily* (May 22, 1943); UAW to directors, May 22, 1943; interview with Kenneth L. Neijstrom, May 25, 1976.

(15) RJS to UAW, "Plant Location Report," March 13 and 18, 1943.

(16) Interviews with Kenneth L. Neijstrom and Albert F. Curtis, May 25, 1976.

(17) RJS to UAW, "Plant Location Report," March 18, 1943.

(18) RJS to UAW, "Plant Location Report," March 18, 1943.

(19) RJS to UAW, March 25, and June 15, 28 and 30, 1943; UAW to CLH, April

21 and May 22, 1943. At the April 21, 1944 meeting of Aircraft-Marine Products Inc.'s Board of Directors, a resolution was passed authorizing the purchase of the building at 1523 N. Fourth Street for $68,000. Also see UAW to CLH, March 29, 1944, for purchase details.

(20) RJS to UAW, June 30, 1943; The Harrisburg Chamber of Commerce, "Annual Report Covering the Year 1942-43," p. 6. Despite the Harrisburg C of C's statement on its role in bringing Aircraft-Marine Products Inc. to its city, Whitaker apparently continued to agree with Szukala's original assessment that the Chamber was "not 100% helpful" about the move. See Walter Johnson to UAW, June 14, 1945. A moving notice sent to Aircraft-Marine Products Inc. customers stated that after December 10, 1943, the company's headquarters would be located at 1523 N. Fourth Street in Harrisburg, Pa.

(21) UAW to Robert Hixon, November 24, December 1 and 24, 1943; Aircraft-Marine Products Inc., Comparative Profit and Loss Statement, for the Years 1941-1949, inclusive.

(22) UAW to Robert Hixon, December 1, 1943.

(23) UAW to CLH, February 12, March 29, April 27, and May 22, 1944.

(24) GEW, "A Consideration of Post-War Marketing Practices as They Relate to AMP Products Currently Available," April 17, 1944.

(25) RJS to UAW and GEW, March 14, 1944, on a priority for air travel to England; UAW to Lt. Vernon H. Grant, October 19, 1944; RJS to UAW, December 26, 1944 on setting up the Chicago export market office.

In June 1942, Walker addressed the export problem in his sales report for the second quarter of the year. Noting that Great Britain and the dominions were "the only real market available" he pointed out to Whitaker that an agent had been named for Canada while a licensing arrangement was being aggressively pursued for Great Britain. He concluded with the information that "excepting the Dominion of Canada, the possibility of immediate cash return seems to be remote because of the restrictions placed by the Bank of England on the removal of cash from Great Britain." GEW to UAW, June 30, 1942.

In February, 1943, Walker was approached by a representative of a Swedish engineering firm to represent Aircraft-Marine Products Inc. in Sweden after the war. O. Z. Pehrson to GEW, February 11, 1943. In spring 1944, Aicraft-Marine Products Inc. had an export agent for South America. GEW to UAW, April 17, 1944.

(26) UAW to Robert Hixon, May 11, 1944 on the subject of the V Loan.

(27) Aircraft-Marine Products Inc., Stockholder List, July 1, 1944; UAW to CLH, September 15, 1944.

(28) UAW to CLH, October 13, November 14, and December 23, 1944; Supplemental Statement, V Loan Application, Item 14 and Item 15, December 16, 1944.

(29) UAW to Robert Hixon, August 17, 1944. Whitaker wrote his friend Lt. Vernon H. Grant early in fall 1944, optimistically about postwar planning: "We are exceptionally busy in postwar planning, and it's going to be a very big problem to get shifted over to postwar work since almost all our business was developed in connection with war work. In spite of the problems prospects look quite good for us. No doubt we will have some tough periods though." UAW to Lt. Vernon H. Grant, September 20, 1944.

(30) Interview with Kenneth L. Neijstrom and Albert F. Curtis, May 25, 1976. ; L. B. Paules to VEC (cc to UAW), February 14, and March 23, 1945.

(31) GEW to UAW, June 12, 1945.

(32) GEW to UAW, July 30, 1946. The company's General and Miscellaneous Correspondence files for 1945 and 1946 are filled with Walker memos of this type.

(33) K. B. White to UAW, June 8, and August 8, 1945; K. B. White to CJF, January 28, and May 28, 1946.

(34) CJF to UAW, May 17, 1945. A list of employees at various locations, which was requested at the Management Meeting held, May 14, 1945, indicated that a total of 925 were currently employed. UAW to Robert Hixon, December 23, 1944; Aircraft-Marine Products Inc., Comparative Profit and Loss Statement, for the years 1941-1949, inclusive.

(35) UAW to Gordon C. Curry, April 11, 1945.

(36) UAW to Lt. Vernon H. Grant, September 21, 1945.

(37) With increasing numbers of war oriented contract cancellations and terminations, Aircraft-Marine Products Inc. approved a program for production personnel cutbacks. By September, 1945, Whitaker reported that the company was nearly completely converted to postwar business. He told the directors that "indications are that we will suffer no loss from terminations and will probably show a small profit". UAW to Robert Hixon, September 25, 1945.

Notes: Chapter Eleven

(1) Interview with Kenneth L. Neijstrom, May 25, 1976. Whitaker made weekly trips to Westfield, New Jersey where the engineers were quartered to find out who was working on what and how things were going and just to talk about engineering problems in general. See UAW's *Deskaide* for 1942 and 1943 for a record of his regular visits to Westfield. On the other hand, it was G. Earle Walker's perception that Whitaker did not want to be bothered about various matters; rather, he preferred people to handle their own problems and not bring them to him. GEW to WHC, April 5, 1977.

(2) Whitaker's policy about directors' salaries is instructive. At the firm's inception, Whitaker, in line with corporate development during the previous decade, believed that the directors of an enterprise should be compensated on the basis of the business talents and experience contributed by the individuals to the enterprise which they were directing. See Supplemental Statement to the V Loan Application, Item 14, (December 16, 1944). At that time, Hixon received $5,000 a year and Hamilton and Warner, $3,000 each. UAW to Robert Hixon, January 17, 1945.

(3) Interview with George Hastings and Truman Safford, March 24, 1977; interview with Marshall Holcombe, May 18, 1977.

(4) Interview with Albert F. Curtis, May 25, 1976.

(5) Interview with George Hastings and Truman Safford, March 24, 1977; interview with Marshall Holcombe, May 18, 1977. Helen Whitaker once remarked that even at home, Whitaker employed the incentive system in bringing up the children.

(6) For a brief analysis of the electronic industry's takeoff see Harold Vatter, *The U.S. Economy in the 1950's* (New York, 1963), pp. 163-68. CLH to UAW, December 19, 1945, and May 8, 1946.

(7) UAW to CLH, February 13, 1946.

(8) Whitaker kept in touch with his old Hoover Company associate, F. L. Pierce all during the war. Whitaker, in fact, had been largely responsible for Pierce's position at Eureka Vacuum Cleaner Company, having recommended him as a replacement for Verne Carlson who left Eureka to join Whitaker in 1942. See H. W. Burritt, President, Eureka Vacuum Cleaner Co. to UAW, June 12, 1942.

(9) GEW to UAW, July 23, 1945.

(10) Interview with GEW, March 31, 1977. William S. Watts, on his frequent field trips noted the reluctance of some automotive engineers to switch over to the new technology. In spring, 1944, after a Detroit visit, he reported that he had "talked to several of the automotive electric boys in the last few days and find that outside of Chrysler the war had educated a lot of them to be at least slightly inclined toward solderless terminals for postwar cars and trucks." W.S. Watts to UAW, April 7, 1944.

(11) On the potential of automatic machines see GEW memo to UAW, April 24, 1946 in which Walker suggests that 500 machines could be placed on the market in 1946.

(12) John Burchard, *MIT In World War II, Q.E.D.* (New York, 1948), pp. 85-88. Burchard, in a footnote, also described the research work done by MIT's Electrical Engineering Department's Instrument and Material Research Laboratory on Aircraft-Marine Products Inc.'s solderless terminal.

(13) UAW to CLH, December 21, 1942; Burchard, *MIT*, p. 185; "Proposed Report of the Visiting Committee of the Division of Industrial Cooperation," March 12, 1941.

(14) See Burchard, pp. 125-33 for a discussion of MIT's Division of Industrial Cooperation.

(15) UAW to Robert Hixon, June 16, August 1 and 17, 1944; Burchard, *MIT*, p. 187. In December 1943, Whitaker reported to Lt. Vernon H. Grant that the project being developed between Aircraft-Marine Products Inc. and MIT involving the use of Amplifilm in high-voltage capacitors was still in an experimental stage and fairly expensive to produce. UAW to Lt. Vernon H. Grant, December 14, 1943. Also see N. McL. Sage to John Keto, Chief of the Aircraft Radiation Laboratory, Wright Field, Ohio, October 22, 1947, for a summary history of the project. The properties and uses of this material are described in a report entitled "Amplifilm Dielectric Sheet and AMP High-Voltage Capacitors," issued some time in 1950.

(16) Aircraft-Marine Products Inc., Comparative Profit and Loss Statement, for the years 1941-1949, inclusive; UAW to directors, April 20, 1946.

(17) RJS to R. R. Williams, Federal Reserve Bank, Philadelphia, December 17, 1946. In applying for an extension of the loan, Szukala described the past year's business situation in some detail. In part, Szukala listed the economic problems of reconversion, the material shortage, and the lack of engineering help due to layoffs caused by contract cancellations.

(18) RJS to UAW, VEC, CJF, January 22, 1946; UAW to Lt. Col. B. W. Bishop, May 7, 1946 on the copper shortage; UAW to directors, April 20, 1946. Whitaker in his regular report noted that now the company was making over 3,000 different items.

(19) UAW to directors, June 27, 1946; 1946 Operations Letter to Directors, March 10, 1947.

(20) UAW to directors, June 27, 1946 and March 10, 1947. "Report on Automatic Machine Division," W. H. Mavity to GEW, February 18, 1946; UAW to CLH, May 11, 1946.

(21) UAW to directors, August 6, and September 6, 1946; RJS to UAW and CJF, March 21, and July 23, 1946 on conferences with the Federal Reserve Bank; RJS to R. R. Williams, Federal Reserve Bank, Philadelphia, December 17, 1946; UAW to

SWW, November 5, 1946. UAW informed his directors of the terms of the loan on January 6, 1947: "The bank loan with the Federal Reserve Bank of Philadelphia has been completed on a basis of giving us $120,000 plus 90% of receivables with a maximum amount of credit of $350,000. The $120,000 is to paid off at the rate of $10,000 per month. If business continues even fair, we should be able to operate quite satisfactorily under the terms of this loan and will be on a straight receivable basis by the end of the year."

(22) "AMP Incorporated Annual Average Employment Worldwide", Philip G. Guarneschelli, Manager, Industrial Relations, AMP Incorporated, to WHC, July 8, 1976. About 250 people were employeed in Harrisburg, about 50 in Glen Rock and another 40 at Seven Valleys. RJS to UAW, October 23, 1946.

(23) "Employee Relations/Benefits," dated June 27, 1944; RJS to UAW, VEC, CJF, July 3 and 23, 1946; RJS to UAW, May 20, 1947; Notice to Employees from I. Ketner, Personnel Department, July 21, 1947 on paid holidays; RJS to UAW, VEC, CJF, "Wage Survey Memo," August 27, 1948; RJS to All Employees, November 11, 1948 (information on the six paid holidays now awarded Aircraft-Marine Products Inc.'s employees); RJS to VEC, June 24, 1949, "Employee-Management Conference"; UAW to Paul Wagner, Vice-President Fidelity-Philadelphia Trust, April 5, 1949 for information on pension plans. Corporate labor relations policies were summed up by R. J. Szukala in October, 1946: "The company has made a special effort to hire stable, loyal, and industrious people for its organization. The result has been a most satisfactory labor-management relationship with mutual confidence and respect for each other. The employees have not joined any labor organization and have an attitude of mutual cooperation for the success of the company. The nature of the company's operations permits operating divisions geographically separated from each other without any diminution in operating efficiency." RJS to UAW, October 23, 1946.

(24) GEW to UAW, February 4, 1948.

(25) GEW to UAW, March 17, July 8, August 25, and September 22, 1948.

(26) UAW to Investors/Directors, August 6, and December 8, 1948; GEW to UAW, April 11, 1949.

(27) Interview with GEW, March 31, 1977.

(28) GEW to UAW, October 26, 1949; interview with Marshall Holcombe, May 18, 1977.

(29) Dick Leuba, "Automachine Division Job Report," December 12, 1949; F. L. Pierce to SWW, January 5, 1947.

(30) Interview with Kenneth L. Neijstrom, May 25, 1976; interview with Marshall Holcombe, May 18, 1977.

(31) Interview with Helen F. Whitaker, April 13, 1976; UAW Trip Memos, September and December, 1943.

(32) Interview with George Hastings and Truman Safford, March 24, 1977.

(33) SWW to UAW, July 5, 1946; UAW to Portia Burnell, May 31, and June 7, 1946; UAW to Dr. R. T. Warburton, June 7 and June 10, 1946. In all, Whitaker spent between $5,000 and $6,000 on the care of his sister Minnie Frost in 1946.

(34) UAW to Ruth and Portia Frost, May 3, 1946, inviting the girls to spend the summer with the Whitakers in Harrisburg. The girls' father, John Frost, was still alive but in recurrently poor health. In September, Frost reluctantly agreed to the adoption as being in the best interests of his two children. UAW to John M. Frost, September 20, 1946; UAW to John Frost, November 22, 1948 and August 18, 1949; John Frost to UAW, August 15, 1949.

(35) UAW to T. H. Whitaker, February 9, 1945; UAW to SWW, July 18, 1946.

Whitaker negotiated for the sale of his farm holdings for about three years and finally, by the close of 1948 he had disposed of nearly all of it. During the same period Whitaker also extricated himself from McKinley Air Transport. In this case, C. J. Fredricksen did most of the work.' See MAT Correspondence General, 1941-1949; for farm negotiations, see General Farm Correspondence 1938-1946 and 1947-1950.

(36) Interview with George Hastings and Truman Safford, March 24, 1977; also see miscellaneous boat files beginning in 1942 which contain voluminous correspondence and documents relevant to Whitaker's boating interests.

(37) UAW to Harper and Brothers, January 22, 1948.

(38) UAW to W. J. Davis, Federal Reserve Bank of Philadelphia, January 18, 1948; William H. Flentye and Company to UAW, July 11, 1946. Flentye apparently had a client willing to pay between $100,000 and $200,000 to acquire Aircraft-Marine Products Inc. UAW to William H. Flentye, July 18, 1946.

(39) Aircraft-Marine Products Inc. Comparative Profit and Loss Statement, for the years 1941-1949, inclusive.

Notes: Chapter Twelve

(1) *Time* (April 11, 1949)

(2) National Industrial Conference Board, *Let There Be Light. The Conference Board's First 50 Years of Service* (New York, 1966), pp. 10,12,21.

(3) Whitaker saved the programs for all of the conferences and his marginal notes often expressed approval or disapproval of a session's speaker.

(4) A meeting of the NICB held in 1951 featured an afternoon session entitled "Meeting the Communist Menace." Louis Budenz, a leading anticommunist spokesman, and an FBI undercover agent in the Communist Party for several years were the main speakers. National Industrial Conference Board meeting, Waldorf-Astoria, New York City, September 17-18, 1952. Whitaker and C. J. Fredricksen appeared to have attended one session called "Resources: From Abundance to Scarcity by 1975?" Written in the margin opposite this program listing is Whitaker's remark that "someday, somehow, somebody is going to have to pay for the fool thinking that is being done right now." In December 1949, Whitaker received an invitation from General Donovan to join the American Committee. Also see "A Statement of Purpose of the American Committee on United Europe," William J. Donovan, Chairman, Allen W. Dulles and Herbert H. Lehman, Vice-Chairmen.

(5) The 1950 ASME Skytop Conference, "The Manager in a Changing World," was largely devoted to the problem of combatting "isms." Whitaker received a partial "off the record" transcript of the Fifth ASME Skytop Conference held in 1951, which recorded speeches made in defense of "Americanism" and what management could do to "win the peace."

(6) Charles R. Hook, Chairman of the Board, Armco Steel to UAW, February 9, 1949; Douglas McGregor, "Human Relations in Industry: A Challenge for Free Enterprise," Antioch *College Bulletin* (September, 1949). McGregor, president of Antioch College and a former director of industrial relations at MIT, was a friend of Whitaker's and often sent off prints of his articles to Whitaker. This particular essay

stressed the relationship between profit and the continued existence of the free enterprise system. According to patent attorney Marshall Holcombe, McGregor's theories on management organization had a good deal of influence on Whitaker's thinking. McGregor's emphasis on the human factor as a crucial aspect of the free enterprise system blended nicely with Whitaker's own approach to industrial relations. See a news report on McGregor's ideas published in the New York *Times* (September 7, 1949); on the dangers of depression see RJS to UAW, January 6, 1949, and an attached article from *The Economist* (January 1, 1949) on the American business situation. Other materials in Whitaker's files stressed the need for a strong national security program involving the cooperation of business and government. See, for example the letter from J. K. Richards, Executive Director, National Security Industrial Association to UAW, February 23, 1950, which speaks of national security as an insurance policy "against the pitfalls and confusions experienced in prior mobilizations."

In addition to his membership in ASME and the NICB, Whitaker was a strong and active supporter of Americans for the Competitive Enterprise System (ACES) and was instrumental in setting up a Harrisburg chapter. In a Management Committee meeting in 1952, Whitaker requested and received approval for a $500 contribution to what he termed "this worthy cause[ACES]." Curtin Winsor, ACES, to UAW, October 17 and 26, 1951; Stroocom Meeting Minutes, February 19, 1952.

(7) GEW to W. H. Mavity, June 27, 1949; F. L. Pierce to Nat McL. Sage, January 10, 1950; UAW to M. F. Lowrey, The Hoover Company, October 16, 1951.

(8) Whitaker received materials on expansion from a variety of sources including chambers of commerce as far away as Duluth and Canada; Peninsula Industrial Committee, Newport News, Va., W. H. Curtis, Chairman, to UAW, May 14, 1951.

(9) UAW to investors and directors, August 3, 1950.

(10) Paul E. Orr, Jr., Vice-President, Management Planning of Washington, Inc., to UAW, August 17, 1950; on the material shortages see R. E. Weber to UAW, October 10, 1950; UAW to Joseph Gaynor, October 27, 1950; Morgan Prentiss to GEW, November 17, 1951.

(11) Pennsylvania Department of Commerce to UAW, July 16, 1951; Teodoro Moscosco, Jr., Administrator Economic Development Administration, Puerto Rico, to UAW, May 8, 1951.

(12) GEW to UAW, March 15, 1945. Walker sent Whitaker materials about doing business in the United Kingdom which Walker had received from British Commerce officers in Washington, D.C.

(13) George S. Hastings to UAW, September 30, 1949; UAW to George S. Hastings, October 4, 1949. On November 28, 1949, Whitaker returned a signed receipt for 100 shares of American Machine & Foundry Company common stock to Parrish and Company in New York City. Two years later Whitaker bought another 200 shares of American Machine & Foundry Company common stock. Both his original purchase and this additional one were based on the future prospects of the company's automatic pin-setting machine, not its cigarette-making equipment as Whitaker told Aircraft-Marine Products Inc. Director F. C. Hixon in the spring of 1950. UAW to Parrish and Company, January 24, 1951; UAW to F. C. Hixon, May 22 and 26, 1950.

(14) R. C. Conangla to UAW, September 29, 1949.

(15) R. C. Campbell to GEW, July 30, 1951; S. W. Pollock, on his own, visited IBM offices in New York and received the same assurance as did Campbell about the future potential of IBM business in France. See Stroocom Minutes, July 10, 1951. Campbell was a native of Harrisburg, a Carnegie Institute of Technology graduate engineer, and

had attended the Georgetown School of Foreign Service. SWP to David A. Horn, Renner Advertisers, February 5, 1953.

(16) SWP to Thomas V. Hodges, Renner Advertisers, October 10, 1951.

(17) R. C. Campbell to GEW, July 30, 1951.

(18) R. C. Campbell to GEW, July 30, 1951.

(19) GEW to CJF, November 6, 1951; meeting, Aircraft-Marine Products Inc. directors, New York Yacht Club, January 30, 1952.

(20) SWP to Charles H. Ducote, February 11, 1952. Pollock told Ducote the French operation was still in the planning stage and that he, Pollock, was in charge of the organization work; also see R. C. Campbell to SWP, June 20, 1952.

(21) R. C. Campbell to SWP, June 27, July 15, August 1 and 25, and September 1 and 12, 1952.

(22) R. C. Campbell to SWP, October 1, 2, 8, and 22 and November 5, 1952.

(23) R. C. Campbell to SWP, November 29, 1952.

(24) E. Marx came to United States to visit Aircraft-Marine facilties in December, 1948. E. Marx to UAW, December, 1948. Campbell's doubts about Marx were expressed in a confidential memo to G. E. Walker in July, 1951.

(25) R. C. Campbell to GEW, July 30, 1951.

(26) SWP to R. C. Campbell, November 4, 1952. At a management meeting on June 12, 1951, (Stroocom) it was recorded that "Walker reported that Mr. Marx has submitted a draft from their solicitor to Mr. Safford [A-MP's patent counsel] in New York for review of a proposed plan to manufacture terminals in England. It is doubtful whether we will react favorably to such a plan." Walker's remarks were made six weeks before Campbell's analysis arrived.

(27) SWP to Hellerman Ltd. (J. Bowthrope), January 15, 1953; Peters de Laet to GEW, April 8,11,20,23,27, and 28, and May 4 and 18, 1953; R. C. Campbell to SWP, March 4, 1953.

(28) American Pamcor Inc., was officially established at a directors' meeting held in Harrisburg on January 29, 1953. A description of the Puerto Rico manufacturing operation, Pamcor Inc., appeared under personnel changes submitted by V. E. Carlson, Director of the General Products Division, October 30, 1952; GEW to O. W. Holmes, December 8, 1952.

(29) GEW to O. W. Holmes, December 8, 1952, and April 22, 1953.

(30) GEW to UAW, January 4, 1950.

(31) GEW to O. W. Holmes, April 22, 1953.

(32) Walker described the relationship between himself and Whitaker in this way:"despite our differences in personalities we functioned reasonably well together, thus a dialectic of my impatience to be on with the matter at hand and his desire for a more measured pace." GEW to WHC, April 5, 1977.

(33) John T. Burnite Jr., to UAW, October 22, 1953; also Burnite reports on Japan dated August 26, and December 17, 1953.

(34) UAW to Mr. Carl E. Nagel, Vice-President and Managing Director, Council for International Progress in Management (USA), Inc., April 28, 1954. In fact, Aircraft-Marine Products Inc. had been thinking about a manufacturing operation in Brazil for some time. See SWP to Aladar Sator, January 20, 1953. In a memo to Walker in the fall of 1955, Burnite, now in Brazil, noted the deteriorating political situation in Brazil by referring to the Kubtschek administration as "communistically inclined". John Burnite to GEW, October 11, 1955.

(35) George Arisman to UAW, March 26, 1954; UAW to George Arisman, April 12, 1954.

(36) In a letter to another business acquaintance, Whitaker spoke of an ongoing survey of European countries for the establishment of a second continental manufacturing plant. UAW to Dr. A. G. Asoff, August 6, 1953. Also see SWP to R. A. Parsons, Hellerman Ltd., July 28, 1954.

(37) SWP to UAW and CJF, October 11 and 18, 1954; UAW to Burgermeister of Vlaardingen explaining Aircraft-Marine Products Inc.'s decision to settle in 's-Hertogenbosch, October 29, 1954.

(38) SWP to UAW and CJF, February 25, 1955; also see SWP to UAW and CJF, March 3,1955.

(39) SWP to UAW, March 18, 1955.

(40) SWP to UAW, October 6, 1955; UAW trip record 1956 and prior; UAW trip record 1957-58. Whitaker visited London, Glasgow, Paris, Nuremberg, Berlin, Hamburg, and Amsterdam in the period October 15-28, 1955. Also see AMP Incorporated,-Annual Report 1956. By the end of 1952, Aircraft-Marine Products Inc. had established a Canadian subsidiary, and by the end of the decade the company would be operating in Japan, Australia, Italy, and West Germany in addition to France, the Netherlands, and Great Britain. In later years Argentina, Brazil, Mexico, Austria, Finland, Norway, Spain, Sweden, Switzerland, and Singapore would be added with distributors in many other countries.

Notes: Chapter Thirteen

(1) The Editorial Press Bureau, Inc., to UAW, October 23, 1953. An article about Whitaker receiving an honorary degree from Elizabethtown College appeared on the front page of the Hickory County Missouri weekly, The Index, on May 13, 1954.

(2) In a real sense, Aircraft-Marine Products Inc. always had been administrated through committees of one sort or another. In the company's earliest days, Whitaker, C. J. Fredricksen, and George Ingalls met frequently, usually until late in the evening, to discuss company affairs. By the beginning of 1943, these meetings, often held in New York City, were given an official structure and a name — The Coordination Committee — with Vern Carlson joining the group. In mid-1944, regular monthly meetings, usually held in Whitaker's office on Sunday mornings commenced. This committee which came to be called the Executive Committee was made up of the above and G. Earle Walker, sales manager. Then, early in 1945, regular Monday management meetings were instituted with F. L. Pierce and Frank Wells in attendance in addition to the regulars who now, of course, included Walker.

The Management Committee, created shortly after World War II, became the Operations Committee in October, 1950. In the meantime, another group was formed, a planning group, comprised of Whitaker, S. W. Pollock, V. E. Carlson, C. J. Fredricksen and F. L. Pierce. This committee first referred to as OOCOM, went through another stage when it became a steering committee and took on the name STROOCOM and some additional members. The name STROOCOM was dropped at the end of 1953, and in June, 1954, it became the Planning Committee. In brief, regardless of the top level committee's name, its personnel makeup remained much the same over the years–Whitaker, Pollock, Fredricksen, Walker, Wells, and Pierce.

See minutes of the Planning Committee for June 3, 1954; also GEW to CJF, VEC, and SWP, May 7, 1954.

Marshall Holcombe's comments on Aircraft-Marine Products Inc.'s growth and antitrust considerations can be found in a report to the Executive Committee, dated November 30, 1954.

(3) Interview with Marshall Holcombe, May 18, 1977.

(4) There was always a good deal of discussion on the relative merits of working under one set of antitrust laws or another, and Holcombe spent much time and effort researching the attendant problems.

(5) SWP to L. V. Whipple, September 16, 1954; L. V. Whipple to UAW, April 5, 1956. In 1942, L. V. Whipple was hired as a consultant to do the plant relocation survey that led Aircraft-Marine Products Inc. to resettle in Central Pennsylvania.

(6) L. V. Whipple to UAW, April 5, 1956; GEW to UAW, August 29, 1955; L. B. Paules to UAW, October 16, 1958; interview with Marshall Holcombe, May 18, 1977.

(7) GEW to UAW, August 29, 1955.

(8) Planning Committee Meeting Minutes, November 20, and December 18, 1956.

(9) Planning Committee Meeting Minutes, November 20, 1956, and February 19, 1957; Executive Committee Meeting Minutes, July 1, 1957; Research Committee Meeting Minutes, April 16 and July 16, 1957; SWP to UAW, June 27, 1957, regarding the proposed technical evaluation department.

(10) Harold Vatter, *The U.S. Economy in the 1950's*, p. 12. Ralph L. Nelson, *Merger Movements in American Industry 1895-1956* (Princeton New Jersey, 1959), pp. 3-7; 106-126.

(11) On recapitalization planning see R. Miles Warner to UAW, April 29, 1953; UAW to R. Miles Warner, May 1, 1953; Solon Rhode, Jr., to Carl G. Mortenson, June 8, 1953. Also interview with A. H. Gordon of Kidder, Peabody & Co., March 25, 1977, and with C. J. Fredricksen, August 29, 1978.

(12) A. H. Gordn to UAW, April 17, 1956.

(13) Interview with A. H. Gordon, March 25, 1977.

(14) Executive Committee Meeting Minutes, June 11, 1956; Marshall M. Holcombe to UAW, August 22, 1956. At the September 24, 1956, Director's Meeting, the company's name was officially changed to AMP Incorporated. Also see AMP Incorporated Prospectus, November 13, 1956, and AMP Incorporated Annual Report for 1956.

(15) Executive Committee Meeting Minutes, September 17, 1956; E. G. Hefter to Marshall M. Holcombe, October 1, 1956; AMP Incorporated Annual Report, 1956, Letter to Shareholders. On Australia see GEW to UAW, June 6, 1957.

(16) GEW to UAW and all members of the Planning Committee, May 9 and 22, 1957.

(17) William H. Slike to UAW, November 10, 1956; UAW to William H. Slike, November 14, 1956; *Time* (November 12, 1956).

(18) UAW to Robert F. Kennedy, August 18, 1967.

(19) GEW to UAW and all members of the Planning Committee, May 9, 1957; GEW to UAW, George Ingalls, SWP, and CJF, October 2, 1957.

(20) SWP to Planning Committee, August 2, 1957; Marshall M. Holcombe to Leon Whipple, November 18, 1957; GEW to UAW, August 8, 1957.

(21) L. V. Whipple to UAW, September 20, 1957; GEW to UAW, George Ingalls, SWP, and CJF, October 1, 1957; GEW to George Ingalls, October 15, 1957.

(22) GEW to SWP, May 20, 1957. Walker's nose was particularly out of joint when he learned that McGraw-Hill had published a study on the Burndy Corporation and its

method of wire terminations, which was then being used as a college text book. See Report to Walker, Information on Burndy, dated May 13, 1957.

(23) GEW to UAW, September 24, 1957.

(24) As early as April and May, 1957, problems with the IBM account were already being discussed. See Executive Committee Meeting Minutes, April 1, and May 6, 1957; GEW to Joseph Brenner, October 18, 1957; William Lange to GEW, October 16, 1957, "Status of Business with IBM, Report for September, 1957." The September IBM bookings, Lange reported as $254,281. This represented a considerable fall-off in monthly sales to IBM when compared, for example, with a 1954 projection of bookings with IBM at a rate of $300,000 per month. See GEW to UAW, October 9, 1953. Walker sent Lange's October 18 report to Whitaker immediately with a cover statement: "Knowing of your vital interest and concern on the status of IBM business, I believe the attached report from Mr. Lange will be of considerable significance." GEW to UAW, October 18, 1957.

(25) GEW to UAW, October 31, and November 11, 1957. Walker attached clippings about Burndy from *Electronic News*(October 28, and November 4, 1957).

(26) GEW to UAW, November 18, 1957 on "The Exploitation of the Public Utility Market."

(27) Research Committee Meeting Minutes, July 15, 1958. G. Earle Walker, in a letter to Herman Haas, December 27, 1955, explained the purpose of API as follows: "API was developed after the last war to protect our overall volume against the contingency of a slump in manufacturing goods, and I already am developing programs which I hope will increase API business beyond the $5,000,000 figure in five years."

(28) SWP to Members of the Planning Committee, January 16, 1958.

(29) GEW to UAW, George Ingalls, SWP, CJF, and Burton Hendricks, January 22, 1958. In a memo to the Planning Committee, dated January 24, 1958, entitled simply "Recession," Walker took issue with those promises about the availability of new products during 1958 and enclosed another memo from F. E. "Bud" Howell, which, in fact, denied the existence of the new products. GEW to Planning Committee, January 24, 1958, and F. E. Howell to GEW, January 23, 1958.

(30) L. B. Paules to SWP, January 3, 1958.

(31) The ad hoc committee was composed of George Ingalls, Herman Haas, L. B. Paules, Marshall M. Holcombe, and S. W. Pollock. SWP to UAW, January 14, 1958.

(32) Research Committee Meeting Minutes, July 15, 1958. In an unsigned report on AMP Incorporated's activity in the missile field dated January 27, 1958, about three dozen AMP Incorporated customers were listed as actively working on missile contracts. According to the report nearly 150 different types of missiles were in various stages of planning and production in the United States. A Curtiss-Wright Corporation report to its stockholders in Whitaker's correspondence files expressed great alarm over the confusion in the defense program and its administration involving the drastic shift from conventional weapons to missile production.

(33) L. B. Paules to SWP, October 15, 1958.

(34) George Ingalls, now retired from American Machine & Foundry Company, joined AMP Incorporated in August, 1957. Executive Committee Meeting Minutes, May 27, 1958; SWP to UAW, CJF, and George Ingalls, October 16, 1958.

(35) Planning Committee Meeting Minutes, October 21, 1958; interview with Marshall M. Holcombe, May 18, 1977.

Notes: Chapter Fourteen

(1) L. B. Paules to SWP, August 12, and November 11, 1958; interview with SWP, February 23, 1977.

(2) John W. Hooper to UAW, September 2, 1958.

(3) Research Committee Meeting Minutes, May 19, 1959.

(4) Planning Committee Meeting Minutes, June 17, 1958.

(5) GEW to UAW, June 6, 1957. In the fall of 1956, E. G. Hefter favored the Australian market over the Union of South Africa and India. See E. G. Hefter to Marshall M. Holcombe, October 10, 1956.

(6) Planning Committee Meeting Minutes, June 17, and November 18, 1958. At the June 17 meeting, Whitaker asked for similar studies for Spain and Italy.

(7) Minutes of the meeting on AMP-Australia, November 25, 1958.

(8) Planning Committeee Meeting Minutes, December 16, 1958. References to the Japanese operation can be found in Planning Commitee Meeting Minutes through much of 1958. See minutes for March 18, and 21, May 7, June 17, September 16, October 21, and December 16, 1958. Also see Planning Committee Meeting Minutes, June 18, 1957, when "it was decided to continue plans for the Japanese manufacturing operation." At the October, 1957, directors' meeting, the announcement about the Japanese unit was made. G. Earle Walker played an extensive role in setting up the Japanese subsidiary. Interview with G. Earler Walker, March 31, 1977. The English language *Japanese Times* carried the story of the new AMP Incorporated operation on October 1, 1957.

(9) Planning Committee Meeting Minutes, January 20, 1959.

(10) Special Meeting, Planning Committee Meeting Minutes, February 11, 1959.

(11) L. V. Whipple to UAW, December 31, 1958, and January 5, 1959. In July, 1958, in the context of a discussion of a major organizational shift in operations, Whipple expressed both his frustrations and limitations to Whitaker: "More and more I find myself drawn into the area of organization and the interrelations of people with their fellow-workers. My engineering background has not equipped me to handle these affairs easily and efficiently." L. V. Whipple to UAW, July 1, 1958.

(12) Planning Committee Meeting Minutes, February 17, 1959; interview with Albert Curtis, May 25, 1976.

(13) L. V. Whipple to UAW, February 20, 1959. Whitaker was always willing to listen to "experts" on a subject, but his tendency to reject an overly "academic" approach lessened the appeal of the advice he received. In March, 1958, for example, Whitaker attended a NICB meeting for chief executives having complete responsibility for their firms. When asked his reaction to the meeting, Whitaker replied "I did find that the great diversity between the opinions of your staff and the presidents led some to believe that your staff had been entirely too narrow in presenting the material." As a corrective measure Whitaker suggested that perhaps a corporation executive might make a better moderater for the discussion. In part, Whitaker liked a more informal approach; in part, as a corporate executive himself, he disliked long speeches and tangential discussions, usually associated with "expert" types. (UAW to John Sinclair, President NICB, August 5, 1958):

(14) L. V. Whipple to UAW, May 8, May 14, and September 11, 1959; L. V.

Whipple to SWP, June 29, 1959. According to C. J. Fredricksen, Whitaker actually forbade the use of organization charts.

(15) Although Whipple's various plans had little impact, he did provide an indispensable service by acting as a liaison between the engineers and management. Interview with SWP, October 17, 1977.

(16) Planning Committee Meeting Minutes, June 16 and November 17, 1959.

(17) Planning Committee Meeting Minutes, August 11, 1959.

(18) Interview with G. Earle Walker, March 31, 1977; interview with Marshall M. Holcombe, May 18, 1977.

(19) UAW to W. C. Lange, June 19, 1959. AMP Incorporated Annual Report, 1959, Letter to Shareholders; a marketing report in Whitaker's files described the decade in this manner. See Chuman Chung to L. B. Paules, June 26, 1959.

(20) Planning Committee Meeting Minutes, November 18, 1958. Whipple assembled a mass of information on potential locations for new domestic manufacturing facilities before the company made the decision to locate in the Greensboro, North Carolina area. As usual, a key priority was the available labor climate with particular emphasis on the politics, union views, and work habits of potential employees; L. V. Whipple to UAW, February 16, 1959, "new facilities." At first Greensboro was favored over Raleigh; then Raleigh over Greensboro because of the proximity of university facilities near the former. Finally, Greensboro won out because it was determined that more skilled labor was available there, all other labor climate conditions being equal. Planning Committee Meeting Minutes, March 17, and April 14, 1959. AMP Incorporated stock was officially approved on the NYSE on October 22, 1959, and active trading began in late November. Edward Gray, Executive Vice-President, NYSE, to UAW, October 22, 1959. Whitaker was "sold" on listing with the NYSE over the American; see UAW to Phillip L. West, Vice-President and Director, NYSE, September 29, 1959.

(21) GEW to Gerald Englehart, November 6, 1959. As Walker put it, a corporation film is "not just a sales tool, but truly a corporate story to be presented to customers, stockholders, stockbrokers, and AMP employees." GEW to F. E. Howell, August 13, 1959.

(22) The Investment Club Bulletin ([?] 1961), pp. 2-5. At the close of 1975, the year of U. A. Whitaker's death, AMP Incorporated stock recorded sales of over $400 million placing it 348th on Fortune's "500 Largest Industrials." In terms of net income, however, it ranked 46th; AMP Incorporated 1975 Annual Report.

Notes: Chapter Fifteen

(1) E. A. Doepke, Jr. to UAW, October 2, 1951.

(2) Leonard Richards (Chairman of the Harrisburg Hospital Fund) to UAW, December 19, 1955; UAW to Mr. Dunleavy, Assistant Trust Officer, New York Community Trust, February 7, 1957; UAW to Bankers Trust, December 20, 1957, and December 18, 1959; UAW to Ralph Hayes, Director, New York Community Trust, August 31, 1959, and May 10, 1963; UAW, for the years 1961-63, to Kermit L. Lloyd, Rector, All Saints Episcopal Church. An indication of how valuable AMP Incorporated stock became can be seen in this letter from the President of Hood College (Andrew G. Truxal to UAW, March 14, 1962):

> As I look over the past decade one of the nicest things that happened to me at Hood was when you came down to the . . . hotel and handed me [those] shares of stock which you valued at $35,000. Little did I realize that today they would be worth around $250,000 . . . and the income probably carries the full salary of the Whitaker professorship. What a tribute to your business genius!

(3) UAW to N. McL. Sage, August 7 and 23, 1940; N. McL. Sage to UAW, August 20, 1940; UAW to Dr. R. T. Warburton, North Canton, Ohio, August 23, 1946.

(4) J. R. Killian Jr. , President of MIT, to UAW, December 8, 1954, and March 9, 1955; Marshall Holcombe to UAW, May 3, 1955, on reviewing the MIT agreements; Solon Rhode Jr. to Walter H. Gale, March 21, 1950. The AMP Incorporated Executive Committee approved a $10,000 appropriation for another year's renewal in 1957; Executive Committee Meeting Minutes, February 18, 1957; UAW to Truman S. Safford, July 26, 1967.

(5) George P. Wadsworth to UAW, October 30, 1957; UAW to George P. Wadsworth, November 5, 1957; UAW to Ralph Jope, December 20, 1957, with details of stock transfer to MIT.

(6) Dr. Irwin W. Sizer, February 25, 1977; UAW to J. R. Killian, October 30, 1960.

(7) J. R. Killian to UAW, October 28, 1959, and January 13, 1961.

(8) Walter J. Beadle to UAW, June 2, 1961.

(9) Walter J. Beadle to UAW, June 2, 1961; J. R. Killian to UAW, June 16, 1961; UAW to J. R. Killian, June 21, 1961.

(10) J. R. Killian to UAW, June 8, 1961; UAW to J. R. Killian, June 21, 1961.

(11) Interview with Helen Fisher Whitaker, April 13, 1976.

(12) J. R. Killian to UAW, August 14, 1961; R. M. Kimball, Secretary MIT, to UAW, August 15, 1961; UAW to R. M. Kimball, August 18, 1961; Irwin W. Sizer to UAW, December 1, 1961.

(13) In Boston, Whitaker supported the research of Robert Wilkins, M. D. and his team at the Massachusetts Memorial Hospital, beginning in 1958. In Cleveland, with Dr. Irvine Page of the Cleveland Clinic, Whitaker helped co-found the Coronary Club Incorporated to provide coronary victims with information about their condition. Whitaker also financed a new research building for the Cleveland Clinic.

(14) Gerald Englehart to Joseph J. Snyder, Vice-President and Treasurer, MIT, June 6, 1953; J. R. Killian to UAW, November 10, 1964; Walter L. Koltum to UAW, November 15, 1965. Wylie, *MIT in Perspective*, p. 139.

(15) Interview with Irwin W. Sizer, February 25, 1977; *Tech Talk* (September 24,

1975), p. 7; Professor Robert W. Mann of the Department of Mechanical Engineering at MIT was the first recipient of the Whitaker Professorship in Biomedical Engineering.

(16) Interview with Irwin W. Sizer, February 25, 1977; *Tech Talk* (October 19, 1977), pp. 1, 12. In 1978, another dream came true when the Whitaker College of Health Sciences, Technology and Management was officially dedicated.

(17) UAW to Vannevar Bush, July 1, 1965; UAW to Dr. Charles A. Townes, December 23, 1965; UAW to Dr. Jerome B. Wiesner, June 14, 1966; UAW to National Material Research Council, July 9, 1969.

(18) *Town and Country* (May, 1968), p. 97.

(19) UAW to Samuel L. Williams, June 19, 1969; *Forbes* (May 1, 1969), 20-21; 1970 *Fortune* "500" issue.

(20) Whitaker, like many Americans, did not favor gun control, believing that criminals who wanted weapons would remain unaffected by any restrictive legislation. In 1965 and again in 1968-69, he devoted some time and effort to making his opinions felt in Congress. See UAW to Representative John R. Kunkle, May 25, 1965, miscellaneous telegrams and letters to Pennsylvania Senator Hugh Scott, and even one communication to President-elect Richard Nixon in January, 1969.

(21) Whitaker's political contributions are documented in his files in various folders, the most important being Political Contributions 1964-1975 and Political Contributions, Miscellaneous, 1968-1975. See for example Nixon for President Committee, Maurice Stans, Chairman, to UAW, February 16, September 25, and November 20, 1968, thanking Whitaker for his contributions. Also J. T. Simpson to UAW, September 16, 1968.

(22) UAW to Portia Burnell, June 20, 1968, and January 22, 1969.

(23) UAW to George Misner, October 31, 1968.

(24) UAW to George Misner and Samuel L. Williams, October 21, 1974.

(25) Peter Drucker in Sterling F. Slappey, Ed. *Pioneers of American Business* (New York, 1973), pp. ix-x.

(26) Joseph Sweeney to UAW, May 14, 1966.

(27) UAW to Marshall Holcombe, May 25, 1971.